P9-BZB-067

Folsom Lake College Library

Reparations for Slavery

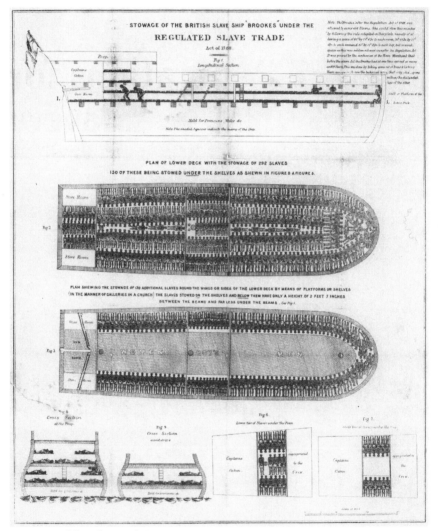

STOWAGE OF THE BRITISH SLAVE SHIP "BROOKES" UNDER THE
REGULATED SLAVE TRADE
Act of 1788

Courtesy of the Library of Congress

Reparations for Slavery

A Reader

Edited By
Ronald P. Salzberger
and
Mary C. Turck

ROWMAN & LITTLEFIELD PUBLISHERS, INC.
Lanham • Boulder • New York • Toronto • Oxford

ROWMAN & LITTLEFIELD PUBLISHERS, INC.

Published in the United States of America
by Rowman & Littlefield Publishers, Inc.
A wholly owned subsidary of The Rowman & Littlefield Publishing Group, Inc.
4501 Forbes Boulevard, Suite 200, Lanham, Maryland 20706
www.rowmanlittlefield.com

PO Box 317
Oxford
OX2 9RU, UK

Copyright © 2004 by Rowman & Littlefield Publishers, Inc.

All rights reserved. No part of this publication may be reproduced,
stored in a retrieval system, or transmitted in any form or by any
means, electronic, mechanical, photocopying, recording, or otherwise,
without the prior permission of the publisher.

British Library Cataloguing in Publication Information Available

Library of Congress Cataloging-in-Publication Data

Reparations for slavery : a reader / edited by Ronald P. Salzberger and Mary C. Turck.
    p. cm.
  Includes bibliographical references and index.
    ISBN 0-7425-1475-7 (hardcover : alk. paper)—ISBN 0-7425-1476-5 (pbk. : alk.
paper)
    1. African Americans—Reparations. 2. Slavery—United States—History. 3.
Slavery—United States—Public opinion. 4. Public opinion—United States. I.
Salzberger, Ronald P., 1945– II. Turck, Mary.
E185.89.R45R475 2004
323.1196'073—dc22

                                                            2003028314

Printed in the United States of America

⊗™ The paper used in this publication meets the minimum requirements of American
National Standard for Information Sciences—Permanence of Paper for Printed Library
Materials, ANSI/NISO Z39.48-1992.

Contents

IMPORTANT SUBSIDIARY ISSUES

Acknowledgments

The editors and publisher thank the following for permission to use copyrighted material.

Beacon Press, for selections from Martha Minow, *Between Vengeance and Forgiveness: Facing History after Genocide and Mass Violence*. Boston: Beacon Press, 1998.

Blackwell Publishing, for Nicholas Rescher, "Collective Responsibility," *Journal of Social Philosophy* 29 (1998): 46–58.

Center for the Study of Popular Culture, for David Horowitz, "Ten Reasons Why Reparations for Blacks Is a Bad Idea for Blacks and Racist Too," FrontPageMagazine.com, January 3, 2001.www.frontpagemag.com/Articles/Printable .asp?ID=1153 (accessed 1 January 2004).

Harper's Magazine, for "Making the Case for Racial Reparations: Does America Owe a Debt to the Descendants of Its Slaves? A Forum." *Harper's*, November 2000, 37–41.

HarperCollins Publishers, Inc., for James Forman, "Black Manifesto: To the White Christian Churches and the Jewish Synagogues in the United States of America and All Other Racist Institutions." In *The Black Manifesto and the Challenge to White America*, edited by Arnold Schuchter. Philadelphia: J. B. Lippincott, 1970, pp. 191–202.

Oxford University Press, for Janna Thompson, "Historical Obligations," *Australasian Journal of Philosophy* 78, no. 3 (2000): 334–45.

Parliament of the U.K. Parliamentary copyright material is reproduced with the permission of the Comptroller of Her Majesty's Stationery Office on behalf of Parliament, for "The Official Record from *Hansard* of the Debate Initiated by Lord Gifford QC in the House of Lords of the British Parliament on 14th March 1996 Concerning the African Reparations," HL Deb (1996) col. 1040–1059.

Philosophy in the Contemporary World, for Stephen Kershnar, "The Case against Reparations," *Philosophy in the Contemporary World* 8, no. 1 (2001): 41–46.

Princeton University Press, for Samuel Scheffler, "Relationships and Responsibilities," *Philosophy and Public Affairs* 26, no. 3 (1998): 189–209, and for George Sher, "Ancient Wrongs and Modern Rights," *Philosophy and Public Affairs* 10 (1980): 3–17.

Regents of the University of California and the University of California Press, for "Wealth Matters," in Dalton Conley, *Being Black, Living in the Red: Race, Wealth, and Social Policy in America*. Berkeley: University of California Press, 1999.

The Black Scholar, for Earnest Allen Jr. and Robert Chrisman, "Ten Reasons: A Response to David Horowitz," *The Black Scholar* 31, no. 2 (2001).

The Institute for Philosophy and Public Policy, for Robert K. Rullinwider, "The Case for Reparations." Report of the Institute for Philosophy and Public Policy (2000), www.puaf.umd.edu/1PPP/Summer00/case_for_reparations.htm (accessed 9 September 2003).

The Monist, for Hugo Bedau, "Summary of Compensatory Justice and the Black Manifesto," *The Monist* 56 (1970): 20–42.

The University of Chicago Press, for Janna Thompson, "Historical Injustice and Reparations: Justifying Claims of Descendents," *Ethics* 112, no. 1 (2002): 114–35, and for Jeremy Waldron, "Superseding Historical Injustice," *Ethics* 103 (1992): 4–28.

The authors also wish to acknowledge permissions granted by Janna Thompson, Jeremy Waldron, and Steven Kershnar.

Introduction

The process of seeking reparations, and of building communities of support while spreading knowledge of the violations and their meaning in people's lives, may be more valuable, ultimately, than any specific victory or offer of a remedy. Being involved in a struggle for reparations may give survivors a chance to speak and to tell their stories. If heard and acknowledged, they may obtain a renewed sense of dignity. The reparations themselves cannot undo the violence that was done. Yet even inadequate monetary payments or an apology without any reparations can afford more opportunities for a sense of recognition and renewal for survivors, observers, and offenders than would an unsuccessful struggle for an apology, for reparations, or for the restitution of property, or a relative's bones. When the victimized and their supporters push for monetary compensation, for restitution of wrongly appropriated artifacts or property, or for official apologies, they also are engaged in obtaining acknowledgement of the violations and acceptance of responsibility for wrongdoing as much as they press for a specific remedy.

—Martha Minow, *Between Vengeance and Forgiveness*

This book is offered in the hope that Martha Minow, quoted above, is right. A public discussion of reparations may provide some of the remedies sought through reparations themselves.

This book accordingly brings together materials to facilitate an intelligent discussion of the question of whether reparations should be paid for the slavery and its aftermath in the United States. Most of the argumentative essays are written by philosophers, though only a very few require any philosophical background of the reader.

The book was conceived as a result of attempts to teach an interdisciplinary course on the subject at Metropolitan State University in St. Paul, Minnesota.

This course had three instructors: a philosopher and two members of the Ethnic Studies Department. The team found that while published works on the subject were few and far between, abundant material was nonetheless available, though salted away in a variety of disciplines and sources. The team also discovered that even among students who voluntarily signed up for a course on reparations for historical injustices, few students had more than a hazy idea of what those injustices consisted of.

The experience of the team suggested the structure of this book.

Accordingly, the book begins with a historical part, "Why Reparations? Slavery and Its Aftermath," that chronicles the abduction of slaves from Africa, the horrendous passage from Africa to the New World, the rigors of slavery, and the legacy of slavery through the years of Reconstruction and Jim Crow. It concludes with a philosophical essay addressed to the question of how we might conceive of and what weight we should attach to the idea that the harms of slavery persist to the present day, not only as lost wealth, but also as moral, spiritual, and psychological injuries.

The second part, "Early Reparations Initiatives," surveys a nineteenth-century effort to win for ex-slaves some consideration for what they had lost and for the disadvantages from which they suffered following emancipation. Also included here are more recent discussions and initiatives during the mid- and late twentieth century to do likewise, including the lightning rod "Black Manifesto," a set of demands to the religious communities of the United States, first delivered at the Riverside Church in New York City in the 1960s.

These two parts are wrapped together in a section called "Indispensable Preliminaries."

The second section, "The Main Questions," begins with a part, "The Contemporary Debate Over Restitution," containing essays that are examples of the current debate, running from the 1970s through the early twenty-first century, as it occurred in both the popular media and in scholarly, principally philosophical, discussion.

The fourth part, "Underlying Questions of Responsibility and Entitlement," includes essays that tackle questions about collective and historical responsibility. How, if at all, is responsibility for an injustice to be justly distributed among members of a group when some of those members were not themselves the causes of the deeds that cry out for remedy? How are we to deal with old, even ancient injustices, when the current population contains neither the immediate victims nor the perpetrators?

Section three, "Important Subsidiary Issues," begins with a part, "Some Devilish Details," that presents essays on associated legal and economic matters. If a legislative strategy to produce reparations fails, what if any legal recourse remains? On the economic side, an essay redirects the discussion of reparations from the loss of wages and unjust enrichment to the problem of capital formation or wealth in the current African-American community. Finally, the section, and book, concludes with a part on alternatives to reparations, "Alternatives," that considers a number of alternatives to compensation and weighs their merits.

The essays chosen for this book were selected on the basis of their quality, their representativeness, their historical importance, and their accessibility to readers with little or no background in philosophy. When greater expertise is desirable, the fact is noted in the chapter's introductory remarks.

We would like to thank a generation of civil rights leaders who awoke us as kids to the ideas of civic and moral responsibility and provided such heroic examples of how these duties could be fulfilled. They were everyday folks, and they were giants.

INDISPENSABLE PRELIMINARIES

I

WHY REPARATIONS?
SLAVERY AND ITS AFTERMATH

In order to address the question of reparations, it is necessary first to understand the injuries for which reparations are sought. This part will sketch a history of slavery and the resulting and continuing injuries that it brings to African Americans.

Chapter 1 describes the conditions of slavery, from the beginning of the European slave trade through the U.S. Civil War and the legal abolition of slavery in the United States. It draws on first-person accounts, from Olaudah Equiano's description of his capture in Africa and his subsequent sale and voyage on a slave ship, to Harriet Jacobs's firsthand description of the horrific conditions of slavery in the United States, to statesman and former slave Frederick Douglass's eloquent "What to the Slave Is Your 4th of July?" This introductory chapter also sketches differences between slavery in Africa and in the United States, discusses difference between indentured servitude and slavery, notes the racialization of slavery in the United States, and describes continuing resistance and rebellion by slaves.

Chapter 2 describes the legal end of slavery in the United States and its aftermath, from Reconstruction to the legal discrimination and repression embodied in Black Codes, Jim Crow laws, lynchings, and terror. Reverend Elias Hill, in testimony before a congressional committee, recounts the terrorist attack he endured at the hands of the Ku Klux Klan in 1871. Thomas Hall, an ex-slave, describes his life experience in compelling detail in a narrative from the archives of the Federal Writers' Project. Historical narrative continues through the Great Migration, the two World Wars, and the civil rights movement, to the end of legal segregation.

Chapter 3, "The Continuing Injuries of Slavery and Jim Crow," describes how segregation continues and affects African Americans, even after the legal victories of the civil rights movement. This final portion of the historical narrative moves into the twenty-first century.

The last portion of this part, chapter 4, is a philosophical essay by Ronald Salzberger discussing the continuing, nonmaterial injuries of slavery. What are these injuries, and how are they attributable to slavery? The essay argues that slavery has produced two sorts of "insults" to African Americans, one moral and another spiritual and psychological. It takes up the ticklish questions of whether slavery, Jim Crow, and discrimination generally have produced dishonor or any pathology among their victims and the victims' descendants. The essay touches on the work of Orlando Patterson, Glen Loury, and others.

1

The Conditions of Slavery

The European slave trade began in 1442, when Portuguese explorers brought ten African captives back from the west coast of Africa. Over the next century, Europeans built trading posts along the west coast, and these posts traded more and more in human beings. By 1500, more than two hundred thousand Africans had been sold into European slavery.

Then came colonization of the Americas. The Spanish and Portuguese colonies of South America and the Caribbean found African slave labor most profitable on their plantations. By 1619, a million Africans had been brought as slaves to Portuguese, Spanish, and French colonies in the Americas.

Slavery existed in Africa before the arrival of the Europeans, but it was markedly different from the European institution of slavery. In Africa, slaves were captives taken in war or kidnapped in raids. They might win or earn their freedom. African slaves were not different from their African masters, except by accident of fortune. They might be slaves for a time, and then free men and women again. Their children were not slaves.

The status of African slaves in Africa resembled that of English indentured servants. English settlers in the Americas brought indentured servants with them. More than half the European immigrants to North America during the seventeenth century arrived as indentured servants.

English indentured servants worked for a period of time—usually seven years—and then were released from servitude with "freedom dues" that commonly included land and seed for planting. When a Dutch ship brought the first Africans to Virginia in 1619, the English colonists were at first inclined to treat them also as indentured servants. Some of the Africans became substantial property holders after earning their freedom.

Slavery took root insidiously and gradually. In 1641, Massachusetts recognized slavery as a legal status. Other colonies followed.

Laws codified the emerging social ideas of race and difference. Laws gradually redefined all African servants as slaves, and made their children slaves as well.

In an early and striking example, three servants—a Scotsman, a Dutchman, and an African—ran away from a Virginia plantation in 1640. Captured, they were taken before a court and found guilty of breaking their contracts. The court sentenced all three to be whipped, and added one year to the indentured servitude contracts of the Scotsman and the Dutchman. Much harsher punishment awaited John Punch, the African servant. The court ordered that he "serve his said master or his assigns for the time of his natural life."[1]

Plantation agriculture made slave owning profitable. Virginia found tobacco a highly lucrative crop. Raising tobacco required labor to clear fields and break ground, to plant, tend, and harvest the crop. Slavery provided that labor.

In 1705, the Virginia Assembly established race-based slavery as the law of the state. The 1705 act said that, "All servants imported and brought into the Country. . . who were not Christians in their native Country . . . shall be accounted and be slaves. All Negro, mulatto and Indian slaves within this dominion . . . shall be held to be real estate."

By 1750, slavery had become law in all thirteen English colonies, as Georgia became the last of the colonies to pass laws establishing slavery.

THE MIDDLE PASSAGE

Slave trading was a high-profit industry. In 1672, the English king chartered the Royal African Company, giving it a monopoly on the British slave trade. Other British merchants protested. They wanted a share in the profits. In 1698, Parliament ended the monopoly and opened the slave trade. Soon the English became the world's leading slave traders, taking more than twenty thousand people from Africa each year.

Before the slave trade ended, more than ten million Africans had been taken as slaves to the Americas. Some estimates put the number as high as one hundred million. In truth, since slaves counted as less than human, no accurate count was ever kept.

The voyage from Africa to the Americas was called the Middle Passage. Before the Middle Passage came the long journey from capture, usually in inland countries of Africa, to the coast. This part of the journey, superintended by African slave traders, ended with sale of the human merchandise to European slavers.

At the end of the Middle Passage, the European slavers sold their cargo. Now the slaves began the final leg of their journey, from American ports to the homes and plantations of their new owners.

Olaudah Equiano was eleven years old when he was kidnapped into slavery. He and his sister were taken from the home of their father, a village leader among the Ibo people in the kingdom of Benin, along the Niger River. He was transported first to Barbados, then to Virginia. Eventually, he became the property of a British naval captain.

During seven years of slavery to Lieutenant Michael Henry Pascal, Equiano studied and worked hard. He bought his freedom in 1766, and eventually became a prominent British abolitionist. His autobiography, published in 1789, reveals much of the nature of the slave trade.

> One day, when all our people were gone out to their works as usual, and only I and my dear sister were left to mind the house, two men and a woman got over our walls, and in a moment seized us both, and, without giving us time to cry out, or make resistance, they stopped our mouths, and ran off with us into the nearest wood. Here they tied our hands, and continued to carry us as far as they could, till night came on, when we reached a small house, where the robbers halted for refreshment, and spent the night. We were then unbound, but were unable to take any food; and, being quite overpowered by fatigue and grief, our only relief was some sleep, which allayed our misfortune for a short time.[2]

Equiano was soon separated from his sister and sold to a chieftain whose family spoke his own language and who treated him well. He stayed there only briefly before being sold again. Like his captors, his owners and purchasers were African. Passed from one owner to another, he was brought by degrees to the coast of Africa.

> The first object which saluted my eyes when I arrived on the coast, was the sea, and a slave ship, which was then riding at anchor, and waiting for its cargo. These filled me with astonishment, which was soon converted into terror, when I was carried on board. I was immediately handled, and tossed up to see if I were sound, by some of the crew; and I was not persuaded that I had gotten into a world of bad spirits, and that they were going to kill me. . . . When I looked round the ship too, and saw a large furnace of copper boiling, and a multitude of black people of every description chained together, every one of their countenances expressing dejection and sorrow, I no longer doubted of my fate; and, quite overpowered with horror and anguish, I fell motionless on the deck and fainted.

In some ways, Equiano was fortunate. Other captives were marched in long slave caravans for hundreds of miles, with as many as half dying en route to the coast. They might be kept in underground dungeons at the coast, waiting for months to be sold and shipped. After this first passage from the interior of Africa to the slave-trading forts on the coast, the captives faced the horrors of the Middle Passage to the Americas, a voyage that took two to four months. Equiano recounts his experience of the Middle Passage:

> At last, when the ship we were in, had got in all her cargo, they made ready with many fearful noises, and we were all put under deck. . . . The stench of the hold while we were on the coast was so intolerably loathsome, that it was dangerous to remain there for any time, and some of us had been permitted to stay on the deck for the fresh air; but now that the whole ship's cargo were confined together, it became absolutely pestilential. The closeness of the place, and the heat of the climate, added to the number in the ship, which was so crowded that each had scarcely room to turn himself, almost suffocated us. This produced copious perspirations, so that the air soon became unfit for respiration, from a variety of loathsome smells, and brought on a sickness among the slaves, of which many died—thus falling victims to the improvident avarice, as I may call it, of their purchasers. This wretched situation was again aggravated by the gaffing of the chains, now became insupportable, and the filth of the necessary tubs, into which the children often fell, and were almost suffocated. The shrieks of the women, and the groans of the dying, rendered the whole a scene of horror almost inconceivable. . . .

Weakened by sickness, Equiano was soon taken up to the deck. The fresh air kept him alive.

> One day, when we had a smooth sea and moderate wind, two of my wearied countrymen who were chained together (I was near them at the time), preferring death to such a life of misery, somehow made through the nettings and jumped into the sea; immediately, another quite dejected fellow, who, on account of his illness, was suffered to be out of irons, also followed their example; and I believe many more would very soon have done the same, if they had not been prevented by the ship's crew, who were instantly alarmed. Those of us that were the most active, were in a moment put down under the deck. . . . However, two of the wretches were drowned, but they got the other, and afterwards flogged him unmercifully, for thus attempting to prefer death to slavery.

European slave traders regarded the Africans as subhuman and treated them as commodities and cargo. They bought slaves from the African traders who brought them to the coast. They rejected any who were lame or sickly or otherwise deemed unsuitable. They packed their ships with as much cargo as possible, in order to reap greater profits at the other end of the voyage. Their only concern was maximizing profit—not the comfort, convenience, or even the lives of the human cargo their ships carried in the Middle Passage from Africa to the Americas.

Alexander Falconbridge, a ship's surgeon on several slave trading vessels, also wrote an account of the Middle Passage.[3] He describes how African slaves are stowed beneath decks "so close, as to admit of no other position than lying on their sides." The decks were too low to allow anyone to stand. Sometimes platforms were built to increase the number of slaves carried, "a kind of shelf, about eight or nine feet in breadth, extending from the side of the ship toward the centre. They are placed nearly midway between the decks, at the distance of two or three feet from each deck. Upon these the Negroes are stowed in the same manner as they are on the deck underneath."

Falconbridge describes the "necessary tubs" mentioned by Equiano in greater detail.

In each of the apartments are placed three or four large buckets, of a conical form, nearly two feet in diameter at the bottom and only one foot at the top and in depth of about twenty-eight inches, to which, when necessary, the Negroes have recourse. It often happens that those who are placed at a distance from the buckets, in endeavoring to get to them, rumble over their companions, in consequence of their being shackled. . . . In this distressed situation, unable to proceed and prevented from getting to the tubs, they desist from the attempt; and as the necessities of nature are not to be resisted, ease themselves as they lie. This becomes a fresh source of boils and disturbances and tends to render the condition of the poor captive wretches still more uncomfortable. The nuisance arising from these circumstances is not infrequently increased by the tubs being much too small for the purpose intended and their being usually emptied but once every day.

Like Equiano, Falconbridge reports that some of the captives would rather die than continue. For this, too, the ship captains had remedies.

Upon the Negroes refusing to take sustenance, I have seen coals of fire, glowing hot, put on a shovel and placed so near their lips as to scorch and burn them. And this has been accompanied with threats of forcing them to swallow the coals if they any longer persisted in refusing to eat. These means have generally had the desired effect.

CONDITIONS OF SERVITUDE

Herded into holding pens upon their arrival, the Africans awaited a fate they could hardly imagine. Equiano describes his fear of being eaten by the strange men of this new land, and his astonishment at seeing the brick buildings and unfamiliar animals such as horses. The slave buyers, of course, could not speak African languages, so they evaluated the new arrivals in the same way that they would inspect livestock. They felt the muscles of one, forced open another's mouth to inspect his teeth, by gestures instructed a third to jump or stand or squat to demonstrate mobility. Sometimes slaves were sold individually; sometimes in lots; and sometimes at so much per head for as many as a slave-buyer could group and tie together.

Those few who were fortunate enough to have been captured with friends or family members and somehow remain with them to the end of the Middle Passage now might find themselves torn from their last human relationships. Slave traders knew nothing and cared less of familial or communal bonds. Soon the new arrivals were transported to plantations to begin a slave's life among strangers, who might not even speak an understandable language.

But there was little time to grieve, to remember, or to think. Work on a tobacco or rice or cotton plantation began at dawn and continued until evening.

ECONOMICS OF SLAVERY

Throughout the Americas, slave labor formed the foundation of national wealth. Slave labor produced goods for domestic consumption and for export—indigo and rice from the Carolinas and coastal marshlands; tobacco in Virginia; sugar in the Caribbean; sugar, gold, and diamonds in Brazil; and finally cotton in the United States.

In 1793, the cotton gin was invented, paving the way for cotton to become the most profitable crop throughout the southern and western states. The cotton gin processed picked cotton. Only human hand labor could plant, chop, and pick the cotton for the gin. Slaves provided the hand labor to feed the gins and make cotton profitable. U.S. production of cotton grew from $150,000 in 1793 to $8,000,000 a decade later. Cotton plantations also made possible and profitable a booming textile trade in northern states.

Most Southerners owned no slaves. They were impoverished farmers or laborers, working on the brink of destitution. They supported the institution of slavery, in part, because it lifted them off the bottom rung of the social ladder. Slavery, and the racist ideology that underlay it, afforded them the status of the second-lowest class rather than the lowest.

Among slave owners, most owned fewer than twenty slaves. Those who owned few slaves often had to work in the fields beside their slaves, barely maintaining their higher status as landowners and slaveholders.

Wealthy plantation owners presided over large farms and many slaves. A small percentage of the slaves worked as household servants—cooking, cleaning, raising the master's children (and often bearing them as well). Most slaves, however, labored in the fields, backs bent under a scorching sun.

White overseers used whips as needed to squeeze the maximum amount of work from their charges—or in some cases, to satisfy their own twisted desires for power and domination. Too often, and too easily, the psychological and economic motivations combined.

Worse even than the back-breaking work was the condition of slavery itself. Pierce Butler inherited family plantations in Georgia and 730 slaves. When he gambled himself deep into debt, he sold the slaves, breaking up families and exiling slaves from the only home they and their parents had ever known. The two-day sale was held at a Georgia racetrack in 1859. The largest single slave sale ever recorded in the United States, it was remembered as "The Weeping Time."

The possession of absolute, life-and-death power over their slaves often brought out the worst in the slave-owners. Even pro-slavery writers worried about what slaveholding did to the character of masters and their children.

The account of Harriet Jacobs in *Incidents in the Life of a Slave Girl* describes the murder of a slave by his owner, a murder unrecognized under law.[4]

Harriet Jacobs: "Incidents in the Life of a Slave Girl"

In my childhood I knew a valuable slave, named Charity, and loved her, as all children did. Her young mistress married, and took her to Louisiana. Her little boy, James, was sold to a good sort of master. He became involved in debt, and James was sold again to a wealthy slaveholder, noted for his cruelty. With this man he grew up to manhood, receiving the treatment of a dog. After a severe whipping, to save himself from further infliction of the lash, with which he was threatened, he took to the woods. He was in a most miserable condition—cut by the cowskin, half-naked, half-starved, and without the means of procuring a crust of bread.

Some weeks after his escape, he was captured, tied, and carried back to his master's plantation. This man considered punishment in his jail, on bread and water, after receiving hundreds of lashes, too mild for the poor slave's offence. Therefore he decided, after the overseer should have whipped him to his satisfaction, to have him placed between the screws of the cotton gin, to stay as long as he had been in the woods. This wretched creature was cut with the whip from his head to his foot, then washed with strong brine, to prevent the flesh from mortifying, and make it heal sooner than it otherwise would. He was then put into the cotton gin, which was screwed down, only allowing him room to turn on his side when he could not lie on his back. Every morning a slave was sent with a piece of bread and bowl of water, which were placed within reach of the poor fellow. The slave was charged, under penalty of severe punishment, not to speak to him.

Four days passed, and the slave continued to carry the bread and water. On the second morning, he found the bread gone, but the water untouched.

When he had been in the press four days and five nights, the slave informed his master that the water had not been used for four mornings, and that a horrible stench came from the gin house. The overseer was sent to examine into it. When the press was unscrewed, the dead body was found partly eaten by rats and vermin. Perhaps the rats that devoured his bread had gnawed him before life was extinct. Poor Charity! Grandmother and I often asked each other how her affectionate heart would bear the news, if she should ever hear of the murder of her son. We had known her husband, and knew that James was like him in manliness and intelligence. These were the qualities that made it so hard for him to be a plantation slave. They put him into a rough box, and buried him with less feeling than would have been manifested for an old house dog. Nobody asked any questions. He was a slave; and the feeling was that the master had a right to do what he pleased with his own property. And what did he care for the value of a slave? He had hundreds of them. When they had finished their daily toil, they must hurry to eat their little morsels, and be ready to extinguish their pine knots before nine o'clock, when the overseer went his patrol rounds. He entered every cabin, to see that men and their wives had gone to bed together, lest the men, from over-fatigue, should fall asleep in the chimney corner, and remain there till the morning horn called them to their daily task. Women are considered of no value, unless they continually increase their owner's stock. They are put on a par with animals. This same master shot a woman through the head, who had run away and been brought back to him. No one called him to account for it. If a slave resisted being whipped, the bloodhounds were unpacked, and set upon him, to tear his flesh from his bones. The master who did these things was highly educated, and styled a perfect gentleman. He also boasted the name and standing of a Christian, though Satan never had a truer follower.

I could tell of more slaveholders as cruel as those I have described. They are not exceptions to the general rule. I do not say there are no humane slaveholders. Such characters do exist, notwithstanding the hardening influences around them. But they are "like angels' visits—few and far between."

REBELLION, REVOLT, AND FEAR

While importation of slaves was banned in 1808, American slave owners turned to breeding programs to replenish and increase their human stock. Since slavery recognized no family ties, husbands were sold away from wives, children away from their parents, multiplying misery. The number of slaves increased from 575,000 in 1781 to 900,000 in 1800 to two million in 1830 and four million in 1860.[5]

As the slave population grew, so did white fear of slave revolts. One of the first recorded revolts took place in 1739. A slave named Jemmy rallied others to flee Carolina for what he thought would be freedom in Spanish-owned

Florida. As he and his followers marched south from Stono, they killed dozens of whites before white colonists overtook them and executed them, displaying the severed heads of the rebels on posts along the road.

Other slaves made common cause with Indians and with white indentured servants, throughout the colonies. Rebellions invariably met with deadly and cruel punishment, including burning at the stake.

Though most blacks were slaves, significant numbers also lived as free men and women. The number of free blacks grew from 59,000 in 1790 to 319,000 in 1830. In 1830, more than half of the free blacks lived in the South.[6]

Philadelphia offered a home to a large and growing free black population. Quakers denounced slavery and eventually barred slaveholders from membership in the Society of Friends. They also helped to educate black children and adults. By 1830, all black people living in Philadelphia were free, and they made up almost ten percent of the population. Philadelphia's black population included business owners and professionals as well as large numbers of skilled and unskilled laborers. Black men formed a mutual aid society, the Free African Society, in 1787, and black women were active in abolitionist work and members of the Philadelphia Female Anti-Slavery Society.

Even Philadelphia, however, was hardly a model of equality or even of tolerance. Racial hostility led to frequent clashes between whites and blacks, most churches remained strictly segregated, and proposals for bans on black immigration and for special taxes on black households were offered in the legislature in the early years of the nineteenth century. Throughout the North, blacks lived in segregated neighborhoods and were segregated in all manner of public accommodations.

Everywhere, free blacks lived in danger of kidnapping. If a white person testified that someone was a fugitive slave, the unfortunate captive could be sent south into slavery. The law did not allow blacks to testify in court. Kidnapping of children was even easier.

The slave revolt in St. Domingue in 1791, which resulted in the formation of the free nation of Haiti, struck fear into the hearts of slave owners throughout the Americas. Blacks in St. Domingue outnumbered whites by a 10:1 ratio, and many returned the extreme brutality that had been their lot for generations. Although the blacks were victorious, France refused to give up, sending twenty thousand troops to Haiti in 1802 to retake the island and reimpose slavery. Though this attempt was ultimately unsuccessful, the ensuing war cost more than 135,000 lives.

Slave rebellions continued in the United States, from Gabriel's revolt in 1800 to the alliance of African Americans and Choctaw Indians at the "Negro Fort" in Florida in 1815 to Denmark Vesey's Carolina attempt in 1822 to Nat Turner's Virginia insurrection in 1831.

COLONIZATION AND ABOLITION

Alarmed by the growing numbers of slaves and the prospect of slave rebellions, some southern slave owners decided that the population must be limited. To this end, they joined forces with antislavery northerners to form the American Colonization Society in 1817. The ACS limited its membership to whites, and planned for transportation of free blacks to Africa, there to found a new colony and spread Christianity among the Africans.

Many blacks opposed the idea of colonization, insisting that they had a right to live as free men and women in the United States. Pro-abolitionist whites also opposed the scheme, arguing that it was only an evasion of the real question of the evil of slavery. Some black and white people, however, saw colonization as the only way to win real freedom for blacks, believing that they could never be treated as free and equal citizens in the country that had enslaved them.

While the colonization movement attracted some adherents and congressional support, the movement for abolition far outpaced it. Strong abolition societies began in Pennsylvania in the early 1800s, and multiplied across the northern United States. As the United States acquired more and more territory, repeated compromises divided the new states between slave and free, never to the satisfaction of either side.

Freed and escaped slaves told their horror stories, and preachers appealed to whites to recognize the humanity of blacks. Among the most eloquent advocates of abolition was Frederick Douglass. In 1852, he spoke to a meeting sponsored by the Rochester Ladies' Anti-Slavery Society.[7]

Frederick Douglass: "What to the Slave Is the 4th of July?"

Fellow-citizens, above your national, tumultuous joy, I hear the mournful wail of millions! whose chains, heavy and grievous yesterday, are, to-day, rendered more intolerable by the jubilee shouts that reach them. . . .

For the present, it is enough to affirm the equal manhood of the Negro race. Is it not astonishing that, while we are ploughing, planting, and reaping, using all kinds of mechanical tools, erecting houses, constructing bridges, building ships, working in metals of brass, iron, copper, silver and gold; that, while we are reading, writing and ciphering, acting as clerks, merchants and secretaries, having among us lawyers, doctors, ministers, poets, authors, editors, orators and teachers; that, while we are engaged in all manner of enterprises common to other men, digging gold in California, capturing the whale in the Pacific, feeding sheep and cattle on the hill-side, living, moving, acting, thinking, planning, living in families as husbands, wives and children, and, above all, confessing and worshipping the Christian's God, and looking hopefully for life and immortality beyond the grave, we are called upon to prove that we are men! . . .

What, am I to argue: that it is wrong to make men brutes, to rob them of their liberty, to work them without wages, to keep them ignorant of their relations to their fellow men, to beat them with sticks, to flay their flesh with the lash, to load their limbs with irons, to hunt them with dogs, to sell them at auction, to sunder their families, to knock out their teeth, to burn their flesh, to starve them into obedience and submission to their masters? Must I argue that a system thus marked with blood, and stained with pollution, is wrong? . . .

What, to the American slave, is your 4th of July? I answer; a day that reveals to him, more than all other days in the year, the gross injustice and cruelty to which he is the constant victim. To him, your celebration is a sham; your boasted liberty, an unholy license; your national greatness, swelling vanity; your sounds of rejoicing are empty and heartless; your denunciation of tyrants, brass fronted impudence; your shouts of liberty and equality, hollow mockery; your prayers and hymns, your sermons and thanksgivings, with all your religious parade and solemnity, are, to Him, mere bombast, fraud, deception, impiety, and hypocrisy—a thin veil to cover up crimes which would disgrace a nation of savages. There is not a nation on the earth guilty of practices more shocking and bloody than are the people of the United States, at this very hour.

Go where you may, search where you will, roam through all the monarchies and despotisms of the Old World, travel through South America, search out every abuse, and when you have found the last, lay your facts by the side of the everyday practices of this nation, and you will say with me, that, for revolting barbarity and shameless hypocrisy, America reigns without a rival. . . .

NOTES

1. "Africans in America." WGBH, 1998. www.pbs.org/wgbh/aia/home.html (accessed February 10, 2003).

2. Olaudah Equiano, *The Interesting Narrative of the Life of Olaudah Equiano, or Gustavus Vassa, the African* (London: 1793), online at www.pbs.org/wgbh/aia/part1 /1h320t.html (accessed February 10, 2003).

3. Alexander Falconbridge, *Black Voyage: Eyewitness Accounts of the Atlantic Slave Trade* (Boston: Little, Brown and Company, 1788).

4. Harriet Jacobs, *Incidents in the Life of a Slave Girl* (1861). Reprint, North Carolina: Academic Affairs Library, the University of North Carolina at Chapel Hill, 1998.

5. Howard Zinn, *A People's History of the United States* (New York: Harper-Collins, 1980, 1995), 167.

6. "Africans in America." WGBH, 1998. www.pbs.org/wgbh/aia/home.html (accessed February 10, 2003).

7. Frederick Douglass, *The Life and Writings of Frederick Douglass*, vol. 2, *Pre-Civil War Decade, 1850–1860* (New York: Philip S. Foner International Publishers Co., Inc., 1950).

2

Restoring White Supremacy: Jim Crow

WAR, RECONSTRUCTION, AND REGRESSION

The election of Abraham Lincoln in 1860 led directly and inevitably to the secession of seven Southern states and the beginning of the Civil War. While Lincoln was no friend of slavery, he did not initially aim to abolish it. He wrote to Horace Greeley during the war, saying, "My paramount object in this struggle is to save the Union, and is not either to save or destroy Slavery. If I could save the Union without freeing any slave, I would do it; and if I could save it by freeing all the slaves, I would do it; and if I could do it by freeing some and leaving others alone, I would also do that. What I do about Slavery and the colored race, I do because it helps to save this Union."

Toward the end of the same letter, Lincoln makes clear his personal position: " I have here stated my purpose according to my view of *official* duty, and I intend no modification of my oft-expressed *personal* wish that all men, everywhere could be free."[1]

In the end, Lincoln gets the credit for ending slavery in the United States — despite the fact that the Emancipation Proclamation was a wartime measure designed to free only slaves in states not under the control of the Union. After four years of Civil War and more than 600,000 deaths, the Union endured, and the Thirteenth Amendment to the Constitution ended slavery in the United States. The Fourteenth Amendment granted citizenship and guaranteed equal protection under law to people of all races.

The Fifteenth Amendment guaranteed all males the right to vote: "The right of citizens of the United States to vote shall not be denied or abridged by the United States or by any State on account of race, color, or previous condition of servitude." Flocking to the polls, Southern blacks elected two black U.S. senators from Mississippi and twenty congressional representatives, as well as state legislators and other state public officials. Their political freedom proved short-lived. In 1868, the Georgia legislature voted to expel its twenty-five black members. Other black legislators were removed by threats, disenfranchisement, and various stratagems. By 1901, not a single Negro served in the U.S. Congress.

As slaves seized upon their new opportunities for education, southern whites tried to maintain subjugation and ignorance. Many schools were taught by Northerners. White women who had worked or prayed for an end to slavery came south to teach. These volunteers met eager black pupils and hostile white Southerners.

Edmonia Highgate was one of the Northern white ladies. She taught in Lafayette Parish, Louisiana, after the war, and wrote of her experience.

The majority of my pupils come from plantations, three, four and even eight miles distant. So anxious are they to learn that they walk these distances so early in the morning as never to be tardy.

There has been much opposition to the School. Twice I have been shot at in my room. My night school scholars have been shot but none killed. A week ago an aged freedman just across the way was shot so badly as to break his arm and leg. The rebels here threatened to burn down the school and house in which I board yet they have not materially harmed us. The nearest military protection is 200 miles distant at New Orleans.[2]

Thomas Hall, a former slave, described both slavery and its aftermath to a Federal Writers Project interviewer in 1937.[3]

My name is Thomas Hall and I was born in Orange County, N.C. on a plantation belonging to Jim Woods whose wife, our missus, was named Polly. I am eighty one years of age as I was born Feb. 14, 1856. My father Daniel Hall and my mother Becka Hall and me all belonged to the same man but it was often the case that this was not true as one man, perhaps a Johnson, would own a husband and a Smith own the wife, each slave goin' by the name of the slave owners family. In such cases the children went by the name of the family to which the mother belonged.

Getting married an' having a family was a joke in the days of slavery, as the main thing in allowing any form of matrimony among the slaves was to raise more slaves in the same sense and for the same purpose as stock raisers raise horses and mules, that is for work. A woman who could produce fast was in great demand and brought a good price on the auction block in Richmond, Virginia, Charleston, South Carolina, and other places. . . .

Conditions and rules were bad and the punishments were severe and barbarous. Some marsters acted like savages. In some instances slaves were burned at the stake. Families were torn apart by selling. Mothers were sold from their children. Children were sold from their mothers, and the father was not considered in any way as a family part. These conditions were here before the Civil War and the conditions in a changed sense have been here ever since. The whites have always held the slaves in part slavery and are still practicing the same things on them in a different manner. Whites lynch, burn, and persecute the Negro race in America yet; and there is little they are doing to help them in anyway.

Lincoln got the praise for freeing us, but did he do it? He give us freedom without giving us any chance to live to ourselves and we still had to depend on the southern white man for work, food and clothing, and he held us through our necessity and want in a state of servitude but little better than slavery. Lincoln done but little for the Negro race and from a living standpoint nothing. White folks are not going to do nothing for Negroes except keep them down.

. . . The Yankees helped free us, so they say, but they let us be put back in slavery again.

When I think of slavery it makes me mad. I do not believe in giving you my story 'cause with all the promises that have been made the Negro is still in a bad way in the United States, no matter in what part he lives it's all the same. Now you may be all right; there are a few white men who are but the pressure is such from your white friends that you will be compelled to talk against us and give us the cold shoulder when you are around them, even if your heart is right towards us.

You are going around to get a story of slavery conditions and the persecutions of Negroes before the Civil War and the economic conditions concerning them since that war. You should have known before this late day all about that. Are you going to help us? No: you are only helping yourself. You say that my story may be put into a book, that you are from the Federal Writer's Project. Well, the Negro will not get anything out of it, no matter where you are from. . . . No matter where you are from I don't want you to write my story cause the white folks have been and are now and always will be against the Negro.

FROM BLACK CODES TO WHITE KNIGHTS AND LYNCHING

Before the Civil War, laws known as slave codes limited and prescribed the lives of slaves, forbidding them to learn to read and write or to travel or to own guns or to testify in court or to exercise any of a myriad of the rights of free people.

Immediately after the war, new Black Codes reimposed restrictions on liberty, restructuring laws to constrain newly freed black men and women. Because Black Codes were state laws, their provisions varied from state to state. In Mississippi, for example, freedmen were forbidden to rent or lease farms — they were allowed to work only on property owned by someone else. Curfews limited the hours that black people could be out of their residences. When

Black Codes were held unconstitutional or repealed, other segregation laws took their place.

Black Codes sometimes restricted the jobs available to black people, and almost invariably required that they work or go to jail as vagrants. This left black workers between a rock and a hard place. To get or keep a job, they had to agree to any demand made by an employer. Breaking a labor contract was also punishable by imprisonment.[4]

Nor did federal law offer much protection. The Civil Rights Act of 1875 was repealed in 1883. Supreme Court decisions gutted the promise of equal protection offered by the Fourteenth Amendment. In *Plessy v. Ferguson*, decided in 1892, the Supreme Court upheld Homer Plessy's Louisiana conviction for the crime of riding in a "white" railroad car. The court held that "separate but equal" facilities were constitutionally permissible.

Southern courts offered no protection to black men or women. Throughout the South, night riders terrorized blacks and Republicans. Some were organized into chapters of the White Knights of the Ku Klux Klan, while others were semiorganized mobs bent on ad hoc beating, burning, or lynching.

Klan members swore secrecy and dressed in masks and sheets to conceal their identities. Their symbol was (and is) a burning cross. Though the KKK faded away, it was revived in the early part of the twentieth century, on an "all-American" platform that included Jews, Catholics, foreigners, and labor unions as objects of hatred, along with blacks.

The KKK might burn a cross on someone's front lawn as a warning, but their primary purpose was delivery of terror. Masked night riders dragged whole families out of their homes, stripping and whipping their victims, from parents to young children. Homes were sometimes burned, women were sometimes raped, and victims were often killed. The KKK punished victims for "offenses" ranging from talking back to a white man to registering to vote. Often, however, their object seemed to be maintenance of terror, rather than punishment of any specific person for a real or imagined offense.

Elias Hill, a former slave, was crippled by disease from the age of seven, but nonetheless managed to teach himself to read and write and became a Baptist minister. His father had purchased his mother's freedom, and Elias, who had the stature of a dwarf, had been thrown in as a way of getting rid of a useless burden. In 1871, Reverend Hill testified before a congressional committee:

> On the night of the 5th of last May, after I had heard a great deal of what they had done in that neighborhood, they [the Ku Klux Klan] came. It was between 12 and 1 o'clock at night when I was awakened and heard the dogs barking, and something walking, very much like horses. . . . At last they came to my brother's door, which is in the same yard, and broke open the door and attacked his wife,

and I heard her screaming and mourning. . . . At last I heard them have her in the yard. She was crying and the Ku- Klux were whipping her to make her tell where I lived. . . . Some one then hit my door. It flew open. One ran in the house, and stopping about the middle of the house, which is a small cabin, he turned around, as it seemed to me as I lay there awake, and said, "Who's here?" Then I knew they would take me, and I answered, "I am here." He shouted for joy, as it seemed, "Here he is! Here he is! We have found him!" and he threw the bed-clothes off of me and caught me by one arm, while another man took me by the other and they carried me into the yard between the houses. . . . The first thing they asked me was, "Who did the burning? Who burned our houses?"—gin-houses, dwelling-houses and such. Some had been burned in the neighborhood. I told them it was not me; I could not burn houses; it was unreasonable to ask me. Then they hit me with their fists, and said I did it, I ordered it. They went on asking me didn't I tell the black men to ravish all the white women. No, I answered them. They struck me again with their fists on my breast, and then they went on. . . .

They pointed pistols at me all around my head once or twice, as if they were going to shoot me, telling me they were going to kill me; wasn't I ready to die, and willing to die? Didn't I preach? That they came to kill me—all the time pointing pistols at me. . . . One said "G—d d—n it, hush!" He had a horsewhip, and he told me to pull up my shirt, and he hit me. He told me at every lick, "Hold up your shirt." I made a moan every time he cut with the horsewhip. I reckon he struck me eight cuts right on the hip bone; it was almost the only place he could hit my body, my legs are so short—all my limbs drawn up and withered away with pain. . . . They all had disguises on. I then thought they would not kill me. One of them then took a strap, and buckled it around my neck and said, "Let's take him to the river and drown him. . . ."

They said "Look here! Will you put a card in the paper next week like June Moore and Sol Hill?" They had been prevailed on to put a card in the paper to renounce all republicanism and never vote. I said, "If I had the money to pay the expense, I could." They said I could borrow, and gave me another lick. They asked me, "Will you quit preaching?" I told them I did not know. I said that to save my life. They said I must stop the republican paper that was coming to Clay Hill. It has been only a few weeks since it stopped. The republican paper was then coming to me from Charleston. It came to my name. They said I must stop it, quit preaching, and put a card in the newspaper renouncing republicanism, and they would not kill me; but if I did not they would come back the next week and kill me.[5]

As a tool of terror and control, lynchings loomed large in both public imagination and reality. Lynching means mob punishment of someone accused of a crime, without due process of law. A report published by the NAACP documented 3,224 lynchings between 1889 and 1918.[6] Lynchings were not limited to the South, or to the immediate postwar period. Three black men were lynched in Duluth, Minnesota, in 1920.[7] Tens of thousands of people, mostly black, were lynched between 1867 and the 1930s.

Unlike the crimes of night riders, lynchings frequently took place in broad daylight, before crowds of people, sometimes in an almost festive atmosphere. In 1916, a white woman was found beaten to death near Waco, Texas. A seventeen-year-old black neighbor, who worked for her family, came under suspicion. To avoid an immediate lynching, the sheriff kept him in an out-of-town jail for a few days until a swift trial could be arranged. Though no medical evidence of rape was presented, Jesse Washington was pronounced guilty of murder and rape after a brief trial attended by hundreds of gun-toting citizens. Jury deliberations took only four minutes, and as soon as the verdict was read, the mob seized the young man. The story is retold by Philip Dray in his excellent book, *At the Hands of Persons Unknown: The Lynching of Black America.*[8]

> As he was prodded and dragged along, Washington was kicked, stabbed, hit with bricks and shovels, and had most of his clothes torn off; then was forced naked onto the pyre. The chain around his neck was looped over a tree limb, and he was jerked into the air. His body was sprinkled with coal oil, as were the boxes and scraps of wood below. There was a momentary delay when it was discerned that the tree itself, which adorned the city square, would be destroyed by the fire, but by now the crowd was huge and pressing in from all sides—students from Waco High on their lunch hour, secretaries, and businessman had wandered over to take in the event—and there was no stopping what was about to occur.
>
> Washington was lowered down one last time so that participants could cut off his fingers, ears, toes, and finally his penis, then with the crowd's delirious roar of approval, the oil-soaked boxes were lit and Washington's body began to be consumed by the flames. "Such a demonstration as of people gone mad was never heard before," recorded the *Waco Times*. When Washington was dead, a man on a horse lassooed the charred remains and dragged them through town, followed by a group of young boys. The skull eventually bounced loose and was captured by some of the boys, who pried the teeth out and offered them for sale.
>
> A local professional photographer, Fred A. Gildersleeve, had documented the lynching for the inevitable souvenir postcards.[9]

Race riots, too, functioned as a means of control. A 1906 riot in Atlanta, Georgia, was sparked by newspaper calls for the lynching of a black man who had allegedly spoken disrespectfully to (but not touched) a prominent white woman. In three days, white mobs killed nearly fifty black residents.[10] In 1917, a riot in East St. Louis drove six thousand people from their homes and left thirty-nine black people and eight whites dead.[11] During the "Red Summer" of 1919, race riots occurred in more than twenty cities. In 1921, rioting whites in Tulsa, Oklahoma, were supported by police and, according to some witnesses, even by airplanes dropping bombs on the black community.

Somewhere between seventy-five and three hundred members of the black community of Tulsa were killed by guns, bombs, and fires, some 1,100 homes destroyed, and black businesses looted and burned.

THE GREAT MIGRATION AND TWO WORLD WARS

What laws required in the South, custom accomplished in the North, segregating residential neighborhoods, employment, education, and even churches. Yet, for all that, the North offered greater freedom and opportunity than the South. During the early decades of the twentieth century, Southern blacks moved north in droves.

Workers followed jobs, as World War I stopped the flow of European immigrants to northern factories. The new immigrants sent word south of their new conditions and of the new freedoms they enjoyed. Hundreds of thousands of blacks had migrated from south to north in search of freedom from fear and opportunities for a better life for themselves and their children. They settled in Detroit and Chicago and New York, in segregated districts that they soon transformed into vibrant communities. They found work in Cleveland and Pittsburgh. From 1910 to 1920, Detroit's black population grew from five thousand to more than forty thousand.[12] By 1930, two million black people had come north.[13]

Though they enjoyed greater freedom in the urban North than they had in the rural South, white fear and racism quickly rose against them. White people organized in various cities to restrict the neighborhoods in which black people could live. Restrictive covenants were written into housing contracts, forbidding the sale or rental of property to black people. Residential segregation made school segregation easy.

White working-class prejudices against black people were reinforced by employers who hired black employees to defeat union organizing or as strikebreakers. Employers played on white fears that black workers would undercut hard-won wage and hour gains.

Many black men enlisted in the armed forces to fight in World War I. Upon their return, they were met with violence from whites who feared that the soldiers might want to claim some rights in the country for which they had fought. Wilbur Little, returning to his home in Georgia, was met by a mob at the train station and forced to take off his uniform and walk home in his underwear. A few days later, when he again appeared in uniform, he was killed.[14] Other returning black soldiers were also lynched in 1919.

In 1930, the majority of black people still lived in the South, mostly as tenant farmers or sharecroppers. With the onset of the Great Depression, the bottom fell out of the cotton market, and prices plummeted from 18 cents per pound in 1929 to 6 cents per pound in 1933. Black farmers were hard-hit. Many were forced off the land and into Southern cities, where, by 1932, more than half were unemployed. And the traditionally "last hired, first fired" black workers in the North also found themselves mostly unemployed.[15]

New Deal work programs clearly discriminated in favor of whites. They were administered by local officials, who refused to hire blacks or segregated them into the worst available jobs. To the dismay of whites, black workers found a champion in Eleanor Roosevelt. While they never came near parity with whites, the Roosevelt New Deal eventually opened some jobs to black workers, and extended some relief payments to impoverished, sometimes starving, black families.

Hundreds of thousands of black men and women enlisted in the U.S. Armed Forces to fight during World War II. From soldiers to poets to politicians, black people recognized the irony of fighting to preserve freedoms that they could not enjoy at home. They fought and died in mostly segregated units, leading the NAACP to protest that "A Jim Crow Army cannot fight for a free world."[16]

Returning from war, having fought for their country, black men were prepared to live in peace and with the honor that they had earned. Instead, they found themselves and their families hemmed in by new restrictions imposed by a fearful white majority. North and South, whites denounced the "cocky" attitudes of returning soldiers and decried the dangers presented by these "uppity Negroes."

For their part, the returning veterans were loath to recede into subservience. They had fought for their country—they intended to take their place in it. They demanded equality, if not integration, and were met with violence.

DYING TO BE FREE: THE CIVIL RIGHTS MOVEMENT

Jim Crow meant segregation for more than a century. Segregation permeated all areas of life—from restaurants and hotels and theaters to schools and libraries and public parks to workplaces and hospitals and cemeteries.

> It shall be unlawful to conduct a restaurant or other place for the serving of food in the city, at which white and colored people are served in the same room, unless such white and colored persons are effectually separated by a solid partition extending from the floor upward to a distance of seven feet or higher, and unless a separate entrance from the street is provided for each compartment.—Alabama

> The officer in charge shall not bury, or allow to be buried, any colored persons upon ground set apart or used for the burial of white persons.—Georgia

All marriages of white persons with Negroes, Mulattos, Mongolians, or Malaya hereafter contracted in the State of Wyoming are, and shall be, illegal and void.—Wyoming

Any person . . . who shall rent any part of any such building to a negro person or a negro family when such building is already in whole or in part in occupancy by a white person or white family shall be guilty of a misdemeanor.—Louisiana

No colored barber shall serve as a barber to white women or girls.—Georgia

Any negro man and white woman, or any white man and negro woman, who are not married to each other, who habitually live in and occupy in the nighttime the same room, shall each be punished by imprisonment not exceeding 12 months, or by fine not exceeding five hundred dollars.—Florida

There shall be maintained by the governing authorities of every hospital maintained by the state for treatment of white and colored patients separate entrances for white and colored patients and visitors, and such entrances shall be used by the race only for which they are prepared.—Mississippi

Any person guilty of printing, publishing or circulating matter urging or presenting arguments in favor of social equality or of intermarriage between whites and negroes, shall be guilty of a misdemeanor.—Mississippi

Any public hall, theatre, opera house, motion picture show or place of public entertainment which is attended by both white and colored persons shall separate the white race and the colored race.—Virginia

It shall be unlawful for a negro and white person to play together or in company with each other at any game of pool or billiards.—Alabama

The schools for white children and the schools for negro children shall be conducted separately.—Florida

In the mid-twentieth century, people in the civil rights movement fought, bled, and, often, died to overturn segregation in the United States. Equality and justice were not new ideas, nor was the civil rights movement a new cause.

During the nineteenth century, prominent black campaigners for equal rights included Frederick Douglass, Sojourner Truth, and Ida B. Wells, who devoted her life to campaigning against lynching. By the beginning of the twentieth century, two poles of thought were represented by W. E. B. Dubois and Booker T. Washington.[17]

No black leader was safe. Mobs tried to prevent Sojourner Truth from speaking in the 1860s. Ida B. Wells campaigned for passage of federal laws to stop lynchings in the late nineteenth century. She fled Memphis in 1892, under threat of being stripped and whipped because of her fiery newspaper columns. White men attacked and beat Booker T. Washington in New York City in 1911.[18] No one who spoke for the rights of black people was safe. National Association for the Advancement of Colored People executive secretary John Shillady, a white man, was arrested, released, and then beaten by a mob in Texas in 1919, barely making it out of the state alive.[19]

When even prominent figures could be attacked in public places, the danger to ordinary black citizens was even greater. A black tenant farmer who dared to demand even his fair share of the crop or an honest accounting might find himself and his family the victims of night riders or simply evicted from their home and blacklisted in the community so they could farm no other land.

The National Association for the Advancement of Colored People, founded in 1909, dominated the civil rights landscape for more than half a century. As a collaborative effort including both black and white founders and members, the NAACP carried on the tradition—and some of the conflicts—of the abolitionist movement and earlier organizations that promoted equal rights. And, while the civil rights movement burst upon the national consciousness of white America and the world in the 1960s, it had never vanished from the consciousness or communities of black America.

Despite danger and death threats, the civil rights movement grew inexorably. NAACP lawyers sued to end segregation in schools. After many years and battles, the cases consolidated as *Brown v. Board of Education* were decided by the Supreme Court in 1954. The Court declared public school segregation illegal and ordered schools to integrate "with all deliberate speed."[20]

The next year, Rosa Parks and the young Reverend Martin Luther King Jr. led an ambitious, and ultimately successful, effort to desegregate public transportation in Atlanta. Both a year-long boycott and legal action were needed to win this victory, and the campaign saw innumerable acts of courage in response to intimidation, arrests, beatings, and bombings.

The *Brown* decision and the Montgomery bus boycott catapulted the civil rights movement into national prominence. They were soon followed by lunch-counter sit-ins, demonstrations, rallies, marches, and Freedom Rides. As the civil rights movement grew, so did the violence that opposed it.

Police clubbed demonstrators, jailed them, beat them, doused them with fire hoses, set dogs on them, and protected angry whites who did even worse. Mobs attacked the buses carrying Freedom Riders, set the buses on fire, and beat the men and women who stumbled out of the burning buses until they fell, bloodied, to the ground, some suffering permanent damage to brains, eyes, and limbs. Arsonists burned black churches and homes.

Herbert Lee, a black Mississippi farmer and father of nine who dared to attend voter registration classes, was murdered by a white Mississippi legislator.[21] William Moore, a white postal worker on a solitary freedom march, was assassinated beside an Alabama highway. NAACP field secretary Medgar Evers was shot to death outside his front door.

The list of martyrs grew—Denise McNair, Addie Mae Collins, Cynthia Wesley, Carole Robertson, Jimmy Lee Jackson, Viola Liuzzo, James Reeb, Vernon Dahmer, Andrew Goodman, James Chaney, Michael Schwerner . . . and eventually Martin Luther King himself.

Through, and because of, the suffering and deaths of so many, the civil rights movement won the Civil Rights Act of 1964, the Voting Rights Act of 1965, and the Fair Housing Act of 1968.

Legal—*de jure*—segregation, that segregation required or allowed by law, was finally abolished throughout the United States. But the end of segregation laws did not end segregation. *De facto* segregation continued, and continues into the twenty-first century.

NOTES

1. James W. Loewen, *Lies My Teacher Told Me* (New York: Simon & Schuster, 1995).

2. Loewen, *Lies,* 194.

3. *Born in Slavery: Slave Narratives from the Federal Writers' Project, 1936–1938* (Washington, D.C.: Library of Congress, 1941). Online at http://memory.loc.gov/ammem/snhtml/snhome.html

4. Howard Zinn, *A People's History of the United States* (New York: Harper-Collins, 1980, 1995), 194.

5. Elias Hill, Testimony before Congressional Committee. Report of the Joint Select Committee to Inquire into the Condition of Affairs in the Late Insurrectionary States (Washington, 1872). Online at http://vi.uh.edu/pages/mintz/44.htm.

6. National Association for the Advancement of Colored People, *Thirty Years of Lynching in the United States, 1889–1919.* New York: NAACP, 1919.

7. Philip Dray, *At the Hands of Persons Unknown* (New York: Random House, 2002), 259.

8. Dray, *At the Hands of Persons Unknown.*

9. Dray, *At the Hands of Persons Unknown,* 218 et seq.

10. Taylor Branch, *Pillar of Fire* (New York: Simon & Schuster, 1998), 31–32.

11. Dray, *At the Hands of Persons Unknown,* 234.

12. Ronald Takaki, *A Different Mirror* (New York: Little, Brown), 341.

13. Takaki, *A Different Mirror,* 347.

14. Dray, *At the Hands of Persons Unknown,* 247–48.

15. Takaki, *A Different Mirror,* 366–67.

16. Takaki, *A Different Mirror,* 396.

17. Booker T. Washington believed that battles against white supremacy were fruitless and instead advocated hard work and accommodation with whites as the route to success, avoiding confrontation. His critics charged him with a willingness to trade political rights for economic opportunities. W. E. B. DuBois, a founder of the NAACP, demanded equal rights and loudly and eloquently protested injustice. DuBois rejected compromise and accommodation.

18. Dray, *At the Hands of Persons Unknown*, 187–89.

19. Dray, *At the Hands of Persons Unknown*, 248–49.

20. *Brown v. Board of Education*, 347 US 483 (1954).

21. Taylor Branch, *Parting the Waters* (New York: Simon & Schuster, 1988), 509–11.

3

The Continuing Injuries of Slavery and Jim Crow

De facto segregation is segregation-in-fact, achieved without the assistance of explicit segregation laws. When a city is divided into black neighborhoods, white neighborhoods, Hispanic neighborhoods, and Asian neighborhoods, that is *de facto* segregation. An example from the northern city of Chicago illustrates the force of *de facto* segregation in the 1960s.[1]

Bridgeport Library Branch, Chicago, IL. Circa 1963.

Two friends and I visited the Bridgeport Library Branch in Chicago, Illinois.

Bridgeport was the neighborhood of former Mayor Richard J. Daily [*sic*] and is all white. We were three Black young men of 11 and 12 years old. We visited the Bridgeport Branch because we couldn't find the books we needed at the Oakland branch, in the Black neighborhood. We crossed the color line to the other side of the tracks. We were young and didn't know. We were more afraid of avoiding the Black street gangs on the other side of the projects (Stateway Gardens).

After we got our books, we started to walk back home. We had no particular problems at the library other than strange looks (e.g., like "what are you niggers doing here"). Half way back to our neighborhood we were chased by a mob of white youths. They were out for blood. I remember the shouts of "kill those niggers."

We split up and ran in panic. One made it back to the library, one got caught in a storefront, and I ran like hell back to the neighborhood. I didn't make it. One of the mob members crashed his bike in front of me, a few hundred yards in front of the rest of the mob. We prepared to duke it out, before the rest of the mob arrived. I remember an old white man stopped his car and boomed, "leave that boy alone." I was surely saved from a severe beating. I was literally saved by a stranger. The mob held back and I suffered no more than a few scrapes and bruises.

As I reached the overpass on the Dan Ryan highway at 35th Street, I stopped and waited for my buddies. To my surprise, one stepped off a CTA bus (the one who returned to the library). He was escorted to the bus by the librarian. More surprising was that my other buddy was being escorted by the store owner and a few more white adults to the overpass. He only suffered a bruised jaw from a sucker punch.

I was never so scared in all of my life. We were attacked by a white mob for our brazen boldness to use the white library branch. My mother had to return my books.

Epilogue. I read a few years ago that another Black youth was attacked by a white mob in Bridgeport for playing on a softball field. He suffered severe head trauma and last I heard he was in a coma. I was lucky, he wasn't. The more things change, the more they stay the same.

—Kenneth M. Stone, CPA, St. Louis, Missouri

SEGREGATION AND RESEGREGATION

While segregation laws were more prevalent in southern states, most northern whites also subscribed to the popular notion of white superiority. During the early twentieth century, best-selling books included *The Negro: A Beast*, by Charles Carroll, *The Negro: A Menace to American Civilization*, by Robert W. Shufeldt, and *The Clansman: A Historical Romance of the Ku Klux Klan*, by Thomas Dixon.[2] The latter became the Hollywood hit, *The Birth of a Nation*, in 1915. The white prejudices embedded in the culture preserved *de facto* segregation and continued discrimination against black people.

These attitudes and their effects persist in the country today as patterns of relative race privilege and disadvantage continue to be maintained by individuals and social institutions.

- In 1993, the average white household owned assets worth $45,740. The average black household owned assets worth $4,418.
- In 1999, white male full-time workers earned an average of $40,100 annually. Black male full-time workers earned an average of $30,900. The income gap was reversed for full-time male workers with less than a high school education, which black males averaging $22,100 and white male workers averaging only $19,400. As educational levels rose, black male workers fell farther and farther behind their white counterparts.[3]

In 1954, when *Brown v. Board of Education* outlawed *de jure* school segregation, seventeen states had school segregation laws in place. A decade later, 98 percent of black students in the South still attended totally segregated schools.[4] Nationwide, 64 percent of black students attended schools that were 90 to 100 percent minority in 1968. Only in the decade following passage of the 1964 Civil Rights Act did school desegregation in the South move rapidly and consistently. The South became the nation's most integrated region.

Public, and especially federal governmental, support for integration diminished in the 1970s. Nationwide, the trend toward integration slowed but continued into the 1980s. In 1986, only 32.5 percent of black students attended 90- to 100-percent-minority schools.

In the late 1980s and continuing to the present, schools have been resegregating.[5] Resegregation accelerated after the U.S. Supreme Court rejected plans that required integration across city-suburban boundaries in *Milliken v. Bradley*.[6] The percentage of black students attending mostly-minority schools rose to 70 percent by 2000.[7]

School segregation, of course, is highly correlated to residential segregation. Across the nation, the 2000 census showed continuing racial segregation in housing. A study of Chicago housing found that patterns of segregation moved from the central city to the suburbs.[8]

We have not overcome the divisions of the color line, but are in the midst of a struggle in which the inequities of the past continue to reproduce themselves. In the six-county Chicago Metropolitan Area African-American and Latino people continue to live in segregated communities. This phenomenon is no longer the result of the divide between cities and suburbs. Today 27 percent of African-Americans and 39 percent of Latinos living in the Metropolitan Area live in the suburbs. Yet the suburbs they live in are segregated from those in which Whites live. Fifty percent of African-Americans living in incorporated suburbs live in just 13 of the six-county area's 264 suburbs; 50 percent of suburban Latinos live in just 17 of the incorporated suburbs. Looking at the data from the perspective of the educational opportunities of children: 50 percent of African-American children live in just 15 of the 245 elementary suburban school districts in the six-county area; and 50 percent of Latino children live in just 17 school districts in the six-county area. . . .

Segregation in the Chicago metropolitan persists in the twenty-first century in much the same way as it persisted in the twentieth century. The one major difference is that the color line is no longer within the city or between the city and its suburbs. It now separates the suburbs themselves and suburban school districts. We are reproducing the segregation in the suburbs with the same force as people 100 years ago first produced it in the city. The data on the way in which the metropolitan area has changed over the past 10 years show that there are plenty of opportunities for racial and ethnic integration to take hold in the metropolitan area. There are now many more areas where minorities and Whites live side by side. But this integration is, for the most part, only temporary. The trends are clear—if a municipality, school district, or census tract is integrated it will likely resegregate. White people, led by upper-and middle-income Whites, seem hell-bent on fleeing minorities.

At the beginning of the twentieth century, W. E. B. DuBois asserted that the color line would be the problem of the new century. At the beginning of the twenty-first century, the color line persisted and race continues to be the problem of the century, playing out in divided U.S. communities, in continuing economic inequality, and in international relations between the white-identified United States and Europe and the overwhelmingly nonwhite world.

NOTES

1. American Radioworks, "Children of Jim Crow," in *Remembering Jim Crow,* online at www.americanradioworks.org/features/remembering/children.html#14 (accessed August 23, 2003).

2. Taylor Branch, *Parting the Waters* (New York: Simon & Schuster, 1988), 31.

3. Glenn C. Loury, *The Anatomy of Racial Inequality* (Cambridge: Harvard University Press, 2002), 178, 175.

4. Gary Orfield, "Schools More Separate: Consequences of a Decade of Resegregation," *Rethinking Schools* 16:1, online at www.rethinkingschools.org/archive/16_01/Seg161.shtml (accessed August 23, 2003).

5. Erika Frankenberg and Chungmei Lee, "Race in American Public Schools: Rapidly Resegregating School Districts." Report of the Civil Rights Project (Cambridge: Harvard University), online at www.civilrightsproject.harvard.edu/research/deseg/reseg_schools02.php#fullreport (accessed August 23, 2003).

6. *Milliken v. Bradley*, 418 U.S. 717 (1974).

7. Orfield, "Schools More Separate," 8.

8. Guy Stuart, "Integration or Resegregation: Metropolitan Chicago at the Turn of the New Century." Report of the Civil Rights Project (Cambridge: Harvard University), online at www.civilrightsproject.harvard.edu/research/deseg/reseg_schools02 .php#fullreport (accessed August 23, 2003).

4

Slavery's Insults:
The Continuing Nonmaterial Injuries of Slavery

Since reparations are typically understood to involve compensation for the effects of slavery and its aftermath, reparations advocates almost invariably concentrate on the economic harms suffered by slaves and their descendants. Thus we hear about unpaid labor, seized inheritances, unjust enrichment, and opportunity usurped.

In reparations circles we hear much less often about continuing injury that is not economic or material. There are, however, discussions of continuing nonmaterial injuries that we should listen to as well.

Slavery was an insult in two senses. In the first, slavery was a kind of moral *stain*. Africans in America were demeaned by slavery. Slavery also insulted in the medical sense. It created psychological *injury*.

MORAL STAIN OR TAINT

How could slavery, a practice that ended in the mid-nineteenth century, continue to stigmatize? If it does, what sort of stain or mark does it apply? Finally, how does the stigma damage the descendants of slaves today?

It is hard to imagine how slavery in one's family's past can stain one today, particularly in today's America, where intergenerational moral ties seem to be especially weak. In America, the relationships between the generations are so tenuous and loose that it is possible for philosophers to ask quite soberly, "What if anything do adult children owe their parents?"[1] The all-but-spoken background assumption to this question is, "Whatever children owe their parents, it cannot be much, perhaps only gratitude and that only sometimes." Moral ties between generations are, in general, not felt to be particularly strong.

While we may be somewhat unclear whether we have backward-looking obligations to our ancestors, we are generally quite certain that "the sins of the fathers" are not to be visited upon the "sons." No misdeed of previous generations, we are inclined to say, reflects on subsequent generations. No shame of theirs is a shame of ours.

If the subject is slavery, the idea that there is a legacy of shame seems even less credible. If one's ancestors were slaves, what about that fact should provoke shame in them, let alone in their descendants? Why should suffering any form of injustice reflect badly on the unfortunate victims? The injustice is the perpetrators', not the victims'. If there is no stigma in being the object of unjust treatment, then there can be no inherited stigma in being the descendants of victims. If anyone is morally tainted by slavery and its aftermath, it should not be African Americans but slaveholders, white supremacists, and anyone who benefited by slavery or the subordination of black people.

What sort of moral calculation, then, can it be that assigns moral taint to those who suffer injustice but are not responsible for it? And how could the stain become a legacy? To suggest that either victim or descendant is stained seems to be an improper, even wicked, assessment. In actual fact, however, reparations proponents argue that African Americans, the descendants of slaves and other dark-skinned people associated with them, remain stigmatized in America today.

We can and will say two things about this: (a) It is possible to diagnose stigma as no moral taint at all but rather a bad attitude that is in the eye of the beholder (whether that beholder is consciously racist otherwise). Or, (b), we can continue to understand stigma or taint as a moral phenomenon attaching to slaves and their descendants, and we can attempt to understand, at the same time, not so much whether this makes sense but of what sort of a moral scheme or system it might make sense.

(a) First, stigma as a bad attitude in the eye of the beholder. Stigma, in this account, cannot be anything like a moral fault, failing, or any sort of morally denigrating characteristic because attaching such to an innocent victim is morally outrageous. So, stigmatization is no more than the negative regard in which a person is viewed by the stigmatizer, together with the consequences of that negative regard. To be stigmatized is just to be viewed and treated by others as though one bears some taint.

What are the characteristics of stigma or taint?

The British philosopher J. L. Austin reminded us that in matters philosophical, ordinary language, though not the Last Word, might indeed be the First Word. In that spirit, consider what is said of the transitive verb *stigmatize*. *To stigmatize* means to brand or label as *disgraceful* or *shameful,* and it is said to be synonymous with the verbs *stain, brand*, and *anathematize.* Related words include *dishonor, reproach, stamp, malign*, and *smear.*

Stigmatized people are smeared, morally stained, or maligned. Their situation is somehow disgraceful or shameful.

But how can the condition of daughters and sons, let alone that of great-great-great grandchildren, be made shameful by the unjust treatment of their forebears? So far, we have suggested that they cannot be shamed by this—none of them, neither descendants nor the victims themselves. So, the stigma mars, not slaves or their descendants, but those who would attach it to them.

(b) Second, how slavery taints slaves and their descendants.

But do we really *believe* this, that there is no taint in having been a slave or in being a slave's progeny? Or is this just what we *say we believe* when we actually believe contrary things and act in other, contrary ways?

Consider a somewhat analogous case, the case of historical anti-Semitism and the Jews.[2]

Jews are viewed by themselves and by others as belonging to a group that has been the target of one or another sort of viciousness for centuries and indeed for millennia. Despite anti-Semitic allegations to the contrary, almost everyone would agree that historically Jews have been the innocent victims of horrendous historical injustices.

Still, you have only to raise the question, *Why have the Jews been targeted so often?* and you produce embarrassment, hesitation, and defensiveness as Jews and others cast about for a satisfactory answer to the question.

Now, this is certainly not to suggest that Jews, Judaism, or Jewry are in any way deserving of the atrocities visited upon them historically. Nor need it suggest that Jews do morally unobjectionable things that nonetheless bring the ill treatment upon them.

Instead, I want here to draw attention only to the fact that there is something in the question that sticks. The question suggests to most hearers the presence of some sort of moral, spiritual, religious, or whatever *defect* in Jews, Judaism, or Jewry. I want to say further that this defect is attached to the circumstance of *being a victim*. For Jews this is a particularly disturbing association because, for most Jews and others, Jewish history is the history of victimization (that some have termed *Leidensgeschiche*, literally *suffering history*).[3] In this popular view, to be a Jew is to be a member of this group regularly abused across all of its history.

The problem is that there seems to be some sort of disgrace attached to being a victim.

In modern discourse, *victim* typically has one of two meanings:

victim n   *(1) an unfortunate person who suffers from some adverse circumstance*
(2) a person who is tricked or swindled (synonym: dupe)

For the most part, the first sense captures the meaning of the word as it is most often used in America, but the associations of the second sense seem to be present as a residue.

Acknowledging that one is a victim or that one has been victimized is an uncomfortable thing to do in contemporary America. The acknowledgment carries with it often an unspoken suspicion of the presence of some unguarded weakness, a condition against which one would have been defended or fortified if one were wise and not foolish.

The unspoken presumption seems to be that for any case of victimization there was an antecedent vulnerability about which one could be ashamed. When we bring this presumption to consciousness and moral reflection, the presumption seems wrong. If we have not been negligent or unreasonably lacking in foresight, then what befalls us, befalls us. It is not a matter for which we have any responsibility, and so we ought not to feel shame over such consequences.

The "official view" of our moral culture is that if one is not responsible for what happens, then one bears no moral stain. Our everyday assessment, however, is often quite different. Who we are, as persons and as "moral agents," is sometimes more than what we do; it is also sometimes what befalls us.

Perhaps we might challenge this notion of responsibility and its relationship to shame. Might it be that in some moral scheme shame might accrue where there is no responsibility? Might it be that this is sensible somehow?

Before we proceed too far, it would be helpful to bear in mind a distinction alluded to above that Bernard Williams makes in his book on the ancient Greeks, *Shame and Necessity*.[4] Williams cautions us there that before we can make any headway on this very matter, we must distinguish between *what we think* and *what we think we think*.

What we think we think is that actions or states of affairs for which we bear no responsibility are, morally speaking, no reflection on us whatsoever. *What we think we think* also is that we, as individuals, almost never bear any responsibility for what our forbears did nor for what our adult offspring will do.

What we think, however, is that there are indeed conditions in which we find ourselves, conditions over which we had no say, that are nonetheless shameful. Having been victimized is one. *What we think* is also that our forbears' and our offspring's conduct and condition do indeed reflect on us.

About *what we think* we could say, "How foolish and unreflective." This is what is thought before *real thinking* has happened. And about *what we think we think* we might congratulate ourselves.

The residue is, however, hard to wipe away. Why? One reason is that we are the heirs of a powerful moral tradition that we seem not yet ready to abandon, perhaps, as Williams believes, for good reason. Whether Williams is right about his estimate of the enduring merit of this moral tradition is not our subject. What it involves, however, is.

That tradition is to be found in classical Greece and Roman literature. To understand it, we are guided by the work of Orlando Patterson, who discusses it explicitly in the context of slavery.

ORLANDO PATTERSON ON THE
DEGRADED STATUS OF THE SLAVE

In *Slavery and Social Death: A Comparative Study,* Harvard sociologist Orlando Patterson argues that a slave is a person utterly deprived of honor.[5] Honor is intimately connected with power, specifically the power to exercise one's will effectively, especially over others. The inability to do so denudes one of honor and reduces one to shame. There is virtually nothing more shameful then than being a slave.

Patterson's discussion of honor, slavery, and shame is cross-cultural but draws a good deal of its support from his analysis of ancient Greek and Roman sources.

Perhaps the most famous ancient discussion of slavery, though not noted by Patterson, is in Aristotle. Aristotle distinguishes between slaves by nature and slaves by accident. Slaves by accident are slaves whose inferior status is an accident of war, politics, or other contingencies. Slaves by nature are those whose constitutions fit them for lives of subordination and nothing more.

Though Aristotle seems to establish two distinct categories of slaves, only one of which involves persons who actually deserve to be slaves, his discussion is a bit murkier than this clear dichotomy would suggest.

First we will briefly review Aristotle's general doctrine on slavery.[6] Then we will review the distinction among slaves that Aristotle purports to draw. Then, with this review in mind, we will return to Patterson's discussion.

Slaves and masters, as well as males and females, says Aristotle, are classified as "those who cannot exist without one another. . . ." and their relation is a "natural" one.

> For that which can foresee by the exercise of the mind is by nature intended to be lord and master, and that which can with its body give effect to such foresight is a subject, and by nature a slave.

Aristotle contends that the relation is not contrary to nature and that some are from their birth clearly meant to rule, others to be slaves. Given their natural propensities, the relation is just, and also expedient (the best arrangement from the standpoint of utility). The dominion of masters is total.

Now, instruments are of various sorts; some are living, others lifeless . . . a slave
is a living possession. . . .
. . .The slave is not only the slave of his master, but wholly belongs to him.
Hence we see what is the nature and office of a slave; he who is by nature not
his own but another man's, is by nature a slave; and he may be said to be another's man who, being a human being, is also a possession.

Slavery is not just a relation among men, but a cosmological principle.
Like Plato, Aristotle understands order (cosmos), harmony, as the subjection
of elements to their proper ruler.

. . . for all things which form a composite whole and which are made up of parts,
whether continuous or discrete, a distinction between the ruling and the subject
element comes to light. Such a duality exists in living creatures, but not in them
only; *it originates in the constitution of the universe.*[7]

The soul and the body stand as master to slave:

[In living creatures, the duality] consists of soul and body; and of these two, the
one is by nature the ruler, and the other the subject.
. . . the soul rules over the body with a despotical rule, whereas the intellect
rules the appetites with a constitutional and royal rule.
From the standpoint of their capacities, slave souls are unable to arrive at
principles or give themselves rules to follow, though they are able to understand
and apply such rules and principles.

This analysis of the capacities of slaves and their natural rulers will play itself out in two ways: one in terms of cognitive capacity and its presumed relationship to one's status as a slave or freeman, and one in terms of the kind
of political organization associated with freemen and slaves.
The capacity to "apprehend . . . rational principles" emerges as the kind of
contemplation philosophers engage in, and so (a) only those who are able to
engage in the kind of abstract discourse philosophers do will be thought to be
naturally free men; and (b) those who can form a state (as opposed to traditional forms of social organization not created as the result of deliberation
[e.g. tribalism, kingship, etc.]) are free, but those who haven't created such a
political form are going to be declared "natural slaves." Slaves "have no share
in happiness or in a life of free choice"; that is, they cannot undertake the activities that are constituent in *eudaimonia* or human flourishing, one of which
is the contemplation of first principles and the ability to give them to oneself.
Returning to the question of the aptness of drawing a distinction between
slaves by nature and slaves by law, Aristotle concedes that the distinction has
a point, but then he proceeds to take it all back.

First, he asserts that there are indeed slaves by nature.

> But is there any one thus intended by nature to be a slave, and for whom such a
> condition is expedient and right, or rather is not all slavery a violation of nature?
>   There is no difficulty in answering this question, on grounds both of reason
> and of fact. For that some should rule and others be ruled is a thing not only
> necessary, but expedient; *from the hour of their birth, some are marked out for
> subjection, others for rule.*

On the one hand, Aristotle notes that the critics of the idea of natural slavery (that there are persons who are "fit" for slavery) are persons who abhor
the idea that because "one man has the power of doing violence and is superior in brute strength, another shall be his slave and subject." There seems to
be notion in play that superior strength does not entail by itself moral superiority that would justify the rule of the stronger over the weaker. Might does
not make right. And Aristotle thinks they have a point.

> But that those who take the opposite view have in a certain way right on their
> side, may be easily seen. For the words slavery and slave are used in two senses.
> There is a slave or slavery by law as well as by nature. The law of which I speak
> is a sort of convention—the law by which whatever is taken in war is supposed
> to belong to the victors. But this right many jurists impeach, as they would an
> orator who brought forward an unconstitutional measure: they detest the notion
> that, because one man has the power of doing violence and is superior in brute
> strength, another shall be his slave and subject. Even among philosophers there
> is a difference of opinion.

Thus Aristotle seems to be committed to the view that not all persons who
are slaves in fact are slaves by nature. Some are slaves by convention, by hap-
penstance, by "law," in the sense that they have been enslaved under provisions of some local custom (such as the custom that prisoners of war may be
enslaved) and are therefore not slaves by nature. Bad things happen and not
all of them are justified or justifiable.
     On the other hand, Aristotle is quite persuaded that *superiority is superior-
ity*, that if one possesses certain characteristics preeminently, then one is also
somehow preeminent in excellence (virtue). He says,

> . . . and as superior power is found only where there is superior excellence of
> some kind, power seems to imply virtue. . . . (*Politics* 1.6)

Then the rule of the stronger is not just a case of the rule of someone who
is *merely stronger,* but of the one who is someone of "superior excellence" or
"virtue." Thus the distinction between slave by nature and slave by convention
seems to collapse into a single category—slave by nature.

In our day, we tend to indulge in Aristotle's reasoning when we suppose that there is some moral or other *weakness* in those who find themselves subjugated at every turn. We tend to think that there must be something constitutionally deficient or inferior in those who, time after time, find themselves with the short end of the stick or at the bottom of the pile.

In these passages, Aristotle simply puts the same kind of reasoning in the affirmative. If someone dominates, then there must be something to his superiority. Elsewhere, however, Aristotle's reasoning is very much like our own: For example, in section 39, *Politics* 1285a (18)–1285b (29), he notes that servility is signaled by a failure to rebel against despotism.

In any event, while Aristotle allows that in principle it is possible that not all slaves are slaves by nature, in practice, something about the ability of some to dominate others suggests, he thinks, their natural superiority and at the same time some natural inferiority in those subject to the domination of another's will.

Returning to Patterson's discussion of slavery and dishonor, we may note that in his *Introduction,* Patterson quotes the early modern English philosopher Thomas Hobbes.

> The manifestation of the Value we set on one another, is that which is commonly called *Honouring* and *Dishonouring*. To Value a man at a high rate is to *Honour* him; at a low rate is to *Dishonour* him. But high and low, in this case, is to be understood by comparison to the rate that each man setteth on himself.

The link between honor and power is direct:

> To obey is to Honour; because no man obeys them, whom they think have no power to help, or hurt them. And consequently to disobey is to Dishonour.

Somewhat cynically Hobbes observes that it really does not matter "whether an action . . . be just or unjust: for Honour consisteth onely in the opinion of power."[8]

The slave can have no honor, says Patterson, because he has no power. His dishonor is a general condition, unlike that of the free man, who may suffer occasions of dishonor. The slave's dishonor is perpetual and unremitting. Patterson notes that the first century B.C.E. writer Publilius Syrus, himself once a slave, wrote that "the height of misery is to live at another's will."[9]

In his chapter, "Honor and Degradation," Patterson sets out to make three principal points.

1. In all slave societies the slave was considered a degraded person.
2. The honor of the master was enhanced by the subjection of his slave;

3. Wherever slavery became structurally very important, the whole tone of the slaveholders' culture tended to be highly honorific. (In many societies, the sole reason for keeping slaves was in fact their honorific value.)[10]

As to the nature of honor, Patterson says that there is an anthropological consensus to be found in the work of Julian Pitt-Rivers:

It is a sentiment, a manifestation of this sentiment in conduct, and the evaluation of this conduct by others, that is to say, reputation. It is both internal to the individual and external to him—a matter of his feelings, his behavior, and the respect he receives.[11]

Honor, Patterson believes, is a sentiment, a set of behaviors one engages in, and a social response to these, but all of them concern one's place in the social order, which Patterson, like Plato and Aristotle, assumes must involve ranks and ranking.

To belong to a community is to have a sentence of one's position among one's fellow members, to feel the need to assert and defend that position, and to feel a sense of satisfaction if that claimed position is accepted by others and a sense of shame if it is rejected.[12]

Asserting and defending one's position is in part a matter of power. Patterson quotes Pitt-Rivers:

. . . the claim of honor depends always in the last resort upon the ability of the claimant to impose himself. Might is the basis of right to precedence, which goes to the man who is bold enough to enforce his claim, regardless of what may be thought of his merits.[13]

So honor and might are intimately connected, because honor is centrally identifiable with the power to enforce one's will. Slaves with no power have no effective will and so are fundamentally degraded and without honor.[14]

The question is, of course, Does this attitude toward being a slave have any merit? But this question rests on two others, one narrow and one much broader.

The narrow question is this: Does the mere fact of subordination reveal something faulty in the will or actions of those who are dominated? The contemporary answer we are inclined to give this question is no. Unless there has been some negligence in preparation or defense, unless there has been an avoidable lack of foresight, unless there has been a regrettable failure of will, losing out to superior force is blameless. To conclude otherwise is to commit the sin of "blaming the victim." This is *what we say we think* about such things.

The broader question concerns whether our moral stature or status can be adversely affected by what befalls us as well as by what we do. Contemporary orthodoxy answers this question with a "no" as well. "Ought" implies "can," *we think we think*. In order to be blameworthy or to be the subject of any kind of moral approbation, we must be capable of doing otherwise. I can be held accountable morally for *x* only if *x*-ing was something I did voluntarily. If *x* is coerced, if it is forced upon me, if I cannot have avoided doing *x*, then I am free of any taint that *x*-ing might carry with it. What befalls me is no reflection on me.

Do we really think this? I think not. First of all, recall our earlier discussion of the discomfort experienced by Americans in acknowledging victimization. A portion of the backlash to feminism in America rests on the claim that feminists portray women as *victims,* and this is, say the antifeminists, a very bad way to see women. Many persons involved in initiatives to end violence against women note that one of the obstacles standing in the way of battered women seeking help is the shame felt in being victimized. It seems that whatever we say about voluntariness, some shame and some moral taint attach to those circumstances where bad things befall us.

That this kind of moral stigmatization can occur has to do with the fact that honor and shame attach not only to action but also to identity. Williams is especially helpful in understanding this.

Williams draws our attention to two characters from ancient Greek tragedy, Oedipus and Ajax. Each winds up, through no fault of his own, being involved in circumstances that each finds intensely shameful, despite the fact that they bore, we would say, no responsibility for the outcomes.

Oedipus, despite acting resolutely to avoid fulfilling a prophecy that he would kill his father and marry his mother, unwittingly winds up doing both. On the basis of what information and power he had, Oedipus does all the right things to avoid fulfilling the prophecy, and still, things end up badly.

Williams frames his discussion in the following way:

> So far we have been concerned with responses that are demanded by some people, or by a legal system, of other people. But there is another aspect to responsibility, which comes out if we start on the question, not from the response that the public or the state, or the neighbors, or the damaged parties demand of the agent, but from what the agent demands of himself.[15]

The moral relation here is not between self and others but is self-regarding, instead. Calling it *responsibility* may mislead.[16] What Williams has in mind here is our moral *status* or *stature* in our own eyes.[17] The moral assessment is by the agent of herself.

Oedipus says of his misadventures, "I have done it with my own hand," and while Oedipus comes to regard the punishments he inflicts on himself for these unintended deeds as excessive, the shape his life has assumed appalls him. Williams writes:

> Not even Oedipus as he is represented in his last days, thought that blinding and exile had to be the response. But should there be no response? Is it as though it had never happened? Or rather, to put the right question: Is it as though such things had happened, but not by his agency—that Laius [Oedipus' father] had died for instance, indeed had been killed, but as Oedpus first believed, and then, for a short while hoped, by someone else? The whole of *Oedipus Tyrannus*, that dreadful machine, moves to the discovery of just one thing, that *he did it*. Do we understand the terror of his discovery only because we residually share magical beliefs in blood-guilt, or archaic notions of responsibility? Certainly not: we understand it because we know that in the story of one's life there is an authority exercised by what one has done, and not merely by what one has intentionally done.[18]

That the deeds were done by Oedipus's own hand and not someone else's is the salient fact whether or not he intended to do them, whether or not he had full responsibility for their commission. That they occurred at all was regrettable, but that they occurred as a result of his personal undertakings is appalling to him. It is *his life*, Oedipus thinks, not just the history of the world, which is stained. Oedipus's life is ruined, and whose would not be?

Now, I am arguing that this is, in Williams's terms, *what we think* and not *what we think we think*. Our ordinary line on "responsibility" leaves us free of any taint for acts in which we could not have done otherwise, unintentional acts, and their unintended consequences. In fact, says Williams—and I agree—we would be appalled to find ourselves in Oedipus's situation. We would not say our case was simply regrettable but no "reflection" on us. We would, moreover, be appalled by someone who failed to be appalled upon finding themselves the murderer of one parent and spouse of the other.

This is a hard fact about the moral universe we seem to inhabit: We are indeed vulnerable to the slings and arrows of outrageous fortune. That an action is not intended and its consequences unforeseeable does not make us morally invulnerable. We are sometimes in the wrong though we have done no wrong.

How can this be?

Consider Williams's next discussion of another figure of Greek literature, the hero Ajax in the play by Sophocles. Having been slighted by the leaders of the Greek expedition to Troy, Ajax sets about to kill them all. Athena makes Ajax mad to forestall his murderous project. Thinking he is murdering Odysseus and his men, Ajax instead kills the Greeks' sheep. When he wakes up, he realizes what he has done and how he has made himself absurd. He, the warrior giant, greatest Greek warrior after Achilles, the "bulwark," has heroically slaughtered a herd of sheep! Ajax realizes, says Williams, that hereafter he, Ajax, will be a laughingstock to the world, and that this is intolerable.

Williams says, "Being what he is, he could not live as the man who had done these things: it would be merely impossible in virtue of the relations between what he expects of the world and what the world expects of a man who expects that of it."[19] Ajax understands himself as a man of certain kind—as a man with a particular identity, and his conduct is inconsistent with what he expects from a man with that identity. In fact, his deeds are permanently inconsistent with that identity: no one could be the Ajax that existed before the sheep were slaughtered and yet slaughter the sheep. That Ajax is now gone, given what he and the world expect of the anterior Ajax. That Ajax might be said to have died with the sheep. The diminished Ajax therefore decides upon suicide.

Nor will it do to tell Ajax to "lighten up," or to argue with him that what others think of him, his reputation, really is of no consequence. Williams concludes,

> People do not *have* to think that they could not live in that situation; they do not *have* to think any such thing . . . but they may sensibly think it if their understanding of their lives and the significance their lives possessed for other people is such that what they did destroyed the only reason they had for going on. Still more, they may recognize that what they unintentionally did, if it did not destroy their lives, changed them radically, and changed them because they did that thing, not just because of what happened to them.[20]

One's identity, then, can be affected by matters over which one has no control. One's acts, however hemmed in by necessity or contingency, by bad luck or by the power of others, can nonetheless adversely affect one's identity. That a slave is dishonored is another hard fact of our moral universe. His genuflections, his inability to protect those dearest to him, his utter inability to claim a place and respect for that place, nonetheless can come to form who he is.[21]

Is such dishonor transmissible across generations? The answer, I think, is, likewise, that it needn't be but that it may be. Most of us understand who we are, our identities, in part in terms of our origins and the history of our ancestors. Where we "came from" is often a central consideration in who we understand ourselves to be. We needn't, perhaps, think of ourselves in this manner, but we often do. Insofar as we do, then, we may feel a certain historical shame and dishonor. We certainly sometimes claim pride and honor for the culture and achievements of our forebears. And to the degree that our identities are thought to be collective, that we are thought of prominently as members of groups, we should expect such things to transfer.

So, the descendants of slaves may still have the dishonor of slavery to contend with.

SPIRITUAL AND PSYCHOLOGICAL INJURY

It never ends. I watched him through the spyglass to see what the game would be. There were five of them. He gets them all gathered at the river's edge and they are nervous. If they haven't done this before, they've heard about it. First he reads to them from the bible. I don't have to hear it to know what passage it is. Then they have to strip, which takes no time as they are wearing only linen pantaloons. One by one they must grasp the rope, swing over the water, and drop in. It's brutally hot; the cool water is a relief, so they make the best of it. He encourages them to shout and slap at one another once they are in the water. Then they have to come out and do it again, only this time they hang on the rope two at a time, which means one has to hold on to the other. They had gotten this far when I looked.

Two boys were pulling the rope, one holding on while the other clutched his shoulders. They were laughing because they were slippery. The sun made their bodies glisten and steam like a horse's flanks after a long run. The boy on the round ran down the bank and off they went, out over the water releasing the rope at the highest point of its arc and crashing into the smooth surface below like wounded Black geese. He hardly watched them. He was choosing the next two, directing one to catch the rope on its return, running his hands over the shoulders of the other, which made the boy cower and study the ground. I couldn't watch anymore.

They have to keep doing this, their little young bodies displayed to him in various positions. When he gets them up to three or four at a time, he watches closely. The boys rub against each other; they can't help it. Their limbs become entwined, they struggle to hang on, and it isn't long before one comes out of the water with his member raised. That's what the game is for. This boy tries to stay in the water, he hangs his head as he comes out, thinking every thought he can to make the tumescence subside. This is what proves they are brutes, he says, and have not the power of reason. A white man, knowing he would be beaten for it, would not be able to raise his member.

He has his stick there by the tree . . . Sometimes the offending boy cries out or tries to run away, but he's no match for this grown man with his stick. . . . If he can find the boy's mother, and she's pretty, she will pay dearly for rearing an unnatural child. . . .

. . .This is only one of his games . . .

Often, as I look through the glass I hear in my head an incredulous refrain: *This is my husband, this is my husband.*[22]

This is fiction, from a novel that appeared in early 2003, written about life on a sugar plantation north of New Orleans Ascension Parish, Louisiana, in

1828. According to Joyce Carol Oates, while the story is not drawn from any one incident, the author, Valerie Martin, "[drew] upon numerous slave narratives compiled by the Library of America, as well as books about the antebellum South like Herbert Aptheker's *American Negro Slave Revolts,* John Hope Franklin and Loren Schweninger's *Runaway Slaves,* Walter John's *Soul by Soul: Life Inside the Antebellum Slave Market,* as well as on the journals of two Louisiana plantation owners."[23]

Fiction has certain advantages: It allows a distillation or compression of several events, phenomena, and players into a single scene or line of action in order to reveal their characteristic forms. In the quotation above, we can see clearly the concatenation of force, domination, sexual oppression, and the distortion in family relations that occurs as a result. All of these features were characteristic and definitive of American slavery. Their consequences are not easily or thoroughly extinguished.

As to the historical relevance of this fictional scene, consider an essay by the eminent historian of slavery, David Brion Davis. In his essay "Life and Death in Slavery," Davis discusses a book by Melton A. McLaurin about a young black woman, named only Celia, age fourteen, who was purchased by a farmer in Missouri, in 1850, to be used as a sexual slave on his plantation in the bottom lands due west of St. Louis.[24] Celia is made noteworthy, not as a victim of sexual predation (because in this respect she was characteristic of her class), but because ultimately she killed her tormentor and went to trial over the homicide.

While the reciprocal violence is unusual, Celia's situation, Davis tells us, is not, though her story, as recounted by McLaurin, "presents glimpses of slavery that are almost never revealed in other accounts."[25] The story involves, says Davis, individuals and events that are nonetheless not at all unusual: What distinguished the planter Robert Newsom was that he was murdered by his own slave.[26]

Robert Newsom, described by McLaurin as "the fulfillment of the Jeffersonian dream," and "the self-sufficient yeoman farmer," was sixty years old when he bought Celia, who at fourteen was the same age as his youngest daughter. His intention was to use her for sex while presenting her as ostensibly a servant for his daughters. He raped her on the road from the point of purchase.

It is unlikely, Davis reasons, that Newsom's family could have been unaware of his relationship with Celia, however hard they tried to look away. Newsom's oldest daughter, Virginia, either widowed or separated, lived with Newsom and managed the household after the death of his wife one year before Celia's arrival. She could hardly have missed her father's frequent trips to Celia's cabin, fifty yards from the house, nor could she have been utterly in the dark about the parentage of Celia's light-skinned children. The same might be said for the other Newsoms living in the household, two brothers and another sister.

Celia, who had fallen in love with one of Newsom's young slaves, George, began to resist Newsom's advances. On a Saturday night in June 1855, she killed Newsom with a club, Though it is likely that someone else probably assisted a woman of her size, no one else was charged with the murder.

Celia confessed and was tried. Her legal team consisted of a former congressman and two young attorneys, all of whom had come from slaveholding families. The defense team did not offer self-defense as their theory, even though at the time some southern states allowed such a defense to slaves accused of capital crimes. Instead they defended Celia in terms of sexual honor, which under Missouri law entitled "any woman" to use deadly force to protect her "honor" against forcible intercourse.

The rub of course was that it was unlikely a black woman would be allowed to count as "any woman" protected by the Missouri statute despite the obvious scope of the phrase. The judge's instructions to the jury apparently made this impossible, and, as a result, the defense called the judge's instructions "illegal" and moved for a new trial. This was unsuccessful, and Celia was hanged on December 21. The defense petition for a stay was denied, despite their contention that "the greater portion of the community here are much interested in her behalf."[27]

Celia's trial was extraordinary because her oppression had been so obvious that it had driven the sons of slaveholders in a slavery state to defend her "honor" and found sympathy even among the white community. But her life was marked by what were for slavery characteristic features: force and violence, predatory sexuality, and the derangement of family life, both for slaves and slaveholders.

Historian Nell Irvin Painter has explored the consequences of this life for slaves and their offspring in her essay, "Soul Murder and Slavery."[28] Soul murder, says Painter, results from "sexual abuse, emotional deprivation and physical and mental torture," that "compromises" the identity of children so that

they cannot register what it is that they want and what it is that they feel. . . . [T]hey often identify with the person who has abused them, and they may express anger toward themselves and others. Abused persons are more at risk for the development of an array of psychological problems that include depression, anxiety, self-mutilation, suicide attempts, sexual problems, and drug and alcohol abuse. Victims of soul murder do not inevitably turn into abusers—there is no direct and predictable line of cause and effect—but people who have been abused or deprived as children grew up at risk psychologically.[29]

In the literature on slavery, little has been written recently about slavery's psychological damage. Painter notes that since the publication of Stanley Elkins's important study, *Slavery: A Problem in American Institutional and Intellectual Life*, historians have been reluctant to speculate about any pathology that slavery produced in slaves. Elkins argued in 1959 that the system of total oppression in which the slaves lived had "produced psychologically crippled adults who were docile, irresponsible, loyal, lazy, humble and deceitful, in short, who were Sambos."[30] The responses to Elkins's diagnosis, some of which were quite heated, were crafted in terms of the resources that enabled slaves to escape samboization. There was revisionist criticism of Elkins's methodology, since he had relied on psychological theory rather than on archival evidence. There was extensive writing about slave resistance, about the mitigating effect of black communities, and about the ability of the black family to insulate its members to some degree from the brutalities of slavery.

The responses to Elkins had three major flaws. First, the ability of the "black community" and the black family to mitigate the horrors of slavery may have been considerable for some, but in many cases, if not most, it was unavailable. Take the case of Celia. In 1850 her slaveholder, Richard Newsom, owned eight hundred acres of land, eighteen horses, six milk cows, twenty-seven beef cattle, seventy pigs, twenty-five sheep, two oxen, and five slaves, one of whom has a five-year-old boy. The farm was in rural Missouri, at some distance from the nearest town. Newsom's farm provided little of either a "black community" or a "black family." In 1850, contrary to common historical memory, only 36 percent of the slave labor force was involved in cotton growing, and 43 percent of the slave population lived on plantations or farms with fifteen or fewer slaves.[31]

Secondly, the reluctance to find black pathology as a result of slavery can be quelled somewhat by a recognition that the psychology produced by slavery deformed not only blacks but also whites. That is, not only did slavery result from white pathology but it produced it as well. Thomas Jefferson, echoing a number of fellow Southerners, discusses the deformation in the character of white children whose families are slaveholders.[32] Northerner and Southerner, slaver and abolitionist, alike, noted the moral liabilities of slaveholding. And in circumstances like Celia's, commentators have commented on the perversion of white family life that slavery often entailed.

Thirdly, the reluctance to take up the question of black pathology, Painter argues, is ironically a sort of well-intentioned discrimination. White people are acknowledged to be the sort of complex psychological beings who undergo development of a certain sort and who are susceptible to psychological injury in the presence of various factors. Failing to attribute the same sort of development and liabilities to black folk is an odd move, and certainly,

Painter believes, one that impoverishes the writing of the history of slavery as well as working-class history generally. But for the most part, historians have acted as though "Any analysis hinting that Black people suffered psychological traumas a result of the vicious physical and emotional practices that slavery entailed [was treated as] tantamount to recapitulating Elkins and admitting the defeat of the race at the hands of bigots."[33]

Everyone agrees, says Painter, that slavery was an institution everywhere bounded by violence or the threat of violence. Work was forced on pain of the lash and other physical punishments. Masters beat or threatened to beat slaves. They beat children to make them into good slaves.

But slave children were also beaten by black folk, including their parents. Older slaves beat children to make them into compliant workers, a condition necessary for the very survival of these children.

So parents had to prepare their own children for subordination and had to do so physically. Moreover, they had to suppress whatever anger they had over this and about their general circumstances. They had to teach their children to quash *their* anger at being beaten. Anger, says Painter, was not allowable in a slave, at least insofar as its display in front of whites was concerned.

We now, says Painter, know what happens under these conditions. We now call the conditions "child abuse." They "have certain fairly predictable effects on [their] victims: feelings of degradation and humiliation, impaired identity formation, suppression of vitality and creativity, deadening of feeling of self [soul murder], anger, hatred, and self-hatred on an individual level and violence on the social level."[34]

Violence was not the only legacy of slavery for its children: there was also neglect.

> Slave children, particularly those whose mothers worked in the fields, were also very likely to suffer physical and emotional neglect, because their mothers were rarely allowed much time off the job to spend with their children. Childcare by people other than mothers could be adequate. . . . But in other instances, the caretakers of children might be too old, too young, or too infirm to provide adequate supervision. Ex-slave narratives illustrate child-rearing patterns that forced hardworking parents to neglect their children and that, as a consequence, often denied babies the opportunity to attach to a parent or parental figure securely.[35]

Painter concludes,

> In slave societies, neglect was routine, abuse was rampant, and anger was to be suppressed. The question regarding the neglect and physical abuse of slave children is not whether they took place—everyone agreed that they did—but rather,

what they meant to the children and adults who experienced them. Did the whipping that was so central a part of child rearing and the enforcement of discipline among slaves affect them and their families as child abuse traumatizes twentieth-century victims?

There is evidence that the child abuse of slavery imposed enormous costs. The relationship between abuse and repercussion is not simple or predetermined, but the damage is frequent enough to be recognizable. For countless women and children, these injuries were magnified by the intimate nature of the abuse.[36]

The same story, the same questions, and the same conclusions hold for sexual abuse during slavery. There was sexual predation, and it had consequences, and these are as observable in the historical record as they are in the twenty-first century.

Psychologists say that children and young women who are sexually abused, like children who are beaten, tend to blame themselves for their victimization and consequently have very poor self-esteem. They may also see their sexuality as their only means of binding other people to them as friends or allies. Recent scholarship outlines a series of long-term psychological repercussions of sexual abuse and incest: depression, difficulty sleeping, feelings of isolation, poor self-esteem, difficulty in relating to other people, contempt for all women including oneself, revictimization, and impaired sexuality that may manifest itself in behavior that can appear as frigidity or promiscuity. It is doubtful that slaves possessed an immunity that victims lack today.[37]

The remaining question is, of course, the degree to which these effects are transgenerational. Is there a "cycle of violence" that inclines those who are abused to become abusers themselves? The answer is, with qualifications, yes.

Cathy S. Widom, professor of psychiatry in the department of psychiatry at the New Jersey Medical School, and Michael G. Maxfield, professor of criminal justice at Rutgers University, conclude in "Research in Brief: An Update on the 'Cycle of Violence'" the following:

[B]eing abused or neglected as a child increased the likelihood of arrest as a juvenile by 59 percent, as an adult by 28 percent, and for a violent crime by 30 percent.[38]

Widom and Maxfield list as other "key findings" of this 1994 update of a study first performed in 1988 that:

- Maltreated children were younger at the time of their first arrest, committed nearly twice as many offenses, and were arrested more frequently.
- Physically abused and neglected (versus sexually abused) children were the most likely to be arrested later for a violent crime.

- In contrast to earlier research findings, the new results indicate that abused and neglected females were also at increased risk of arrest for violence as juveniles and adults.
- White abused and neglected children were no more likely to be arrested for a violent crime than their nonabused and nonneglected white counterparts. In contrast, black abused and neglected children in this sample showed significantly increased rates of violent arrest compared with black children who were not maltreated.
- An out-of-home placement was not related to the number of arrests among those who were removed from their homes [solely because of] abuse or neglect.

The study relied on relatively clear definitions of abuse and neglect. "Physical abuse" refers to injuries like bruises, welts, burns, abrasions, lacerations, wounds cuts, etc. "Sexual abuse" was determined to be present through charges ranging from arrests for nonspecific assault and battery "with intent to gratify sexual desires" to "fondling or touching in an obscene manner." Neglect was understood as occurring when parents were found to have failed to provide adequate food, clothing, shelter, and medical attention to the children for whom they had responsibility.

Everyone agrees that such conditions were realized under slavery: physical abuse, sexual abuse, and neglect. There is, therefore, reason to believe that the children of slaves, and their children as well, were, to the degree that the numbers suggest, captured in the "cycle of violence" and suffer from the same pathologies, soul murder as well as a disposition toward violence and neglect, as contemporary victims of abuse and neglect.

It may be reasonable to suppose that time heals all wounds. Over several generations one might suppose that the effects of slavery diminish until they finally wash out. Two considerations, however, make this assumption somewhat dubious.

First, while slavery ended with the Civil War, the subordination of African Americans and their vulnerability to unpunished violence did not end simultaneously. Even where physical assault diminished, the liability to social humiliation did not. Sexual crimes were more likely to be alleged against African Americans than against whites, and blacks were more likely to be punished severely. The economic conditions that make for neglect were more likely to be found among the African American population than in the population generally. If there is any cutoff date for these phenomena, it would have to be the conclusion of the civil rights movement, but the heirs of abuse and neglect are alive today.

Secondly, even if we suppose that the effects of such treatment tend to diminish across generations, there is nonetheless a compounding effect that works against the social perception that the incidence of such pathology has diminished. Reputation generally lags reality, and in this case, there is a social mechanism to ensure that the lag is great or that perception never changes. Even if the pathology disappears over time, the stigma will remain, and the perception, paradoxically, will nonetheless be supported by the evidence.

In his ingenious study, *The Anatomy of Racial Inequality,* Glenn C. Loury introduces the notion of a "self-confirming stereotype."[39] Though Loury notes that the idea of *stereotype* usually carries with it the implication that it misleads, the way he wants to use the term is compatible with the reasonableness of the generalization that some stereotype comprises. A stereotype involves the classification of a domain into groups of members and the association with each group of a set of statements purporting to be fact. So a domain of objects comes to be broken into groups A, B, C, etc., and for each of these subgroups, there is a class of associated statements. A Lourian *stereotype* is the set of statements associated with each group such that there is some basis in fact supported by the statements.

What's important to emphasize about the Lourian idea of *stereotype* is that, in his estimation, the framing of a stereotype as yet involves no statistical or moral error. Ordinarily when we hear a characterization called a stereotype, we think something has already gone wrong, either in the statistical projection onto individual members of the group or by way of a viciously motivated projection of a false characteristic onto either an individual or group. Loury has neither in mind when he speaks of stereotypes.[40] So, for Loury, a stereotype needn't be false, and indeed, he wants to introduce the notion of a "self-fulfilling stereotype."

> A "self-fulfilling stereotype" is a statistical generalization about some class of persons regarding what is taken *with reason* to be true about them as a class, but cannot be readily determined as true or false for a given member of the class. Furthermore, the generalization is "reasonable" in the specific sense that it is *self-confirming.* [The emphases are Loury's].[41]

Self-confirming stereotypes have a certain logic. They begin as generalizations in the form of expectations that are warranted by limited factual information. That is, given the information available to social actors, these generalizations have some reasonable basis. But the expectations or generalizations then take on a causal life of their own, shaping subsequent behavior in a way that tends to conform to the generalization. So, ultimately, the generalization, initially supported only by limited information, comes to enjoy even greater empirical support. Belief and behavioral evidence are "in equilibrium," as belief-based behavior creates evidence and evidence supports belief.

[I]f [real estate] agents hold a negative stereotype about blacks, they may think (correctly) that, on the average and all else equal, commercial loans to blacks pose a greater risk of default or black residential neighborhoods are more likely to decline. But this can hardly be the end of the story. What about the possibility that race conveys this information only because agents expect it to, and then act in ways that lead to the confirmation of their expectations? What if blacks have trouble getting further extensions of credit in the fact of a crisis, and to default more often? Or what if nonblack residents panic at the arrival of blacks, selling their homes too quickly and below the market value to lower-income buyers, thereby promoting neighborhood decline?[42]

Here race markers are useful in assessing financial risk but by their very use they tend to increase the risk, thereby worsening the prospects for African American home ownership. No one in the initial information-gathering phases in the real estate industry has much incentive to ask whether the race-markers actually have "intrinsic significance." They seem to work, and they are truer all the time.

Consider another useful example Loury provides. Taxicab drivers often refuse to pick up black men at night, believing them to be a real risk of robbery. Crime news reporting, we could add to Loury's example, mentions race most prominently when the race of some alleged offender is not white. We hear more of drug offenses committed by nonwhites in the inner city than of similar offenses committed by whites in the suburbs. So, there's an information-supported fear of black males at nighttime.

Now the population divides into young black men who at night are intent on robbery and those who simply need a ride home. Young black men who need a ride home at night are well advised to seek means of transportation other than taxicabs, knowing that cabbies will be reluctant to pick them up. Those intent on robbery will know that their prospects of successful robbery are diminished by fearful cab drivers,

But a person bent on robbery will not be so easily deterred. Even though he knows most cabs are unlikely to stop, he only needs one to do so to get in his night's work. . . . [T]he driver's reluctance to stop will discourage relatively more of the law abiding than of the robbers among blacks. . . . Hence, through a process that economists call "adverse selection," the set of young black men actually seen to be hailing taxis after dark may well come to contain a noticeably larger than average fraction of robbers, precisely the circumstance presumed by the drivers in the first place.
. . . Clearly, once a convention employing the self-confirming stereotype has been established, the drivers' beliefs and actions are defensible on the basis of reason. And yet the deeper conclusion—that there is an intrinsic connection between race and crime—is altogether unjustified.[43]

The question for Loury then becomes, Why hasn't "the deeper conclusion" been successfully challenged? The reason, he says, is racial stigmatization. The stigmatization takes this form: Where the subject is a member of a racially stigmatized group, there is little or no incentive for social learning. The holder of a stereotyped belief faces no social situation that inclines him to see below the race marker to the underlying mechanism producing certain behaviors.

What would impel the cabbie to attempt to explain the disproportionate number of young black male robbers in a way that includes his own reluctance to pick up black males at nighttime in his cab?

Loury explains that no individual cabbie has reason to believe that an information search or a review of the limits of his generalization would pay, since blacks are stigmatized. The dishonor of their historical slave position, together with the contemporary presence of easily observable markers that locate them among the class of persons whose ancestors were slaves, issue in easy assumptions by white observers (and by some African Americans as well) of their otherness and danger.

In short, stigmatization blocks the possibility of any further refinement of the generalization or stereotype and the stereotypes often produce self-fulfillment in the form of evidence supporting the stereotype simply because the stereotype is believed or unchallenged, bearing in mind here that the stereotype has justification of a limited sort, on Loury's analysis.

So stigma works to inhibit the refinement of stereotypes that themselves are self-fulfilling. And, in this analysis, the stigma dates to the convergence of dishonor and race that was American slavery.

NOTES

1. Jane English, "What Do Grown Children Owe Their Parents?" in *Having Children*, ed. Onora O' Neill (New York: Oxford University Press, 1979), 351–56.

2. There is no intention here of equating the social conditions of American Jews and African Americans, now or at any time in their American sojourns. Jews may once have been nonwhites or "provisional whites" in America, but they were never slaves and are now, in virtually all the ways that matter, white folks. However, they continue to bear the marks of a stigmatization with respect to their collective histories similar to that burdening African Americans, as we will discuss below.

3. Salo Baron, quoted in Albert S. Lindeman, *Esau's Tears* (Cambridge: Cambridge University Press, 1997), 15. Baron's term is generally rendered as "lachrymose history" with an intentional derisory tone. Baron himself disputes this view of Jewish history, arguing that "it is quite likely . . . that even the average medieval Jew, compared to his average Christian contemporary . . . was the less unhappy and destitute

creature—less unhappy and destitute not only by his own consciousness, but even if measured by such objective criteria as standard of living, cultural amenities, and protection against individual starvation and disease" (p. 11).

4. Bernard Williams, *Shame and Necessity* (Berkeley: University of California Press, 1993).

5. Orlando Patterson, *Slavery and Social Death: A Comparative Study* (Cambridge: Harvard University Press, 1987).

6. The selections from Aristotle are drawn from his *Politics*, 1, 2–8.

7. The idea, common to Plato and Aristotle, is that order is maintained only in a hierarchy where superior rules subordinate. Here is Gregory Vlastos's conclusion to his essay, "Slavery in Plato's Thought," in *Platonic Studies* (Princeton, N. J.: Princeton University Press, 1973):

> This study does not suggest that Plato deduced his political theory, his psychology or his ontology from his concept of slavery. No such deduction is to be found in his writing. . . .What it does suggest is that his views about slavery, state, man, and the world illustrate a single hierarchic pattern, and that the key to the pattern is his idea of *logos*. . . . The slave lacks *logos;* so does the multitude [most of the people] in the state, the body in man, and material necessity [physical causation] in the universe. Let to itself each of these would be disorderly and vicious in the sense of the untranslatable Greek word *hybris.* Order is imposed upon them by a benevolent superior: master, guardian, mind, demiurge. Each of these rules in his own domain. The common title to authority is the possession of *logos* [loosely—*reason of a high order*]. In such an intellectual scheme slavery is "natural": in perfect harmony with one's notions about the nature of the world and of man. (pp. 161–62)

8. Patterson, *Slavery and Social Death*, 10.

9. Patterson, *Slavery and Social Death*, 77.

10. Patterson, *Slavery and Social Death*, 79,

11. Patterson, *Slavery and Social Death*, 79.

12. Patterson, *Slavery and Social Death*, 79.

13. Patterson, *Slavery and Social Death*, 80.

14. It should be noted that Patterson introduces a serious complication in the idea of honor here. He says, "although its existence is revealed, and its claims proven in acts of honor, such acts are always epiphenomenal. . . . Acting honorably is not the same thing as *being* honorable. . . . Honor is never evaluated in teleological terms [by its end or results]" (p. 80). Patterson's remarks here seem to imply that honor is more than the claiming and defense of social position. Whatever his final view of the matter, it is clear that he thinks that the successful claim and defense of position—in the ability to exercise one's will socially—is a necessary if not a sufficient condition of honor.

15. Williams, *Shame and Necessity*, 68.

16. The term *responsibility* suggests that of two persons, one is liable to the other, or one has a justifiable claim against the other, etc., and also seems to involve some assumption about fault, voluntariness, etc. Williams actually means to clear our minds of these things when thinking about such self-regarding assessments as Oedipus's and Ajax's.

17. This, by the way, makes the claim regarding the Greeks that theirs was a "shame culture," exclusively concerned with reputation, where honor is just a matter of how others think about you, manifestly false.

18. Williams, *Shame and Necessity*, 69.

19. Williams, *Shame and Necessity*, 71.

20. Williams, *Shame and Necessity*, 74.

21. As Williams notes, that Ajax's life was now intolerable to Ajax was a fact about Ajax. One can imagine circumstances where this is not true. But one can equally imagine a sensible person thinking it was true and not being wrong. Frederick Douglass's self-esteem went unimpaired, though he was once a slave (but he, after all, was Frederick Douglass).

22. Valerie Martin, *Property* (New York: Doubleday, 2003), 3–4.

23. Joyce Carol Oates, "Desire and Dread: A Review of *Property* by Valerie Martin," *New York Review of Books,* May 1, 2002. Online at www.nybooks.com/articles/16213.

24. David Brion Davis, *In the Image of God: Religion, Moral Values, and Our Heritage of Slavery* (New Haven: Yale University Press, 2001), 248–59. The book Davis discusses is *Celia: A Slave,* by Melton A. McLaurin (Athens, Ga.: University of Georgia Press, 1991).

25. Davis, *In the Image of God*, 250.

26. Davis, *In the Image of God*, 249.

27. Quoted in Davis, *In the Image of God*, 254.

28. Nell Irvin Painter, "Soul Murder and Slavery: Toward a Fully Loaded Cost Accounting," in *U.S. History as Women's History*, eds. L. Kerber, A. Kessler-Harris, and K. Kish Sklar (Chapel Hill: University of North Carolina Press, 1995), 125–46.

29. Painter, "Soul Murder and Slavery," 128.

30. Painter, "Soul Murder and Slavery," 131.

31. Davis, *In the Image of God*, 249.

32. Here is a frequently quoted passage by Jefferson, quoted in Benjamin Schwarz, "What Jefferson Helps to Explain," *The Atlantic Monthly,* vol. 279, no. 3 (March 1997), pp. 60–72.

The whole commerce between master and slave is a perpetual exercise of the most bois-terous passions, the most unremitting despotism on the one part, and degrading submis-sions on the other. Our children see this, and learn to imitate it. . . . If a parent could find no motive either in his philanthropy or his self-love, for restraining the intemperance of passion towards his slave, it should always be a sufficient one that his child is present. But generally it is not sufficient. The parent storms, the child looks on, catches the lineaments of wrath, puts on the same airs in the circle of smaller slaves, gives a loose to the worst of passions, and thus nursed, educated, and daily exercised in tyranny, cannot but be stamped by it with odious peculiarities. The man must be a prodigy who can retain his manners and morals undepraved by such circumstances.

33. Painter, "Soul Murder and Slavery," 131.

34. Painter, "Soul Murder and Slavery," 134.

35. Painter, "Soul Murder and Slavery," 134.

36. Painter, "Soul Murder and Slavery," 134.
37. Painter, "Soul Murder and Slavery," 138.
38. Cathy Spatz Widorm and Michael G. G. Maxfield, "An Update on the 'Cycle of Violence.'" Research Brief. 2/2001. National Institute of Justice. Online at www.ojp.usdog.gov/nij.
39. Glenn C. Loury, "Racial Stereotypes," chap. 2 in *The Anatomy of Racial Inequality* (Cambridge: Harvard University Press, 2002), 15–54, passim.
40. This is characteristic of Loury's approach to racial inequality and its causes. Specifically, pernicious moral principles or attitudes he thinks are *not now* at the roots of racial inequality. A manner of classification of social reality and the failure to address this precisely in the remedies proposed for racial inequality, he thinks, is the problem. In sum, Loury thinks that, left to themselves, individual and small groups will continue to classify and gather information about African Americans in a way that adversely affects that group. A bottom-up strategy to improve the conditions of African Americans has not and will not work but not because of the morally defective character of either small groups or individual white Americans.
41. Loury, "Racial Stereotypes," 23.
42. Loury, "Racial Stereotypes," 25.
43. Loury, "Racial Stereotypes," 30–31.

II

EARLY REPARATIONS INITIATIVES

The idea of reparations for slavery is hardly a new one. The first limited discussions of reparations began before slavery ended. After the Civil War, the "Radical Republicans" in Congress mounted an unsuccessful effort to legislate reparations. With their defeat, the issue faded, only to be revived in the midst of the twentieth-century civil rights movement. This chapter traces the historical roots of the reparations debate in the nineteenth century, outlines the debate over the "Black Manifesto" at mid-twentieth century, and moves forward to the continuing political debate over reparations today.

5

The Nineteenth Century

Even before slavery ended, earnest Quakers joined in an unlikely alliance with southern slaveholders to form the American Colonization Society. The ACS worked to repatriate slaves to a "homeland" in Africa that they had never seen. The slaveholders were motivated by fear of slave revolts and simply wanted to diminish the number of free black men and women in the United States. The Quakers, on the other hand, believed that the nation owed amends to Africans it had enslaved. For the ACS, those amends took the form of resettlement in Liberia—furnishing transportation, start-up funds, and supplies so that free black men and women from the United States could begin a new life in Liberia.

In 1822, the ACS shipped the first eighty-six immigrants to Africa. About nineteen thousand followed over the next forty years. A similar colony, organized by Britons, took root in neighboring Sierra Leone.

In 1847, the nation of Liberia declared its independence. England and France recognized the new country, and its U.S.-born president, Joseph J. Roberts, visited Queen Victoria and Napoleon III. Though the American repatriates controlled Liberia, named its capital Monrovia after U.S. President James Monroe, modeled its economic and social life after the United States, and modeled its government on the form of the United States, the U.S. government did not recognize the new country until 1862.

The U.S. Civil War slowed the flood of immigrants to Liberia to a trickle. Millions of newly free African Americans focused on building new lives in their own country—the United States.

The idea of reparations flourished in the Civil War era. As in many wars, the defeated enemy should, many argued, be obliged to make reparations to the victors. Logically, decisions on reparations would include reparations to former slaves.

Revisionist history aside, the Civil War was about slavery. Arguments that the war was "really" about states' rights, or sovereignty, or a southern way of life ignore historical fact. The states' rights in question were rights to buy, sell, recapture, and control human beings held as slaves. State sovereignty meant state immunity from any federal regulation of the peculiar institution of slavery. The southern way of life was built on the backs of slave laborers and could not survive without the economic benefits accruing to whites from the coerced services of blacks.

Even after the war, however, neither North nor South could quite concede the full humanity of black Americans, nor fully acknowledge the depth of harm done to them. In the end, North and South united in sweeping under the carpet the pressing questions of justice and reparations for slavery. For eighty years, reparations remained a dead issue. Then, resurrected by the civil rights movement and given voice by James Forman in his 1969 Black Manifesto, reparations again seized the national stage and demanded a national debate.

CIVIL WAR AND THE FREEDMEN'S BUREAU

As Union armies marched south, freed and runaway slaves flooded into army camps. Tens of thousands enlisted and fought in the war. Many others, including women and children, could not become soldiers. Providing for the noncombatant refugees became another responsibility assigned to Union generals.

Some Union generals had confiscated estates and property of rebels and set freedmen to work on these plantations. Victorious General Sherman ordered, "The islands from Charleston south, the abandoned rice fields along the rivers for thirty miles back from the sea, and the country bordering the St. John's River, Florida, are reserved and set apart for the settlement of Negroes now made free by act of war." Sherman's promises were popularized in the slogan of "forty acres and a mule," due to freed slaves as reparations for years of servitude and as a means of making a fresh start.

The first post–Civil War attempt by the U.S. government to make reparations for slavery was embodied in the Freedmen's Bureau, established in 1865. This official government agency joined more than fifty nongovernmental organizations (then styled "benevolent societies"), some in existence for decades before the war, whose aim was to offer freed slaves assistance in the form of food, clothes, money, employment, and education.[1]

The Freedmen's Bureau was formally named the "Bureau of Refugees, Freedmen, and Abandoned Lands," and was created within the War Department to operate during the war and for one year thereafter. Abandoned lands were given to the bureau to be leased and sold to ex-slaves in forty-acre parcels. Though it established the Freedmen's Bureau, Congress did not provide funds for it to carry out its mission.

The first commissioner of the bureau was thirty-five-year-old Maj. Gen. Oliver O. Howard, a veteran of Gettysburg and of Sherman's march to the sea. He supervised the Freedmen's Bureau in its multitudinous tasks, which included registering marriages, births, and deaths of freedmen, setting up or supervising schools, protecting freedmen from white violence, and establishing court systems, as well as distributing land.

Since the Freedmen's Bureau lacked funding, it relied heavily on the military to do its work. The South was, after all, barely out of war and the army still occupied it, providing at least a military government. Congress reluctantly, but repeatedly, renewed the mandate of the Freedmen's Bureau annually to 1872. The educational work of the Bureau continued through 1876.

The end of the war brought Confederate soldiers back to their abandoned homes and farms. At every turn, they sabotaged the work of the Freedmen's Bureau. Writing about the work of the Bureau, Frederick Douglass summarized the reasons for its failure:

In a time of perfect calm, amid willing neighbors and streaming wealth, the social uplifting of 4,000,000 slaves to an assured and self-sustaining place in the body politic and economic would have been an herculean task; but when to the inherent difficulties of so delicate and nice a social operation were added the spite and hate of conflict, the Hell of War; when suspicion and cruelty were rife, and gaunt Hunger wept beside Bereavement,—in such a case, the work of any instrument of social regeneration was in large part foredoomed to failure.[2]

REPUBLICANS AND REPARATIONS

During and after the Civil War, Republicans were the party of radicals, the political home of anyone who believed in some measure of racial equality. When Lincoln was assassinated, the new president, Andrew Johnson, sought to win back some measure of southern support by restraining the "radicalism" of his fellow Republicans.

Nowhere was that radicalism more apparent than in the fiery rhetoric of Representative Thaddeus Stevens of Pennsylvania.[3] Stevens denounced former slaveholders as "dethroned tyrants" deprived of the "luxuries of despotism." He insisted that God was the advocate for the freed slaves and, on their behalf, introduced a reparations bill, H.R. 29, in Congress in 1867. The bill was not passed.

There were other nineteenth-century initiatives, such as the ex-slave pension movement.[4]

Reparations Bill for the African Slaves in the United States—
The First Session Fortieth Congress[5]

—March 11, 1867, Thaddeus Stevens of Pennsylvania, H.R. 29.

Whereas it is due to justice, as an example to future times, that some future punishment should be inflicted on the people who constituted the "confederate States of America." Both because they, declaring on unjust war against the United States for the purpose of destroying republican liberty and permanently establishing slavery, as well as, for the cruel and barbarous manner in which they conducted said war, in violation of all the laws of civilized warfare, and also to compel them to make some compensation for the damages and expenditures caused by the said war: Therefore,

Be it enacted by the Senate and House of Representatives of the United States of America in Congress assembled. *That all the public lands belonging to the ten States that formed the government of the so-called confederate States of America shall be forfeited by said States and become forthwith vested in the United States.*

SEC. 2. And be it further enacted. That the President shall forthwith proceed to cause the seizure of such of the property belonging to the belligerent enemy as is deemed forfeited by the act of July 17, A. D. 1862, and hold and appropriate the same as enemy's property, and to proceed to condemnation with that already seized.

SEC. 3. And be it further enacted,

That in lieu of the proceeding to condemn the property thus seized enemy's property. As is provided by the act of July A. D. 1862, two commissions or more, as by him may be deemed necessary. Shall be appointed by the President for each of the said "confederate States," to consist of three persons each, one of whom shall be an officer of the late or present Army, and two shall be civilians, neither of whom shall be citizens of the State for which he shall be appointed; that the said commissions shall proceed adjudicate and Condemn the property foresaid, under such forms and proceedings as shall be prescribed by the Attorney General of the United States, whereupon the title to said property shall become vested in the United States.

SEC. 4. And be it further enacted.

That out of the lands thus seized and confiscated the slaves who have been liberated by the operations of the war and the amendment to the constitution or otherwise, who resided in said "confederate States" on the 4th day of March, A.D. 1861, or since, shall have distributed to them as follows, namely: to each male person who is the head of a family, forty acres; to each adult male, whether the head of a family or not, forty acres, to each widow who is the head of a family, forty acres-to be held by them in fee-simple, but to be inalienable for the next ten years after they become seized thereof.

For the purpose of distributing and allotting said land the Secretary of War shall appoint as many commissions in each State as he shall deem necessary, to consist of three members each, two of whom at least shall not be citizens of the State for which he is appointed. Each of said commissioners shall receive a salary of $3,000 annually and all his necessary expenses. Each commission shall be allowed one clerk, whose salary shall be $2,000 per annum. The title to the homestead aforesaid shall be vested in trustees for the use of the liberated persons aforesaid. Trustees shall be appointed by the Secretary of War, and shall receive such salary as he shall direct, not exceeding $3,000 per annum. At the end of ten years the absolute title to said homesteads shall be conveyed to said owners or to the heirs of such as are then dead.

SEC. 5. And be it further enacted,

That out of the balance of the property thus seized and confiscated there shall be raised, in the manner hereinafter provided, a sum equal to fifty dollars, for each homestead, to be applied by the trustees hereinafter mentioned toward the erection of buildings on the said homesteads for the use of said slaves; and the further sum of $500,000,000, which shall be appropriated as follows, to wit: $200,000,000 shall be invested in United States six per cent, securities; and the interest thereof shall be semi-annually added to the pensions allowed by law to pensioners who have become so by reason of the late war; $300,000,000, or so much thereof as may Be needed shall be appropriated to pay damages done to loyal citizens by the civil or military Operations of the government lately called the "confederate States of America." [Emphasis added]

Stevens spoke eloquently in support of his bill, but it never passed. His speech in support of the bill sets out three rationales for economic reparations. First, reparations are a matter of economic justice, restoring to the freed slaves some of the economic benefits produced by their labor and confiscated by slave-holders. Second, reparations are required by a just God. Finally, reparations must be made or the country will experience continuing racial hatred, inequality, and strife.

Thaddeus Stevens, Quoted Speaking to the U.S. House of Representatives on Section 4 of H. R. 29—The 1867 Slave Reparation Bill[6]

"The fourth section provides first that out of the lands thus confiscated each liberated slave who is a male adult, or the head of a family, shall have assigned to him a homestead of forty acres of land, (with $100 to build a dwelling), which shall be held for them by trustees during their pupilage.

"Let us consider whether this is a just and politic provision.

"Whatever may be the fate of the rest of the bill I must earnestly pray that this may not be defeated. On its success, in my judgment, depends not only the happiness and respectability of the colored race, but their very existence. Homesteads to them are far more valuable than the immediate right of suffrage, though both are their due.

"Four million persons have just been freed from a condition of dependence, wholly unacquainted with business transactions, kept systematically in ignorance of all their rights and of the common elements of education, without which none of any race are competent to earn an honest living, to guard against the frauds which will always he practiced on the ignorant, or to judge of the most judicious manner of applying their labor. But few of them are mechanics, and none of them skilled manufacturers. They must necessarily, therefore, be the servants and the victims of others unless they are made in some measure independent of their wiser neighbors. The guardianship of the Freedmen's Bureau, that benevolent institution, cannot be expected long to protect them. It encounters the hostility of the old slaveholders, whether in official or private station, because it deprives these dethroned tyrants of the luxury of despotism. In its nature it is not calculated for a permanent institution. Withdraw that protection and leave them a prey to the legislation and treatment of their former masters, and the evidence already furnished shows that they will soon become extinct, or be driven to defend themselves by civil war.

"Withhold from them all their rights, and leave them destitute of the means of earning a livelihood, the victims of the hatred or cupidity of the rebels whom they helped to conquer, and it seems probable that the war of races might ensue which the President feared would arise from kind treatment and the restoration of their rights. I doubt not that hundreds of thousands would annually be deposited in secret, unknown graves. Such is already the course of their rebel murderers; and it is done with impunity. The clearest evidence of that fact has already been shown by the testimony taken by the 'Central Directory.' Make them independent of their old masters, so that they may not be compelled to work for them upon unfair terms, which can only be done by giving them a small tract of land to cultivate for themselves, and you remove all this danger. You also, elevate the character of the freedman.

"Nothing is so likely to make a man a good citizen as to make him a freeholder. Nothing will so multiply the productions of the South as to divide it into small farms. Nothing will make men so industrious and moral as to let them feel that they are above want and are the owners of the soil which they till. It will also be of service to the white inhabitants. They will have constantly among them industrious laborers, anxious to work for fair wages. How is it possible for them to cultivate their lands if these people were expelled? If Moses should lead or drive them into exile, or carry out the absurd idea of colonizing them, the South would become a barren waste.

"When that wisest of monarchs, the Czar of Russia, compelled the liberation of twenty-five million serfs, he did not for a moment entertain the foolish idea of depriving his empire of their labor or of robbing them of their rights. He ordered their former owners to make some compensation for their unrequited toil by conveying to them the very houses in which they lived and a portion of the land which they had tilled as serfs. The experiment has been a perfect success. It has brought the prosperity which God gives to wisdom and justice. Have they not a right to it? I do not speak of their fidelity and services in this bloody war. I put it on the mere score of lawful earnings. They and their ancestors have toiled, not for years, but for ages, without one farthing of recompense. They have earned for their masters this very land and much more. Will not he who denies them compensation now be accursed, for he is an unjust man? Have we not upon this subject the recorded decision of a Judge who never erred? Four million Jews were held in bondage in Egypt. Their slavery was mild compared with the slavery inflicted by Christians. For all recorded slavery—Pagan, heathen, or Mohammedan—Christian slavery has been the most cruel and heartless; and of all Christian slavery American slavery has been the worst. God, through no pretended, but a true Moses, led them out of bondage, as in our case, through a Red Sea, at the cost, as in our case, of the first born of every household of the oppressor. Did He advise them to take no remuneration for their years of labor? No!! He understood too well what was due to justice. He commanded the men and the women to borrow from their confiding neighbors 'jewels of silver and jewels of gold and raiment.' They obeyed him amply, and spoiled the Egyptians, and went forth full handed. There was no blasphemer then to question God's decree of confiscation. This doctrine then was not 'satanic.' He who questions it now will be a blasphemer, whom God will bring to judgment. If we refuse to this downtrodden and oppressed race the rights which Heaven decreed them, and the remuneration which they have earned through long years of hopeless oppression, how can we hope to escape still further punishment if God is just and omnipotent? It may come in the shape of plagues or of intestine [sic] wars—race against race, the oppressed against the oppressor. But come it will. Seek not to divert our attention from justice by a puerile cry about fatted calves!"

Stevens's Reparations Bill failed, of course. The North, as well as the South, wanted an end to the Civil War and a return to prosperity. The North, no less than the South, believed that black men and women were different, inherently lower in intelligence, suited to manual labor, unworthy of equal rights or opportunities.

The Freedmen's Bureau was swept away in the tide of anti-Reconstruction sentiment that effectively returned control of the South to its former owners. Whether by foreclosure or by terrorist threats, most black families lost the land they had purchased. Without land, they were once again reduced to dependence on white landowners and employers.

NOTES

1. W. E. B. DuBois, "The Freedmen's Bureau," *The Atlantic Monthly*, March 1901, online at www.theatlantic.com/issues/01mar/dubois.htm (accessed February 10, 2003).

2. DuBois, "The Freedmen's Bureau."

3. Stevens was born in Danville, Vermont, on April 4, 1792. He graduated from Dartmouth College in 1814, then moved to York, Pennsylvania, where he taught

school and studied law. He practiced law in Gettysburg and Lancaster. Stevens was a member of the Pennsylvania state legislature before going to Congress in 1848 as an antislavery Whig. After opposing the fugitive slave law and the Compromise of 1850, Stevens was reelected to Congress as a member of the antislavery Republican Party. As a "Radical Republican" of that period, Stevens advocated emancipation and black suffrage.

4. See Walter B. Hill Jr., "The Ex-Slave Pension Movement: Some Historical and Genealogical Notes," *Negro History Bulletin* 59, no. 4 (1996): 7–11.

5. U.S. Congress, House of Representatives. Reparations Bill for the African Slaves in the United States. 40th Cong., 1st sess., 1867.

6. Speech of the Hon. Thaddeus Stevens of Pennsylvania, Delivered in the House of Representatives, March 19, 1867, on the Bill (H. R. No. 20) Relative to Damages to Loyal Men, and for Other Purposes, online at http://chnm.gmu.edu/courses/122/recon/stevens.htm.

6

The Mid-Twentieth Century

THE BLACK MANIFESTO—1969

About a hundred years after the Slave Reparation Bill, another dramatic call for reparations was sounded. James Forman, an activist formerly with the Student Nonviolent Coordinating Committee (SNCC), seized the imagination of the National Black Economic Development Conference in April 1969. Forman proposed nothing less than payment of $500 million in reparations by the white Christian and Jewish churches and synagogues of the United States.

The National Black Economic Development Conference was sponsored by the Interreligious Foundation for Community Organization (IFCO). IFCO was created by Christian and Jewish religious bodies in 1967, as an agency that could coordinate their financial support for community development and community organization. The religious organizations saw IFCO as a bridge between their mostly white governing bodies and people of color.

More than eight hundred people attended the NBEDC in Detroit, a turnout that was larger than organizers anticipated. As an official of SNCC, Forman read his "Manifesto" to the NBEDC meeting, which voted 187–63 in favor of adopting it.

The demands of the Manifesto are addressed to religious bodies, not to the nation as a whole. Perhaps this reflects the civil rights movement's greater confidence in religious institutions, in contrast to a generalized distrust of the political and governmental structure.

Forman entered Riverside Church at a Sunday morning communion service on May 4, 1969. Without permission of the presiding minister, he read
six demands from the Manifesto, and ended with a call to action:

Our patience is thin.
Time is running out.
We have been slaves too long.
The Church is racist.
The Church has profited from our labor.
We are men and women, proud black men and women.
Our demands shall be met.
Reparation or no Church!
Victory or Death.

James Forman: "The Black Manifesto"—1969[1]

We the black people assembled in Detroit, Michigan for the National Black Economic Development Conference are fully aware that we have been forced to
come together because racist white America has exploited our resources, our
minds, our bodies, our labor. For centuries we have been forced to live as col-
onized people inside the United States, victimized by the most vicious, racist
system in the world. We have helped to build the most industrial country in the
world.
    We are therefore demanding of the white Christian churches and Jewish syn-
agogues which are part and parcel of the system of capitalism, that they begin
to pay reparations to black people in this country. We are demanding
$500,000,000 from the Christian white churches and the Jewish synagogues.
This total comes to 15 dollars per nigger. This is a low estimate for we maintain
there are probably more than 30,000,000 black people in this country. $15 a
nigger is not a large sum of money and we know that the churches and synagogues have a tremendous wealth and its membership, white America, has profited and still exploits black people. We are also not unaware that the exploitation of colored peoples around the world is aided and abetted by the white
Christian churches and synagogues. This demand for $500,000,000 is not an
idle resolution or empty words. Fifteen dollars for every black brother and sister
in the United States is only a beginning of the reparations due us as people who
have been exploited and degraded, brutalized, killed and persecuted. Underneath all of this exploitation, the racism of this country has produced a psychological effect upon us that we are beginning to shake off. We are no longer
afraid to demand our full rights as a people in this decadent society.
    We are demanding $500,000,000 to be spent in the following way:

1. We call for the establishment of a Southern land bank to help our brothers and sisters who have to leave their land because of racist pressure for
   people who want to establish cooperative farms, but who have no funds.

We have seen too many farmers evicted from their homes because they have dared to defy the white racism of this country. We need money for land. We must fight for massive sums of money for this Southern Land Bank. We call for $200,000,000 to implement this program.

2. We call for the establishment of four major publishing and printing industries in the United States to be funded with ten million dollars each. These publishing houses are to be located in Detroit, Atlanta, Los Angeles, and New York. They will help to generate capital for further cooperative investments in the black community, provide jobs and an alternative to the white-dominated and controlled printing field.

3. We call for the establishment of four of the most advanced scientific and futuristic audio-visual networks to be located in Detroit, Chicago, Cleveland and Washington, D.C. These TV networks will provide an alternative to the racist propaganda that fills the current television networks. Each of these TV networks will be funded by ten million dollars each.

4. We call for a research skills center which will provide research on the problems of black people. This center must be funded with no less than 30 million dollars.

5. We call for the establishment of a training center for the teaching of skills in community organization, photography, movie making, television making and repair, radio building and repair and all other skills needed in communication. This training center shall be funded with no less than ten million dollars.

6. We recognize the role of the National Welfare Rights Organization and we intend to work with them. We call for ten million dollars to assist in the organization of welfare recipients. We want to organize the welfare workers in this country so that they may demand more money from the government and better administration of the welfare system of this country.

7. We call for $20,000,000 to establish a National Black Labor Strike and Defense Fund. This is necessary for the protection of black workers and their families who are fighting racist working conditions in this country.

8. We call for the establishment of the International Black Appeal (IBA). This International Black Appeal will be funded with no less than $20,000,000. The IBA is charged with producing more capital for the establishment of cooperative businesses in the United States and in Africa, our Motherland. The International Black Appeal is one of the most important demands that we are making for we know that it can generate and raise funds throughout the United States and help our African brothers. The IBA is charged with three functions and shall be headed by James Forman:

   (a) Raising money for the program of the National Black Economic Development Conference.

   (b) The development of cooperatives in African countries and support of African Liberation movements.

(c) Establishment of a Black Anti-Defamation League which will protect our African image.

9. We call for the establishment of a Black University to be funded with $130,000,000 to be located in the South. Negotiations are presently under way with a Southern University.

10. We demand that IFCO allocate all unused funds in the planning budget to implement the demands of this conference.

In order to win our demands we are aware that we will have to have massive support, therefore:

(1) We call upon all black people throughout the United States to consider themselves as members of the National Black Economic Development Conference and to act in unity to help force the racist white Christian churches and Jewish synagogues to implement these demands.

(2) We call upon all the concerned black people across the country to contact black workers, black women, black students and black unemployed, community groups, welfare organizations, teacher organizations, church leaders and organizations, explaining how these demands are vital to the black community of the U.S. Pressure by whatever means necessary should be applied to the white power structure of the racist white Christian churches and Jewish synagogues. All black people should act boldly in confronting our white oppressors and demanding this modest reparation of 15 dollars per black man.

(3) Delegates and members of the National Black Economic Development Conference are urged to call press conferences in the cities and to attempt to get as many black organizations as possible to support the demands of the conference. The quick use of the press in the local areas will heighten the tension and these demands must be attempted to be won in a short period of time, although we are prepared for protracted and long range struggle.

(4) We call for the total disruption of selected church sponsored agencies operating anywhere in the U.S. and the world. Black workers, black women, black students and the black unemployed are encouraged to seize the offices, telephones, and printing apparatus of all church sponsored agencies and to hold these in trusteeship until our demands are met.

(5) We call upon all delegates and members of the National Black Economic Development Conference to stage sit-in demonstrations at selected black and white churches. This is not to be interpreted as a continuation of the sit-in movement of the early sixties but we know that active confrontation inside white churches is possible and will strengthen the possibility of meeting our demands. Such confrontation can take the form of reading *The Black Manifesto* instead of a sermon or passing it out to church members. The principle of self-defense should be applied if attacked.

(6) On May 4, 1969 or a date thereafter, depending upon local conditions, we call upon black people to commence the disruption of the racist churches and synagogues throughout the United States.

(7) We call upon IFCO to serve as a central staff to coordinate the mandate of the conference and to reproduce and distribute en masse literature, leaflets, news items, press releases and other material.

(8) We call upon all delegates to find within the white community those forces which will work under the leadership of blacks to implement these demands by whatever means necessary. By taking such actions, white Americans will demonstrate concretely that they are willing to fight the white skin privilege and the white supremacy and racism which has forced us as black people to make these demands.

(9) We call upon all white Christians and Jews to practice patience, tolerance, understanding, and nonviolence as they have encouraged, advised and demanded that we as black people should do throughout our entire enforced slavery in the United States. The true test of their faith and belief in the Cross and the words of the prophets will certainly be put to a test as we seek legitimate and extremely modest reparations for our role in developing the industrial base of the Western world through our slave labor. But we are no longer slaves, we are men and women, proud of our African heritage, determined to have our dignity.

(10) We are so proud of our African heritage and realize concretely that our struggle is not only to make revolution in the United States, but to protect our brothers and sisters in Africa and to help them rid themselves of racism, capitalism, and imperialism by whatever means necessary, including armed struggle. We are and must be willing to fight the defamation of our African image wherever it rears its ugly head. We are therefore charging the Steering Committee to create a Black Anti-Defamation League to be funded by money raised from the International Black Appeal.

(11) We fully recognize that revolution in the United States and Africa, our Motherland, is more than a one dimensional operation. It will require the total integration of the political, economic, and military components and therefore, we call upon all our brothers and sisters who have acquired training and expertise in the fields of engineering, electronics, research, community organization, physics, biology, chemistry, mathematics, medicine, military science and warfare to assist the National Black Economic Development Conference in the implementation of its program.

(12) To implement these demands we must have a fearless leadership. We must have a leadership which is willing to battle the church establishment to implement these demands. To win our demands we will have to declare war on the white Christian churches and synagogues and this means we may have to fight the government structure of this country. Let no one here think that these demands will be met by our mere stating

them. For the sake of the churches and synagogues, we hope that they have the wisdom to understand that these demands are modest and reasonable. But if the white Christians and Jews are not willing to meet our demands through peace and good will, then we declare war and we are prepared to fight by whatever means necessary. . . .

Brothers and sisters, we no longer are shuffling our feet and scratching our heads. We are tall, black and proud.

And we say to the white Christian churches and Jewish synagogues, to the government of this country and to all the white racist imperialists who compose it, there is only one thing left that you can do to further degrade black people and that is to kill us. But we have been dying too long for this country. We have died in every war. We are dying in Vietnam today fighting the wrong enemy.

The new black man wants to live and to live means that we must not become static or merely believe in self-defense. We must boldly go out and attack the white Western world at its power centers. The white Christian churches are another form of government in this country and they are used by the government of this country to exploit the people of Latin America, Asia and Africa, but the day is soon coming to an end. Therefore, brothers and sisters, the demands we make upon the white Christian churches and the Jewish synagogues are small demands. They represent 15 dollars per black person in these United States. We can legitimately demand this from the church power structure. We must demand more from the United States Government.

But to win our demands from the church which is linked up with the United States Government, we must not forget that it will ultimately be by force and power that we will win.

We are not threatening the churches. We are saying that we know the churches came with the military might of the colonizers and have been sustained by the military might of the colonizers. Hence, if the churches in colonial territories were established by military might, we know deep within our hearts that we must be prepared to use force to get our demands. We are not saying that this is the road we want to take. It is not, but let us be very clear that we are not opposed to force and we are not opposed to violence. We were captured in Africa by violence. We were kept in bondage and political servitude and forced to work as slaves by the military machinery and the Christian church working hand in hand.

We recognize that in issuing this manifesto we must prepare for a long range educational campaign in all communities of this country, but we know that the Christian churches have contributed to our oppression in white America. We do not intend to abuse our black brothers and sisters in black churches who have uncritically accepted Christianity. We want them to understand how the racist white Christian church with its hypocritical declarations and doctrines of brotherhood has abused our trust and faith. An attack on the religious beliefs of black people is not our major objective, even though we know that we were not Christians, when we were brought to this country, but that Christianity was used to help enslave us. Our ob-

jective in issuing this Manifesto is to force the racist white Christian Church to begin the payment of reparations which are due to all black people, not only by the
Church but also by private business and the U.S. government. We see this focus on
the Christian Church as an effort around which all black people can unite.

Our demands are negotiable, but they cannot be minimized, they can only
be increased and the Church is asked to come up with larger sums of money
than we are asking. Our slogans are:

ALL ROADS MUST LEAD TO REVOLUTION
UNITE WITH WHOMEVER YOU CAN UNITE
NEUTRALIZE WHEREVER POSSIBLE
FIGHT OUR ENEMIES RELENTLESSLY
VICTORY TO THE PEOPLE
LIFE AND GOOD HEALTH TO MANKIND
RESISTANCE TO DOMINATION BY THE WHITE CHRISTIAN CHURCHES
    AND THE JEWISH SYNAGOGUES
REVOLUTIONARY BLACK POWER
WE SHALL WIN WITHOUT A DOUBT

As Forman was careful to point out, the half-billion-dollar demand of the
Manifesto was aimed only at "the church power structure." He clearly anticipated further action, saying, "We must demand more from the United States
Government." Those further demands from the United States government and
businesses continue, unmet, to the present day.

Response to the Manifesto was swift. It produced a good deal of fear, outrage, and outright rejection of its demands. There was a very modest positive
response from some churches. The rhetoric of the Manifesto, as much as its
specific demands, was responsible for its generally unfavorable reception.[2]

While some churches and synagogues approved of reparations "in principle," the actual contributions raised in response to the Manifesto were slight.
No money went directly to Forman's group. The Episcopal Church gave
$200,000 to the National Committee of Black Churchmen; the General Board
of the National Council of Churches *pledged* $500,000; the Presbyterians au-
thorized a drive for $50 million for "general works against poverty"; the
(Catholic) National Association of Laymen *requested* the sum of $400 mil-
lion from the U.S. Catholic Church; the World Council of Churches set up a
secretariat on racism with a $15,000 budget, and $200,000 in reserve for "oppressed peoples," and *asked* their members for more.

Progressive leaders were in general unresponsive. Bayard Rustin, head of the
A. Philip Randolph Institute and organizer of the 1963 March on Washington,
said: "The idea of reparations is a ridiculous idea. If my great-grandfather
picked cotton for 50 years, then he may deserve some money, but he's dead and
gone and nobody owes me anything."

Hugo Bedau, a professor of philosophy at Tufts University in Medford, Massachusetts, was a much cooler head at the time. His essay below separates the rhetoric of the Manifesto from its implied arguments and concludes that many have merit.

Hugo Bedau: "Compensatory Justice and The Black Manifesto"[3]

In May 1969, James Foreman interrupted a religious service at Riverside Church in New York to deliver "The Black Manifesto," which included a stunning "demand" of $500 million in "reparations" for black Americans from the white religious establishment. In the period since that date, *The Manifesto* has aroused rather less serious discussion than one might have thought it would.[4] No doubt, the burden of *The Manifesto* has struck many whites and some blacks as so outrageous in its morality, so unrealistic in its politics, so unfeasible in its economics, that intellectuals may have done a public service by consigning *The Manifesto* to relative neglect.[5] Not that *The Manifesto* has had only unfavorable publicity, nor that the churches have ignored it; quite the contrary. What remains true, however, is that the crucial burden of *The Manifesto*, indeed, the precise *argument* it advances for reparations and compensatory justice, has not so far as I can tell received the thoughtful attention it deserves. Until it does, and is appraised with care and fairness, it is impossible either to support or to reject *The Manifesto*'s "demands." Let us try, then, however belatedly, to state and assess the argument of *The Black Manifesto*.

The full text of *The Manifesto* runs to less than three thousand words; its "Introduction" adds another two thousand words. What is needed, however, is neither quotation, excerpt, or summary of these texts but a reconstruction of the argument they contain, since it is the merits of that argument which demand scrutiny and appraisal. The problem immediately evident to any reader of *The Manifesto* is that its argument is elliptical and obscure. The rhetoric of revolution, plain indignation, threats, predictions, and the sketch of how the reparations are to be used once they are in hand—all these confuse and fail to advance the argument implicit in *The Manifesto* and upon which whatever merit it has rests. My first task, therefore, is to take it as it is written and to reconstruct the argument it must contain if its central explicit and manifest assertions and accusations are meant seriously. As a first approximation to a complete reconstruction I offer the following sixteen premise version. [A few of the restated premises] are my interpolations of what I take to be among the tacit assumptions relied upon by the explicit assertions to be gleaned from the published text of *The Manifesto*. Expanded though the argument in my reconstructed version is, I have not tried to make it formally valid; no doubt that could be done, but it is not essential to my purposes here to try to do so. All the really interesting tacit premises I have tried to state.

The Argument of the Black Manifesto[6]

(1) Blacks in U.S.A. since 1619 have been "exploited and degraded, brutalized, killed and persecuted" by whites.

(2) This has been the objective effect of the commitment to "racism, capitalism and imperialism" practiced by the white power structure.

(3) The historic white Christian and Jewish religious establishment is "part and parcel" of the white power structure, "another form of government in this country;" it has actively supported and continues to support this systematic objective exploitation of blacks.

(4) Corporate black America is the heir of the historic victims and includes in its heritage the harm and injury suffered by the parents, grandparents, etc., of living blacks.

(5) The existing white religious establishment is liable to living blacks for whatever harm has been inflicted by its historic organizational forebears upon blacks.

(6) The chief purpose of slavery and its racist aftermath was to develop "the industrial base" of America.

(7) The wealth exacted by this exploitation has been astronomical in the thousands of billions.

(8) Much of this profit is owned or controlled or has otherwise been diverted to the benefit of, the white religious establishment—"the white Christian churches and synagogues."

(9) Little if any of that profit has been returned over the centuries for the benefit of those who were exploited to earn it.

(10) This profit constitutes an unjust enrichment in the hands of white America, including the white religious establishment.

(11) Such unjust enrichment constitutes a basis for justifiable compensation (restitution being impossible in the nature of the case) or "reparations."

(12) The compensation owed should be paid to and on behalf of "all black people," by the white religious establishment.

(13) Just reparations are a sum which will fund the development of those institutions, skills, and services for living blacks and their heirs of which their heritage has deprived them and in virtue of which they cannot compete today as the socio-economic equals of whites.

(14) $500,000,000 (or "$15 per nigger") is part of such a sum; but "it is only a beginning of the reparations due."

(15) The white religious establishment can afford to pay such a sum; it has "tremendous wealth."

(16) The white religious establishment in U.S.A. must pay $500,000,000 indemnity to corporate black America.

There are, at the onset, three kinds of objections to the argument of *The Manifesto* which I wish to state here so as to be relieved of any need to discuss them later. Some will object, first, that *The Manifesto* advances a claim ostensibly for reparations based on past wrongs, when in fact this only disguises the real argument for *redistribution* of currently available social resources given the present unfair disadvantages of blacks. In other words, some will say that the argument for compensatory justice in *The Manifesto* is really a disguised argument for distributive justice.

Others will object, second, that the real argument is not one for reparations nor is it a disguised argument for distributive justice. They will argue that it is really a disguised argument of an entirely different sort, namely, for special benefits to blacks given their special needs, on the ground that the *net social welfare is* maximized by this treatment. These critics of *The Manifesto* think that the entire appeal to justice (compensatory or distributive) is a deception, because the point to be made really relies upon the utility of redistributed wealth. Still others will object, third, that the argument of *The Manifesto* is disguised *extortion,* a veiled threat of violence unless half a billion dollars is transferred from white control to black. Those who view the argument in this third way see nothing moral in it at all.

All of these objections, one must concede, have some force. No doubt the third has the least plausibility, certainly in retrospect. Yet even this notion is not wholly absurd; after all, people do sometimes threaten to harm those whom they believe owe them compensation, especially if the plea for compensation falls on deaf ears. Nevertheless, I urge that we put aside this third possibility, and also the first two as well, because in a certain sense they are neither controversial nor interesting (except among politicians, perhaps, and racists). Hardly anyone (else) denies or contests the claim on behalf of living black Americans to a larger share of the total wealth and power in the nation. Hardly anyone (else) denies it would do them good to have a larger share in the nation's affluence and in its control, quite apart from the debatable question of the advisability of accomplishing these results by granting the demands contained in *The Manifesto.* Nor is it doubtful that present injustices in the distribution of social wealth provide a sufficient justification for transfers of wealth from white hands to black on a scale even greater than that contemplated by *The Manifesto.* Indeed, it may even be that the redistributive or the utilitarian version of the argument of *The Black Manifesto* is really the best way to construe it, given the political and economic realities of the 1970s.[7] After all, one need not shut his eyes to the possibility that the point of a manifest argument for reparations is in fact contained in a coordinated but concealed argument for distributive justice or social welfare.

Nevertheless, all these possibilities should be put clearly off to one side, because they are all alike in being *reinterpretations* of the argument evidently being advanced, and to that extent at least, they are evasions or repudiations of *The Manifesto.* It is as an argument for reparations, for compensatory justice, that *The Manifesto* makes its plain claim upon our understanding, and it simply cannot be taken seriously unless its force (and limitations) as *this sort* of argument are granted at the onset and without reservation.

Let us turn, then, to those objections which take the argument of *The Manifesto* at face value. Fundamentally, of course, any such counter-argument is going to proceed by alleging either that the argument-form itself is invalid, or that some explicit or implicit factual or moral premise is false. We know in advance, thanks to elementary logic, that only if at least one of these faults obtains can the argument be rejected. At the risk of being excessively contentious I propose to canvass possible objections and then rebut them as well as I can, and I shall begin with the least plausible objections and move to the more perplexing and complex ones. My survey will not be thorough, for I shall not try to dissect the reconstructed argument premise by premise, but I think the full range of possible obstacles to accepting the argument will at least be sketched and, I hope, the gravest objections directly stated and answered.

Objection (1). The figure of "$15 per nigger," mentioned in premise (14), is an arbitrary and really senseless sum because it bears no relation to any assessment of the injury suffered or the benefits exploited by whites from blacks.

This objection is partly wrong-headed. It regards the figure of $15 as a charge per head, whereas that figure is merely an arithmetic artifact produced by dividing $500 million by the number, roughly, of living black Americans. Besides, *The Manifesto* does not attempt to show that $15 per head is the upper limit, or anywhere near it, of the liability owed. It claims only that the lower limit of the liability is not below this sum. Whether that is so depends on certain calculations, and I return to this topic below in connection with Objection (10).

Objection (2). *The Manifesto* ignores the fact that the white religious establishment, mentioned in premises (5) and (8), of which white churches are alleged to be a part, is not "lily white" at all. For some decades, black Americans have been part of the congregations and, increasingly, of the clergy in all major national Protestant denominations and in the Catholic church, too. If so, then part of the current wealth and power of these churches has been contributed to them by some of the very group on whose behalf the claim of exploitation is made. This is doubly paradoxical: First, because from this fact of black membership in allegedly white churches, the victim turns out to be at one, as a member in a common institution, with his oppressor; and second, because the wealth of the oppressor has been given to him and not extorted or exploited by him from his victims.

The way to dissolve these paradoxes is by insisting that in fact the numbers of black persons in white churches is insignificant (perhaps one in a hundred, or in a thousand); and consequently, that the portion of white church wealth today which has been obtained from the voluntary contributions of black church members and clergy is equally negligible. The objection, then, is sound in implicitly raising the point (pace Hobbes) that a person or a class cannot "injure" himself, and a fortiori cannot hope to obtain redress for that injury from himself. It is wrong, however, in that the facts in this case do not permit application of this point.

It may also be part of this objection that it is inconceivable that the churches, as institutions, should owe reparations to blacks. This is a complex question, and I shall deal with part of it in my reply to Objection (4) and with more of it in my reply to Objection (10). Here, I would point out that *The Manifesto* asserts racist bias in the historic white churches of America, it implies racist exploitation among the lay and clerical members of white churches, and I think it also assumes corporate continuity of today's predominantly white churches with the historic "lily white" churches. If so, the anti-racism of the contemporary white church will fail to be a barrier against the demand for reparations to the extent that today's churches cannot legitimately deny continuity with their racist predecessors nor point to prior acts of reparation of their own or of their predecessors.

Objection (3). The idea. (introduced in premise (4)) of corporate black America being indemnified is absurd and unworkable. Blacks are no more a corporate body in America than are W.A.S.P.s. And the Black Economic Development Conference, which first formulatcd and publicised *The Manifesto*, cannot claim to speak for blacks; it has no authority to act as their representative or trustee. So, even if the argument were sound, there would be no legitimate body to receive and disburse the indemnification. (One might argue the other way, and claim that insofar as blacks can be thought of corporately or as a class, they can be so only as Jews or W.A.S.P.s are, viz., as a consequence of self-identification and group acceptance. But these two conditions are too imprecise and unpredictable in their actual operation to be sufficient for the purpose of granting the assumption of *The Manifesto*.)

The reply, I believe, is that it is not impossibly difficult to think of ways in which all and only living black Americans might be convened so as to create a truly representative body, or anyway a body with genuine ethnic legitimacy and authority, to receive and administer these reparations. It is not necessary that blacks undertake to effect physical, economic, or legal separation from their white fellow citizens in America in order to be, for the purposes of these reparations, identifiable as a nation within a nation. Likewise, B.E.D.C. or its successor could be established as a trustee, holding the monies received in indemnity until such a legitimate representative of corporate black America emerged. As for criteria of membership in black America, a suitable "grandfather clause" in disjunction with a nativity clause could be used to supplement self-identification and group acceptance, so as to exclude non-American blacks, e.g., Jamaican Negroes, and new black Americans, e.g., Ghanian immigrants provided it was in fact thought necessary or desirable to limit eligibility in corporate black America in such ways.

Objection (4). The argument of *The Manifesto*, in being addressed to the churches, is arbitrary and unfair. The churches as corporate bodies are, if anything, less guilty of racist exploitation than other white institutions.

We may concede that *The Manifesto* does not make clear whether the churches are the only or simply the first white institution to be subjected to demands for reparations. In theory, *The Manifesto* might well be reformulated and addressed to tax-exempt foundations (typically created by the surplus profits of American commercial and industrial enterprise), institutions of higher learning (endowed from the same sources), and other non-profit organizations (such as hospitals, theatres, galleries, museums, libraries). *The Manifesto* explicitly does allude to demands for reparations from "private business and the United States government."[8] However, most of these other white institutions have already been asked to make quasi-restitutionary compensation, rather than monetary reparation. They have been asked to extend their services and open their jobs to blacks. It is an ironic commentary on the state of religious life in America that the chief contribution by way of compensation it is thought white churches can make to black Americans is merely money. Whether other institutions which have more to offer could wholly discharge their debt to black America through compensatory jobs and services, however, is very doubtful, if the argument of *The Manifesto* is sound. As for the complaint that among white institutions the churches are not the most guilty of racist practices, this is irrelevant in two respects. First, it remains true that the guilt of the churches would not vanish before the fact that other white institutions share or even exceed that guilt. But the truth is, the question of guilt is not properly at issue. Guilt carries with it the atmosphere of punitive sanctions, whereas reparations is not a punitive remedy at all. Instead, what is at issue here is corporate *liability*;[9] like guilt, liability admits of degrees and is such that the greater liability does not efface the lesser.

Second, the objection overlooks an important consideration. Churches, more than any other white institution, are specially vulnerable to a demand for reparations because such a demand can be understood perhaps best within the ancient pattern of sinfulness, contrition and penance which is inseparable from the entire historical theology of the Judeo-Christian religion. This religion, in every version and throughout history, teaches that it costs a sinner something to put himself into a right relationship with his God and his fellow-man. Surely, it is this consideration which makes the professedly religious bodies of America the very best place to begin a campaign for reparations.[10] For what other institution is equally susceptible to the demand to confess and make amends? If anything, the difficulty raised by objection (4) lies in quite the reverse direction. If the importance of the pattern of sinfulness, confession and penance—true repentance—is stressed as central to the setting in which this demand for reparations is made, then it will entail that the argument of *The Manifesto* has little or no application to any other white institution! Certainly, no secular corporation, whether it makes a profit or not, will be or will think of itself as susceptible to a demand for reparations cast in this form. Nor is this an idle and inconsequential consideration. If white America owes reparations to black America, then the vast non-church-going bulk of the white population today in this country will evade paying its share of the corporate indemnity, simply by virtue of confining the argument of *The Black Manifesto* exclusively to white churches. Obviously, this was not the intent of *The Manifesto*'s authors and supporters.

There remains, then, a certain tension in the fact that it is the churches to whom *The Manifesto* is officially and initially addressed. If the aptness of addressing the churches is stressed, then no other institutions will be subject to reparations, at least, by the terms of this argument. This is a considerable price to have to pay in order to avoid the charge of unfair and arbitrary selection of the churches as the sole target of *The Manifesto*, when one considers the relatively small percentage of the nation's total wealth in church control.

Since, however, the argument of *The Manifesto* relies upon the idea of corporate black America, and since according to the argument every white American is in some way and to some degree accountable for historic harms visited upon blacks, why doesn't *The Manifesto* ignore all white institutions, such as the churches, and address itself directly to corporate white America? If corporate black America can be viewed as the injured party and the party deserving reparations, why not serve the demand for reparations against corporate white America?

The answer, I think, is twofold. Corporate white America is too unrepresented, too disorganized, too diffuse to be effectively approached by anybody for anything, much less by black spokesmen for something as disturbing as reparations. The churches, by contrast, are well organized and like other voluntary organizations are accessible to black leaders; they meet weekly to transact their spiritual business behind open doors. *The Black Manifesto* is obviously already symbolic enough without being reduced to pure gesture, as it would be if it were addressed to corporate white America as such. Thus, while from a logical point of view, the ideas of corporate black and corporate white America are on precisely equal footing, from a practical point of view as regards the motive for organizing under such a rubric, they could not be farther apart. Moreover, since the churches might be said to be the functional conscience of the nation, addressing *The Manifesto* to them might be viewed legalistically as placing the churches in subrogation for corporate white America: the white churches are made to answer for the liability of all white Americans. (Once again, however, if we accept this latter interpretation, only the churches can ever be made liable for reparations.)

Objection (5). The argument, if not strictly inconsistent, at least poses a dilemma for its advocates. It begins with a radical Marxist critique in its complaint of "exploitation," in premises (1), (3), and (6)–(7). But before it ends, in premises (10)–(12), it shifts into a conventional Liberal demand for "justifiable compensation." Now, the argument cannot be both Marxist and Liberal. If it is the former then it should demand expropriation of the exploiters, a revolutionary redistribution of the product of the worker's labor to all the people, public ownership of the means of production and distribution, etc.[11] For this version of the argument to be sound, it is essential to establish that current wealth in white institutions is the causal product of historic capitalist exploitation. But if the argument is merely Liberal and reformist, as it seems in the end to be, then the initial complaint of exploitation (like the alleged surplus profits) is irrelevant. It is sufficient on this version of the argument to establish only that blacks still suffer from uncompensated wrongs while others (whites) still enjoy the undeserved benefits of those historic wrongs.

The reply to this alleged dilemma is twofold. There is nothing wrong, in Marxist theory, with arguing for half a loaf rather than all. In a pre- or nonrevolutionary situation, there is no reason why a sincere and consistent Marxist should not appeal to reparations, redistribution, or to any other familiar Liberal principle of social justice provided it will succeed in persuading a nominally Liberal (and unquestionably anti-Marxist) society to shift the current allocation of its resources away from protecting the propertied class to assisting the workers. In any case, Liberals have ample reason to press the purely Liberal version of the argument to its conclusion, quite apart from the evident Marxist overtones in the argument as it stands. For others, who are sympathetic to if not imbued with Marxist theory, one might insist that the notion of exploitation used in *The Manifesto*'s argument is truly equivocal. The labor of generations of blacks has created surplus profits of slight or no benefit to them, and this labor was originally stolen and thenceforth made captive under conditions of structured injustice which a Hume, a Mill, or a Rawls would be able to recognize as such. The slave and Jim Crow heritage, therefore, constitutes both a moral and an economic exploitation. Blacks in America have been doubly exploited, so their argument for compensation is entitled to take this into account and it does. To put it another way, we might view *The Black Manifesto* as attempting to invoke not merely one or another version of conventional Liberal principles of justice, nor of Marxist justice—if there is such a thing—[12] but what might be called socialist justice (the full outline of which, I would concede, is nowhere as yet stated).

Objection (6). *The Manifesto*'s argument rests on racist (i.e., immoral racial) assumptions. It concedes that the claimant is not the party directly injured, and that the party liable to pay up is not the party who directly inflicted the injury. Yet it argues that it is just to make the heirs of the former pay the heirs of the latter because the one continues to profit from the injury as the latter continues to suffer from it. But to do this the argument must imply that blacks as a class or a race have been injured; how can this be true unless every black has been injured? Likewise, if whites as a class have inflicted the injury, is not every white responsible? But these implications are very probably false and certainly not proved. True, *The Manifesto*'s argument does not impute fault to every white distributively, any more than it imputes benefits to every white distributively from the slavery of blacks and its aftermath. But it does allege that whites as such have benefited and blacks as such have suffered at their hands. This pattern of reasoning does, therefore, rely upon the idea of liability or responsibility (if not guilt) by mere racial association, as well as the suffering of injury by mere racial association. Any argument relying upon such concepts is morally unsound. Moreover, the nature of the argument is such that no evidence of good faith, either individually or collectively, by whites or white institutions towards blacks prior to the levy of the demand for reparations in *The Manifesto* would seem to exempt such whites from its thrust.

The basis of the rebuttal must lie in the incontestable fact that blacks in America have been regarded as a class historically by slave and post-slavery segregation legislation and coordinate social practices. However difficult it may be, according to anthropologists, to develop an adequate empirical basis for a sound theory of races, this difficulty has not stood in the way of a practical development of the concept of a *black* as distinct from a *white* race in this country. Consequently, it is possible that various other practical relations, including injury, liability, benefit, and redress should obtain between the parties so defined, despite spatial, temporal, and hereditary dispersals among the members of the two classes (races). There is, in short, no purely logical or conceptual reason why there should not be liability and the rest by virtue of merely racial association or membership in a racially defined class. Whether there is any factual basis for such a doctrine is a separate question.

As for guilt by association, where criminal guilt before a court of law is the question, it is perfectly fitting that such guilt should be attacked and repudiated. Criminal guilt and individual fault, however, are not in question here. Therefore, any criticism of *The Manifesto* based on complaint against the immorality of guilt by association is simply beside the point. The appeal to corporate or institutional liability is legitimate just in case the facts show participation in and profit from racial slavery and segregation by the institution in question. The record is far from complete, but in so far as the liability of the white churches of America is in question, it would appear even without the exhaustive researches scholars have yet to provide that it ill-behooves contemporary defenders of the major American religious denominations to repudiate the moral legitimacy of the notion that their churches as institutions are liable for claims of reparations based on the fact that they are beneficiaries and preservers of racist practices against blacks.[13]

Objection (7). The argument of *The Manifesto* relies upon tacit analogy either with reparations exchanged between sovereign nations (as in German war reparations, under the Versailles Treaty) or with indemnities granted by a sovereign nation to one of its dependent or custodial peoples (as in our government's indemnities to certain American Indian tribes). Neither analogy is plausible. In the latter class of cases, there is always some specific treaty violation which serves as the basis of the claim for reparations; but no such treaty exists between black and white America. In the former class of cases, we have a very dangerous analogy because only the defeated ever pay war reparations and they look upon them not as just compensation owed to the victims of their unjust aggressive war, but rather as the tribute exacted from the loser under the time-honored doctrine that to the victor belongs the spoils.

First, while it is of course true that no legal treaty binds black and white Americans together, the federal Constitution and the host of federal "Civil Rights" legislation and decisional law do testify to a kind of implicit social contract among racial equals. Black Americans are entitled to argue that individually they are parties to this implicit contract but that as a class they have yet to receive their full and fair share under its terms. Second, the parallel with war reparations only points to the truth that it is unreasonable to demand reparations from a party who has made no concession of liability, and today it is doubtful whether white America has conceded its liability for wrongs visited upon black America. Yet one can make too much of this. It is true that it is unreasonable, in the face of white intransigence and the absence of overwhelming black power, to *demand* reparations, just as it is futile to threaten to take property or services valued in the amount of the reparations demanded unless they are paid promptly and in full. Some, may have found such intentions in *The Manifesto*, because near its end we read: ". . . we are not opposed to force and we are not opposed to violence."[14] However, it is not necessary to construe this remark as a genuine threat. For those without any access to an appropriate court room, part of an ef-

fective strategy to get someone who is liable for reparations to accept that liability is to press upon him a well-reasoned argument imputing liability and demanding compensation. This is what (with perhaps less than perfect success)
The Black Manifesto attempts to do.[15]

A better rebuttal to the complaint based on the weakness of the analogy proceeds by denying that the argument relies on any such analogy at all. The argument of *The Manifesto*, as I have reconstructed it, relies not on analogy with
treaty violations or war reparations, but upon the common legal notion of *unjust enrichment* (see premises [6]–[12]). Arnold Kaufman has correctly emphasized this idea, though without using the term, when he asserted:

> The sons of privilege are being asked to compensate the sons of slaves whether or
> not the former are responsible for the disabilities of the latter. . . . The sons of
> slave-masters continue to profit, the sons of slaves to suffer the disabilities of the
> original iniquity. Under these conditions the sons of slaves have rights of compen-
> sation against the sons of slave masters.[16]

In this, there is no argument by analog at all. Instead, there is a straightforward
appeal to the fundamental principles of compensatory justice on the assumption
that the facts of the situation of black Americans today vis-a-vis white Americans
(or, at least, the white churches of America) satisfy those principles.[17] Moreover,
there is reason to see some disanalog between compensation for black Americans and the German war reparations, because the latter case does not rely
upon the notion of unjust enrichment. It relies upon the idea of criminal harm,
or at least tortious injury: the deliberate waging of aggressive and unprovoked
warfare with peaceful neighbors. But an analogous complaint against the
churches is at most obliquely asserted in *The Manifesto*.

Objection (8). The argument of *The Manifesto* is sufficiently legalistic that it invites criticism on at least two legalistic grounds: (a) the defense of belatedness of
claim, and (b) the defense of unsought benefits. (a) Claims of compensatory desert
based on harms that occurred decades, generations, even centuries ago are not
payable because civilized society cannot be expected to entertain such claims on
grounds of justice over an indefinitely long period. The parties who were originally
liable are not now around to pay up, and it is unfair to expect their unknowing
and innocent heirs to pay in their stead. Blacks as a class have no right today to
ask the white churches or any other white institutions for reparations for ancient
wrongs. (b) "A person is not ordinarily required to pay for benefits which were
thrust upon him with no opportunity to refuse them. The fact that he is enriched
is not enough, if he cannot avoid the enrichment."[18] But if *The Manifesto*'s assumptions about racism in America are correct, this is precisely the predicament
of most whites, including white institutions, in this society. The wealth which the
churches have is obtained entirely through their members' voluntary contributions
and the subsequent profitable investment of the unspent portions. This wealth derives from persons all of whom possess the unsought advantages of color and race,
advantages of which they cannot divest themselves. There is a certain tragedy and
pathos in this for blacks, but no occasion for reparations from whites.

The objection in (b) is easily met. The defense of unsought benefits in law is clearly designed to protect the recipient of a gift forced upon him from having to make restitution to the donor upon demand at a later date. The donor is entitled to restitution only when he affords the donee an opportunity to decline the benefit or else has a reasonable excuse for failure to do so.[19] But the special advantages accruing to whites in virtue of their race and color are not benefits given to or conferred upon whites by blacks. Historically, they have been exacted from blacks by whites only by the utmost use of terror and violence. So, while it may be true that many whites have enjoyed unsought advantages deriving from their race and color, it is false that these advantages were somehow inherent in race and color themselves, just as it is false that these advantages were thrust upon whites by blacks choosing to disadvantage themselves.

The objection in (a) is based on what might be called a moral statute of limitation, or a moral analogy to the legal bar of laches (i.e., "negligence in the performance of any legal duty, or delay in asserting a right, claiming a privilege, or making application for redress"[20]). Equity, we are told in an old maxim, aids only the vigilant; and a victim of another's injustice who is negligent in the assertion of his right to compensation may discover that his negligence bars him from remedy. The passage of time may result in unfair hardship for the defendant, or for third parties, or increase the likelihood of substantial change of error regarding the relevant facts.[21] It is for these reasons that statutes of limitation and the equitable defense of laches are available to protect defendants. No doubt they have comparable force in the forum of conscience as well. Whether they should work to defeat the claim for reparations advanced in *The Black Manifesto* is doubtful. One might argue persuasively that it is only in recent years that black spokesmen have been in a position to advance and press a claim for reparations, and thus that their failure to do so in earlier decades is not evidence of black negligence so much as it is a measure of the severity of black disabilities. In addition, the churches cannot plead that they are unable to pay the compensation demanded or that it would bankrupt them to do so. But only this kind of severe hardship enables a defendant to successfully invoke laches. Whether, however, the enormous passage of time—more than three centuries, over which the injury to blacks was inflicted and the unjust enrichment by whites was reaped is so great as to make incalculable the injury and the benefit, and for this reason something like laches should enter, this is a difficulty to which I will turn in Objection (10).

Objection (9). Although *The Manifesto* claims that "black people are the most oppressed group of people inside the United States,"[22] its authors do not and could not claim that blacks alone have been exploited by others to create profits in which they have not shared, because the same is true of most white and other non-white immigrants throughout the history of the nation. This creates the possibility of destroying the argument of *The Manifesto* by reducing it to absurdity through constructing parallel arguments for compensatory reparations on behalf of other exploited and disadvantaged groups. The aboriginal American Indians are survived by tribes whose title to such reparations is every bit as good of that of erstwhile African blacks; the same is true of Mexican Americans in the Southwest and of Puerto Ricans on the eastern seaboard. But then the same is also true of the East Boston Irish, the North End Italians, the West End Jews, etc., etc. Every minority has been exploited by the established society of its day, so the heirs of every exploited minority have a right to file a claim comparable to that levied in *The Manifesto*. Now, since each such argument is valid only if all are valid, none is valid—because it is absurd for all to be valid. It is simply preposterous to imagine seriously working out the details of the cross-claims for class indemnities which would be established by this multitude of valid claims for reparations.

Again, there are two replies to this objection, one of which concedes the assumption in question and the other of which denies it. It is true that the spectacle of a whole series of claims and cross-claims for compensation by each American ethnic group against all others boggles the mind. But this is not a theoretical objection to entertaining such a complex set of intertwined claims. Lawyers are paid every day to work on cases nearly as complex. Practically, of course, it would be extremely difficult to work out a suitable scale of historic injury and to parcel out the relative degrees of liability among the various groups in question. One might hypothesize, on behalf of *The Manifesto*'s authors, that if such cross-claims in indemnity were worked out, we would discover that they would cancel out so far as all the claims among white ethnic groups are concerned, leaving only the massive claim of blacks against whites, one portion of which is the explicit preoccupation of *The Manifesto*.

However, I think it is more likely to suppose that the authors of *The Manifesto* did not anticipate this kind of objection, because it seems in fact to be frivolous. It may be that *The Manifesto*'s claim of compensation rests upon the assumption that blacks are historically only the nation's most exploited and least rewarded ethnic group, and that for this reason only their claim for compensation goes to the head of the list. Certainly, nothing in *The Manifesto* as such implies that no other ethnic group in America also deserves reparations from whites. But the economic, psychological, and other societal facts have convinced most observers that the unique history of forced immigration (in contrast to free immigration) and chattel slavery (in contrast to indentured servitude and "wage slavery") has left a heritage of defeat among blacks incomparably more devastating than that suffered by any other initially disadvantaged immigrant minority group. Likewise, the evidence that blacks as a class, like Irish, Italian, Jewish, and other non-W.A.S.P. immigrants, can take the upwardly mobile route to its own economic prosperity and social diffusion throughout society at all levels without special compensatory efforts is doubtful at best.

There is, nevertheless, one other rival claimant to the unique status advanced by *The Manifesto* on behalf of blacks: the Indians. Only the American Indian as an ethnic minority has suffered what might be called (after British criminal law) "constructive genocide," a fate even more brutal in its effects than forced immigration and chattel slavery. The legitimacy of the Indians' claim, on Liberal if not on Marxist assumptions, is if anything more valid and incontestable than the claim of blacks.[23] Without the mineral resources and real estate bargained, wrested and stolen from the Indians, white culture in this nation would lack the material base for the past century's agricultural and industrial growth and the ensuing wealth in its possession. One reply to this objection, therefore, is that the Indians are entitled to make a claim against whites in terms no less stark than those used in *The Manifesto*. What we need alongside *The Black Manifesto* is a Red Manifesto; but this concession is not sufficient to establish a *reductio ad absurdum* at all.

Finally, we should not overlook a purely logical point. The argument of *The Manifesto* cannot be shown to be unsound merely by the possibility that if the form of argument it employs were valid, then infinitely many other versions of the same argument would also be valid. For this is uninteresting unless it is likely that because *The Manifesto*'s argument is sound, so are all or many of these other compensatory arguments. However, that cannot happen so long as at least one premise is false in every other version of the argument. In my criticism above, I have relied on precisely this outcome, with the one notable exception already discussed.

Objection (10). In order to make out a claim for compensatory justice, one needs to know the value of the loss suffered, the benefit derived therefrom by another, the causal connection between the injured and injuring parties, and the acts committed by the latter upon the former for which reparations are sought. But in this case, we cannot (and *The Manifesto* does not) identify with sufficient precision the specific harm suffered by blacks as a class nor the specific benefits secured by and on behalf of the white churches, nor the causal relation between the two. The argument for recompense depends on some assessment of how blacks would be today as a class if they had not been exploited historically. Otherwise, their loss cannot be calculated; but there is no way to establish the value of this loss, nor the wealth unjustly in white hands. The result is that the demand of any given amount in reparations is hopelessly unmoored from the necessary factual base. It is hardly surprising that the militant authors of *The Manifesto* themselves are unable to settle upon a proper sum for reparations. Although they initially announced the sum as $500 million, within two months they had raised it by a factor of six.[24]

Many will think this is the most fundamental and unanswerable objection of them all, so it deserves careful consideration. To take the last point first, the fact that the authors of *The Manifesto* upped their claimed indemnity is perhaps owing as much to the rapid change in their knowledge of the assets controlled by white churches as it is either to greed or to the sobering costs of the programs to be financed with the reparation money. Quite apart from any other considerations, if reparations are owed blacks as a class by the white churches, it does not seem unreasonable that they should amount to a sum equivalent to (what has been reasonably estimated as) 3% of the total real estate holdings of the churches,[25] or perhaps one year's worth of, Sunday morning church offerings.

The Manifesto is not clear as to the precise mechanisms of white enrichment at the expense of black slavery and discrimination, and a certain sympathetic inventiveness on behalf of the authors of *The Manifesto* is required if we hope to do justice to their argument. I suggest that we view the wealth of the churches as created by white membership and administered by white clergy on behalf of implicitly racist (or with indifference to anti-racist) policies, in which the actual creation and perpetuation of slavery itself played an important but not decisive part. Thus, whether black chattel slavery was or was not itself a profitable institution on these shores (a matter much debated by historians)[26] is not crucial to *The Manifesto*'s complaint at all. We are to think of the wealth in the churches today as created bit by bit over the generations, and as representing in part the surplus profits available only to whites because of the racist character of the larger society. Presumably, if blacks had been paid their fair share (i.e., at the same rates as whites doing equivalent jobs) during these centuries for the services they rendered to white employers, there would have been proportionately less wealth now in the control of the white churches, and the position of blacks today would be more nearly that of whites as well.

Blacks, we know, arrived on these shores virtually penniless and with few exceptions remained that way generation after generation thanks to the repressive forces harnessed in slavery. Economic research, theoretically at least, should be able to give us estimates at, say, fifty year intervals throughout our entire history and at decennial intervals during the past century of the total wealth in the control of corporate black America and corporate white America, respectively. If we were to plot these data on a graph, so as to get a representation of the economic growth rate of blacks vs. whites in America since the earliest days, we know without any question both that (a) the rate of slope for black growth would be much shallower than for whites, and that (b) the growth curve for blacks would start at the point of origin on the graph and remain nearly there for decades, whereas the comparable curve for whites would begin above zero and without faltering would continue to rise. What we don't know and could not calculate is the shape the curve for blacks would have taken had they been free men from the start and had they suffered discriminations in degree and in kind no worse than the average of those discriminations imposed by the dominant white groups upon the immigrant white groups. We might get some idea of what that curve would look like by plotting, if we could, on our graph the economic growth rate for every other identifiable ethnic group which has landed on these shores. One can assert with fair confidence that (a) and (b) above will be true no matter what white ethnic group's growth rate curve is compared with the blacks!

Given, then, that *The Manifesto*'s argument is entitled to rely upon proof of continuous severe racial discrimination by whites against blacks in this country, proof of continuous severe economic disadvantages for blacks as against whites, proof that the latter is in considerable part explained by the former, the only fundamental question which remains is whether $500 million (or $3 billion, or any given amount) can be said to be an adequate measure of the reparations owed, given the cost to blacks of their losses and the unjust wealth accrued by whites and transferred to their churches. The only honest thing one can say is that we do not know whether it is or whether it isn't.[27] Between ludicrous extremes (such as asking for $10,000 in reparation, or asking for black control of the total wealth and income of all the churches) there are many equally plausible sums to fix upon, because our economic knowledge about the matters discussed in this and the preceding paragraph is too vague for more precision. Both $500 million and $3 billion seem to me to be within that plausible range and not at all ludicrous. Beyond that I cannot venture. One sympathizes with the predicament of white church leaders and the black authors of *The Manifesto*, for none of them has knowledge on these economic questions adequate to being more confident and more precise than I have been.

Yet further difficulties beyond the ten objections I have discussed can be imagined. It might be argued that if whites as a class are liable to blacks as a class for reparations, then not even if all voluntary nongovernmental white institutions make reparations will all whites have paid their fair share; only the government, through the use of its tax monies, can truly compensate blacks for centuries of slavery, injury, and degradation. Or, as another objection, one might urge that the entire argument of *The Manifesto*, resting as it does, upon the concept of desert, is anachronistic, because desert is a concept of declining relevance in the adjustment of social relations where inequalities suffered on the scale of those which burden American blacks are concerned.[28] Or one could argue that *The Manifesto* constitutes an example of what has elsewhere been called "inflated desert" claims; that is, *The Manifesto* commits the fallacy of inferring from the true conclusion that blacks as a class deserve reparations to the unproved further conclusion that blacks as a class ought to be paid $3 billion in reparations.[29] Or, to mention a fourth possibility, one might object that

> . . . the Negro's past suffering seems beyond the remedy of society to redeem. There is no payment that can supply its balance. It would be a sign of contempt for the Negro should the white community offer to compensate this debt, for there are trials of the spirit too large and awesome to stand comparison with any good that might be proposed as their measure. . . . The strictly compensatory act of payment for past suffering is impossible . . .[30]

There is no end to the objections that might be raised.

Perhaps, however, it is enough to have come as far as we have. I hope I have shown what the basic structure of the argument of *The Black Manifesto* is, and that although it can be subjected to various criticisms, these in turn, with varying degrees of finality, can be rebutted. Little I could add now would make the argument significantly more persuasive for those to whom it is addressed. Nor do I wish to stand in impartial judgment on the demands of *The Manifesto* and deliver any final verdict. Once in a while, at least, it ought to be enough for philosophers to try to understand and not at the same time judge, much less to change, the world.[31]

The last half of the twentieth century was marked by another American legislative effort to secure reparations for Black America. A bill sponsored by Rep. John Conyers, H.R. 40, never made it out of committee.

H. R. 40, IH 33, 106th Congress, 1st Session[32]

106th CONGRESS
1st Session
H. R. 40

To acknowledge the fundamental injustice, cruelty, brutality, and inhumanity of slavery in the United States and the 13 American colonies between 1619 and 1865 and to establish a commission to examine the institution of slavery, subsequently de jure and de facto racial and economic discrimination against African-Americans, and the impact of these forces on living African-Americans, to make recommendations to the Congress on appropriate remedies, and for other purposes.

IN THE HOUSE OF REPRESENTATIVES
January 6, 1999
Mr. CONYERS (for himself, Mr. FATTAH, Mr. HASTINGS of Florida, Mr. HILLIARD, Mr. JEFFERSON, Ms. EDDIE BERNICE JOHNSON of Texas, Mrs. MEEK of Florida, Mr. OWENS, Mr. RUSH, and Mr. TOWNS) introduced the following bill; which was referred to the Committee on the Judiciary.

A BILL
To acknowledge the fundamental injustice, cruelty, brutality, and inhumanity of slavery in the United States and the 13 American colonies between 1619 and 1865 and to establish a commission to examine the institution of slavery, subsequently de jure and de facto racial and economic discrimination against African-Americans, and the impact of these forces on living African-Americans, to make recommendations to the Congress on appropriate remedies, and for other purposes.

Be it enacted by the Senate and House of Representatives of the United States of America in Congress assembled,

SECTION 1. SHORT TITLE.
This Act may be cited as the 'Commission to Study Reparation Proposals for African-Americans Act'.

SEC. 2. FINDINGS AND PURPOSE.
(a) FINDINGS—The Congress finds that—

(1) approximately 4,000,000 Africans and their descendants were enslaved in the United States and the colonies that became the United States from 1619 to 1865;

(2) the institution of slavery was constitutionally and statutorily sanctioned by the Government of the United States from 1789 through 1865;

(3) the slavery that flourished in the United States constituted an immoral and inhumane deprivation of Africans' life, liberty, African citizenship rights, and cultural heritage, and denied them the fruits of their own labor; and

(4) sufficient inquiry has not been made into the effects of the institution of slavery on living African-Americans and society in the United States.

(b) PURPOSE—The purpose of this Act is to establish a commission to—

(1) examine the institution of slavery which existed from 1619 through 1865 within the United States and the colonies that became the United States, including the extent to which the Federal and State Governments constitutionally and statutorily supported the institution of slavery;

(2) examine de jure and de facto discrimination against freed slaves and their descendants from the end of the Civil War to the present, including economic, political, and social discrimination;

(3) examine the lingering negative effects of the institution of slavery and the discrimination described in paragraph (2) on living African-Americans and on society in the United States;

(4) recommend appropriate ways to educate the American public of the Commission's findings;

(5) recommend appropriate remedies in consideration of the Commission's findings on the matters described in paragraphs (1) and (2); and

(6) submit to the Congress the results of such examination, together with such recommendations.

SEC. 3. ESTABLISHMENT AND DUTIES.

(a) ESTABLISHMENT—There is established the Commission to Study Reparation Proposals for African-Americans (hereinafter in this Act referred to as the 'Commission').

(b) DUTIES—The Commission shall perform the following duties:

(1) Examine the institution of slavery which existed within the United States and the colonies that became the United States from 1619 through 1865. The Commission's examination shall include an examination of—

(A) the capture and procurement of Africans;

(B) the transport of Africans to the United States and the colonies that became the United States for the purpose of enslavement, including their treatment during transport;

(C) the sale and acquisition of Africans as chattel property in interstate and intrastate commerce; and

(D) the treatment of African slaves in the colonies and the United States, including the deprivation of their freedom, exploitation of their labor, and destruction of their culture, language, religion, and families.

(2) Examine the extent to which the Federal and State governments of the United States supported the institution of slavery in constitutional and statutory provisions, including the extent to which such governments prevented, opposed, or restricted efforts of freed African slaves to repatriate to their home land.

(3) Examine Federal and State laws that discriminated against freed African slaves and their descendants during the period between the end of the Civil War and the present.

(4) Examine other forms of discrimination in the public and private sectors against freed African slaves and their descendants during the period between the end of the Civil War and the present.

(5) Examine the lingering negative effects of the institution of slavery and the matters described in paragraphs (1), (2), (3), and (4) on living African-Americans and on society in the United States.

(6) Recommend appropriate ways to educate the American public of the Commission's findings.

(7) Recommend appropriate remedies in consideration of the Commission's findings on the matters described in paragraphs (1), (2), (3), and (4). In making such recommendations, the Commission shall address, among other issues, the following questions:

(A) Whether the Government of the United States should offer a formal apology on behalf of the people of the United States for the perpetration of gross human rights violations on African slaves and their descendants.

(B) Whether African-Americans still suffer from the lingering affects of the matters described in paragraphs (1), (2), (3), and (4).

(C) Whether, in consideration of the Commission's findings, any form of compensation to the descendants of African slaves is warranted.

(D) If the Commission finds that such compensation is warranted, what should be the amount of compensation, what form of compensation should be awarded, and who should be eligible for such compensation.

(c) REPORT TO CONGRESS—The Commission shall submit a written report of its findings and recommendations to the Congress not later than the date which is one year after the date of the first meeting of the Commission held pursuant to section 4(c).

SEC. 4. MEMBERSHIP.

(a) NUMBER AND APPOINTMENT—

(1) The Commission shall be composed of 7 members, who shall be appointed, within 90 days after the date of enactment of this Act, as follows:

(A) Three members shall be appointed by the President.

(B) Three members shall be appointed by the Speaker of the House of Representatives.

(C) One member shall be appointed by the President pro tempore of the Senate.

(2) All members of the Commission shall be persons who are especially qualified to serve on the Commission by virtue of their education, training, or experience, particularly in the field of African-American studies.

(b) TERMS—The term of office for members shall be for the life of the Commission. A vacancy in the Commission shall not affect the powers of the Commission, and shall be filled in the same manner in which the original appointment was made.

(c) FIRST MEETING—The President shall call the first meeting of the Commission within 120 days after the date of the enactment of this Act, or within 30 days after the date on which legislation is enacted making appropriations to carry out this Act, whichever date is later.

(d) QUORUM—Four members of the Commission shall constitute a quorum, but a lesser number may hold hearings.

(e) CHAIR AND VICE CHAIR—The Commission shall elect a Chair and Vice Chair from among its members. The term of office of each shall be for the life of the Commission.

(f) COMPENSATION—

(1) Except as provided in paragraph (2), each member of the Commission shall receive compensation at the daily equivalent of the annual rate of basic pay payable for GS-18 of the General Schedule under section 5332 of title 5, United States Code, for each day, including travel time, during which he or she is engaged in the actual performance of duties vested in the Commission.

(2) A member of the Commission who is a full-time officer or employee of the United States or a Member of Congress shall receive no additional pay, allowances, or benefits by reason of his or her service on the Commission.

(3) All members of the Commission shall be reimbursed for travel, subsistence, and other necessary expenses incurred by them in the performance of their duties to the extent authorized by chapter 57 of title 5, United States Code.

SEC. 5. POWERS OF THE COMMISSION.

(a) HEARINGS AND SESSIONS—The Commission may, for the purpose of carrying out the provisions of this Act, hold such hearings and sit and act at such times and at such places in the United States, and request the attendance and testimony of such witnesses and the production of such books, records, correspondence, memoranda, papers, and documents, as the Commission considers appropriate. The Commission may request the Attorney General to invoke the aid of an appropriate United States district court to require, by subpoena or otherwise, such attendance, testimony, or production.

(b) POWERS OF SUBCOMMITTEES AND MEMBERS—Any subcommittee or member of the Commission may, if authorized by the Commission, take any action which the Commission is authorized to take by this section.

(c) OBTAINING OFFICIAL DATA—The Commission may acquire directly from the head of any department, agency, or instrumentality of the executive branch of the Government, available information which the Commission considers useful in the discharge of its duties. All departments, agencies, and instrumentalities of the executive branch of the Government shall cooperate with the Commission with respect to such information and shall furnish all information requested by the Commission to the extent permitted by law.

SEC. 6. ADMINISTRATIVE PROVISIONS.

(a) STAFF—The Commission may, without regard to section 5311(b) of title 5, United States Code, appoint and fix the compensation of such personnel as the Commission considers appropriate.

(b) APPLICABILITY OF CERTAIN CIVIL SERVICE LAWS—The staff of the Commission may be appointed without regard to the provisions of title 5, United States Code, governing appointments in the competitive service, and without re-

gard to the provisions of chapter 51 and subchapter III of chapter 53 of such title relating to classification and General Schedule pay rates, except that the
compensation of any employee of the Commission may not exceed a rate equal
to the annual rate of basic pay payable for GS-18 of the General Schedule under section 5332 of title 5, United States Code.

(c) EXPERTS AND CONSULTANTS—The Commission may procure the services of experts and consultants in accordance with the provisions of section
3109(b) of title 5, United States Code, but at rates for individuals not to exceed the daily equivalent of the highest rate payable under section 5332 of
such title.

(d) ADMINISTRATIVE SUPPORT SERVICES—The Commission may enter into
agreements with the Administrator of General Services for procurement of financial and administrative services necessary for the discharge of the duties of
the Commission. Payment for such services shall be made by reimbursement
from funds of the Commission in such amounts as may be agreed upon by the
Chairman of the Commission and the Administrator.

(e) CONTRACTS—The Commission may—

(1) procure supplies, services, and property by contract in accordance with
applicable laws and regulations and to the extent or in such amounts as are provided in appropriations Acts; and

(2) enter into contracts with departments, agencies, and instrumentalities of
the Federal Government, State agencies, and private firms, institutions, and
agencies, for the conduct of research or surveys, the preparation of reports, and
other activities necessary for the discharge of the duties of the Commission, to
the extent or in such amounts as are provided in appropriations Acts.

SEC. 7. TERMINATION.
The Commission shall terminate 90 days after the date on which the Commission submits its report to the Congress under section 3(c).

SEC. 8. AUTHORIZATION OF APPROPRIATIONS.
To carry out the provisions of this Act, there are authorized to be appropriated
$8,000,000.
END

The rest of the English-speaking world went much further in the twentieth
century than did the United States in addressing issues of the historical injustices of the nineteenth century. Canada, Australia, and New Zealand all apologized in part to or compensated portions of their indigenous populations for
the displacement, disenfranchisement, disinheritance, and degradation suffered by these groups as a result of national policy.

Included below is a 1996 debate in the British House of Lords on the subject of responsibility of Britain for slavery and the correction of the harms it
inflicted.

The Official record from Hansard of the Debate
Initiated by Lord Gifford QC
in the House of Lords of the British Parliament
on 14th March 1996
Concerning the African Reparations[33]

9.18 P.M.

Lord Gifford rose to ask Her Majesty's Government whether they will make appropriate reparation to African nations and to the descendants of Africans for the damage caused by the slave trade and the practice of slavery.

The noble Lord said: My Lords, the Question raises an issue which is being debated with increasing vigour and intensity by African people around the world; and by African people I mean people of African descent, wherever they live, whether in Africa itself, in the United States, in Great Britain or in the Caribbean, where I now live and practise law.

The issue is this. The under-development and poverty which affect the majority of countries in Africa and in the Caribbean, as well as the ghetto conditions in which many black people live in the United States and elsewhere, are not, speaking in general terms, the result of laziness, incompetence or corruption of African people or their governments. They are in a very large measure the consequences the legacy of one of the most massive and terrible criminal enterprises in recorded human history; that is, the transatlantic slave trade and the institution of slavery.

The thesis that I advance tonight is that in accordance with international law and with basic human morality, measures of atonement and reparation are due from the successors of those who instigated and carried out the trade and who profited massively from it to the descendants of the victims of the criminal enterprise who still suffer in many different ways from the effects of the crime.

The horrendous nature of the enterprise of African slavery is well known and documented. Around 20 million young people were kidnapped, taken in chains across the Atlantic and sold into slavery in the plantations of the New World. Millions more died in transit in the dungeons of the castles such as Gore, Elmina and Cape Coast, or in the hell holes under the decks of the slave ships. It was without doubt, in the fullest sense of the term, a crime against humanity.

A vast proportion of sub-Saharan Africa from Senegal right round to Angola and on the other side from Mozambique into Malawi and Tanzania was depopulated. Its young men and women were taken away. Population estimates show that Africa's population remained static at around 100 million between 1650 and 1850 while in the same period the populations of Europe and Asia increased between twofold and threefold. It is small wonder that the great kingdoms of Africa such as Mali, Songhai and Ghana fell into decline while the slave-trading nations prospered mightily. Whole cities such as Liverpool and Bristol grew wealthy on the triangular trade of manufactured goods going to Africa, slaves going from Africa to the colonies, and sugar coming back from the colonies to Britain. No calculations can measure the loss suffered by the African continent from that massive depopulation of its young people, for which no compensation was ever paid.

African governments today. who have tried to rectify the under-development which they have inherited from history, have borrowed from the financial institutions of the West and are now in a virtually uncontrollable spiral of debt. In reality—and in morality—I suggest that it is the West which is in debt to Africa, not Africa which is debt to the West.

On the other side of the Atlantic, the African captives were cut off from their families, their land and their language. They were forced to be owned as chattels and to work as beasts of burden. When, finally, emancipation day came—in the British colonies, in 1838—the ex-slaves received nothing. It was the ex-slave owners who were compensated for the loss of their property.

The slavery experience has left a bitter legacy which endures to this day in terms of family breakdown, landlessness, under-development and a longing among many to return to the motherland from which their ancestors were taken. Once again, in the Caribbean the need to finance development programmes has bound Caribbean governments and peoples in fresh shackles, the shackles of debt. In Jamaica, where I live, between 40 per cent. and 50 per cent. of the national budget has had to be paid out in debt servicing over the past 10 years. In many African countries, the proportion is much higher. The effects are crippling in that every public service, such as schools, health facilities, transport and roads, prisons and justice systems, is so squeezed that it is failing to deliver at even a minimum standard.

As well as the consequences in Africa and the Caribbean, there is a further element in the legacy of the slave trade which is the damage done within Britain, within the United States and other Western societies. The inhuman philosophy of white supremacy and black inferiority was inculcated into European peoples to justify the atrocities which were being committed by a Christian people upon fellow human beings. That philosophy continues to poison our society today.

On one short visit back to Britain this month, I come across reports of racism in the Armed Forces and the police. Equal rights legislation has not been enough. It is necessary to look more deeply, to understand why the crimes of the past are poisoning the present for all people, white and black, and then to do something effective to repair the wrong. That will assist both African and European, black and white, to lance the poison and to heal the wounds.

The concept that reparations are payable where a crime against humanity has been committed by one people against another is well established in international law and practice. Germany paid reparations to Israel for the crimes of the Nazi Holocaust. Indeed, the very creation of the State of Israel can be seen as a massive act of reparation for centuries of dispossession and persecution directed against Jews.

Japan apologised only last year, 50 years on, for its wartime atrocities and is still being urged, rightly, to pay compensation to the victims. The USA made apology and restitution for the internment of Japanese Americans during the Second World War. Going further back into history, Her Majesty the Queen, only last November in New Zealand, personally signed the Royal Assent to the Waikato Raupatu Claims Settlement Bill through which the New Zealand Government paid substantial compensation in land and in money for the seizure of Maori lands by British settlers in 1863. She apologised for the crime and recognised a long-standing grievance of the Maori people. Other indigenous peoples have similar just claims for the dispossession which their ancestors suffered.

African people, too, have a massive and long-standing grievance. It is no use saying that it all happened a long time ago, and we should just forget about it. The period of colonialism which succeeded the period of slavery, continued the exploitation of Africa and the Caribbean in new ways. Further acts of brutality were committed, and the peoples of those regions, until recently, were denied the status of sovereignty and independence with which alone could themselves demand the redress of the wrongs which were done.

But the wrongs have not been forgotten. The peoples of Africa and the Caribbean live with their consequences still. A group of eminent Africans under the auspices of the Organisation of African Unity is beginning to articulate the claim for reparation.

What is meant by the claim for reparations? The details of reparations settlement would have to be negotiated with an appropriate body of representatives of African people around the world. I would anticipate that some of the elements of an appropriate package would be, first, as with other precedents, an apology at the highest level for the criminal acts committed against millions of Africans over the centuries of the slave trade. His Holiness the Pope set the example when he visited the slave dungeons of Goree in Senegal in February 1992 when he said:

"From this African sanctuary of black pain,
we implore forgiveness from Heaven."

Secondly, there would be the cancellation of the intolerable burden of debt, which has overloaded the economies of Africa and the Caribbean. There are powerful economic and social arguments for debt cancellation which were most recently deployed by former President Kaunda of Zambia during a visit to Scotland in February 1996. He said of the present state of Africa:

"It is a human tragedy. People are dying by their thousands every day, children are dying. These things bring social disorder to countries".

Thirdly, there would be the return of treasures and works of art which come from the African continent, many of which are to be found in Britain's museums as a result of acts of theft and robbery. I refer, for instance, to the Benin Bronzes in the Museum of Mankind.

Fourthly, there would be measures to facilitate the repatriation and resettlement of those who wish to return to Africa. The word "repatriation" has an ugly ring in the mouth of racists who want to drive black people out of Britain. However, it expresses, too, a yearning among many descendants of Africans which is as powerful as was the yearning of the Jewish people for the Promised Land.

Fifthly, there would be a reparations settlement which would involve programmes of development, without strings attached, in Africa, the Caribbean,

Brazil and elsewhere, including programmes to promote equal rights and justice within the countries of the West.

As we move to the next millennium, none of us can deny that there is a growing divide between north and south, between black and white, across frontiers and within frontiers. It is in the interests of all of us to recognise that the reasons for that divide lie in a shameful past. If we realise that, we will be on the way to doing something to repair the wrong which was done, even though it may cost heavily in terms of pride and revenue. The steps to be taken will bring a happier world for all our children.

In asking this Question on an issue which may be new and difficult for many of your Lordships, I ask the Government and the Opposition parties for a positive and open-minded response. I believe that this issue will remain with us and will gather momentum. Today's governments and parties are not guilty of fostering the slave trade. But they would be responsible if they did nothing to remedy the injustice, the suffering, the poverty and the racism which the slave trade and the institution of slavery inevitably engendered into the present day.

Lord Burnham: My Lords, before the noble Lord sits down, can he tell the House which country first stopped the slave trade?

Lord Gifford: My Lords, after carrying it on and profiting massively from it, the slave trade was stopped by the nations of Europe. I pay tribute to the ancestor of the noble and learned Lord, Lord Wilberforce, who played a leading part in stopping the trade. However, no compensation was paid when it was stopped and the unredressed grievance remains with us today.

9.33 P.M.

Lord Willoughby de Broke: My Lords, I fear that seldom have so few people come together to do so little. I respect the noble Lord's concern and no doubt your Lordships were enlightened by his expose of the slave trade, albeit slightly coloured by his attitude to the Question. However, I too wish to point out to the House that Britain was the first country in Europe to stop the slave trade 30 years before it was stopped in America. It is not remotely realistic to start talking about reparations at this stage. Reparations can be dangerous; one only has to think of the Versailles Treaty to realise what reparations brought in their wake. Reparations breed envy and distrust and stir up hatred. Far better is what we have done, which is to give aid to help countries to rebuild their prosperity and future.

Britain has a good record in relation to aid to sub-Saharan African countries. I have looked up some of the figures. I am able to tell the noble Lord that between 1979 and 1995 Great Britain paid out 11,610,000,000 dollars to sub-Saharan Africa. Even the noble Lord, Lord Judd, might agree that that is not just small change; it is a considerable sum of money. Even if a regrettable amount of that goes into the pockets of neo-Marxist military dictators, it is to be hoped that some of it is properly administered and will help the developing countries in Africa.

If the noble Lord, Lord Gifford, is concerned about slavery, perhaps I may suggest that he should direct his energies towards the countries which are still

Folsom Lake College Library

practising slavery today. A number of countries are doing that, including countries which are more developed; for example, India and China.

While I am on the subject of money, as a fully paid-up member of the taxpayers' club, I wonder whether the Minister will tell me how much it has cost to research the answer to this Question which seems to me to be slightly irrelevant in terms of reality. I respect the concern of the noble Lord, Lord Gifford. But is it realistic to talk about reparations when so much has been done by this country and other countries to help Africa? I do not believe that it is. I should like to hear what the noble Lord has to say about that.

I had not intended to thank the noble Lord, Lord Gifford, for asking this Question but I am indebted to him because, looking at the clock, I find that I have missed my train home and I shall claim appropriate reparations by way of an overnight allowance.

9.37 P.M.

Lord Wilberforce: My Lords, I am grateful, as no doubt are other noble Lords, for this opportunity to ascertain something of the Government's views on slavery, the slave trade and its consequences, even though I have difficulty with some of the tenor of the speech of the noble Lord, Lord Gifford.

I declare at once an interest in this subject as a joint president of Anti-Slavery International. I agree with the noble Lord that, in principle, one cannot object to the idea of the concept of compensation to individuals for wrongs which they have suffered. There is certainly no wrong more grievous, after the wronged loss of life, than loss of liberty. There is no doubt that compensation has been paid in certain circumstances to individuals who suffered ascertained wrongs. The noble Lord referred rightly to the compensation to the Jews and the Jewish nation which was directed by Chancellor Adenauer and to the compensation paid by sections of German industry to individual Jewish persons and refugees.

There are other cases. The noble Lord mentioned some. One could mention the situation of the Sudeten Germans who have been individually thought to be entitled to compensation. On the Japanese side, it is true, I believe, that Japanese prostitutes in the course of the war have received compensation for the wrongs they endured.

However, in all those cases one finds unquestioned guilts and unquestionable responsibility of a particular person. In the case of the Jews, it was the German state. There are identifiable victims of the wrong and direct and assessable consequences. I do not find that those conditions are satisfied, or anywhere near satisfied, in the present case.

Of course, there is still slavery in Africa. One notices that the Question refers specifically to compensation to African nations and compensation to be paid by the British Government, but not international compensation to a whole mass of people all over the world.

We know that slavery still exists in Africa and that there is still slave trading in the area. But for neither of those things can the responsibility realistically, fairly or properly be laid on Her Majesty's Government. On the contrary, as the noble

Lord, Lord Willoughby de Broke indicated, ever since 1833 when slavery was abolished in the British Empire (which covered a great many of the states of Africa), British governments have striven by law, by force, by use of their navy, by influence and by the expenditure of money, to have slavery abolished in African countries, to stop the trade in human beings, and to mitigate the consequences. The difficulty of assessing the consequences and reparation were adverted to by the previous speaker. I feel sure that the Minister will deal with that view of the matter supported by facts. I am quite happy to leave that aspect of the matter to him.

However, I believe that we should carry the case a little further. For that I believe we are indebted to the noble Lord who tabled the Question. We can perhaps look wider than the precise narrow point outlined by the noble Lord. I shall put my main point very shortly. However good our historical record may be— and I believe it to be a very good one—however much direct responsibility for the existence of slavery and of the slave trade may rest now upon independent states in Africa and elsewhere, however difficult, indeed impossible, it is to assess compensation or reparation, we nevertheless—and this also applies to other western and first world countries—have a very strong moral responsibility now and always to do two things; first, to bring about as far as possible the abolition of slavery wherever it still exists, and, secondly, to do whatever we can both practically and realistically to alleviate the consequences.

On the first task, we know that slavery exists in Africa. There are the known examples of the Sudan, Mauritania and probably Mozambique. It is worth underlining again, with reference to the noble Lord's Question, that, in the case of Mozambique, responsibility there is entirely that of the Portuguese who ruled the country until 1974. We have no conceivable responsibility either directly or indirectly. On the other hand, our duty is a strictly humanitarian one, owed by man to man.

What we have to do and what we can do as regards abolishing slavery is, first, to establish beyond doubt where it exists and in what countries. That means supporting with money directly and indirectly those organisations, of which ASI is one, which are able to do so. We must support the United Nations with influence and money, particularly its working groups and reporters who are charged with ascertaining the facts. Again, we must support with influence and, if necessary, money, the higher organisations in the United Nations which are able to bring about change. For example, in Mauritania slavery still exists, although it was abolished by law in 1980. However, we know that that is not the end of the matter; indeed, it is only the beginning of the story. What is needed to make progress is land reform, education and a new labour system based on liberty, all of which need strong international support and someone to give a lead. I believe that we can fairly look to Her Majesty's Government in that respect.

Above all, we must press—this is something we can do and which we do do—all countries which have not done so to ratify the supplementary convention of 1956. There are many African countries among the non-signatories. So much, very briefly, for taking action to abolish slavery where it still exists. I have rather confined myself to Africa because that was the tenor of the noble Lord's Question.

We have a moral responsibility—I go along entirely with the noble Lord to that extent to do what we can to mitigate the consequences of slavery, either of pre-existing slavery, as in 19th century economic slavery, or of existing slavery, as it has been in our time. The main consequences which we can identify and which we are in a position to do something about are well known. They are low prices for commodities and the burden of debt, which is itself a form of slavery. This has been referred to, and the noble Lord, Lord Judd, made a persuasive point at Question Time yesterday. The proportion of income from exports that is now needed to pay for debts is impossibly large and is bringing about what is, in effect, a state of economic slavery in many areas. There is also the question of unfair trading, which can be attacked through application of the Uruguay Round. Civil wars which have existed in so many countries, and which still exist in Africa, bring about, inevitably, conditions of slavery, and the consequences of that. I need only mention the Sudan in that connection.

We all know that these consequences of slavery occur. We can see them. I believe that Her Majesty's Government use their influence internationally to mitigate those consequences. I hope that the Minister will comment on the possibility of action to combat those consequences. Often this matter is discussed in the context of self-interest. It is argued that if we attack forms of slavery, that will bring prosperity to us. I have no objection to the argument of self-interest being used; any argument which helps in this connection is welcome. However, I still believe that the case is basically a moral one based on the history of the western powers and their development—if I may use that colourless word—of Africa and its resources in the past. I believe that the case rests on the drawing of boundaries by the western powers which has led inevitably to stress, wars, poverty and underdevelopment. That point was touched on by the noble Lord who tabled the Question.

I wish to reaffirm that I believe that the case for action and any sort of compensation should not be based on guilt, nor on an expedient expenditure of money. We should base the case for giving help on morality. That is entirely in line with the beliefs of the original great reformers. Just west of this House, in Westminster Abbey, there is a bust of Zachary Macaulay, one of the original strong abolitionists. As your Lordships know, he was governor of Sierra Leone—a colony of freed slaves. The bust is dedicated to a man, "who during 40 successive years rescued Africa from the woes, and the British Empire from the guilt of slavery and the slave trade".

The case now is not one of guilt but of morality. I commend it as such to your Lordships.

9.48 P.M.

Lord Gisborough: My Lords, the noble Lord, Lord Gifford, painted a moving picture of the slave trade, and one cannot argue with the picture he painted. Slavery is an age-old matter. It goes back to the Greeks and the Romans who had slaves on their galleys. Slavery has existed on all continents for as far back as can be recorded. Some people were enslaved by press gangs, or were enslaved after being captured in wars. Others were enslaved as a form of punishment. One must not forget that many slaves were sold into slavery by their parents or by the chiefs of their villages. There is the case of the blacks in the sugar plantations but, as has already been mentioned, slavery has occurred in many countries and people were enslaved in Europe during the past war. It is a phenomenon which is far from confined to the black nations.

As regards compensation, therefore, one has to ask how far it would be proposed to go back in time. The noble Lord suggests that we go back 300 years to the slave trade, and the descendants of those involved. Why not go back 1,000 years to the descendants of the Greeks? Where would it stop? And who would pay compensation? Almost every country was responsible for slavery in those days, including the French, the Spanish and the blacks themselves. Therefore, it is absurd to ask Her Majesty's Government to make reparations for the slave trade.

Lord Gifford: My Lords, I thank the noble Lord for giving way. Of course I recognise that if there were a positive answer to this Question that would give a lead to the other European governments which profited similarly. It would be a joint international venture.

Lord Gisborough: My Lords, I appreciate that. However, the suggestion is particularly rich because, as has already been mentioned, the British led the anti-slavery campaign. We can read about Gordon, whose object was entirely anti-slavery. Then there was the struggle for central Africa in the 1880s. Again that was a matter of Europeans going into Africa, and often fighting the Arab slavers who ran the slave trade. A new book entitled *The Scramble for Africa* paints the whole picture.

The purpose of my speaking was not to go into history but to reinforce the remarks about modern day slavery. We cannot do much about the slavery of old, but we can and we must do something about the slavery that is going on at the moment.

There was a television documentary the other day which showed that, for example, Filipinos were going to Saudi Arabia, having been promised wages. However, when they reached Saudi Arabia their employers took their passports away and they were not paid. If they attempted to escape they were accused of theft, with the obvious consequences if they were found guilty. Slavery of Filipinos in Saudi Arabia is rampant. That is only one example. There are many examples in other countries, which have already been mentioned.

The General Assembly of the United Nations issued a declaration in 1948 about the abolition of slavery, which was fully agreed. However, it has not been implemented by many countries in Africa and in Asia.

All possible action must be taken by the Government to try to stop slavery now. Aid should be restricted to countries where slavery takes place. The Government should bring great pressure on every country where slavery is known to take place even though it may not be legal. It is unacceptable for slavery to be so widespread in 1996.

9.53 P.M.

The Viscount of Falkland: My Lords, I should like to thank the noble Lord, Lord Gifford, for giving us the opportunity today to speak on a very complicated subject. I agree broadly with a good deal of what the noble Lord said. I agree also with the noble and reamed Lord, but I part company with him to some extent on the tone of his speech, and in particular some of the phrases that he used and the way that he ran some of the issues together, although, in view of the constraints of time, I understand why he did that.

I made my maiden speech in this House some 12 years ago, !ate at night about this time, on the subject of the problems in sub-Saharan Africa. That is a subject about which I know something because for 10 years I had done a good deal of work in East Africa. In that debate I had the great privilege to have as fellow speakers some very distinguished noble Lords, many of whom are not with us today. One in particular, who became a particular friend of mine in this House, was the late and great Lord Pitt of Hampstead. If the noble Lord had been alive today, I am sure that he would have spoken in the debate. He himself was the descendant of a slave. He came from the island of Grenada. My father lived in Grenada for some years. Like many of the inhabitants of that island, Lord Pitt had a particular charm and an easy going nature, but underneath a firm resolve to deal with problems of racism and those of sub-Saharan Africa in which he took a close interest.

I have always taken an interest in history and I knew a certain amount about slavery at that time. However, Lord Pitt introduced me to the works of Eric Williams, Prime Minister of Trinidad and Tobago and perhaps the greatest West Indian historian of his period.

Slavery is a fascinating and at the same time horrifying subject. Apart from the fact of our mercantile growth through slavery over a period of a century or more, one of the great shames is that subsequently in our education in schools so little attention has been paid to slavery as a factor governing the development of this country as we now know it. Barbados was the jewel in the colonial crown at the beginning of the 17th century. One can make a quite clear link between the first importing of slaves from the coast of West Africa into the Caribbean islands, in particular Barbados, and the growth of our mercantile trade and our struggles with other countries which sought to outdo us, through financing the Industrial Revolution to where we find ourselves today. To that degree, I agree absolutely with what the noble Lord, Lord Gifford, said. Where I part company with him is the way in which he has somewhat abbreviated and compressed history.

I agree absolutely that racism has been one of the legacies of slavery. It was not racism that caused slavery, it was economic necessity. Before slaves were taken to Barbados, other West Indian islands and certain colonies in the United States, we used other forms of labour. That has been referred to by other noble Lords. We used petty criminals who had not been condemned for capital offences. We press-ganged—if that is the right word; I believe that it was called "Barbadosing"—vagrants and others who seemed superfluous in our society and bundled them off in ships to the islands where they were to all intents and purposes slaves. Those people were probably treated worse than the slaves themselves because they were there for a limited time and not until perpetuity. The flogging and the misery were suffered as much by those of European origin as by slaves later.

The reason that slavery suddenly developed in our islands was through our race against other nations to develop agricultural products. The great prize of expansion was to replace minerals. There was a great race to develop the sugar crop. Sugar has been and is still the great evil. I have given it up for Lent. Sugar is the crop that perhaps has created the most misery and degradation of all the agricultural crops. It was a luxury product which then became a common product in more advanced countries for sweetening tea and coffee.

The cane sugar plant originally came from Polynesia. It was tried by the Portuguese who first used slaves in Madeira and the Cape Verde Islands. It was then taken by the British to Barbados but it could only be produced in economic quantities with a supply of labour which was robust and relatively docile. The West Africans filled that bill and thus the great triangular trade began which has been accurately referred to by other noble Lords. There was the movement of goods from Britain, Manchester, down to the west coast of Africa, then slaves to the West Indies and then back again with products. That resulted in about 12 million slaves—I am not sure of the figures—in that trade in the 18th century going from West Africa.

I pay tribute to the great reformers. Presumably one of them was the direct ancestor of the noble and learned Lord, Lord Wilberforce. I must include the Quakers who were persistent opponents of slavery in these islands: the great Joseph Sturge whose descendant, the noble Baroness, Lady Eccles of Moulton, sits in this House today. He was a great and popular Quaker reformer in Bristol.

Lord Gifford: My Lords, the noble Viscount is interesting and erudite in his history, but I am sure he will accept that it was the Danes who were the first European nation legally to abolish the slave trade. We followed them six years later.

The Viscount of Falkland: My Lords, I am most grateful to the noble Lord, as I am sure are other noble Lords, for answering a point which was put to him. I do not wish to sound cynical but I am sure that there were reasons other than philanthropic ones for abolishing slavery in this country. When it was abolished, the sugar islands became uneconomic. We hastened the end of slavery because we did not wish competitors to continue in the islands which they held which were still marginally fertile. I agree that it was a hideous crime against humanity which was used for economic reasons. A great deal of wealth was created which had a well-known effect on our history.

Reparation was the main drift of the noble Lord's speech. Whether it is appropriate I do not pretend to know. I look forward with anticipation to what the Minister will tell us. Even having heard the noble Lord, Lord Gifford, it seems to me a complicated area. How does one judge whether reparations are appropriate? How much should they be? What mitigating factors should be taken into account? It has not yet been mentioned that the end of slavery in West Africa caused a great deal of upheaval among African native slave traders and the kingdoms because they made a good deal of profit from the trade. In particular, what is now southern Nigeria and the Bight of Benin, a highly populated part of West Africa, found themselves in a position where they had to go back to old and barbaric ways of thinning out their populations. They were paid compensation by the British in many cases for their loss of revenue from the slave trade. I believe that the experiment in palm oil was an agricultural activity promoted—rather like our groundnut scheme centuries later—in order in some way to try to compensate.

That is a different matter from the reparations to which the noble Lord refers. The way we viewed it was that our reparations should be to compensate those who had helped us. That is where I part company with the noble Lord, Lord Gifford, when he referred to kidnapping. It would have to be taken into account. If we considered reparations, we would have to calculate the amount of co-operation that took place at that time with the African states.

I shall say no more about the history of slavery. I absolutely agree that it is an appalling episode in the history of the world. It can be explained. It is well documented. I do not like to confuse what we were discussing on that night in 1984—namely the proper support of sub-Saharan countries, with the debt that it is proposed we owe either African nations or others for the slavery period. The need for us to take a completely new, more positive and more constructive look at the need to help the development of Africa stands on its own feet.

The situation facing us in 1984 which we all rightly foresaw, of great famines in Africa which have taken place with horrifying consequences and misery to countless numbers of men, women and children, still exists. The only problem now, as the noble Lord, Lord Judd, well knows and may mention, is that, since the world has changed and the great imperatives of East-West confrontation have disappeared, the African problem has become somewhat marginalised. The attention of the world has been turned towards central Europe and the Far East. I am much concerned about the development of southern Africa, except of course for the enormously encouraging events that have taken place in South Africa.

There is another reason why I do not absolutely go along with the noble Lord, Lord Gifford. I have worked for a long time in central and eastern Africa. We have the evidence of what has happened with President Mandela, and before him President Kenyatta. In my experience, the African people are immensely forgiving. They have forgiven the indignities that they suffered in recent times. To encourage the kind of attitude of fervent desire for reparation suggested here would go against the grain, certainly among Africans, because it is not in their nature. What we owe to Africans is a renewed and more energetic attitude, and a greater amount of material, constructive and well thought-out aid for sub-Saharan Africa. Perhaps I may also say that that is true for the Caribbean islands as well. There are slightly different problems there.

I see the issues as quite separate. The issues of slavery need to be open and need to be discussed. We need more debates like this. More children need to know more about the history of their country, about what is good and what is bad. They need to face that appalling period.

I still believe, as did Lord Pitt, in a multi-racial society in this country. It is one of the great tragedies of my life that we have not achieved it. Whether we can achieve it going down the road suggested by the noble Lord, Lord Gifford, I do not know. I remain to be persuaded.

10.04 P.M.

Lord Judd: My Lords, all of us should certainly be grateful to my noble friend Lord Gifford for the opportunity of this short debate this evening. It has been a good little debate. When we are debating slavery we all particularly value the thoughts of the noble and learned Lord, Lord Wilberforce.

My noble friend has always championed human rights and colonial freedom. I recall serving under his chairmanship on the British committee for freedom in Mozambique, Angola and Guinea before the revolution against tyranny in Portugal itself, in the days when Portugal was seen by many in this House and the other place as a NATO ally under no circumstances to be criticised and thereby, paradoxically, provoking the extension of Communist influence among those struggling for their freedom in Africa.

My noble friend speaks in the tradition of George Fox, Glanville, Sharp, William Wilberforce, Josiah Wedgwood, Thomas Clarkson and the other determined Quakers, evangelicals and people of principle and vision who achieved the abolition of the slave trade in the Act of 1807 and the abolition of slavery itself in British colonies between 1834 and 1840.

It was a tough, demanding struggle which required unyielding consistency and integrity. Coupled with the courage of those who sought to emancipate the grotesquely exploited working classes, who, although not categorised as slaves, suffered acutely and enjoyed precious little freedom in our own society, it is a powerful lesson to all of us in the age of sound-bite, spin-doctor politics. We should never forget those who devoted themselves to those struggles. More importantly, we should never forget the appalling plight of the slaves and the exploited themselves. The story of slavery goes back for perhaps 10,000 years to the origins of farming itself and the use of prisoners of war on the land; and, as we have been reminded this evening, it continues in many parts of the world today, together with the associated evil of racism, to which my noble friend so powerfully referred.

We should never be tempted to romanticise. Between the 1500s and 1800s, Europeans shipped about 12 million black slaves in hellish conditions from Africa to the western hemisphere. As my noble friend reminded us, nearly 2 million died in transit. Those who survived to reach the United States and other destinations played a major part in economic development, clearing wildernesses, building canals, roads and railways and, to use the term with meaning, slaving away in cotton and sugar plantations, usually more than 16 hours a day.

I hope that I shall be forgiven if, at this point, I quote from Josiah Henson, who wrote of his experience as a field hand. He said that "Our dress was of tow-cloth

. . . and a pair of coarse shoes once a year. We lodged in log huts. Wooden floors were an unknown luxury. In a single room were huddled, like cattle, ten or a dozen persons, men, women and children. . . . There were neither bed-steads nor furniture. . . . Our beds were collection of straw and old rags. . . . The wind whistled and the rain and snow blew in through the cracks, and the damp earth soaked in the moisture fill the floor was miry as a pig sty."

Slavery was only legally abolished in the United States as a whole in 1865 and in Latin America some 20 years later. I agree with my noble friend; it is sad that there has never been proper reparation for that cruel evil by the exploiters and their advantaged descendants.

If, on all sides of the House, we take an opportunity to pause and reflect on the sober realities and lessons of history, it is not only slavery but colonialism and indeed its aftermath that we have to examine. In some cases, the colonial period fuelled the growth of ethnic tension from which we are still reaping the results today. In Rwanda, for example, under first the Germans and then the Belgians, the minority Tutsi were favoured in terms of education and posts in the colonial administration over the majority Hutu. At independence, the Belgian switched support to the majority Hutu government. Both those factors have been cited by the interesting and somewhat disturbing multi-agency Rwanda evaluation study that is just being published as contributory factors, among many others, which led to the build up of ethnic hatred and the 1994 genocide.

Following their so-called independence, assistance to African countries was often based on Cold War loyalties, with few questions asked about the governance record of the country in question on the basis, I believe, that "It doesn't matter if he is a bastard, provided he is our bastard." Consequently, large amounts of money were "invested" in propping up some fairly dubious regimes. In retrospect, long-term British assistance to the Banda regime in Malawi was almost certainly one such example, although latterly, greatly to the credit of the noble Baroness, the Minister, we froze aid when it became clear just how cruel and repressive that tyranny had become.

It is, frankly, grimly ironic that, in historic terms, so soon after the age of direct or indirect colonialism, we should see freedom again set aside with ruthless unrepresentative oppressive governments in countries like Sudan, Nigeria, the Gambia and, until now, Sierra Leone—though we all pray that in the case of Sierra Leone the elections and peace negotiations may help to pave the way to a better future.

I am sure we would all agree that the thoughts of the noble Viscount, Lord Falkland, were particularly interesting. Indeed, he is right. Since the end of the Cold War, sub-Saharan Africa has been of much less strategic importance in the West and, given its limited economic importance, it is increasingly falling off the map world concern. Declining aid budgets in the United States, Canada, Italy and the United Kingdom reflect declining political support for the principle of development co-operation.

While the Overseas Development Administration's fundamental expenditure review claims to address the problem by proposing to focus 85 per cent. of the bilateral programme on 20 countries in sub-Saharan Africa and South Asia, I hope the noble Lord opposite will forgive me if I say that there is inevitably strong scepticism—cynicism even—lest that is little more than a smoke-screen for managing decline. The Overseas Development Administration's figures demonstrate that, even if the Government moved from 69 per cent. to 85 per cent. being spent in the priority 20 countries over the next two or three years, because country programmes are anyway scheduled to decline over that period the Government would only be able to maintain existing assistance to those 20 countries in cash terms rather than holding it in real terms, let alone increasing it.

In the Caribbean the situation with regard to aid is even worse. The fundamental expenditure review makes it clear that the Caribbean is a non-priority area, despite our historical debt to those islands underlined by the purpose of the debate this evening. The economies of many of those countries are already in peril. Some, having been encouraged by their colonial powers to live off the proceeds of growing a single crop—bananas—now find themselves threatened by the single European market which opens them up to competition from cheaper bananas produced in Latin America. In the face of that, at a time when Britain, as a former colonial power, clearly has a moral duty to assist with diversification, it appears that instead we shall be turning our backs.

The colonial legacy for many African and Caribbean countries has been that the traditional, balanced self-sufficiency, with well-tried coping mechanisms for hard times, has been replaced by over-dependence on a single commodity making them extremely vulnerable to fluctuations in commodity prices on the world market. In sub-Saharan Africa commodities account for 80 per cent. of exports. Between 1980 and 1993 prices for non-oil commodities fell by more than half relative to prices for manufactured goods. The estimated loss to developing countries over that period was 100 billion US dollars—more than twice the total flow of aid in 1990.

Again, Rwanda is a pertinent example. Rwanda is heavily dependent on coffee and the slump in world coffee prices, combined with other factors such as bad weather and economic policies, led to a per capita fall in incomes of 40 per cent. between 1989 and 1993. That hit the Rwandan peasantry particularly hard, increasing social and economic pressure within society—another factor quoted by the multi-agency evaluation report as contributing to the tragic events of 1994.

The conclusion of the last Uruguay Round was held as a triumph which would benefit everyone; everyone, that is, apart from sub-Saharan Africa which, on the basis of OECD figures, will be the only region to be a net loser under the terms of the agreement. Indeed, if we are talking about reparations, what about some compensation to sub-Saharan Africa for what it is going to lose out on under the Uruguay Round?

While no one should deny that adjustment is necessary, the fact remains that the social costs of adjustment in many African countries have been high. Cuts in public expenditure have encouraged the introduction of user fees for basic health and education services, putting them beyond the reach of the poorest sections of society. During the 1980s real per capita spending on education in Africa fell by one-third while two-thirds of the countries in the region also reduced spending on health. Surely it is imperative for essential social spending to be protected in countries undergoing structural adjustment. It is unforgivable that the innocent should be confronted with the bill for the transgressions of irresponsible—frequently selfish—leaders and equally irresponsible lenders in the past. The poor have no access to those foreign bank accounts.

My noble friend emphasised debt. Perhaps nowhere is our legacy to Africa more apparent than in the spiraling debt burdens under which many countries in sub-Saharan Africa are labouring. Uganda spends 17 dollars per person on debt for every three dollars it is able to spend on health. Zambia spent 37 million dollars on primary education from 1990 to 1993 while it spent 1.3 billion dollars on debt repayments. Tanzania spends twice as much on debt as it spends on access to clean water. The human costs of debt are enormous and existing debt release initiatives have done little to solve the problem. Today's report in the *Financial Times* about a new initiative, if true, is encouraging. The IMF/World Bank meeting in April really must end the misery by agreeing a comprehensive solution to the debt crisis incorporating bilateral, multilateral and commercial debt suitably funded from within the multilateral institutions themselves, including the use of World Bank reserves and IMF gold stock and special drawing rights aimed at restoring debt repayments to sustainable levels by the year 2000.

Slavery was abolished as the result of inspired and tireless efforts by the campaigners coupled with a growing doubt about its material economic advantages, a point to which the noble Viscount referred. Similarly, I hope that the efforts of those like my noble friend Lord Gifford—and others like him whom we are able to hear more regularly in this House and the other place—coupled with a growing realisation of the unproductive madness of diverting as much as £3 billion annually, directly or indirectly, from bilateral aid programmes intended to promote sustainable long-term development into debt servicing of multilateral debt, will encourage the Government to work relentlessly for a comprehensive strategy for debt reduction at the forthcoming meeting in April of the International Monetary Fund and the World Bank. That, I believe, would be a practical first step in the direction so powerfully advocated by my noble friend.

10.23 P.M.

Lord Chesham: My Lords, we all agree that slavery was shameful. Indeed, my right honourable friend the Prime Minister, speaking in Cape Town in September 1994, described slavery as a moral outrage. No one can feel proud about the traffic in human beings, a traffic which is still taking place today, as many noble Lords have said, in various parts of the world, including Africa. Indeed, one of the worst aspects of the slavery of which we read today is the encompassment of child prostitution with it. The Government totally deplore that slavery. I can assure the noble and learned Lord, Lord Wilberforce, and my noble friend Lord Gisborough that the Government are doing whatever they can to see that it is stopped wherever it occurs.

I turn now to the Atlantic slave trade. Attributing responsibility for that is difficult; it is not straightforward. Slavery existed in Africa for centuries before outsiders began to engage in the trade, and continued after they had stopped. Far more people were enslaved internally in Africa than were ever exported across the Atlantic. The first outside slave traders were in fact North African Arabs, plying across the Sahara. That took place at least some seven or eight centuries before the first Europeans began to practise the trade. The Atlantic trade first began by tapping that long-standing trans-Saharan slave trade to North Africa. In East Africa, the trade was almost entirely in the hands of Arabs from Oman and the Gulf. Nor, as has been mentioned, is slavery a monopoly of Africa: it existed in the Greek and Roman empires, and in many other parts of the world.

At the height of the transatlantic slave trade, considerable numbers of African slavers and middlemen were involved. African rulers could open and close the market at will, at a time when European penetration of Africa was limited. Traders made their own arrangements with African rulers for slaves, supplied by fellow Africans, and had to pay gifts and taxes to various African rulers along the West African coast. African societies often had control of the slaves until they were loaded on to European ships. That is supported by a large body of academic research.

To claim that the Atlantic slave trade was imposed by Western nations on powerless African communities is to deny Africa's political history. African leaders were themselves active participants with the capacity to determine how trade with Europe developed. Many of the highly impressive African kingdoms and empires in West Africa were built on the foundations of slavery, such as the Asante kingdom in present-day Ghana.

Africans, Arabs and Europeans participated in the slave trade. Responsibility for British involvement in the transatlantic slave trade does not rest on the shoulders of the British Government. British participation in the trade was not conducted by the Government but by individual traders and companies. After the abolition of the slave trade in 1807, the Royal Navy played an honourable part in suppressing the transatlantic slave trade by maintaining naval patrols off the West African coast. British also drew up anti-slavery treaties with African leaders in an attempt to suppress the slave trade. As was written in the *Chronicle of Abuju*, written in Hausa by the two brothers of the Emir of Abuja in 1945, "when the British came, those men who had been earning a rich living by this trade saw their prosperity vanish, and they became poor men."

The case for reparations for slavery rests on the premise that the effects of slavery are still being felt on Africans now living in Africa and the Diaspora. There is no evidence of that. Current historical research has revised the thinking on the numbers involved in the Atlantic trade and its effects on demography and depopulation. The main areas of slaving, for example, in the Niger delta and Benin, are now among the most densely populated parts of Africa. The majority of slaves exported were male and not female, and this has less impact on demography due to the widespread practice of polygamy. A comparison with Europe illustrates that the economic long-term effects of the Atlantic slave trade are often exaggerated. Emigration from southern Europe, particularly from Italy, to the New World between 1880 and 1914 is estimated at about 30 million. The total of the Atlantic slave trade over a far greater period is now generally accepted to number between 20 million and 25 million.

Mention has been made of the growing support for the campaign for reparations for slavery. However, African leaders increasingly accept that many of the economic problems have arisen from policies pursued since independence. As former Nigerian head of state General Obasanjo said in 1991 at the Africa Leadership Forum Conference in Nigeria: "the major responsibility of our present impasse must be placed squarely on the shoulders of our leaders".

General Obasanjo is currently detained in Nigeria.

Many noble Lords have mentioned the problem of racism, which is an undoubted evil. No one condones it. Any manifestation needs to be fought. To attribute racism to slavery is too simplistic. Racism occurs not just between black and white, but between different ethnic groups all over the world. It is not just a pure black and white problem.

Much has been said about debt relief. We see no linkage between the debts owed by African countries and the legacy of the slave trade. Any practical claim for reparations may serve to undermine the good and widely recognised arguments for reducing Africa's debt burden. The British Government have been active in promoting debt relief for African countries, because such debts constitute a serious obstacle to development.

The British Government have written off the aid debts of 31 of the world's poorest countries to the total value of £1.2 billion. That includes 18 countries in Africa. Additionally, and exceedingly helpfully, for many years all new aid to the poorest countries has been on grant terms so as not to increase their debt burden. The British Government have taken the lead in pressing for solutions to the official bilateral and multilateral debt burdens of the poorest and most indebted countries. At the Paris Club of government creditors, 14 countries benefited from Naple's terms' rescheduling.

The British Government have taken the lead also in pressing for action on multilateral debt. At last year's annual meetings of the IMF and World Bank, the Chancellor called upon all international financial institutions to examine further measures to deal with the problems of multilateral debt for the poorest most indebted countries, as mentioned by the noble Lord, Lord Judd. That work is currently under way, and we expect firm proposals at the April 1996 meetings of the World Bank and IMF.

I touched earlier on the responsibility for slavery. I wish to return to that. Arabs, Europeans, Americans and Africans were all directly involved in the trade, but even if it could be decided to whom the bill should be sent, to whom should any proceeds go? Which Africans would benefit and how? Which descendants of slaves living in America, the Caribbean. or the UK should benefit? To whom, incidentally, should the UK send the bill for the naval squadrons that patrolled the waters of West Africa for half a century to prevent the Spaniards, Brazilians and others from slaving long after we had abolished it? We should remember also the large percentage of slaves who were prisoners of war in ethnic clashes who would otherwise just have been killed.

I return to the subject of aid: 40 per cent of our bilateral aid (over 386 million (UK Pounds Sterling) in 1994–95) went to countries in sub-Saharan Africa. We also make a substantial contribution through multilateral aid. The EU's aid programme to sub-Saharan Africa from 1990 to 1995 was the equivalent of £6 billion. The UK's share of that was £1.25 billion. However, we are quite aware that the poorest countries of sub-Saharan Africa will continue to require substantial amounts of aid. These countries have been, and will continue to be, a high priority for British aid. Many have embarked on structural re-adjustment and policy reform programmes which take time to bear fruit. Their external funding needs are substantial in order to reconstruct their economies and to provide better living standards.

Comment has been made about international precedents. In May 1991 in Lagos Chief Anyaoku, Secretary General of the Commonwealth, devoted an entire speech to the legacy of slavery. However, he stated that, although the moral case was strong, there was no precedent for reparations outside the post-war settlement. The fact that reparations for war crimes have been paid in this century— for example, Germany, Japan and Iraq—is a red herring. It provides no historic parallel. They were among the terms for peace imposed at once by victors in the wars upon vanquished governments and could be precisely catalogued.

The noble Lord, Lord Gifford, mentioned the Queen's apology to the Maoris. Her Majesty's apology to a New Zealand Maori tribe for the killings and seizure of land that it suffered under Queen Victoria was at the instigation of her New Zealand Ministers; in other words, the New Zealand Government, which is constitutionally distinct from the British Government. It was not a personal apology from the Queen. It was an acknowledgement of the breach of the treaty signed in 1840. The situation is therefore entirely different. It was not a question of slavery but one of the possession of land resulting from war.

The noble Lord, Lord Judd, surprisingly mentioned the fundamental expenditure review. He is aware, as are all noble Lords, that every government must balance the many public expenditure priorities and demands. The ODA's job is to ensure that the resources allocated to development are spent well and make a real difference to the lives of poorer people. The FER concluded that development assistance has, by and large, been effective and there is a continuing need for Britain to provide concessional aid. It reaffirmed both the moral argument for this country being involved in the development effort and that of enlightened self interest. The Government agree.

Lord Judd: My Lords, I am grateful to the Minister for giving way. If is he drawing on the substance of the fundamental expenditure review, would he not agree that virtually in words of one syllable the authors of that review questioned whether the resources of our aid programme were now sufficient to meet the commitments which have been undertaken?

Lord Chesham: My Lords, I shall be dealing with that point, if I may be allowed to continue. The FER recommended that we should define better our basic purpose and the aims that serve that purpose. We have done so. Our purpose is stated clearly; that is, to improve the quality of life for people in poorer countries by contributing to sustainable development and reducing poverty and suffering. It is important to note that all our work will be directed to meeting that overarching purpose of poverty reduction and sustainable development.

The FER recommended concentration. In principle, I agree with the recommendation that the ODA's bilateral resources should be concentrated. We are working in more countries and undertaking more complex activities than ever before. Focusing our regular bilateral country programmes on fewer recipients will improve the quality and impact of our aid and maximise our influence. Other countries will continue to benefit from British partnership schemes, the heads of mission schemes and smaller-scale projects often provided with local NGOs. I believe that that answers the question put by the noble Lord, Lord Judd.

Lord Judd: My Lords, with great respect, I am deeply grateful to the noble Lord for endeavouring to meet the point. However, if he reads carefully what he said, he will see that he has not done so. He talks about concentrating the aid programme and establishing priorities but he has not dealt with the criticism in the report that there are not sufficient resources to meet the commitments. Furthermore, he has not dealt with the point that I raised; namely, that the report talks about the possible need to reduce support in the Caribbean at a time that the Caribbean, at a time of the single market and the European Community, is facing new challenges as it should be trying to diversify away from exclusive dependence on bananas.

Lord Chesham: My Lords, at this hour, I do not believe that it is appropriate to become involved in a discussion on banana regimes, the EU/ACP Lome V agreement which is in existence at the moment and which was signed in Mauritius in early November of last year.

Of course, as has been said a number of times from this Dispatch Box, the ODA would rather have more funds to expend. However, we have also discussed from the Dispatch Box the restrictions which are imposed by our friends in the Treasury. Therefore, we have decided that as far as possible, we wish to concentrate the funds that we do have in the best possible way.

The return of artifacts was mentioned. As I am sure the noble Lord, Lord Gifford, knows, in this country that is a matter for the trustees of the museums who are independent. In the past the British Museum has said that it is prevented from disposing of any part of its collection by the British Museum Act 1963.

My noble friend Lord Willoughby de Broke asked about the cost of researching and preparing for this Question. I do not have those figures, but all Questions are expensive to prepare and research at this time of night. Of course, that should not necessarily discourage any noble Lord from tabling a Question.

To suggest that the Government should make reparations to the African nations and the descendants of Africans for the damage caused by the slave trade is clearly, from what I have said, not appropriate. A great deal of our aid—40 per cent. of our bilateral country programmes—is accounted for by Africa. That recognises the fact that Africa contains many of the world's poorest countries. Therefore, we are playing a major part in helping Africa to overcome its problems of poverty and under-development. But those problems have nothing to do with the slave trade. Slavery has not had the enduring effect claimed for it and the Government do not accept that there is a case for reparation.

House adjourned at seventeen minutes before eleven o'clock.

NOTES

1. Forman, James. *Black Manifesto: To the White Christian Churches and the Jewish Synagogues in the United States of America and All Other Racist Institutions.* Reprinted in Murray Kempton, "The Black Manifesto," *New York Review of Books,* July 10, 1969, pp. 31–33.

2. See Jerry K. Frye, "The 'Black Manifesto' and the Tactic of Objectification," *Journal of Black Studies* 4, no. 1 (1974): 65–76.

3. Hugo Bedau. 1972. "Compensatory Justice and the Black Manifesto," *Monist* 56: 20–42.

4. See, however, Murray Kempton, "The Black Manifesto," *New York Review of Books,* July 10, 1969, pp. 31–33; Michael Harrington and Arnold S. Kaufman, "Black Reparations: Two Views," *Dissent* (1969): 317–20; Robert S. Lecky and H. Elliot Wright, eds., *Black Manifesto: Religion, Racism, and Reparations* (New York: Sheed & Ward, 1969); Arnold Schuchter, *Reparations* (Philadelphia: Lippincott, 1970).

5. The Manifesto, said Murray Kempton (p. 31), is "not so much argument as incantation"; according to Michael Harrington, in "Black Reparations: Two Views," it is an "outlandish scheme" (p. 317), and an "impossible vision" (p. 318).

6. All page references are to the version published by Lecky and Wright, eds., pp. 114–26. The full text is also available in Kempton, and in Schuchter.

7. Thus, Michael Harrington objected to *The Black Manifesto* mainly on the ground that taking it seriously would "divert precious political energies from the actual struggle" to remedy "unequal income distribution in America" (p. 318). Murray Kempton went even further in the direction of repudiating the apparent burden of the *Manifesto*, for he insisted that its "indictment" was "not of a genuine deprivation but of a totally fancied reward" (p. 31). Arnold Kaufman, while emphasizing the legitimacy of its literal compensatory nature, endorsed the argument because he thought it would "strengthen . . . the political will to support vast enlargement of compensatory *governmental* programs" (p. 319; italics in original). Similarly, Calvin B. Marshall, chairman of the Black Economic Development Conference, has criticized the failure of the churches to respond to the *Manifesto*'s appeal as evidence of their "refusing to consider human need . . ." (*New York Times,* June 10, 1970, p. 53). But "human need," like "unequal income distribution," and the rest, are not concepts central to an argument for *reparations* and *compensatory* justice.

8. Lecky and Wright, 126.

9. For a discussion of the difference between the idea of (criminal) guilt and the idea of (civil) liability, and of the need to confine corporate responsibility to the latter, see Joel Feinberg, "Collective Responsibility," in his *Doing and Deserving* (Princeton: Princeton University Press, 1970), 231–33.

10. This point is persuasively argued by William Stringfellow, "Reparations: Repentance As a Necessity to Reconciliation," in Lecky and Wright, 52–64.

11. The "Introduction" to the Manifesto does speak of "taking the wealth away from the rich people such as General Motors, Ford, Chrysler, the DuPonts, the Rockefellers, the Mellons" (p. 117). The Manifesto continues, ". . . we are dedicated to building a socialist society inside the United States where the total means of production and distribution are in the hands of the State . . ." (p. 118).

12. "The common image of Marx as a prophet of social justice is a false one. . . . To Marx's mind . . . socialists like Proudhon who preached social justice were misguided because they failed to see the irrelevance of the idea of justice to the social problem." Robert Tucker, "Marx and Distributive Justice," in *Nomos VI: Justice*, eds. Carl J. Friedrich and John M. Chapman (New York: Atherton Press, 1963), 309, 323.

13. See Schuchter, *passim*, and esp. appendix B, "Slavery and the Churches."

14. Lecky and Wright, 126.

15. In the first year after it released the Manifesto, B.E.D.C. admitted it had raised only 1/170 of the $500 million originally sought from the churches. It was also reported, however, that as much as one-third of the total had been pledged. *New York Times, loc. cit.*

16. Kaufman, 319.

17. 1 have tried to set out those principles in a general analysis of compensatory justice in another paper (unpublished), versions of which were presented to several audiences in conjunction with earlier versions of this paper.

18. John W. Wade, *Cases and Materials on Restitution,* 2nd ed. (Brooklyn, N.Y.: Foundation Press, 1966), 1198.

19. Wade, *Cases and Materials on Restitution*, 1212.

20. *Oxford English Dictionary*, 2nd ed., 1989.

21. Wade, *Cases and Materials on Restitution,* 455–56.

22. Lecky and Wright, 116; cf. 117.

23. See, e.g., Dee Brown, *Bury My Heart at Wounded Knee* (New York: Harper, Row and Winston, 1971) and Vine de Loria, ed., *Of Utmost Good Faith* (San Francisco: World Publishing Co., 1971). Much the same point has been made, along with other valuable suggestions, in Graham Hughes, "Reparations for Blacks?" *New York University Law Review* 43 (1968): 1063–74.

24. See Lecky and Wright, 50, and *New York Times, loc. cit.*

25. For evidence as to the wealth of the churches in the United. States, see Lecky and Wright, 176, and Schuchter, 175–78.

26. See, e.g., Eric Williams, *Capitalism and Slavery* (New York: Capricorn Books, 1966), and Robert S. Starobin, *Industrial Slavery in the Old South* (New York: Oxford University Press, 1971).

27. If we were not required to use the model of unjust enrichment, we could take a very different approach to this question. It is clear from actual cases at law where

compensation *is* successfully sought for incommensurables that it *will* be adequate to compensate him for his loss if he decides that it is. It does not follow from this that an eye is "worth" $10,000, or an unsullied reputation "worth" $50,000 because these sums are not to be construed as measures (e.g., an eye blinded in industrial accident, a reputation damaged by libel or slander), the injured party can accept a certain sum as his indemnity and of the value of the thing lost, but only as compensation for injury to them, and an imperfect remedy at best.

28. Cf. Brian Barry, *Political Argument* (New York: Humanities Press, 1965), 113.

29. Cf. Joel Feinberg, "Justice and Personal Desert," in *Nomos VI*, ed. Friedrich and Chapman, 94.

30. Richard Lichtman, "The Ethics of Compensatory Justice," *Law in Transition Quarterly* 1 (1964): 87; italics in original. Professor Lichtman has informed me that his current views on these issues are very different from what they were when he wrote this essay.

31. Earlier versions of this paper were read before a number of audiences during 1970 and 1971. 1 am especially grateful for stimulus and criticism to many colleagues who discussed it with me at colloquia arranged by the departments of philosophy at the University of Waterloo and at the University of Michigan, by faculty at Boston College Law School, and at the Boston Area Political Theory Conference.

32. H. R. 40, 106th Congress, 1999.

33. Slavery: Legacy the Official Record from Hansard of the Debate Initiated by Lord Gifford QC in the House of Lords of the British Parliament on 14th March 1996 Concerning the African Reparations. Official Hansard; Africa Reparations Movement, 1996. Online at www.arm.arc.co.uk/LordsHansard.html (accessed September 9, 2003).

THE MAIN QUESTIONS

III

THE CONTEMPORARY MORAL DEBATE OVER RESTITUTION

The first portion of this part, "The Contemporary Moral Debate over Restitution," begins with an antireparations broadside that was published in newspapers across America. Before David Horowitz placed his paid advertisement, "Ten Reasons Why Reparations for Blacks Is a Bad Idea for Blacks—and Racist Too," in college newspapers in the spring of 2001, the most prominent public discussion of reparations was Randall Robinson's book, *The Debt*, and the responses of its admirers and detractors. Horowitz's ad established him for a time as the central figure in the reparations debate in America, an achievement much hoped for by Horowitz and much lamented by reparations advocates.

David Horowitz is the president of the Center for the Study of Popular Culture, a best-selling author and editor, and a sometime columnist for the online journal, *Salon*. He is a leading neoconservative critic of the American left, a spot on the American political spectrum that he once called home. Horowitz attended Columbia University and the University of California at Berkeley in the 1960s and was part of the radical student leadership of the era. He went on to edit *Ramparts Magazine*, one of the principal journals of the New Left. But he changed his mind. In his 1989 book, *Destructive Generation: Second Thoughts about the Sixties,* he took it all back, repudiating his earlier politics and excoriating everyone to the left of the Reagan administration.

The ad, "Ten Reasons Why Reparations for Blacks Is a Bad Idea for Blacks—and Racist Too," was placed in a number of college newspapers. While the ad has its defenders on the right and in certain civil libertarian circles, its publication was rejected by some papers, and its appearance was condemned at others. This led Horowitz and others to retarget his attack—from reparations to "political correctness" and the loss of free speech he thought it entailed. For example, the black conservative sociologist, Thomas Sowell, lamented, in the pages of *The Washington Times,* that

> Despite media proclamations of "the public's right to know" and frequent invocations of the First Amendment, there has been a deafening silence from the national media over the storm trooper tactics used on college campuses against student newspapers that carried a paid advertisement by David Horowitz, outlining the case against reparations for slavery.[1]

Horowitz recorded this further controversy in a new book, *Uncivil Wars: The Controversy Over Reparations for Slavery.*[2] About *Uncivil Wars* and Horowitz's antireparations campaign generally, Alan M. Dershowitz, author of *Shouting Fire: Civil Liberties in a Turbulent Age* and a professor at Harvard Law School, had this to say:[3]

> David Horowitz, whose provocative ad against reparations for slavery generated a firestorm on college campuses during the spring of 2001, assures the readers of *Uncivil Wars,* his self-serving account of that controversy, that the book's "subject is not me, nor is it the advertisement that provoked such a reaction." He claims that the subject of his book is an idea: the "dubious idea of reparations" and, in a larger sense, "the intellectual vulgarities of American universities in an age of 'political correctness.'"

This is a misleading characterization of *Uncivil Wars,* which is, in fact, all about Horowitz and his in-your-face brand of confrontation. Reparations are an important symbol of black solidarity on college campuses, and his ad was calculated to stir raw emotions. If it was accepted for publication, he knew it would create a backlash against the editors who agreed to publish it. If it was rejected, he knew he could cry "censorship." An editor at the *Daily Princetonian,* whose column Horowitz quotes in *Uncivil Wars,* got it exactly right when he wrote:

> Horowitz plays a clever game. He played it with several of our peer college papers in the past few weeks. And he won. When Horowitz submits an ad to a college paper, he hopes that one of two things will happen: Either the paper refused to print the ad, so he can tell the world that conservative ideas are being censored by the liberal college press, or the paper prints the ad and campus activists protest. Both ways, Horowitz gets what he wants. . . .

While there were scores of replies to Horowitz, we have chosen as a response a careful answer originally published in *The Black Scholar.* The essay was coauthored by Professor Ernest Allen Jr., Associate Chair of African-

American Studies at the University of Massachusetts–Amherst, and Robert Chrisman, a poet and essayist and the founding editor and publisher of *The Black Scholar, Journal of Black Studies*.

The second pair of essays in this chapter were written by philosophers. Their articles appeared in either university-related publications or scholarly journals. They represent one species of philosophical writing about reparations. That is, they take up several aspects of the reparations debate rather than concentrating on a subtopic, as do the later essays in this anthology that examine collective responsibility or historical obligation, subjects embedded in the consideration of reparations but more general than the question of reparations itself.

Robert Fullinwider, the first philosopher, received his Ph.D. in philosophy from Purdue University and is currently senior research scholar, Institute for Philosophy and Public Policy, University of Maryland, where he has worked since 1979. Fullinwider argues here that common objections to reparations fail to understand that the "culprit" is neither *individuals* nor *racial* or *ethnic groups* (e.g., whites) but is instead *corporate* in nature (i.e., attributable to society or the government, or the United States of America). Says Fullinwider,

> When "society" is understood corporately, however, the "wrongdoing" of society does not distribute to each of its members. Individual citizens may be blameless for the wrongs of their nation. That the burden of payment for national wrongdoing falls to them simply reflects their civic roles and not anything about their persons. In making the case for reparations, it is a mistake to go looking for personal complicity on the part of those who must pay. And worse yet, it is a mistake to turn the putative personal complicity into guilt-by-blood.

Nonetheless, Fullinwider says, the case for reparations should not be based on the fact of slavery, neither on the harm inflicted by slavery itself nor on the unjust enrichment of white Americans who benefited from it.

> However, basing reparations on slavery and on the great benefits accrued to whites invites complication and controversy. I suggest the case is actually strengthened by dropping both slavery and the benefits reaped by whites as grounds for reparations.

What is this alternative basis for reparations? Fullinwider offers this:

> Had the federal government done nothing after 1865 except vigorously protect the civil and voting rights of blacks, the legacy of slavery would have faded considerably if not wholly by now through the industry of blacks themselves. That the legacy still persists owes much, if not all, to the post–Civil War oppression

of African Americans and it is this wrong that offers the most direct and salient basis for reparations.

Dr. Stephen Kershnar, author of the second philosophical article, is assistant professor of philosophy at SUNY Fredonia. Professor Kershnar has published numerous essays on such socially contentious topics as affirmative action, reparations, and immigration. In his paper, "The Moral Status of Harmless Adult–Child Sex,"[4] he writes:

Nonforcible adult–child sex is thought to be morally wrong in part because it is nonconsensual. In this paper, I argue against this notion. In particular, I reject accounts of the moral wrongfulness of adult–child sex that rest on the absence of consent, concerns about adult exploitation of children, and the existence of a morally primitive duty against such sex.

In "There Is No Moral Right to Immigrate to the United States,"[5] Kershnar argues

U.S. citizens have a right to exclude potential immigrants. This right rests in part on the threat immigration poses to change the character of the institutions to which the current citizens have consented and, in part, on the threat immigrants pose to the citizens' rights to collective property. With the exception of those cases relating to unjust and harmful acts by the U.S. government, the right to exclude potential immigrants is not opposed by a special right to immigrate.

Finally, in another article, Kershnar writes against "strong affirmative action,"[6] reasoning that:

In the context of state educational institutions, young white males are owed a duty to respect their legitimate desert and interest claims. Not all white males have waived this duty since many white males have not performed the relevant types of culpable wrongdoing. Merely having benefited from an unjust injuring act or being a member of a community that owes compensation to racial minorities and women, are not sufficient grounds to override the duty owed to the white male. Hence, the compensatory justice justification for strong affirmative action programs at state educational institutions, probably fails to justify such programs.

His position on reparations in the essay below is made clear by the title, "The Case against Reparations." Such a case, he thinks, is "overwhelming." Kershnar argues here that any claims for compensation by slaves or their descendants have faded over time for various reasons, and moreover, the social liabilities suffered by African Americans have other explanations and rest on factors for which others are not responsible.

NOTES

1. Thomas Sowell, Commentary, *Washington Times*, 24 March, 24, 2001, A12.
2. David Horowitz, *Uncivil Wars: The Controversy Over Reparations for Slavery* (San Francisco: Encounter Books, 2003).
3. Alan M. Dershowitz, "Uncivil Wars: The Controversy Over Reparations for Slavery," *The Los Angeles Times*, Book Reviews, June 2, 2002.
4. Stephen Kershnar, "The Moral Status of Harmless Adult–Child Sex," *Public Affairs Quarterly* 15, no. 2 (2001): 111–32, in *Philosopher's Index: 1940–2003*, online at www:ovid.com (accessed September 4, 2003).
5. Stephen Kershnar, "There Is No Moral Right to Immigrate to the United States," *Public Affairs Quarterly* 14, no. 2 (2000): 141–58, in *Philosopher's Index: 1940–2003*, online at www:ovid.com (accessed September 4, 2003).
6. Stephen Kershnar, "Strong Affirmative Action Programs at State Educational Institutions Cannot Be Justified Via Compensatory Justice," *Public Affairs Quarterly* 11, no. 4 (1997): 345–63, in *Philosopher's Index: 1940–2003*, online at www:ovid.com (accessed September 4, 2003).

7

Reparations for Slavery in the Popular Press

David Horowitz: "Ten Reasons Why Reparations for Blacks
Is a Bad Idea for Blacks—and Racist Too"[1]

One: There Is No Single Group Clearly Responsible
for the Crime of Slavery.

Black Africans and Arabs were responsible for enslaving the ancestors of African-Americans. There were 3,000 black slave-owners in the ante-bellum United States. Are reparations to be paid by their descendants, too?

Two: There Is No One Group That Benefited Exclusively from Its Fruits.

The claim for reparations is premised on the false assumption that only whites have benefited from slavery. If slave labor created wealth for Americans, then obviously it has created wealth for black Americans as well, including the descendants of slaves. The GNP of black America is so large that it makes the African-American community the 10th most prosperous "nation" in the world. American blacks on average enjoy per capita incomes in the range of twenty to fifty times that of blacks living in any of the African nations from which they were kidnapped.

Three: Only a Tiny Minority of White Americans Ever Owned Slaves,
and Others Gave Their Lives to Free Them.

Only a tiny minority of Americans ever owned slaves. This is true even for those who lived in the ante-bellum South, where only one white in five was a slaveholder. Why should their descendants owe a debt? What about the descendants of the 350,000 Union soldiers who died to free the slaves? They gave their lives.

What possible moral principle would ask them to pay (through their descendants) again?

Four: America Today Is a Multiethnic Nation, and Most Americans Have No Connection (Direct or Indirect) to Slavery.

The two great waves of American immigration occurred after 1880 and then after 1960. What rationale would require Vietnamese boat people, Russian refuseniks, Iranian refugees, and Armenian victims of the Turkish persecution, Jews, Mexicans Greeks, or Polish, Hungarian, Cambodian and Korean victims of communism, to pay reparations to American blacks?

Five: The Historical Precedents Used to Justify the Reparations Claim Do Not Apply, and the Claim Itself Is Based on Race, Not Injury.

The historical precedents generally invoked to justify the reparations claim are payments to Jewish survivors of the Holocaust, Japanese Americans and African-American victims of racial experiments in Tuskegee, or racial outrages in Rosewood and Oklahoma City. But in each case, the recipients of reparations were the direct victims of the injustice or their immediate families. This would be the only case of reparations to people who were not immediately affected and whose sole qualification to receive reparations would be racial. As has already been pointed out, during the slavery era, many blacks were free men or slave-owners themselves, yet the reparations claimants make no distinction between the roles blacks actually played in the injustice itself. Randall Robinson's book on reparations, *The Debt*, which is the manifesto of the reparations movement, is pointedly sub-titled "What America Owes to Blacks." If this is not racism, what is?

Six: The Reparations Argument Is Based on the Unfounded Claim That All African-American Descendants of Slaves Suffer from the Economic Consequences of Slavery and Discrimination.

No evidence-based attempt has been made to prove that living individuals have been adversely affected by a slave system that was ended over a hundred and fifty years ago. But there is plenty of evidence the hardships that occurred were hardships that individuals could and did overcome. The black middle-class in America is a prosperous community that is now larger in absolute terms than the black underclass. Does its existence not suggest that economic adversity is the result of failures of individual character rather than the lingering aftereffects of racial discrimination and a slave system that ceased to exist well over a century ago? West Indian blacks in America are also descended from slaves but their average incomes are equivalent to the average incomes of whites (and nearly 25% higher than the average incomes of American born blacks). How is it that slavery adversely affected one large group of descendants but not the other? How can government be expected to decide an issue that is so subjective—and yet so critical—to the case?

Seven: The Reparations Claim Is One More Attempt to Turn African-Americans into Victims. It Sends a Damaging Message to the African-American Community.

The renewed sense of grievance—which is what the claim for reparations will inevitably create—is neither a constructive nor a helpful message for black leaders to be sending to their communities and to others. To focus the social passions of African-Americans on what some Americans may have done to their ancestors fifty or a hundred and fifty years ago is to burden them with a crippling sense of victimhood. How are the millions of refugees from tyranny and genocide who are now living in America going to receive these claims, moreover, except as demands for special treatment, an extravagant new handout that is only necessary because some blacks can't seem to locate the ladder of opportunity within reach of others—many less privileged than themselves?

Eight: Reparations to African-Americans Have Already Been Paid.

Since the passage of the Civil Rights Acts and the advent of the Great Society in 1965, trillions of dollars in transfer payments have been made to African-Americans in the form of welfare benefits and racial preferences (in contracts, job placements, and educational admissions)—all under the rationale of redressing historic racial grievances. It is said that reparations are necessary to achieve a healing between African-Americans and other Americans. If trillion-dollar restitutions and a wholesale rewriting of American law (in order to accommodate racial preferences) for African-Americans is not enough to achieve a "healing," what will?

Nine: What about the Debt Blacks Owe to America?

Slavery existed for thousands of years before the Atlantic slave trade was born, and in all societies. But in the thousand years of its existence, there never was an anti-slavery movement until white Christians—Englishmen and Americans—created one. If not for the anti-slavery attitudes and military power of white Englishmen and Americans, the slave trade would not have been brought to an end. If not for the sacrifices of white soldiers and a white American president who gave his life to sign the Emancipation Proclamation, blacks in America would still be slaves. If not for the dedication of Americans of all ethnicities and colors to a society based on the principle that all men are created equal, blacks in America would not enjoy the highest standard of living of blacks anywhere in the world, and indeed one of the highest standards of living of any people in the world. They would not enjoy the greatest freedoms and the most thoroughly protected individual rights anywhere. Where is the gratitude of black America and its leaders for those gifts?

Ten: The Reparations Claim Is a Separatist Idea That Sets African-Americans against the Nation That Gave Them Freedom.

Blacks were here before the *Mayflower*. Who is more American than the descendants of African slaves? For the African-American community to isolate itself even further from America is to embark on a course whose implications are troubling. Yet the African-American community has had a long-running flirtation with separatists, nationalists, and the political left, who want African-Americans to be no part of America's social contract. African-Americans should reject this temptation.

For all America's faults, African-Americans have an enormous stake in their country and its heritage. It is this heritage that is really under attack by the reparations movement. The reparations claim is one more assault on America, conducted by racial separatists and the political left. It is an attack not only on white Americans, but on all Americans—especially African-Americans.

America's African-American citizens are the richest and most privileged black people alive—a bounty that is a direct result of the heritage that is under assault. The American idea needs the support of its African-American citizens. But African-Americans also need the support of the American idea. For it is this idea that led to the principles and institutions that have set African-Americans—and all of us—free.

Ernest Allen Jr. and Robert Chrisman: "Ten Reasons: A Response to David Horowitz"[2]

David Horowitz's article, "Ten Reasons Why Reparations for Slavery Is a Bad Idea and Racist Too," recently achieved circulation in a handful of college newspapers throughout the United States as a paid advertisement sponsored by the Center for the Study of Popular Culture. Since then it has appeared in numerous other mainstream publications. While Horowitz's article pretends to address the issues of reparations, it is not about reparations at all. It is, rather, a well-heeled, coordinated attack on black Americans which is calculated to elicit division and strife. Horowitz reportedly attempted to place his article in some 50 student newspapers at universities and colleges across the country, and was successful in purchasing space in such newspapers at Brown, Duke, Arizona, UC Berkeley, UC Davis, University of Chicago, and University of Wisconsin, paying an average of $700 per paper. His campaign has succeeded in fomenting outrage, dissension, and grief wherever it has appeared. Unfortunately, both its supporters and its foes too often have categorized the issue as one centering on "free speech." The sale and purchase of advertising space is not a matter of free speech, however, but involves an exchange of commodities. Professor Lewis Gordon of Brown University put it very well, saying that "what concerned me was that the ad was both hate speech and a solicitation for financial support to develop antiblack ad space. I was concerned that it would embolden white supremacists and antiblack racists." At a March 15 panel held at UC Berkeley,

Horowitz also conceded that his paid advertisement did not constitute a free speech issue.

As one examines the text of Horowitz's article, it becomes apparent that it is not a reasoned essay addressed to the topic of reparations: it is, rather, a racist polemic against African-Americans and Africans that is neither responsible nor informed, relying heavily upon sophistry and a Hitlerian "Big Lie" technique. To our knowledge, only one of Horowitz's ten "reasons" has been challenged by a black scholar as to source, accuracy, and validity. It is our intention here to briefly rebut his slanders in order to pave the way for an honest and forthright debate on reparations. In these efforts we focus not just on slavery but also the legacy of slavery, which continues to inform institutional as well as individual behavior in the U.S. to this day. Although we recognize that white America still owes a debt to the descendants of slaves, in addressing Horowitz's distortions of history we do not act as advocates for a specific form of reparations.

1. There Is No Single Group Clearly Responsible for the Crime of Slavery.

Horowitz's first argument, relativist in structure, can only lead to two conclusions: (1) societies are not responsible for their actions and (2) since "everyone" was responsible for slavery, no one was responsible. While diverse groups on different continents certainly participated in the trade, the principal responsibility for internationalization of that trade and the institutionalization of slavery in the so-called New World rests with European and American individuals and institutions. The transatlantic slave trade began with the importation of African slaves into Hispaniola by Spain in the early 1500s. Nationals of France, England, Portugal, and the Netherlands, supported by their respective governments and powerful religious institutions, quickly entered the trade and extracted their pieces of silver as well. By conservative estimates, 14 million enslaved Africans survived the horror of the Middle Passage for the purpose of producing wealth for Europeans and Euro-Americans in the New World.

While there is some evidence of blacks owning slaves for profit purposes—most notably the creole caste in Louisiana—the numbers were small. As historian James Oakes noted, "By 1830 there were some 3,775 free black slaveholders across the South . . . The evidence is overwhelming that the vast majority of black slaveholders were free men who purchased members of their families or who acted out of benevolence."[3]

2. There Is No Single Group That Benefited Exclusively from Slavery.

Horowitz's second point, which is also a relativist one, seeks to dismiss the argument that white Americans benefited as a group from slavery, contending that the material benefits of slavery could not accrue in an exclusive way to a single group. But such sophistry evades the basic issue: who benefited primarily from slavery? Those who were responsible for the institutionalized enslavement of people of African descent also received the primary benefits from such actions. New England slave traders, merchants, bankers, and insurance companies all profited from the slave trade, which required a wide variety of commodities ranging from sails, chandlery, foodstuffs, and guns, to cloth goods and other items for trading purposes. Both prior to and after the American Revolution, slaveholding was a principal path for white upward mobility in the South. The white native-born as well as immigrant groups such as Germans, Scots-Irish, and the like participated. In 1860, cotton was the country's largest single export. As Eric Williams and C. L. R. James have demonstrated, the free labor provided by slavery was central to the growth of industry in western Europe and the United States; simultaneously, as Walter Rodney has argued, slavery depressed and destabilized the economies of African states. Slaveholders benefited primarily from the institution, of course, and generally in proportion to the number of slaves that they held. But the sharing of the proceeds of slave exploitation spilled across class lines within white communities as well.

As historian John Hope Franklin recently affirmed in a rebuttal to Horowitz's claims:

> All whites and no slaves benefited from American slavery. All blacks had no rights that they could claim as their own. All whites, including the vast majority who had no slaves, were not only encouraged but authorized to exercise dominion over all slaves, thereby adding strength to the system of control.
>
> If David Horowitz had read James D. DeBow's "The Interest in Slavery of the Southern Nonslaveholder," he would not have blundered into the fantasy of claiming that no single group benefited from slavery. Planters did, of course. New York merchants did, of course. Even poor whites benefited from the legal advantage they enjoyed over all blacks as well as from the psychological advantage of having a group beneath them.

The context of the African-American argument for reparations is confined to the practice and consequences of slavery within the United States, from the colonial period on through final abolition and the aftermath, circa 1619–1865. Contrary to Horowitz's assertion, there is no record of institutionalized white enslavement in colonial America. Horowitz is confusing the indenture of white labor, which usually lasted seven years or so during the early colonial period, with enslavement. African slavery was expanded, in fact, to replace the inefficient and unenforceable white indenture system.[4]

Seeking to claim that African-Americans, too, have benefited from slavery, Horowitz points to the relative prosperity of African-Americans in comparison to their counterparts on the African continent. However, his argument that, "the GNP of black America makes the African-American community the 10th most prosperous 'nation' in the world" is based upon a false analogy. GNP is defined as "the total market value of all the goods and services produced by a nation during a specified period." Black Americans are not a nation and have no GNP. Horowitz confuses disposable income and "consumer power" with the generation of wealth.

3. Only a Tiny Minority of White Americans Ever Owned Slaves, and Others Gave Their Lives to Free Them.

Most white union troops were drafted into the union army in a war which the federal government initially defined as a "war to preserve the union." In large part because they feared that freed slaves would flee the South and "take their jobs" while they themselves were engaged in warfare with Confederate troops, recently drafted white conscripts in New York City and elsewhere rioted during the summer of 1863, taking a heavy toll on black civilian life and property. Too many instances can be cited where white northern troops plundered the personal property of slaves, appropriating their bedding, chickens, pigs, and foodstuffs as they swept through the South. On the other hand, it is certainly true that there also existed principled white commanders and troops who were committed abolitionists.

However, Horowitz's focus on what he mistakenly considers to be the overriding, benevolent aim of white union troops in the Civil War obscures the role that blacks themselves played in their own liberation. African-Americans were initially forbidden by the Union to fight in the Civil War, and black leaders such as Frederick Douglass and Martin Delany demanded the right to fight for their freedom. When racist doctrine finally conceded to military necessity, blacks were recruited into the Union Army in 1862 at approximately half the pay of white soldiers—a situation which was partially rectified by an act of Congress in mid-1864. Some 170,000 blacks served in the Civil War, representing nearly one third of the free black population.

By 1860, four million blacks in the U.S. were enslaved; some 500,000 were nominally free. Because of slavery, racist laws, and racist policies, blacks were denied the chance to compete for the opportunities and resources of America that were available to native whites and immigrants: labor opportunities, free enterprise, and land. The promise of "forty acres and a mule" to former slaves was effectively nullified by the actions of President Andrew Johnson. And because the best land offered by the Homestead Act of 1862 and its subsequent revisions quickly fell under the sway of white homesteaders and speculators, most former slaves were unable to take advantage of its provisions.

4. Most Living Americans Have No Connection (Direct or Indirect) to Slavery.

As Joseph Anderson, member of the National Council of African-American Men, observed, "the arguments for reparations aren't made on the basis of whether every white person directly gained from slavery. The arguments are made on the basis that slavery was institutionalized and protected by law in the United States. As the government is an entity that survives generations, its debts and obligations survive the lifespan of any particular individuals. . . . Governments make restitution to victims as a group or class."[5]

Most Americans today were not alive during World War II. Yet reparations to Japanese Americans for their internment in concentration camps during the war was paid out of current government sources contributed to by contemporary Americans. Passage of time does not negate the responsibility of government in crimes against humanity. Similarly, German corporations are not the "same" corporations that supported the Holocaust; their personnel and policies today belong to generations removed from their earlier criminal behavior. Yet, these corporations are being successfully sued by Jews for their past actions. In the same vein, the U.S. government is not the same government as it was in the pre-Civil War era, yet its debts and obligations from the past are no less relevant today.

5. The Historical Precedents Used to Justify the Reparations Claim Do Not Apply, and the Claim Itself Is Based on Race Not Injury.

As noted in our response to "Reason 4," the historical precedents for the reparations claims of African-Americans are fully consistent with restitution accorded other historical groups for atrocities committed against them. Second, the injury in question—that of slavery—was inflicted upon a people designated as a race. The descendants of that people—still socially constructed as a race today—continue to suffer the institutional legacies of slavery some one hundred thirty-five years after its demise. To attempt to separate the issue of so-called race from that of injury in this instance is pure sophistry. For example, the criminal (in)justice system today largely continues to operate as it did under slavery—for the protection of white citizens against black "outsiders." Although no longer inscribed in law, this very attitude is implicit to processes of law enforcement, prosecution, and incarceration, guiding the behavior of police, prosecutors, judges, juries, wardens, and parole boards. Hence, African-Americans continue to experience higher rates of incarceration than do whites charged with similar crimes, endure longer sentences for the same classes of crimes perpetrated by whites, and, compared to white inmates, receive far less consideration by parole boards when being considered for release.

Slavery was an institution sanctioned by the highest laws of the land with a degree of support from the Constitution itself. The institution of slavery established the idea and the practice that American democracy was "for whites only." There are many white Americans whose actions (or lack thereof) reveal such sentiments today—witness the response of the media and the general populace to the blatant disfranchisement of African-Americans in Florida during the last presidential election. Would such complacency exist if African-Americans were considered "real citizens"? And despite the dramatic successes of the Civil Rights movement of the 1950s and 60s, the majority of black Americans do not enjoy the same rights as white Americans in the economic sphere. (We continue this argument in the following section.)

6. The Reparations Argument Is Based on the Unfounded Claim That All African-American Descendants of Slaves Suffer from the Economic Consequences of Slavery and Discrimination.

Most blacks suffered and continue to suffer the economic consequences of slavery and its aftermath. As of 1998, median white family income in the U.S. was $49,023; median black family income was $29,404, just 60% of white income. (2001 *New York Times Almanac*, p. 319) Further, the costs of living within the United States far exceed those of African nations. The present poverty level for an American family of four is $17,029. Twenty-three and three-fifths percent (23.6%) of all black families live below the poverty level.

When one examines net financial worth, which reflects, in part, the wealth handed down within families from generation to generation, the figures appear much starker. Recently, sociologists Melvin L. Oliver and Thomas M. Shapiro found that just a little over a decade ago, the net financial worth of white American families with zero or negative net financial worth stood at around 25%; that of Hispanic households at 54%; and that of black American households at almost 61%.[6] The inability to accrue net financial worth is also directly related to hiring practices in which black Americans are "last hired" when the economy experiences an upturn, and "first fired" when it falls on hard times.

And as historian John Hope Franklin remarked on the legacy of slavery for black education: "laws enacted by states forbade the teaching of blacks any means of acquiring knowledge—including the alphabet—which is the legacy of disadvantage of educational privatization and discrimination experienced by African-Americans in 2001."

Horowitz's comparison of African-Americans with Jamaicans is a false analogy, ignoring the different historical contexts of the two populations. The British government ended slavery in Jamaica and its other West Indian territories in 1836, paying West Indian slaveholders $20,000,000 pounds ($100,000,000 U.S. dollars) to free the slaves, and leaving the black Jamaicans, who comprised 90% of that island's population, relatively free. Though still facing racist obstacles, Jamaicans come to the U.S. as voluntary immigrants, with greater opportunity to weigh, choose, and develop their options.

7. The Reparations Claim Is One More Attempt to Turn African-Americans into Victims. It Sends a Damaging Message to the African-American Community.

What is a victim? Black people have certainly been victimized, but acknowledgment of that fact is not a case of "playing the victim" but of seeking justice. There is no validity to Horowitz's comparison between black Americans and victims of oppressive regimes who have voluntarily immigrated to these shores. Further, many members of those populations, such as Chileans and Salvadorans, direct their energies for redress toward the governments of their own oppressive nations—which is precisely what black Americans are doing. Horowitz's racism is expressed in his contemptuous characterization of reparations as "an extravagant new handout that is only necessary because some blacks can't seem to locate the ladder of opportunity within reach of others, many of whom are less privileged than themselves." What Horowitz fails to acknowledge is that racism continues as an ideology and a material force within the U.S., providing blacks with no ladder that reaches the top. The damage lies in the systematic treatment of black people in the U.S., not their claims against those who initiated this damage and their spiritual descendants who continue its perpetuation.

8. Reparations to African-Americans Have Already Been Paid.

The nearest the U.S. government came to full and permanent restitution of African-Americans was the spontaneous redistribution of land brought about by General William Sherman's Field Order 15 in January, 1865, which empowered Union commanders to make land grants and give other material assistance to newly liberated blacks. But that order was rescinded by President Andrew Johnson later in the year. Efforts by Representative Thaddeus Stevens and other radical Republicans to provide the proverbial "40 acres and a mule" which would have carved up huge plantations of the defeated Confederacy into modest land grants for blacks and poor whites never got out of the House of Representatives. The debt has not been paid.

"Welfare benefits and racial preferences" are not reparations. The welfare system was set in place in the 1930s to alleviate the poverty of the Great Depression, and more whites than blacks received welfare. So-called racial preferences come not from benevolence but from lawsuits by blacks against white businesses, government agencies, and municipalities which practice racial discrimination.

9. What About the Debt Blacks Owe to America?

Horowitz's assertion that "in the thousand years of slavery's existence, there never was an anti-slavery movement until white Anglo-Saxon Christians created one," only demonstrates his ignorance concerning the formidable efforts of blacks to free themselves. Led by black Toussaint L'Ouverture, the Haitian revolution of 1793 overthrew the French slave system, created the first black republic in the world, and intensified the activities of black and white anti-slavery movements in the U.S. Slave insurrections and conspiracies such as those of Gabriel (1800), Denmark Vesey (1822), and Nat Turner (1831) were potent sources of black resistance; black abolitionists such as Harriet Tubman, Frederick Douglass, Richard Allen, Sojourner Truth, Martin Delany, David Walker, and Henry Highland Garnet waged an incessant struggle against slavery through agencies such as the press, notably Douglass's *North Star* and its variants, which ran from 1847 to 1863 (blacks, moreover, constituted some 75% of the subscribers to William Lloyd Garrison's *Liberator* newspaper in its first four years);

the Underground Railroad, the Negro Convention Movement, local, state, and national anti-slavery societies, and the slave narrative. Black Americans were in no way the passive recipients of freedom from anyone, whether viewed from the perspective of black participation in the abolitionist movement, the flight of slaves from plantations and farms during the Civil War, or the enlistment of black troops in the Union army.

The idea of black debt to U.S. society is a rehash of the Christian missionary argument of the 17th and 18th centuries: because Africans were considered heathens, it was therefore legitimate to enslave them and drag them in chains to a Christian nation. Following their partial conversion, their moral and material lot were improved, for which black folk should be eternally grateful. Slave ideologues John Calhoun and George Fitzhugh updated this idea in the 19th century, arguing that blacks were better off under slavery than whites in the North who received wages, due to the paternalism and benevolence of the plantation system which assured perpetual employment, shelter, and board. Please excuse the analogy, but if someone chops off your fingers and then hands them back to you, should you be "grateful" for having received your mangled fingers, or enraged that they were chopped off in the first place?

10. The Reparations Claim Is a Separatist Idea That Sets African-Americans against the Nation That Gave Them Freedom.

Again, Horowitz reverses matters. Blacks are already separated from white America in fundamental matters such as income, family wealth, housing, legal treatment, education, and political representation. Andrew Hacker, for example, has argued the case persuasively in his book *Two Nations*. To ignore such divisions, and then charge those who raise valid claims against society with promoting divisiveness, offers a classic example of "blaming the victim." And we have already refuted the spurious point that African-Americans were the passive recipients of benevolent white individuals or institutions which "gave" them freedom.

Too many Americans tend to view history as "something that happened in the past," something that is "over and done," and thus has no bearing upon the present. Especially in the case of slavery, nothing could be further from the truth. As historian John Hope Franklin noted in his response to Horowitz:

> Most living Americans do have a connection with slavery. They have inherited the preferential advantage, if they are white, or the loathsome disadvantage, if they are black; and those positions are virtually as alive today as they were in the 19th century. The pattern of housing, the discrimination in employment, the resistance to equal opportunity in education, the racial profiling, the inequities in the administration of justice, the low expectation of blacks in the discharge of duties assigned to them, the widespread belief that blacks have physical prowess but little intellectual capacities and the widespread opposition to affirmative action, as if that had not been enjoyed by whites for three centuries, all indicate that the vestiges of slavery are still with us.
>
> And as long as there are pro-slavery protagonists among us, hiding behind such absurdities as "we are all in this together" or "it hurts me as much as it hurts you"

or "slavery benefited you as much as it benefited me," we will suffer from the inability to confront the tragic legacies of slavery and deal with them in a forthright and constructive manner.

Most important, we must never fall victim to some scheme designed to create a controversy among potential allies in order to divide them and, at the same time, exploit them for its own special purpose.[7]

NOTES

1. David Horowitz, 2001. "Ten Reasons Why Reparations for Blacks Is a Bad Idea for Blacks—and Racist, Too." *FrontPageMagazine.com*, January 1, 2003: www.frontpagemag.com/Articles/ReadArticle.asp?ID=1153 (accessed August 23, 2003).

David Horowitz is editor in chief of *FrontPageMagazine.com* and president of the Center for the Study of Popular Culture

2. Ernest Allen Jr. and Robert Chrisman, "Ten Reasons: A Response to David Horowitz," *Black Scholar* 31, no. 2 (June 2001): 49 et seq.

3. James Oakes, *The Ruling Race: A History of American Slaveholders* (New York: Vintage Books, 1983), 47–48.

4. Abbot Emerson Smith, *Colonists in Bondage: White Servitude and Convict Labor in America, 1607–1776.* Published for the Institute of Early American History and Culture at Williamsburg, Virginia (Chapel Hill: University of North Carolina Press, 1947).

5. *San Francisco Chronicle*, March 26, 2001, A21.

6. Melvin L. Oliver and Thomas M. Shapiro, *Black Wealth/White Wealth: A New Perspective on Racial Inequality* (New York: Routledge, 1995), 87.

7. Works Cited:

2001 *New York Times Almanac*. New York: Penguin Books, 2000.

———. *The Negro in the Civil War*. Boston: Little, Brown, 1953.

America, Richard F. *Paying the Social Debt: What White America Owes Black America*. Westport, Conn.: Praeger, 1993.

Berlin, Ira, et al. *Slaves No More: Three Essays on Emancipation and the Civil War*. New York: Cambridge University Press, 1992.

Conley, Dalton. *Being Black, Living in the Red: Race, Wealth, and Social Policy in America*. Berkeley: University of California Press, 1999.

Cornish, Dudley Taylor. *The Sable Arm: Black Troops in the Union Army, 1861–1865*. rpt. Lawrence: University Press of Kansas, 1956, 1987.

Cox, LaWanda. "The Promise of Land for the Freedmen." *Mississippi Valley Historical Review* 45 (December 1958): 413–40.

DeBow, J. D. B. "The Interest in Slavery of the Southern Non-Slaveholder," in *Slavery Defended: The Views of the Old South*, ed. Eric L. McKitrick, 169–77. Englewood Cliffs, N.J.: Prentice-Hall, 1963.

Foner, Eric. *Free Soil, Free Labor, Free Men: The Ideology of the Republican Party before the Civil War*. New York: Oxford University Press, 1970.

Franklin, John Hope, and Alfred A. Moss Jr. *From Slavery to Freedom: A History of African-Americans*, 7th ed. New York: McGraw-Hill, 1994.

Hacker, Andrew. *Two Nations: Black and White, Separate, Hostile, Unequal.* rev. ed. New York: Ballantine Books, 1995.

Horton, James Oliver, and Lois E. Horton. *In Hope of Liberty: Culture, Community, and Protest among Northern Free Blacks, 1700–1860.* New York: Oxford University Press, 1997.

Huston, James L. "Property Rights in Slavery and the Coming of the Civil War." *Journal of Southern History* 65 (1999): 249–86.

Oakes, James. *The Ruling Race: A History of American Slaveholders.* New York: Vintage Books, 1983.

Oliver, Melvin L., and Thomas M. Shapiro. *Black Wealth/White Wealth: A New Perspective on Racial Inequality.* New York: Routledge, 1995.

Quarles, Benjamin. *Black Abolitionists.* New York: Oxford University Press. 1969.

Rodney, Walter. *How Europe Underdeveloped Africa.* Washington, D.C.: Howard University Press, 1981.

Salzman, Jack, David Lionel Smith, and Cornel West, eds. *Encyclopedia of African-American Culture and History.* 5 vols. New York: Macmillan Library Reference, 1996. USA: Simon & Schuster Macmillan; London: Simon & Schuster and Prentice Hall International, 1996.

Schemo, Diana Jean. "An Ad Provokes Campus Protests and Pushes Limits of Expression." *New York Times*, March 21, 2001, A1, A17.

Smith, Abbot Emerson. *Colonists in Bondage: White Servitude and Convict Labor in America, 1607–1776.* Published for the Institute of Early American History and Culture at Williamsburg, Virginia. Chapel Hill: University of North Carolina Press, 1947.

Solow, Barbara L., and Stanley L. Engerman, eds. *British Capitalism and Caribbean Slavery: The Legacy of Eric Williams.* New York: Cambridge University Press, 1987.

Williams, Eric. *Capitalism & Slavery.* rpt. New York: Russell & Russell, 1944, 1961.

8

Reparations for Slavery in Scholarly Writing

Robert K. Fullinwider: "The Case for Reparations"[1,2]

Because of its visibility, Randall Robinson's new book, *The Debt: What America Owes to Blacks*, may rekindle a broad public debate on reparations. The issue is not new, nor is public debate about it. In 1969, the civil rights leader James Forman presented the Black Manifesto to American churches, demanding that they pay blacks five hundred million dollars in reparations. The Manifesto argued that for three and a half centuries blacks in America had been "exploited and degraded, brutalized, killed and persecuted" by whites. This treatment was part of a persistent institutional pattern of, first, legal slavery and, later, legal discrimination and forced segregation. Through slavery and discrimination, the Manifesto went on to contend, whites have extracted enormous wealth from black labor with little return to blacks themselves. These facts constitute grounds for reparations on a massive scale. American churches were but the first institutions asked by Forman to discharge this great debt.

The Manifesto achieved immediate notoriety and stimulated debate in newspapers and magazines. Within a short period, however, public excitement died away.

The issue of reparations has always found favor within the African American community itself, taking root not long after the freeing of the slaves during the Civil War. It flourished around World War I with the Marcus Garvey movement and later found voice in Forman's Black Manifesto. It has recently regained vitality, given new life by a recent precedent, the Civil Liberties Act of 1988, in which Congress authorized payment of reparations to Japanese American citizens who had been interned during World War II. In each session of Congress since 1989, Representative John Conyers has introduced a bill to create a commission to study reparations for slavery and segregation. Although the bill has made no legislative headway, the publication now of Randall Robinson's new book reflects the growing sense among many African Americans that the time is right to push reparations back onto the public agenda.

If public debate is to prove fruitful, however, both proponents and opponents of reparations will have to sidestep certain common but toxic confusions. In a long article in *The Washington Post* last December, these confusions were much on display. The article's lead questions—"Should the U.S. pay reparations to the descendants of slaves?" and "[W]hy shouldn't the great grandchildren of those who worked for free and were deprived of education and were kept in bondage be compensated?"—were countered by another—"Why should Americans who never owned slaves pay for the sins of ancestors they don't even know?" The article quoted Congressman Henry Hyde's firm answer to the last question: "The notion of collective guilt for what people did [200-plus] years ago, that this generation should pay a debt for that generation, is an idea whose time has gone. I never owned a slave. I never oppressed anybody. I don't know that I should have to pay for someone who did [own slaves] generations before I was born." His response didn't satisfy at least one African American, whose letter-to-the-editor noted, "Henry Hyde, like many whites, is quick to say, 'I never owned a slave'. . . . Why should I pay . . . for something my ancestors did? . . . Well, because some people are descendants of slave owners and have profited from the labor of blacks who were never paid for their labor."

Personal Versus Civil Liability

The demand for reparations to African Americans cannot be casually dismissed. It is grounded in a basic moral norm, a norm presupposed, for example, in the Biblical injunction at Exodus 22: "If a man steal an ox, or a sheep, and kill it, or sell it; he shall restore five oxen for an ox, and four sheep for a sheep." You must make good the wrongs you do. This principle in one form or another underlies every mature moral and legal system in the world. At the same time, however, Henry Hyde's distaste for collective guilt seems equally well-founded: "The father shall not be put to death for the children, neither shall the children be put to death for the fathers: every man shall be put to death for his own sin" (Deuteronomy 24:16). We must not penalize one person for another's misdeeds. Does, then, the demand for reparations pose a conflict between two distinct and equally basic moral principles? Not if the demand is properly understood.

Henry Hyde echoes a common but confused sentiment. If personal liability for slavery or past racial oppression were being imputed to him, then the Congressman's response would be appropriate. He denies personal responsibility for the wrongs to be made good. But personal responsibility and liability are not at stake. The real issues are corporate responsibility—the responsibility of the nation as a whole—and civic responsibility—the responsibility of each citizen to do his fair part in honoring the nation's obligations. When Congress passed the Civil Liberties Act of 1988, no one assumed that individual Americans were being held accountable for personal wrongdoing. The interning of Japanese Americans was an act of the United States government and its agents. At the time, the government acted for putatively good reasons. Following the Japanese attack on Pearl Harbor, American officials were concerned about the security of the West Coast from similar attack or sabotage. Whether the government actually acted for honorable motives or not, the point remains that with the passage of time thoughtful Americans—and the government itself—have come to view the internment as an unjustified response to the war with Japan, and one that wronged its victims. The Civil Liberties Act, and the token reparations it paid ($20,000 to each interned Japanese American or to his or her surviving spouse or children), represented an official apology and a small step toward making whole the material losses incurred by the internees. The reparations were appropriated out of general revenues. Consequently, Henry Hyde, as taxpayer, contributed a small portion, not because he had any personal responsibility for the internment but because as a citizen he is required to bear his share of the government's necessary expenditures.

One can make a parallel argument for reparations to African Americans. Although countless individual Americans throughout our history exploited their power or standing to oppress African Americans, that power and standing itself derived from law—first from the latitude of the English Crown, then from the Constitution of 1787 (which accepted slavery in the states where it was established), and finally from the tissue of post-Civil War "Jim Crow" laws, rules, and social conventions that enforced de jure and de facto racial segregation. The chief wrongs done to African Americans, thus, were not simply the sum of many individual oppressions added together but were the corporate acts of a nation that imposed or tolerated regimes of slavery, apartheid, peonage, and disenfranchisement. Just as it was the nation that owed Japanese Americans reparations, so it is the nation that owes reparations to African Americans. And so it is that Americans not as individuals but as citizens owe support for the nation's debt.

Confusions about Liability

The foregoing seems simple and plain enough. Why then do so many opponents of reparations confuse the matter? We might content ourselves to speculate unflatteringly about their motives, were it not for the fact that the proponents of reparations often fall into the same and worse confusions. A recent spate of articles in law reviews demonstrates that the distinctions among corporate, civic, and personal liability prove elusive. These articles try to make the case for reparations and answer objections to it. To accept the reasonableness of reparations, they contend, we have to abandon the "individualistic" models characteristic of American law and think in terms of group rights and group wrongs. "The guiding paradigm of traditional remedies law," writes Rhonda Magee in the *Virginia Law Review*, "is the one plaintiff, one defendant lawsuit in which the plaintiff seeks the position she would have occupied 'but for' the wrong committed by the defendant." Within this paradigm, the demand by blacks for reparations seems unsustainable, since we can no longer identify individual successors to slave owners or state agents who promulgated legal oppression of blacks, nor separate out the respective harms to the successors of those who lived under slavery and Jim Crow.

However, at least with respect to the matter of liability, it is not the "individualism" of American law that we need to give up but the assumption, implicitly at work here, that all liability is personal. The argument for reparations fits comfortably enough within the traditional paradigm when we make sure the focus is on corporate liability, for the corporate actor in question, the United States, is an "individual" under law. Indeed, precisely because it is an "individual" that doesn't die, it can acquire and retain debts over many generations, though individual Americans come and go. That is why Henry Hyde can indeed owe something as a result of his ancestors' actions.

Nevertheless, Magee and others insist on the indispensability of "group" conceptions of victims and wrongdoers. In the words of Mari Matsuda, victims of racial oppression "necessarily think of themselves as a group, because they are treated and survive as a group. [Even] [t]he wealthy Black person still comes up against the color line." The "group damage engendered by past wrongs ties victim group members together, satisfying the horizontal unity sought by the legal mind." Similarly, a "horizontal connection exists as well within the perpetrator group." Members of the latter—whites—continue to benefit from past wrongs and from the contemporary privilege their skin-color confers upon them. Finally, a horizontal relation of moral causality obtains between the two groups. The relationship might be represented in this way:

where the arrow represents liability, indicating that W owes reparations to B, and where the respective entitlements and liabilities distribute within each group to its individual members, who are all tied to one another by the "victim"/"victimizer" attributes.

Magee, Matsuda, and other defenders of reparations labor to establish that the harms of slavery and discrimination affect each and every African American (even the wealthy black runs up against the color line) and the culpability for the harms extends to each and every white (every white unjustly benefits from white-skin privilege). This picture, in fact, does not represent some new "group" paradigm at all, but an individualism run rampant, the product of failing to keep distinct personal and civic liability.

The real lines of liability, I contend, run this way:

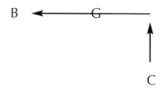

where it is G (the government) that owes B (the victims) and where members of C (citizens) are duty-bound to underwrite government debts. The connection of citizens to the creditor "group" B is indirect and vertical, not direct and horizontal. Thus Henry Hyde owes something not because he is white or a member of the perpetrator "group" but because he is a citizen. The various "horizontal" connections among citizens are irrelevant. Indeed, included in the citizen "group" are African Americans themselves. They too will contribute in support of the government's reparations.

This outcome strikes the writers I am discussing here as an anomaly that needs explaining. In fact, it is no anomaly at all once we appreciate that blacks are citizens as well as victims and that their equal citizenship is reflected in their civic obligation to support government reparations—whether those reparations are paid to Japanese Americans or even to themselves in their capacity as wronged individuals.

Unfortunately, the ghost of personal responsibility is not so easily exorcised from these legal essays. This is especially true in the case of Vincene Verdun, writing in the *Tulane Law Review*. Although self-consciously rejecting "individualistic" thinking in favor of "group" thinking, she nevertheless edges close to the proper conclusion when she observes that the "wrongdoer" owing reparations is American "society." However, her failure fully to grasp the corporate nature of "society" is betrayed by her next move. "Treating society as the wrongdoer," she observes, "necessarily includes the injured parties in the classification of wrongdoer. If society pays, it will do so at least in part with tax dollars, and African Americans pay taxes." Nevertheless, "[t]here is a ring of propriety in having African Americans share in the . . . burdens," observes Verdun. Why? Here we expect Verdun to note that African Americans are citizens like everyone else. Instead, she locates the propriety in their own guilt!

Opponents of reparations are quick to point out that Africans participated in the slave trade and [some] African Americans owned slaves. The truth in these statements cannot be rebutted. Vincent Verdun [the author's father, introduced in a prologue], is an injured party, because he was deprived of his rightful inheritance because his great-great-great grandmother was a slave. On the other hand, his great-great-great grandfather [the offspring of a French plantation owner and his black slave, and who was later emancipated and given land] was a slave owner.

Now, aside from the fact that the situation Verdun describes was fairly rare, what possible connection could there exist between Vincent Verdun, who lived his life as a black man, and his slave-owning great-great-great grandfather that would visit on him the sins of his ancestor? Indeed, what connection between this ancestor and Vincene Verdun herself could lead her to confess, as she later does, that her "heritage," deriving from both "master and slave," makes her not only a victim but one of the "wrongdoers," the group that owes reparations? No connection exists between these two Verduns and their long-ago ancestor except one, blood. Evidently, guilt travels through blood, since neither Vincene nor her father derived any lasting benefit or privilege from the ancestor—indeed, their only significant inheritance was the color of their skin.

The racialist assumption embedded in Verdun's "confession" speaks for itself. What would prompt a level-headed legal scholar to step into such a malodorous swamp? The explanation lies in Verdun's failure, despite her ostensible attachment to "group" thinking over "individualistic" thinking, fully to appreciate the various ontologies of groups and the difference between collective and corporate liability, a failure Magee and Matsuda share with her. She seems to assume that any property that characterizes "society" must characterize each of its members. If "society" is a "wrongdoer," then each member of society must be a wrongdoer. It is easy enough for her to view every white as a "wrongdoer" but she is forced to stretch to include blacks themselves as part of the "wrongdoers" since they, too, are part of "society": they are taxpayers.

When "society" is understood corporately, however, the "wrongdoing" of society does not distribute to each of its members. Individual citizens may be blameless for the wrongs of their nation. That the burden of payment for national wrongdoing falls to them simply reflects their civic roles and not anything about their persons. In making the case for reparations, it is a mistake to go looking for personal complicity on the part of those who must pay. And worse yet, it is a mistake to turn the putative personal complicity into guilt-by-blood.

Randall Robinson himself is less than careful in this regard. Sometimes in his book it is "white society" that must pay reparations, sometimes the "whole society." At one place, the debtors are characterized as those—"nations, individuals, whites as a racial entity"—who benefited from slavery and segregation. Finally, Robinson, too, appeals to blood: the value of the labor stolen from slaves, he says, has been compounding "through the blood lines" of slave owners. Just how blood transmits and compounds debt he does not say.

The imprecision and neo-racialist overtones in *The Debt* evidently caused Robinson some second thoughts. He recently wrote in *The Nation* that "individual Americans need not feel defensive or under attack" as a result of the call for reparations. "No one holds any living person responsible" for slavery or its successor regime of Jim Crow. We must all, "as a nation," address reparations, he writes. That is the right focus.

Making the Case for Reparations

Avoiding the confusion about corporate, civic, and personal liability clears the way to explore more fruitfully the positive case for reparations. How should that case go? The argument mounted by Robinson, Verdun, Magee, and other African Americans bases reparations on the great wrong of slavery as well as the more recent wrongs of legally sanctioned discrimination. Further, the argument stresses the purported benefits that whites over the centuries have extracted from slavery, Jim Crow, and a general social system of white supremacy.

However, basing reparations on slavery and on the great benefits accrued to whites invite complication and controversy. I suggest the case is actually strengthened by dropping both slavery and the benefits reaped by whites as grounds for reparations. Let me explain.

First, although the proposition that whites as a whole have benefited enormously from past racial oppression might seem self-evident, and remains an article of faith among the reparationists, whether slavery and segregation in fact yielded net positive economic benefits to this country and to whom those net benefits flowed (to all or only some whites) are difficult questions to answer. More importantly, trying to answer them is diversionary and unnecessary. A sufficient basis for reparations lies in the wrong done African Americans by the nation, whether or not anyone really benefited from it. After all, the basis of the Civil Liberties Act of 1988 was not some putative benefit Americans had extracted from the internment of Japanese Americans in 1942–45. The basis was the wrong done to the internees.

What wrong to African Americans, then, should current reparations address? Making slavery the basis for reparations is unwise for two reasons. First, doing so invites the retort that America has already paid for the wrong of slavery, not with money but with the blood shed in the Civil War. The attempt successfully to parry this retort leads to complications, since whether to reckon the blood sacrifice of the Civil War as expiation for the sins of the past and how to weigh that sacrifice against any unpaid debt to the newly liberated slaves are questions that invite calculations prone to sophistical quibbling on either side.

A second reason it is unwise to base reparations on the fact of slavery is that the passage of time since abolition has now itself become a morally significant factor. Whatever condition they find themselves in, people have the responsibility to make the best of their circumstances, to provide for themselves even if they start with the most meager resources. For example, between 1865 and 1965, millions of immigrants came to America penniless and with little to offer but their physical labor. By dint of hard work, they and their successor generations eventually blended into the larger American fabric.

Over time one might have expected a similar process to play itself out for the newly liberated slaves, especially since their numbers would have allowed them to possess considerable political power in several states. Yet this process didn't occur. Why not? Because, after having made the newly freed slaves citizens, the federal government abandoned them. It allowed southern whites, through terror and law, to recapture control of state governments, disenfranchise African Americans, and, through the apparatus of Jim Crow, reduce them to virtual peonage. Indeed, America's highest court put its official stamp on state apartheid in its 1896 ruling, *Plessy v. Ferguson*, a ruling that Justice Harlan, in dissent, accurately predicted would one day be viewed by Americans as no less pernicious than the Court's fateful decision in Dred Scott.

In sum, governments—state and federal—made no effort to vindicate the rights to full and equal citizenship the Civil War Amendments extended to blacks, a failure that prevented African Americans from successfully following the immigrant model. That failure persisted into recent times. The U. S. began to expend real effort toward defending the basic rights of blacks only after the 1954 Supreme Court ruling in *Brown v. Board of Education*, an effort far from complete today.

Had the federal government done nothing after 1865 except vigorously protect the civil and voting rights of blacks, the legacy of slavery would have faded
considerably if not wholly by now through the industry of blacks themselves.
That the legacy still persists owes much, if not all, to the post-Civil War oppression of African Americans and it is this wrong that offers the most direct and
salient basis for reparations.

Answering Objections

Some may object that the post–Civil War oppression of African Americans still
leaves the case for reparations unpersuasive. They might insist that reparations
are not possible or, alternatively, that they are not necessary.

Consider the first, that reparations are not possible because we can't now really identify who should get what. I argued earlier that the individualist legal
paradigm creates no real difficulties in dealing with liability for reparations.
However, doesn't it generate problems about entitlement to reparations? To
whom should reparations be paid? Should every individual black person receive
reparations? Quite obviously, different blacks have fared very differently under
past segregation. Most of those affected worst are long dead. How was the
legacy of their wrongful deprivations diffused to their descendants down to the
present moment? How do we trace the damages?

Most living African Americans have incurred their own indignities and damages under discrimination, but how do we match reparations to losses? Do we
pay the same to the child of middle class blacks who immigrated to the United
States from the West Indies twenty years ago that we pay to an elderly retiree
who spent half his life as a field hand in Mississippi? Mari Matsudi says that even
the wealthy black person comes up against the color line. True enough. But the
damage to him has not been the same as the damage to others. A scheme of
reparations like the program for Japanese American internees that pays a flat
sum to every black, whatever his background and economic condition, does not
seem very attractive. So might the opponent of reparations argue.

This objection would carry more force if justice forbade paying reparations unless we could identify the exact victims and the exact degree of their victimization. However, while justice requires that we take special care to identify the
proper "wrongdoers" from whom to extract compensation, it is less insistent that
we scrupulously avoid compensating "victims" who weren't real victims, especially if such avoidance would mean not compensating anyone at all. Because
the effects of a hundred years of racial oppression have been dispersed so widely
throughout the African American community, it makes sense to adopt some
scheme of reparations that morally approximates rather than actually effects the
restoration of victims to their "rightful places"—the positions they would have
occupied but for the past history of oppression. Congress could follow the precedent of post–World War II Germany. Apart from paying compensation to some
identifiable individual victims of its war crimes, Germany made reparation payments to organizations that represented European and world Jewry, including to

the State of Israel, on the reasonable assumption that these organizations in the course of their efforts to resettle displaced Jews would benefit many of the victims of the Nazi regime. Similarly, Congress could fashion a reparations plan to fund specially designated organizations who would act on behalf of the African American community. A reparations program need not involve government indiscriminately writing checks to individual African Americans.

Even if the first objection is not telling, what about the second? Are reparations actually necessary? The opponent of reparations might argue that the country did enough when it passed the civil rights laws of the 1960s. In the words of Jonathan Yardley, these laws "are concrete, purposeful and immensely significant attempts to eliminate the vestiges of slavery, to make the country equally free to all its citizens." Moreover, their "effect has been incalculable." Actually, it might be better to say that their effect is quite calculable. We can easily measure, for example, the growth of the black middle class since 1960, the near-parity between black and white high school graduation rates, and the upsurge in black public officials and legislators. We can also count the growth of African Americans on campus over the last forty years, and calculate the narrowed gap in earnings between similarly skilled black and white workers. Surely, then, we can extrapolate from these improvements to even further progress for African Americans in the near future. What would reparations add?

The answer is that reparations would add something quite important. Although the gains from the civil rights laws of the 1960s are undeniable, they should not be overstated. In particular, the narrowing income gap between whites and blacks masks a tremendous wealth gap. As Dalton Conley points out in an important new study, "At all income, occupational, and education levels, black families on average have drastically lower levels of wealth than similar white families." Moreover, he argues, it is the wealth rather than income of parents that proves pivotal to a child's ascending the academic and economic ladders to the middle class and beyond.

The black-white wealth gap is large, enduring, and damaging. Moreover, it is for the most part a direct legacy of official and unofficial discrimination lasting into the 1960s. Consequently, reparations at this late date would not be gratuitous; there is real work for them to do. A properly structured reparations program enacted by Congress could funnel substantial resources over three or four decades into organizations specifically designed and monitored to create wealth among African Americans—organizations that would assist development of neighborhoods, ownership of homes, creation of businesses, and expansion of human capital. These organizations could direct their energies and investments toward local and small-scale interventions to interrupt the cycle of poverty and hopelessness that traps the black underclass and toward broad-based efforts to secure the growing middle class in its economic purchase on the American dream. Such investments in infrastructure and wealth-creation would go some distance toward repairing for African Americans as a whole the damages occasioned by a hundred years of legal oppression.

The Limits of Reparations

The foregoing represents barely the sketch of a case for reparations. But it does suggest the contours of a specific, "lean" strategy: reparations (1) based on the wrongs done African Americans by the legal regime of racial discrimination that lasted until thirty-some years ago, and (2) designed to stimulate creation of wealth, broadly conceived, in the African American community. It is "lean" because it omits elements many African Americans embrace, particularly the argument about slavery and the wealth that was purportedly extracted from it. Thirty years ago, in discussing a proposal put forward by Yale law professor Boris Bittker that the "post–Civil War wrongs are more than sufficient to support" a claim for reparations, the African American legal scholar Derrick Bell conceded that "the legal argument for reparations improves with the exclusion of the slavery period." Nevertheless, such exclusion, he thought, represents a "tactical loss." It "sacrifices much of the emotional component that provides moral leverage for black reparations demands." To the contrary, excluding slavery not only improves the legal case for reparations, it strengthens both the tactical and the moral cases as well by stripping them of diversionary complications.

It is true, however, that excluding slavery may sacrifice for African Americans some of the emotional resonance of the reparations argument, and this aspect may turn out, in the eyes of some, to be the most vital part of all. Although Randall Robinson's *The Debt* seems on its face to be addressed to a larger public, its real audience is other African Americans. It is a book less about the details of reparations (they receive little more than a nod in the next-to-last chapter) than about Robinson's unrequited anger at slavery and the "staggering breadth of America's crime" against blacks. The real crime of slavery for Robinson? It has "maliciously shorn" African Americans of their "natural identity" and destroyed their self-esteem, leaving a people riven by self-hatred, self-doubt, and self-rejection. The real and continuing injury has been psychic. (Similarly for Vincene Verdun: "It is emotional injury, stemming from the badge of inferiority and from the stigma attached to race which marks every African American, that composes the most significant injury of slavery.")

Thus, for Robinson the emotional resonance of slavery for African Americans is not some unnecessary complicating factor to be trimmed away from a clean argument for reparations, it is the centerpiece for an aggressive, collective demand for redress. By pressuring "white society" to confess its sin of slavery and by "implacably demand[ing]" their full due, African Americans will "find" their own "voice." Fighting the fight for reparations on the basis of slavery will bring "catharsis." African Americans will rediscover their identity and know themselves to be a worthy people, win or lose.

Robinson's vision starkly poses a crucial question: what do African Americans take to be the real stakes in a reparations argument? Is the goal to succeed (with as many allies as possible) against high odds in achieving a reparations enactment by Congress that will bring some limited but vital wealth-creation to African American communities? Or is the goal of reparations to force a debate on their terms, as a vehicle of self-discovery and emotional self-renewal, however socially divisive it becomes and however remote it makes actual enactment of reparations? Readers of *The Debt* will not find a clear rendering of the trade-offs between these goals that Robinson is willing to countenance; but they cannot fail to see his passion for staking out the "sin" of slavery as the field on which to do battle. If this passion is unyielding, however, the debate about reparations may never really engage Americans at large. This would be too bad. A real public debate, stripped of disabling confusions while sharply focused on manageable grounds and practical results, could do every citizen a service.

Stephen Kershnar: "The Case against Reparations"[3,4]

Abstract. *George Schedler raises interesting issues with regard to the amount of reparations owed for slavery, the parties who are owed reparations, and the standard for these reparations. His arguments, however, do not hold up upon analysis. His analysis of the case for the descendants of slaves being owed compensation seriously overestimates the case for such reparations. He does not identify the grounds for such compensation, i.e., either stolen inheritance or the descendants' trustee-like control over the slave's estate, and this results in his not identifying the metaphysical and epistemic problems that accompany the descendants' claim to reparations. In analyzing whether the U.S. government owes compensation, Schedler provides arguments based on its small role in bringing about slavery and the break in national identity that followed the Civil War. Such arguments fail but his conclusion can be supported by other arguments, specifically the nature of the federal government's relation to slavery and the limited nature of its powers. Thus, the case against reparations is overwhelming but not for the reasons Schedler provides.*

Introduction

George Schedler, in his recent book, *Racist Symbols and Reparations*, discusses the case for compensation for slavery.[5] He concludes that the case for the U.S. government owing reparations is problematic. I think his discussion is useful since I think that despite his general negativity toward the case for reparations, he overestimates the case for reparations. By noting the way in which he overestimates this case, we can see the strength of the case against reparations.

The issue of whether compensation for slavery is owed can be more fruitfully explored via an exploration of more particular issues. First, what events or affairs, if any, justify compensation? Second, to whom is compensation owed? Third, who owes compensation? Fourth, what form and amount should compensation take? The topic alone gives us a crude answer for the first issue: slavery justifies compensation. I shall thus focus on Schedler's answer to the other three issues as a way of illuminating the weakness of the case for reparations.

Schedler's Account

Schedler argues that compensation is owed to slaves. On his account, the compensation ought not follow the free worker standard, i.e., the value of the slave's labor measured by the amount of wages a free person performing the labor would have been paid (101, 107–109). Schedler provides two arguments for this claim. First, he argues that this approach does not capture the wrongfulness of slavery. The wrongfulness of slavery, he argues, does not consist in doing certain kinds of work but "in depriving the individuals of freedom to choose some other work (or no work at all)." It is the elimination of opportunities and enjoyment of their own choosing that was wrong, not the failure to compensate for what they were forced to do (107). Second, Schedler argues that the free worker standard violates the ought-implies-can rule. This is because in the relevant world in which slavery does not exist the slave's work is done by others or does not get done (108). He argues that the proper compensation for slavery is the value of the opportunities and enjoyment available if slavery had never existed (108). This consists of compensation for pain and suffering, kidnapping, loss of family, and loss of opportunities (113). Also, on his account, the slaves that were emancipated were owed compensation to allow them to compete on a fair basis with their white counterparts (113).

On Schedler's account, the descendants of first generation slaves are also owed compensation. He argues that a person born into slavery, e.g., a second generation slave, or a descendant of a slave is owed compensation for slavery only if she is worse off than if she had never come into existence (112). However, on his account, compensation for slavery-related harm is owed to the descendants of slaves for whatever damages were owed to their ancestors and which because they were unpaid put them at a disadvantage (114).

Schedler argues that the federal government does not owe compensation because it had a small role in establishing and maintaining slavery and because the prewar federal government is not strictly identical to the postwar federal government (116–117). In addition, if there is any debt, he argues that fairness requires that less of the burden be placed on the postbellum immigrant population and their descendents because these immigrants did not consent to the continuing failure to pay the debt owed to slaves (116, 119).

Schedler on the Issue of the Persons to Whom Compensation Is Owed

I shall argue that Schedler errs in denying the free worker standard for compensation for slaves and that he leaves out important arguments against compensation being owed to the current descendants of slaves.

The Free Worker Standard

In denying the free worker standard, Schedler focuses on the claim that the wrongfulness of slavery does not consist in doing certain kinds of work and not being properly compensated for it where one does not voluntarily waive the claim to compensation. This is false. Consider Schedler's own example. If Holocaust survivors are forced to perform musical work worth $20,000 in addition to other harms, this is a separate wrong that can ground a claim to compensation. This follows from the notion that one act or set of acts can produce multiple harms because it can set back multiple interests.

Schedler argues against the free worker standard on the basis that the relevant baseline is a world in which the work is not done or done by other workers. Still in the world in which slavery occurs the slave's interest in receiving just compensation for one's work is set back. That this work would not otherwise have been done is not determinative of the issue. For example, consider the case where pain and suffering worth $400,000 is imposed on a slave who is raped by her master, where had she not been enslaved she would have been ganged raped (far more frequently) and slaughtered by an aggressor rival tribe in Africa. This is true even if that tribal warfare led to her creation. And this is true even if the master bought her in order to rape her and even if other likely masters would have committed even more brutal rapes of her. This is because token harms, harms individuated by some feature or features of their causal history, are not necessarily determined by the possible world picked out by the absence of the victimizing act or set of acts.

In general, there is no algorithm for determining the baseline world for measuring the degree of harm that a person incurred.[6] Instead, the baseline world must be chosen in a way that allows us to pick out the token harm that the wrongdoer brought about. At times, this is done by picking out the nearest possible world in which the wrongdoer's act or omission, did not occur, whereas at other times the world picked out must be one that lacks both the wrongdoer's act (or omission) and other wrongdoers' acts or omissions. The example involving the slave who is a rape victim is such a case.

At times, it seems as if multiple baseline worlds have to be used in order to pick out the relevant token harms. In the case of slavery, one baseline world may be needed to pick out the harm caused by enslavement relative to the slave's family, community, culture, and liberty. A second baseline world may be needed to pick out the token harm that came about via the forced labor and beatings that the slave was made to endure. An objector might argue that this does not show the need for two baselines since the forced labor and beatings further deviate from the world in which the enslaved person spends her life in Africa.[7] However, given that a careful selection process is needed to pick out the relevant baseline world in order to isolate the relevant token harm, I am not sure what is lost by the use of multiple baseline worlds as an epistemic tool by which to pick out the multiple token harms.

Inheritance Grounds the Compensation Claim of Descendants of Slaves

Schedler does not fully identify the ground of the claim for compensation for the descendants of slaves. He notes that it is the result of the claim to compensation being held by the slave (114). I would argue that at their death one of two things happens to their claim. It may be transferred to their inheritors. Since a person's descendants are usually his inheritors, the descendants then inherit the slave's claim to compensation.[8] This is the account I will adopt. On an alternative picture, the slave retains her moral claim to compensation even after her death and this claim survives her death. On this account, the descendants never own the claim to compensation but merely assert it on behalf of the deceased slave in the same way in which an estate's trustee may claim, both morally and legally, the right to recover money owed to the deceased after she dies. Schedler's account could be clearer in recognizing one or both of these models as grounding the descendant's claim to compensation. His point about the descendant's being at a disadvantage as a result of the loss of inheritance is beside the point unless it means to identify the loss of inheritance as the relevant disadvantage.

Schedler does not focus on some of the main difficulties with the descendants' claim to compensation and this failure leads to his overestimation of the case for compensation.

The Dilution Effect

On the above account, the inherited claim is diluted over successive generations. As a person's descendants branch out over successive generations, each generation gains only a portion of the earlier generation's claim. For example, if a black man is owed $1,000,000 in compensation and his claim is divided up equally between 10 great grandchildren, each will have a claim worth no more than $100,000 plus interest.

Epistemic Problems with Compensation

Over several generations, epistemic problems arise in identifying the descendants of slaves as the inheritors of the slave's claim. The notion that a claim would have been passed on through successive generations is made less likely by the proliferation of factors that lead families over generations to lose wealth, sell off claims in return for immediate benefits, or disinherit one another. It is unlikely that later descendants would have a portion of, let alone the whole, of her share of her ancestor's claim. Even the notion that as a collection, current black descendants of slaves would hold the claims to compensation of the slaves also depends on a denial of transference between the group of descendants and others that is not obvious.

An additional epistemic problem arises with regard to the amount of the original claim. Other than by a counterfactual free market, it seems hard to assign a value to the loss of liberty, pain and suffering, degradation, etc. The slave's (and his family's) ex ante wealth and expectations about quality of life in Africa would play a large role in structuring this counterfactual. In assigning the disvalue of slavery, a potential slave would compare the disvalue of a life in slavery to the value of resources being provided to his family and village. The background idea behind the resources being provided to the slave's family and village rather than herself is that since a slave does not legally own herself any resources given to her can be confiscated by her master, thus making such payments of dubious value.

The epistemic problem cannot be solved via an assumption that but for slavery or past discrimination blacks would have the same income and distribution of positions as whites. This is because there is strong evidence to believe that there are genetic differences in the average intelligence of racial groups and that such differences will likely affect a group's economic performance.[9] Also, there are probably differences in sociocultural beliefs, attitudes, and values between different groups.[10] While not genetic, these are deeply embedded factors that are also likely to affect a group's economic performance. There are also destructive behaviors that are not the result of discrimination and that likely produce inequality between racial groups. For example, in the mid-1990's blacks had nearly a 70 percent out-of-wedlock birthrate.[11] Since out-of wedlock births are associated with many destructive behaviors, e.g., crime, attitudes and activity leading to out-of-wedlock births have harmful effects on the black community. Blacks also commit a disproportionately large amount of violent crimes. For example, during recent periods they have constituted 50–60% of the arrests for murders and 50% of the arrests for rape. These rates match the frequency distribution of victims' reports.[12] Out-of-wedlock births and violent crimes are in general voluntary acts for which moral responsibility rests on the agent who performs them. When such acts form a general pattern in the black community, they produce an unequal distribution of income and wealth when compared to other racial groups. The effects of this destructive behavior must be disentangled from those injuries that result from the loss of inheritance and this is a daunting task. When combined, these epistemic problems make the decision as to the amount of damages owed for lost inheritance highly speculative.

The slaveholders are long dead and the wealth of the taxpayer population has been formed in large part through voluntary actions, thus creating a powerful moral claim against overcompensation of the descendants. This claim rests on the value of respecting reasonable expectations, protecting legitimate property rights, promoting economic efficiency, and perhaps also satisfying economic desert. An extended defense of this claim will take us too far afield but I note that many justifications of property rights and free market transactions are independent of claims about the justice of the initial acquisition of resources.[13] Given this powerful claim on behalf of taxpayers and given the speculative nature of the descendants' claim the case for compensation should be rejected.

Nor can the epistemic problems be solved via a setting of compensation equal to the disgorgement of ill-gotten gains. This is because disgorgement is not directly related to the attempt to return the descendant to the position they would have been in but for the harmful act or omission.[14] In general, a person who injures another may have an unjust gain that differs from the victim's unjust loss. Consider the following case. Jane has $10,000 in the bank and has it invested at a 6% rate of interest. Susan then steals the money and invests it in a risky technology company whose stock subsequently skyrockets, resulting in Susan's stock (at least that part purchased with Jane's money) being worth $200,000. Here Susan's unjust gain is far greater than the sum needed to compensate Jane for her loss.

This last point invalidates another one of Schedler's arguments. He argues that since slave owners did not receive any ill-gotten gains, at least by the end of the Civil War, they do not owe any compensation on these grounds (114–15).[15]

However, given the above point, it can be seen that whether they benefited is irrelevant to the issue of whether they owe damages for the harm they have caused.

The Violent-Crime Offset

While Schedler does point out some offsets to the descendant's claim to compensation, he fails to notice a major one. Blacks commit a substantial number of crimes, including a disproportionately large number of violent crimes. For example, approximately one black male in four is incarcerated at some time for the commission of a felony.[16] Given that crimes that victimize others ground a claim to compensation in the victim, the compensation for lost inheritance must be offset by such claims to compensation against those who have committed such acts or those who have benefited from the inability or refusal of aggressors to pay compensation. To the extent that this affects a substantial portion of the black community, e.g., some criminals and their families, this may reduce the compensation that is owed. Whether this offset exceeds the compensation owed introduces yet another epistemic difficulty and the problem gets even murkier when we consider the party against whom the offset applies.

The Welfare-Benefits Offset

One other offset that is mentioned in the literature and that is worth considering is that accompanying the welfare state. Michael Levin argues that in the U.S. there is an enormous transfer of wealth from whites to blacks every year. He argues that since blacks make considerably less money on average than do whites, since blacks constitute about 40% of welfare dependency, and since income taxes are progressive, there is a net annual white-to-black transfer of about seventy-five billion dollars.[17] Using 1990 dollars, this is equivalent to a Marshall Plan for blacks every three years. It is not clear that such payments are to count toward any reparations owed since the money is given out in a manner that is unrelated to reparations and is instead based on need.

However, this is unclear. Consider the case where a wealthy benefactor, Al, negligently breaks the leg of his grandson Stan. Before he can pay for that injury, Al dies and his estate, using its discretion, decides to transfer to each of his three grandsons, including Stan, $300,000. Does this satisfy the debt? If the estate labels the money to Stan as payment plus a gift then it does, assuming this amount is more than the debt, whereas if it does not do so then the case gets murkier. The problem here is that there is an issue as to whether transfers of wealth that are neither motivated by a desire to satisfy a debt of compensation nor labeled as such can satisfy a debt of compensation. It seems that this is likely not the case where the money is given to the injured party in satisfaction of an independent moral claim, e.g., the moral claim that all those in need receive equal treatment. Hence, this white-to-black transfer will probably not satisfy even a portion of the debt owed for slavery.

Schedler on Who Owes Compensation

Schedler argues that the federal government does not owe compensation because it is not the one that had a role in bringing about slavery and even if it is, it only had a small role in doing so (116–117). In addition. he notes that if there is any debt, fairness requires that a disproportionately smaller burden be placed on the postbellum immigrant population and their descendants (116).

National Identity

Schedler's second argument rests on the notion that the prewar federal government is not strictly identical to the postwar federal government. His argument for this rests on a change in the fundamental assumption of racial inequality that can be seen in the passage of the Thirteenth, Fourteenth, and Fifteenth Amendments (117). This argument is at the least incomplete and probably incorrect. A legal system can change some of its more fundamental laws so long as it does so in a way that satisfies the rule of recognition, the litmus for what shall constitute a law in a particular system of law. If this were not the case, then it would be a contradiction to say that a nation has changed some of its fundamental laws, and it is not. Schedler might argue that the postwar legal changes did not satisfy the rule of recognition because of the process in which the Southern States were coerced into ratifying these amendments. However, at the very least such an argument would have to be made and would require the further argument that a particular system of law is an essential property of a nation.

Schedler's argument is also irrelevant. Consider this analogy. If Sony buys Toyota, then in the absence of a contractual condition to the contrary Sony assumes all of Toyota's debts and assets. If the postwar federal government legitimately replaced the antebellum government, then in the absence of a contractual condition to the contrary the postwar government assumed all of the prewar government's debts and assets. In the case of the alleged two governments, there is no such contractual condition and hence the postwar government would still hold such debts.

On a side note, if one assumes, and I think one should, that the Civil War was an illegal war of aggression, then the federal government's debt to blacks would have to compete with its debt to the South, thus introducing a need for a theory of debt prioritization.

The Federal Government's Role in Permitting Slavery

Schedler argues that the federal government does not owe compensation for slavery because of its small role in bringing it about relative to other parties. However, this would at most show that the federal government should bear only a small portion of the debt.

Schedler should have focused on the nature of the federal government's role. The federal government permitted but did not cause enslavement and the slave trade to occur. Generally, a party does not owe compensation for harm to another for a refusal to act, unless the refusal infringed upon a special duty that was owed to the harmed party. This special duty might rest on either a contract or a special relationship. However, neither is present in this case. There was no contract between the potential slaves and the federal government, nor did the institution of slavery violate the terms of the prewar Constitution. This is because the Constitution explicitly recognized slavery, e.g., Art. I sec. 2. In addition, the federal government's role was explicitly limited, by Art. I sec. 8, to certain enumerated functions. These do not include preventing injustices committed by the states or private individuals. One might argue that the federal government had a special relationship to all of its citizens based on whatever justification warrants the federal government's authority and that this special relationship gave rise to the duty in question. This does not follow however if the government's authority is limited to a specific list of enumerated powers and this structure precludes action designed to satisfy the alleged duty.

A Distribution of the Debt Among Citizens

Even if we think that the federal government owes compensation, Schedler is mistaken in his notion that certain citizens owe less than others on the basis of this lineage. In the absence of a contractual condition to the contrary, a person's consent to be an equal member in a partnership includes a commitment to bear an equal share of the partnership's benefits and burdens. This is true regardless of the responsibility that certain members have for the partnership's debts. Postwar immigrants have consented to be equal partners in this country and have not, as best I can determine, placed a condition on becoming partners. Hence, contrary to Schedler, all citizens should owe an equal share. This includes the families of recent immigrants and the descendants of slaves.

Conclusion

George Schedler raises interesting issues with regard to the amount of reparations owed for slavery, the parties who are owed reparations, and the standard for these reparations. His arguments, however, do not hold up upon analysis. His rejection of the free worker standard to account for the harm caused via forced labor fails because it rejects the notion that such labor is a separate harm and because it fails to recognize the way in which baselines must be chosen so as to identify the token harms. His analysis of the case for the descendants of slaves being owed compensation seriously overestimates the case for such reparations. He does not identify the grounds for such compensation, i.e., either stolen inheritance or the descendants' trustee-like control over the slave's estate, and this results in his not identifying the metaphysical and epistemic problems that accompany the descendants' claim to reparations. In analyzing whether the U.S. government owes compensation, Schedler provides arguments based on its small role in bringing about slavery and the break in national identity that followed the Civil War. Such arguments fail but his conclusion can be supported by other arguments, specifically the nature of the federal government's relation to slavery and the limited nature of its powers. Thus, the case against reparations is overwhelming but not for the reasons Schedler provides.[18]

NOTES

1. Robert K. Fullinwider, *The Case for Reparations*. Report of the Institute for Philosophy and Public Policy. Maryland: Maryland School of Public Affairs, Institute for Philosophy and Public Policy, 2000.

2. *Sources*: Randall Robinson, *The Debt: What America Owes to Blacks* (Dutton 1999); Randall Robinson, "America's Debt to Blacks," *The Nation*, vol. 270 (March 13, 2000); Black Manifesto appears as appendix to Boris Bittker, *The Case for Black Reparations* (Random House, 1973); Henry Hyde quoted from Kevin Merida, "Did Freedom Alone Pay a Nation's Debt? Rep. John Conyers Jr. Has a Question. He's Willing to Wait a Long Time for the Answer," *The Washington Post* (November 23, 1999); see also the letter-to-the-editor from Juanita Adams, *The Washington Post* (November 29, 1999); Rhonda V. Magee, "The Master's Tools, From the Bottom Up: Responses to African-American Reparations Theory in Mainstream and Outsider Remedies Discourse," *Virginia Law Review*, vol. 79 (May 1993); Mari J. Matsuda, "Looking to the Bottom: Critical Legal Studies and Reparations," *Harvard Civil Rights—Civil Liberties Law Review*, vol. 22 (Spring 1987); Vincene Verdun, "If the Shoe Fits, Wear It: An Analysis of Reparations to African Americans," *Tulane Law Review*, vol. 67 (February 1993). A large literature exists on the question of the economic benefits of slavery; a classic work is Eric Williams, *Capitalism and Slavery* (University of North Carolina Press, 1944). See also Alfred H. Conrad and John R. Meyer, *The Economics of Slavery and Other Studies in Econometric History* (Aldine Publishing Co., 1964); Hugh G. J. Aitken, ed., *Did Slavery Pay? Readings in the Economics of Black Slavery in the United States* (Houghton Mifflin, 1971); Robert W. Fogel and Stanley L. Engerman, *Time on the Cross: The Economics of American Negro Slavery* (Little Brown, 1974); Herbert G. Gutman, *Slavery and the Numbers Game: A Critique of Time on the Cross* (University of Illinois Press, 1975); Paul A. David, et al., *Reckoning with Slavery: A Critical Study in the Quantitative History of American Negro Slavery* (Oxford University Press, 1976); Elizabeth Fox-Genovese and Eugene D. Genovese, *Fruits of Merchant Capital: Slavery and Bourgeois Property in the Rise and Expansion of Capitalism* (Oxford University Press, 1983); James Oakes, *Slavery and Freedom: An Interpretation of the Old South* (Alfred A. Knopf, 1990). Concerning whether the Civil War "paid" for slavery, see, for example, letter-to-the-editor by Joseph Lucas, *The Washington Post* (November 29, 1999); also Robert S. McElvaine, "They Didn't March to Free the Slaves," in Roy L. Brooks, ed., *When Sorry Isn't Enough: The Controversy Over Apologies and Reparations for Human Injustice* (New York University Press, 1999), and in that same volume Thomas Geoghegan, "Lincoln Apologizes," and Mary E. Smith, "Clinton and Conservatives Oppose Slavery Reparations." Jonathan Yardley quoted from "Reparations: It's Too Late," *The Washington*

Post (November 29, 1999). Information about black progress and wealth comes from Stephen Thernstrom and Abigail Thernstrom, *America in Black and White: One Nation, Indivisible* (Simon & Schuster, 1997); William Spriggs, ed., *The State of Black America 1999* (National Urban League, 1999); Dalton Conley, *Being Black, Living in the Red: Race, Wealth, and Social Policy in America* (University of California Press, 1999). Derrick Bell quote from "Dissection of a Dream," *Harvard Civil Rights—Civil Liberties Law Review*, vol. 9 (January 1974). For an idea of reparations similar to mine, see Robert Westley, "Many Billions Gone: Is It Time to Reconsider the Case for Black Reparations?" *Boston College Law Review*, vol. 40 (December 1998), which proposes the establishment of a private trust through which reparations would be paid to "any project or pursuit aimed at the educational and economic empowerment of the trust beneficiaries to be determined on the basis of need."

3. Stephen Kershnar, "The Case against Reparations," *Philosophy in the Contemporary World* 8 (1): 41–46.

4. Steven Kershnar teaches in the Department of Philosophy at SUNY.

5. George Schedler, *Racist Symbols and Reparations* (Lanham, Md.: Rowman & Littlefield, 1999), chaps. 7 and 8.

6. A baseline world is a thought experiment whereby we try to imagine what the world would be like if the victimizing act did not occur. By comparing the victim's well-being in this imaginary world to the actual world, we assess the amount of harm she incurred, which then is used to determine the amount of compensation she is owed. Generally, this amount of compensation is the amount of money that would have to be paid to her before the victimization in order to make her indifferent to whether she is victimized and compensated or not victimized and uncompensated. The idea is that compensation should put her in a position at least as good as if she were not victimized at all.

7. I owe this objection to Michael Levin.

8. Stephen Kershnar provides an in-depth discussion of these two models in "Are the Descendants of Slaves Owed Compensation for Slavery?" *Journal of Applied Philosophy* 16 (199): 95–101. The inheritance model can also be found in Bernard R. Boxill, "The Morality of Reparation, in *The Affirmative Action Debate*, ed. Steven M. Cahn (New York: Routledge, 1995), 107–14.

9. Richard J. Herrnstein and Charles Murray argue for the existence of such differences in *The Bell Curve* (New York: The Free Press, 1994), chap. 13.

10. An extended defense of this claim is provided in Thomas Sowell, *Civil Rights: Rhetoric or Reality?* (New York: Quill, 1984).

11. U.S. Department of Commerce, *Statistical Abstract of the United States 2000* (Washington, D.C.: Government Printing Office, 2001), 70.

12. N. A. Wiener. and M. E. Wolfgang, "The Extent and Character of Violent Crime in America, 1969 to 1982," in *Violence*, ed. Neil Alan Weiner et al. (New York: Harcourt Brace Jovanovich, 1990), 32.

13. For example, a classic efficiency-based defense of property rights can be found in Harold Desetz, "Toward a Theory of Property Rights," *American Economic Review*. Proceedings and Papers 57 (1967): 347–59. A desert-based defense of income earned via sacrifice can be found in Joel Feinberg, *Doing and Deserving* (Princeton,

N.J.: Princeton University Press, 1970), 89–94, and a general defense of desert to the object of one's hard work found in George Sher, *Desert* (Princeton: Princeton University Press, 1987), chap. 4.

14. Here I am not committing myself to the stronger claim that compensatory justice allows a debt of compensation to be discharged by a person other than the one that caused the harm. Such a view is defended in Jules Coleman, "Corrective Justice and Wrongful Gain," *Journal of Legal Studies* 11 (1982): 421–40.

15. It should be noted that Schedler is making this argument in the context of a discussion of the free worker standard for compensation.

16. Michael Levin, "Responses to Race Differences in Crime," *Journal of Social Philosophy* 23 (1991): citing "The Black-on-Black Crime Plague," *U.S. News & World Report*, August 22, 1988, p. 54.

17. Michael Levin, *Why Race Matters* (Westport, Conn.: Praeger, 1997), 259. I suspect that Levin underestimates the degree of the transfer since he underestimates the progressivity of the income tax, but I will leave aside such an argument as it is irrelevant in this context.

18. I would like to thank Michael Levin, James Sauer, and George Schedler for their helpful comments and criticisms.

IV

UNDERLYING QUESTIONS OF
RESPONSIBILITY AND ENTITLEMENT

This part, "Underlying Questions of Responsibility and Entitlement," is addressed to questions about *the extension of responsibility*. The first chapter, on collective responsibility, deals with the question of whether and under what conditions responsibilities for bad acts can be extended to persons other than those who originally committed them. The second chapter, on historical responsibility, has to do with that sort of extension of responsibility across large expanses of time, with many intervening events and generations.

In the context of reparations, these questions become paramount. There are no living slaveholders, government officials who enacted or enforced slavery, soldiers who fought against emancipation, nor are there slaves and their children. Who, if anyone, is it who remains responsible? Who, if anyone, is it who deserves recompense? Why?

There is even a controversy over whether there is a controversy about collective responsibility. Here is Gregory Mellema, a philosopher from Calvin College, from the introduction to his book on collective responsibility.[1]

One morning in March 1993, Dr. David Gunn died about two hours after being shot three times in the back by an antiabortion protester named Michael Griffin. Dr. Gunn regularly performed abortions at seven clinics in Florida, Georgia, and Alabama, and was well-known to antiabortion groups. He was shot in the parking lot of an abortion clinic in Pensacola, Florida as he was arriving for work.

Following this incident was a great deal of talk about responsibility: the responsibility of Griffin for killing Dr. Gunn, the responsibility of abortion protesters for the effects of their actions, and the responsibility of Dr. Gunn for taking the lives of unborn victims. But one claim about responsibility was sweeping in breadth. In the wake of this incident, a reporter for National Public

Radio claimed that all Americans are collectively responsible for not doing more to counteract the violence at abortion clinics. Not only were the people immediately involved in the incident responsible for what happened, and not only are antiabortion groups responsible for the harmful effects of their protests, but all Americans are collectively responsible for failing to do more to prevent these harmful effects.

Claims such as this are common in the media and in ordinary conversation. We commonly hear people claim that various groups are collectively responsible for what has happened, and the groups claimed to be responsible are commonly vast in number. To hear someone say that all Americans are collectively responsible for some harmful situation such as the size of the national deficit or the failure to deal with the problem of homelessness is so commonplace as to attract little attention . . .

[C]laims of this type are seldom challenged. By all appearances people seem to believe that they are true. People are willing to grant that they are part of a vast collective responsible for this or that problem. . . .

The equanimity with which these claims are received by most people is ironic. For twentieth-century Western culture is often characterized as thinking in individualistic terms. People in contemporary Western culture think in terms of individual rights, individual liberties, and, presumably, individual responsibilities. According to this characterization of contemporary Western culture, the individual bears moral responsibility for what he or she has done. Moral responsibility is a personal, individual matter, and we should never be expected to bear responsibility for the wrongdoings of another (unless we have agreed to do so voluntarily, as when we take responsibility for the actions of our child, our subordinate, or our senile parent). Moral responsibility is not something which can somehow spread spontaneously through a whole group of people; it is confined to each individual exactly in proportion to what the individual has done or failed to do.

One of the ways in which contemporary Western culture is often contrasted with "primitive cultures" is in the manner in which moral responsibility is conceived. People in some primitive cultures supposedly think in terms of entire tribes bearing responsibility for the violation of mores or breaking of taboos by one member of the tribe. This collective way of thinking about moral responsibility is based upon the idea of the guilt of one individual being transmitted to all members of a clan or tribe and is quite foreign to contemporary Western ways of thinking about moral responsibility. . . . People sometimes argue that collective conceptions of moral responsibility are associated with primitive or even superstitious approaches to morality and have no place in contemporary Western approaches to morality. They credit Western morality that it has managed to overcome these supposedly primitive and superstitious notions by thinking of responsibility in strictly individualist terms.

Given the highly individualistic conception of moral responsibility which supposedly characterizes contemporary Western culture, the fact that ascriptions of collective responsibility are made as commonly as they are and challenged as little as they are is quite ironic. . . .

Professor Melema may be right that in some circles, say, on National Public Radio, there is a certain level of comfort with ideas like collective responsibility, but as the intense debate about reparations itself makes clear, there is an equally vocal opposition to this notion. In general, the intuition is that the closer the liability for wrongdoing comes, the more ready are people to challenge the whole idea of collective responsibility. This is not to say that all who reject the idea of collective responsibility do so out of personal interest—to protect themselves from any liability for restitution of some kind. It is simply to point out that there is indeed a controversy here and it would be odd if there were not.

The first article about collective responsibility is written by Nicholas Rescher. Rescher is University Professor of Philosophy at the University of Pittsburgh. He has held visiting lectureships at Oxford, Constance, Salamanca, Munich, and Marburg. Professor Rescher is the author of some hundred books ranging over many areas of philosophy.

Professor Rescher divides the question of the validity of collective responsibility into a variety of sub-questions and examines each carefully. He concludes that there are occasions on which responsibility for a group's action can rightly be laid upon the shoulders of individual members, but only under certain conditions. Individuals become individually responsible when the group's acts are the result of a certain kind of coordination among the group members' intentions, for example, when individuals sign on individually for a particular course of action or when they voluntarily delegate authority to act for the group to some agent of the group.

Samuel Scheffler, author of the second essay, "Rights and Responsibilities," received his Ph.D. from Princeton. He holds the Class of 1941 World War II Memorial Chair in the philosophy department of the University of California at Berkeley. Since 1997 he has divided his time evenly between the philosophy department and the Jurisprudence and Social Policy Program of the law school.

Professor Scheffler argues that sometimes we have a responsibility to others not because of any interaction with them—not via what was *done*—but just because of the nature of the relationship in which we stand to them, i.e., because of the groups to which we and they belong and the degree to which we value these groups. Relationships, Professor Scheffler says, may generate responsibilities even without voluntary acts or consent. Scheffler's position thus seems to imply that the coordination of intentions, as discussed by Rescher, is not required for the development of responsibility. Scheffler argues that when we value relationships these may carry special obligations with or without voluntary acts binding us in. More precisely, we cannot be said to value a relationship in itself without "seeing it as a source of special responsibilities."

Four articles are next offered that tackle in various ways the question of responsibilities that persist over considerable periods of time, what some call
cross- or multi-generational responsibilities.

In "Ancient Wrongs and Modern Rights," George Sher, Herbert S. Autrey
Professor of Philosophy and department chair at Rice University, asks
whether it makes sense to say that people are owed compensation for the
effects of wrongs done not merely before they were born, but generations
before that. Sher's view is that claims to compensation tend to fade over time.
Given that the weight of claims diminishes over time, achieving a just distribution in society is better served by attending to recent events rather than "ancient" ones.

Jeremy Waldron was admitted as barrister and solicitor of the Supreme
Court of New Zealand, 1978, and received his D.Phil. in philosophy at
Oxford University in 1986. Waldron is the Maurice & Hilda Friedman Pro-
fessor in the school of law of Columbia University.

"Superseding Historical Injustices" examines the question of what response to historic injustice is morally incumbent upon us. He has his eye on
the seizure of lands from indigenous persons by white settlers in North America and Australasia. As Waldron sees the question, arguments calling for compensation are typically based on attempts to estimate what the current situation of these indigenous people would have been had the seizures not
occurred. He concludes that such an estimate cannot be done successfully for
various reasons and that, moreover, in the interval between the original injustice and the present, other, competing, valid claims have arisen. Like Sher,
he is inclined to say that the most serious consideration is the fair distribution
of current resources among present inhabitants, not the question of how
things have gotten to the pass they have.

The last two essays of this chapter are both by Janna Thompson. Thompson, B. Phil. Oxford, is deputy director of the Australian Research Council
Special Research Centre for Applied Philosophy and Public Ethics and
teaches in the philosophy department of La Trobe University. She is the author of a recent study, *Taking Responsibility for the Past: Reparation and Historical Justice*,[2] which represents her reworking and synthesis of the themes
of earlier papers, including the two presented here.

Thompson defines an historical obligation as "a moral responsibility belonging to citizens of a state, or members of some other intergenerational
group, in respect to commitments made, deeds done by their predecessors."
In "Historical Obligations," she says that most accounts of collective responsibility fail to account for these obligations. Thompson argues that citizens do
incur historical obligations. Illustrations in support of this view are drawn
from claims made by indigenous peoples for reparations for injustices done
to them years ago.

In "Historical Injustices and Reparations: Justifying Claims of Descendants," Thompson examines the moral circumstances of claims by descendants of victims of injustices, noting that they are sometimes problematic because the individuals now pressing their claim for restitution are not the persons to whom the injustices were originally done. These claims nonetheless can be justified, she thinks, via the family relationships they bear with the original victims. The perspectives of "heads of families" she argues are among those that must be considered in any comprehensive theory of justice. From this perspective, inheritance and maintenance of family heritage are compelling concerns, not withstanding serious and well-founded worries we might have about the unfairness of the cumulative effects of bequests that privilege subsequent generations by improving their opportunities in comparison with others who do not inherit sizable estates.

Among the lines of thought Thompson develops are two particularly interesting ones that have important implications for questions about reparations. First, she develops the idea that moral seriousness involves the desire that our moral commitments be honored in the future even after our deaths. The second idea is that fairness requires that our binding future generations to commitments that we make—an indispensable condition for civic life and government—means that we must accept the moral obligations that are generated by our predecessors.

NOTES

1. Gregory Mellema, *Collective Responsibility* (New York: Rodopi, 1997). Online at www.calvin.edu/academic/philosophy/writings/crintro.htm (accessed September 2, 2003).

2. Janna Thompson, *Taking Responsibility for the Past: Reparation and Historical Justice* (Cambridge: Polity Press).

9

Collective Responsibility: Am I Responsible for the Misdeeds of Others?

Nicholas Rescher: "Collective Responsibility"[1]

The Issue

Is the U.S. military at large to blame for the massacre at My Lai? Do Americans in general deserve reproach for the plight of the country's Indian reservations? Whom can one fault for the decline of civility in America's cities or the slippage of mathematical competence in its high schools? It is problems of this sort that are at issue in the present deliberations, whose focal questions are as follows: What is involved in a group's being responsible for producing a collective result? What conditions must be satisfied for it to be appropriate for us to praise or blame a group for some result of its doings?

In addressing this problem the natural step is to begin by basing our understanding of group responsibility upon that of individual responsibility. Now here, at the level of individuals, responsibility for a result is clearly a matter of *producing the result through one's own deliberate agency*—barring the intrusion of defeating aberrations such, for example, as duress or deceit. For responsibility to enter in, it is not enough that that untoward result be *produced*, as the causal result of an individual's actions, it must also be *intended* in some appropriate fashion. Carrying this idea over to groups, one thus needs to address two pivotal issues: group agency and group intention. Unfortunately, neither is anything like as simple and straightforward as one might wish.

Problems of Group Agency

The "responsibility" at the focus of the present discussion will be of the sort that opens the door to evaluative and normative appraisals, so that praise and blame will be pivotal considerations.[2] The merely causal "responsibility" of productive contribution is of course neutral in this regard, a merely necessary but not sufficient condition. For authentic responsibility some element of intentionality must always attend to causal participation—the factor of *productive intentionality* is crucial.

All the same, causal or productive involvement is an important part of the picture. And as regards causality, the first thing to note is that a group can bring it about that a certain result obtains without any member of that group having any significant or substantial contributory relationship to the production of that result as such. Thus if every dweller in a town adores his neighbor's cats and hates his dogs, they can collectively produce the result that all the town's cats are loved and all its dogs hated, even though this may occur in such a way that no one ever desires—or even contemplates—this result. And the same sort of thing happens if every driver happens to be out on the road and a traffic jam results. Moreover, in such a case no one contributes more than a minute share to the result, and sometimes, interestingly, the smaller the individual shares—the more people on the road, say—the worse the result. Such situations are legion; groups regularly manage to produce results with which, as such, their members have little or nothing to do.

The fact is that when a group collectively produces a certain result, none of its individual agents need do anything that bears significantly on that result as such. Indeed, often this result is something the individuals could not facilitate if they wanted to—which they well may not. Consider "The affidavits made by Tom and Jerry created a conflict of testimony." Clearly neither agent—acting on his own—did anything that was in and of itself conflict-engendering. Again, suppose that a hardware store carries ten hammers and that ten customers come along and buy them. Among them they have "exhausted the store's supply of hammers." But of course nothing of this sort figures in any of *their* thoughts or actions. In all such cases it makes no visible difference *as far as the individual agent is concerned* whether that contributory act obtains in isolation or in an unwitting, merely fortuitous concert with other agents for the production of an untoward aggregate results. The inherent status of contributing individuals' doings are clearly not affected one way or the other by the essentially accidental circumstances of context. And even should it eventuate that the collectivity is a disaster, the fact remains that the individual's act may well be perfectly innocuous absent any or all personal foresight and understanding in relation to the aggregate end-product. Neither in production nor in contemplation need a group's individual members play a significant role in such cases.

The circumstance that an individual's act constitutes a contributing part certain overall result represents a feature of that act all right—but a contextual feature of it. And this context is in general something over which the individual in question has no control nor even significantly productive influence. (Think, for example, of the "wave" created by spectators at a sporting event, where each individual simply stands up and raises his or her arms—or, even more drastically, think of what happens when a foreign expression enters a language as a "loan word.") Moreover, the contributory aspect of the action may well lie entirely outside the individual's awareness. (That individual's contribution to the wave may simply be an aping of his neighbor in a mere social conformity.)

Problems of Group Intentions

Suppose that someone comes across a nearly unconscious sufferer on a country lane. After providing an effective but rather slow-acting medical remedy, he goes off to get further assistance. Then another person comes and does exactly the same. But these remedial doses, though individually helpful and appropriate, nevertheless create a jointly fatal overdose. The two people acting together have, in effect caused the sufferer's demise by their well-intentioned actions. And this is the polar opposite of what they intended or expected. This "Good Samaritan" mishap illustrates the sort of thing that can—and often does—happen with interactively produced results, where product and intention can readily diverge.

For intention and responsibility, then, distributive activities that collectively engender a result by way of causal production are clearly not enough. Overt purposiveness in relation to this result must be added. Suppose that X wants p, Y wants q, and that they act accordingly. Joined together the group X-and-Y wants p-and-q. Yet neither X nor Y may want this outcome or anything like it. (Indeed, wanting it may be senseless, as when q happens to be not-p.) Accordingly, the overall upshot may well be something seen by both as eminently undesirable, as when X wants to kill Y, and Y to kill X. With groups of agents, the separate intentions of individuals cannot simply be combined. Here wholes that have features which, as far as intentionality is concerned, are nowise mere sums of the parts.

Group responsibility clearly calls for coordination and depends on the extent to which the group acts as a unit within which the actions of individuals are concerted. With the product of a merely fortuitous confluence of individual actions (e.g., a bank run), group responsibility is, clearly, out of the picture. The element of collaborative coordination—a "conspiracy" so to speak, in producing the result—is an indispensable requisite. The difference between acting as a coordinated group and acting as only a collection of disjoint and disaggregated individuals is crucial here.

With group responsibility, as with individual responsibility, this factor of intention is critical. The weaker the element of intentionality, the weaker that of responsibility. Thus consider the series

- active and deliberate participation in the production of a result
- passive agreement in its production
- detached spectatorship
- reluctant acquiescence (going along).

Responsibility clearly fades away as we move down the line here. The closer the "degree of association" of the individual with the production of a collective result, the greater the responsibility (and the greater the extent of blame or credit).

From the causal point of view, individual contributions appear to sum up productively. The individual agents make their causal contributions to the whole, and the whole consists of the sum of the parts—causally speaking. But intentions certainly do not work this way. Groups regularly bring things about that none of their members plan, intend, or indeed even ever envision. Every cowboy just wants to kill his few buffalo—no one contemplates extermination of the species. There is no way to sum up individual intentions to underwrite the imputation of an aggregate intention vis à vis the overall result. The denizens of the city of London rebuilt their city after the great fire of 1661, and the inhabitants of Charleston, South Carolina did the same after the catastrophic destruction wrought by Hurricane Hugo in 1991. Collectively they accomplished the task, but distributively each property owner simply addressed the problems of his or her own situation. Among those who were active in the rebuilding, virtually no one had any intentions in regard to the bigger object—the intentions of each were for the most part focused on the particular micro-task at hand. The overall macroachievement lay outside the reach of anyone's intention. A group's interactively produced macro-results are all too frequently uncontemplated, unforeseen, unplanned, and even undesired by many, most, or even all of that group's individual members.

And so, while the responsibility or intention of groups must indeed derive from and inhere in that of its constituent individuals, it will actually do so only in special circumstances. The coordinative factor of an at least vicarious consent must be there: absent individual participation (of an at least statistical, majoritarian sort), there must at least be centralization through representation. The fact of the matter is that without an appropriate coordination of individual intentions it makes no sense to impute intention to a group.

It makes sense to say that a collectivity wants or intends something only when we have either

- *consensual subscription:* when the macro-objective at issue is something that the generality or the substantial majority of group members want *as such*, thus rendering it into an object of the collective *volonté générale, so* to speak.
  or
- *representative endorsement:* when the duly delegated representatives of the group's members duly agree to producing the result in question.

To be sure, distributive coincidence is not sufficient to yield the sort of intent at issue. The element of collectivity must be present. And there must be the right sort of coordination. The members of a board may distributively happen to be of one mind in all wanting the chairman dead, but this does not mean that the one who goes and shoots him is implementing a group consensus. Their "wanting him dead" does not come to "wanting him killed" let alone "wanting him killed by *X.*" Here those who have remained have certainly not "agreed" to the murder simply in view of their (perhaps reprehensible) attitude. The members may "want him dead" but not agree to his being rendered so by the sort of action at issue. For responsibility the group must constitute something of a "moral person" with a collective unity of mind.

And the conjunctivity at issue means that whenever group responsibility does in fact exist, there must be responsible individuals: group responsibility cannot exist without individual responsibility And this need for a proper grounding in the responsibility of individuals means that it cannot happen that a group does something wrong without there being culpable individuals at whose door some of the blame can be laid. (Note: that it is crucial for the tenability of this statement that it reads "something *wrong*" and not merely "something *bad.*") Group responsibility must have a rooting in the responsibilities of individuals and cannot manage to exist without this.

All the same, collective responsibility is just exactly that—collective. It emphatically does *not* function distributively—it cannot automatically be projected upon the individuals who constitute that collectivity. We can indeed reason from "Tom, Dick, and Harry talked about mathematics" to "Tom and Dick talked about mathematics." But we can no more reason from "Tom, Dick, and Harry carried the piano upstairs" to "Tom and Dick carried the piano upstairs" than we can reason from "Tom Dick, and Harry filled up the sofa" to "Tom and Dick filled up the sofa." Only in very special cases will the doings of collectivities project down to their component units.[3]

Consequences for Collective Responsibility

With these considerations about causation and consent in mind, we can profitably return to our initial question. When the individual actions of diverse agents collectively issue in an overall result, there is, by hypothesis, a collective causality in point of productivity. But does moral responsibility follow from this? Is there also automatically room for guilt and credit, praise and blame, laudation and reprehension?

Given the aforementioned complexities of collective intentionability, the answer is clearly a negative here. For this reason, it would be folly to argue: The individually intentional actions of the members of a group produced a certain result, hence the members of the group are individually responsible for that result. Exactly as in the accidental overdosing case considered above, no single agent in a group whose acts are conjointly disastrous need do anything wrong or blameworthy.

Without the requisite coordination of individual intentions through consensus or delegative authorization it makes no sense to speak of group intentions. So-called guilt by association—by merely being a member of a group that collectively produces a bad result—is just not enough to establish a valid imputation of responsibility. In a bank run every depositor just wants his own money from the bank—no one foresees or intends the ruin and bankruptcy that ensues.

But who is responsible—"everybody and nobody"—and so in the final analysis no one. Except in special conditions and circumstances—when the proper sort of coordination obtains—the intentions of individuals simply do not aggregate into some sort of group product: they do not somehow blend together into a group intention. And where intention is absent, there too responsibility is missing. When a group produces an unintended disaster, the situation as regards culpability is exactly the same as when an individual produces a wholly unintentional disaster—to wit there simply *is no culpability*. Without a normative response that transcends mere causality, there can be no actual guilt. When this sort of thing happens, we can regret but cannot reproach.

The pivotal fact in this connection is that responsibility for the collective transgressions of groups can be projected down upon its component individuals only in special conditions. For only where group malfeasance indeed roots in the informed consent of individuals through coordination or delegation can those individuals be held to blame. And even then only subject to limits. For to be culpable, individuals must form part of that consensus and be party to its consent. The defenses "I was opposed to it" and "I cast my vote against it" must be allowed their due weight in matters of individual exculpation.

Escaping group responsibility by dissociation is thus possible through the spectrum from explicit abstention to actual opposition. The ideological impetus of the ethically inspired resisters to Nazism is a case in point. Their actual efforts were futile and unavailing (perhaps often even incompetent). But symbolically they are of the greatest significance in providing a highly visible token of the fact that the German people in general did not go along here, so that the moral properties require an explicit line to be maintained between Germans and Nazis.

On the other hand, however, individuals can indeed be held responsible for group actions even if in a strict sense they "didn't have anything to do" with the malfeasance at issue. For when their intentionability is betokened by way of consent or consensus, then those evil acts which its agents (few though they be) actually perform on behalf and under the consensual aegis of the wider group will also fall into the responsibility sphere of its individual members. Association is not enough to establish responsibility, but the sort of association involved in being an "accessory" of sorts—be it consensual or delegative—can prove sufficient. And even tacit consent can do so. The acquiescing citizenry is indeed responsible for the authorized actions of its duly delegated agents.

The Legal Aspect: Moral vs. Legal Responsibility

A thorny question now arises. If an appropriately structured coordinative basis in individual responsibility is indeed required for the moral responsibility of a group, then what of collectively produced outrages that are uncoordinated?

Two contrasting positions are possible here. At the one pole there is the "Protestant" position that individuals are the prime (perhaps even the sole!) bearers of responsibility. The position is that agents stand on their own feet in matters of evaluation appraisal. And so, when a group produces a collective result, then its individual agents are responsible ONLY for their own individual acts—and so only for their free and intended individual contributions. They are responsible for and creditable with only those negativities and positivities that they themselves engender through their own suitably deliberate actions. Contextual considerations can be dismissed from the moral point of view. In practical effect we can simply forget about group responsibility as a distinct issue: moral deliberation can be limited to the domain of individuals; group evaluations are at most statistical summaries.

At the other pole is the "Hebraic" position that the community is the prime (perhaps even the sole!) bearer of responsibility for collectively produced results—that what the group collectively does can and must be laid unavoidably at its collective door of responsibility (To be sure, whether this collective responsibility can then be downloaded upon the constituent individual of the community still remains as an additional and potentially controversial question, but the responsibility of the community-as-a-whole remains in any event—irrespective of how we answer this additional question.) In effect, the group is thus treated as a responsible individual in its own right in a way that is essentially independent of the responsibilities of its members. Groups are morally autonomous: they stand on a collective footing—the idea is simply rejected that the responsible actions of groups must inhere in or derive from its individual members.

We thus come to the question: As regards specifically moral responsibility which is the right line to take here: the "Protestant" or the "Hebraic"? At this point the question of law vs. ethics comes to the fore.

To start with, it deserves to be noted that in actual practice we generally allow legality and morality to go separate ways. And we do so for very practical reasons. Some examples will help to make this point.

Strictly speaking, the person who drives home drunk after the office party and has the good luck not to have an accident that injures others is in exactly the same moral position as the person who fails to be so lucky.[4] But legally there is all the difference in the world here: legally the one is (so we suppose) guilty while the other is altogether guilt-free. Here the legal standing of the two is thus very different. The law is concerned with actual results in a way that morality is not. Again, military law holds the commander responsible for mishaps for which there may well be no actual causal responsibility at the personal level. So here there will be situations where one will be morally innocent but legally culpable. And again, in group punishment situations, one charges the "innocent" members of the group with an onus of responsibility that has no moral basis. Here too the law can reflect the society's pragmatic care for results in a way that bypasses moral complications.

The fact is that the law is part of a system of social contract that has other fish to fry than that of fixing moral culpability, and in consequence it often insists on beneficial overall results at the expense of strict justice. The pivotal point is that legal and administrative systems embody a concern for certain social desiderata distinct from strict justice per se. This circumstance makes for a crucial difference between moral and legal responsibility.[5]

From the moral point of view the proper line will have to be that the source and basis of responsibility is always with individuals. Thus moral responsibility belongs to groups only insofar as the individuals are suitably active within them. Groups can only bear responsibility derivatively—either by way of aggregation (consensus) or by way of delegation (via representation). And moral responsibility is in a way inalienable. It remains with those causally contributing individuals even when they transmit it to the group with which they act. But with *legal* responsibility, the situation is different. Groups can be *legal* persons and thus bear legal responsibility. For legal responsibility is alienable and capable of transfer and delegation. Forming a corporation (or "legal person") or imposing a collective sanction on a criminal group or a destructive society makes perfectly good sense.

In this contrast between moral and legal responsibility we thus find a reflection of the contrast between the aforementioned "Protestant" and "Hebraic" positions on responsibility. And as far as moral wrongdoing is concerned, the "Protestant" position is surely plausible: the moral culpability of groups must inhere in that of their individuals—with the result that there can be collective acts that are unfortunate and regrettable, but yet not wrong, owing to the absence of any personal wrongdoing.

Some Lessons

An instructive lesson emerges from these deliberations. If as was insisted above (i) the only avenue to group responsibility/reprehension is indeed via group intention, and moreover (ii) group intention requires coordination—either through an aggregation afforded by consensus or through a centralized delegation to representative deciders—then it follows that (iii) there will unavoidably be many instances where group-engendered outrages will "fall between the stools" as far as responsibility and reprehension goes. And this means that there will thus be group-engendered catastrophes responsibility for which admits of no specific allocation to individuals, since it is a "merely fortuitous confluence of individual actions" that does the mischief.

Who, then, can be held responsible for the carnage on America's roads, the poor performance of its schools, the decay of its social conscience and its public civility? Clearly only those who bear some sort of immediate responsibility. Reproaching the group-as-a-whole makes no sense here, seeing that the requisite element of interpersonal coordination is lacking. Such aggregate negativities are the confluence of the uncoordinated and disjointed actions of innumerable individuals. They result from the causal contributions of many but the intentionality of none. And this lack of intentionality precludes the availability of actual culprits.[6]

Those aggregate effects which come to be realized through the vicissitudes of context lying beyond the ken and control of the individuals involved have to be viewed as "accidents of circumstance" with respect to which the chain of moral responsibility is severed en route to a causal result. As the case of the "Good

Samaritan" overdose illustrates, those terrible overall results have come about through the intentional doings of individuals all right, but there is nothing intentional about them *as such*. The only relevant intentions were fragmentary and disjointed—and so for this very reason were the responsibilities of individuals. That overall catastrophe was never envisioned—let alone intended—by anybody. The responsible actions of people produce disaster, all right, but a disaster which is detached from the responsibility of individuals (in any sense over and above the causal).

Thus the perhaps unwelcome fact of the matter is that individually the actions of people can still be blameless—and perhaps praiseworthy—even in cases where the collective, combined result of their actions is a disaster. (The destabilizing rush of people to the side of the boat from which a cry of "save me" emanates is perhaps something of an example.) When such aggregated mishaps occur as a causal result of people's unconcerted actions, there is nothing that those disaggregated individuals can be held culpable for. There is no occasion for blame allocation: here collective actions can engender aggregate outrages that are entirely culprit-free as far as individual agents are concerned. The prospect of a lack of any suitable basis for attributing a communal intent means that the action of groups can sometimes produce terrible results for which there is neither collective responsibility nor individual fault.

What we have here is a fact of life that moral philosophy and common sense alike simply have to take in stride. For in this regard, group causation is like nature causation—the group in effect acts like an unmanageable natural force rather than a voluntary personal agent. There is no sense in blaming the chair that we stumble over in the dark. When uncooperative nature produces a bad result, there simply is no one who can plausibly be asked to bear the burden of reproach. We regret the result but cannot find someone to blame for it. It's just "one of those #!@?* things" that we have to come to terms with in a difficult world. And much the same thing has to be said when unhappy aggregate effects come about through the disaggregated actions of members of a group. Morally, each individual can, should, and must bear responsibility for his or her own individual acts and intentions. But, to reemphasize, the aggregate effect—however unfortunate—may prove to be just one of those unfortunate things.[7]

This, at least, is how matters stand from the moral point of view. And there is a significant lesson here. Causal and moral responsibility behave very differently in situations of collectivity. By hypothesis, an agent whose intended actions play a contributing part on the side of causal production will thereby and for this very reason bear a share of causal responsibility in relation to the overall product. But of course moral responsibility is not like that, it is not simply a matter of aggregation. For here the whole can be less than the sum of its parts—or more. No causal collective results can exist without individual causal contributions. But collective morally negative or positive results can indeed emerge in situations where individuals make no personal contributions of a morally positive or negative coloration.

But what about group responsibility for faults of omission—for culpable inaction? The pivotal considerations here are a failure to act in the presence of opportunity, when this matter of opportunity pivots on (i) the existence of a suitable *occasion* where action is called for, (ii) an *awareness* that this is so, be it by the group at large or those duly responsible for the conduct of its affairs, and (iii) the availability of the requisite *means* for action. On this basis, the culpable inaction of groups is again something substantially analogous to the situation with regard to individuals. Still, when groups neglect doing something that they (morally speaking) ought to do—that is, to do as a group—can the blame for these omissions be laid at the door of its individuals? The answer is YES-BUT, namely: *but only under special conditions* obtaining when that group neglect is the result of a culpable (or "inexcusable") oversight on the part of individuals. If, as maintained above, it is indeed the case that group responsibility must inhere in individual responsibility and cannot exist without it, then this will also hold insofar as responsibility for omission is concerned. (Q: But just which individuals are responsible for the group's default? A: Exactly those whose intentionality was causally involved. Intentional causation is again the crux—absent the usual array of responsibility deflectors.)

A Review of the Argument

The preceding deliberations, though brief, tell a rather complicated story. It is accordingly useful to pass the overall argument in review:

1. Responsibility presupposes (i) productive agent-causality, and (ii) deliberate intentions.
2. The productive causality of groups can issue from the entirely disconnected and uncoordinated agency of its constituent individuals. There are accordingly two modes of group-productivity: (i) the actually coordinated (ii) the uncoordinated and "accidentally" confluent as it were.
3. For the intentionality of group products there must be a coordinative synthesis of the individuals' intentions. Such coordinative cohesion can take two forms: the informally *consensual* or the formally *representational*. In the former case we have the explicit agreement of (at least most of) the members; in the latter case we have the imputed consent of the members at issue via the mediation of representational institutions.
4. Where the products of group activity are concerned, it only makes sense to speak of group intentions in the case of coordinated productions. Without the synthesis or unification of actions there is no meaningful collective intention.
5. An absence of intentionality means that groups' actions may be disastrous without there being any wrongdoing on the part of individuals.
6. However, group actions cannot be wrong absent individual wrongdoing. For—
7. Intention—and thus responsibility—must initiate with individuals. Groups can achieve such a condition only "by derivation"—that is, via the mechanics of consensuality and/or delegated consent. Accordingly—

8. Group intention/responsibility therefore exists only with coordinated group products produced under conditions of a synthesis of individual intentions via consensus or delegation. Then and only then is it proper to project group responsibility unto its component individuals—and only to the extent that their own intention were causally involved.

Consequences

One significant consequence of these deliberations is that group responsibility can lapse into nothingness where rogue regimes abrogate the normal processes of representative government. The people of Uganda cannot be held responsible for the excesses of Idi Amin's regime, nor the people of the U.S.S.R. for those of Stalin, whose transformations of governmental organism through state terrorism they neither foresaw nor endorsed. On the other hand, the responsibility of Americans for the atomic bombing of Japan in WWII or for the defoliation of crops and the destruction of villages in the Viet Nam war cannot be denied—at any rate not on this basis of flawed intentionality. (But, as noted above, this collective responsibility of the group does not automatically devolve upon its individual members.)

At this point an interesting question arises. For group intentions we have appealed to two coordinative factors: distributive consensus and centralized consent through representational institutions. But what if these two get out of joint with the one pointing in one way and the other in another. What becomes of group responsibility when the group's legally constituted representatives act in the face of a general consensus to the contrary? For example, should one impute to the people of Britain credit for abolishing the death penalty or reprehension for tolerating fox hunting, seeing that Parliament's position on these issues is decidedly out of phase with the opinion polls?

There is—there can be—no simple answer here. What we have is yet another illustration of the fact that conceptual tidiness cannot be secured in a difficult world. In such situations we confront complex questions that require complex answers.

Appendix: Collective Credit

The preceding deliberations have mainly taken into view the negative side of evaluative responsibility in regard to blame and guilt. But of course there is also the positive side of praise and credit. And it is—and should be—reasonably clear that the overall situation here must be regarded as being substantially analogous in this regard.

However, the analogy is not complete. An important and interesting difference arises. When several individuals actively collaborate in doing something bad (say in a murder conspiracy), then each of them is standardly credited with—that is, bears legal and moral blame for—the production of that negative result: each of them is regarded as being "guilty of murder."[8] But when individuals actively collaborate in the production of something good (say in making a scientific discovery or in establishing a museum), then they are credited only with their own particular identifiable contribution. And there is a sound rationale for this. It would seem that the difference in treatment here lies in the practicalities of the matter rather than in purely abstractly theoretical considerations. We systematically seek to *discourage* individual participation in the doing of bad things and to *encourage* the efforts of individuals toward the doing of good. And these desiderata are clearly reflected in the disanalogy at issue.

Let us explore this aspect of the issue a bit further. Anyone who has ever worked on a crossword puzzle with a collaborator realizes that here the whole is greater than the sum of the parts—that the collaboration synergy of two working together is something superior to the mere compilation of their separate achievements. In such collaborative problem-solving situations we encounter the synergetic potentiation of teamwork. The work of one member helps to potentiate that of another. In joining forces the group members pave the way to an entirely new level of achievement. But in such cases to whom does the credit for this advancement—this "collaborative surplus"—belong?

It all depends. There are principally two kinds of teams: those that are leader-directed and/or hierarchical, and those that are purely cooperative and unstructured. In the former case matters of responsibility are once again comparatively straightforward: responsibility and with it credit issues from the top down. But in the latter case there will be some diffusion. When individuals cooperate collectively in the production of something positive, the "surplus" of achievement over and above what individuals accomplish on their own will presumably be allocated [in] proportion with the extent to which they make their individual contributions. Such a principle once again provides for the maximum of reasonable encouragement.

Samuel Scheffler: "Relationships and Responsibilities"[9,10]

How do we come to have responsibilities to some people that we do not have to others? In our everyday lives, many different kinds of considerations are invoked to explain these "special" responsibilities. Often we cite some kind of interaction that we have had with the person to whom we bear the responsibility. Perhaps we made this person a promise, or entered into an agreement with him. Or perhaps we feel indebted to him because of something he once did for us. Or, again, perhaps we once harmed him in some way, and as a result we feel a responsibility to make reparation to him. In all of these cases, there is either something we have done or something the "beneficiary" of the responsibility has done that is cited as the source of that responsibility.

Not all of our explanations take this form, however. Sometimes we account for special responsibilities not by citing any specific interaction between us and the beneficiary, but rather by citing the nature of our relationship to that person. We have special duties to a person, we may say, because she is our sister, or our friend, or our neighbor. Many different types of relationship are invoked in this way. Perhaps the person is not a relative but a colleague, not a friend but a teammate, not a neighbor but a client. Sometimes the relationship may consist only in the fact that we are both members of a certain kind of group. We may belong to the same community, for example, or be citizens of the same country, or be part of the same nation or people. In some of these cases, we may never have met or had any interaction with the person who is seen as the beneficiary of the responsibility. We may nevertheless be convinced that our shared group membership suffices to generate such a responsibility. Of course, claims of special responsibility can be controversial, especially in cases of this kind. While some people feel strongly that they have special responsibilities to the other members of their national or cultural group, for example, other people feel just as strongly that they do not. Nevertheless, it is a familiar fact that such ties are often seen as a source of special responsibilities. Indeed, we would be hard pressed to find any type of human relationship to which people have attached value or significance but which has never been seen as generating such responsibilities. It seems that whenever people value an interpersonal relationship they are apt to see it as a source of special duties or obligations.[11]

However, although it is clear that we do in fact cite our relationships to other people in explaining why we have special responsibilities to them, many philosophers have been reluctant to take these citations at face value. Instead, they have supposed that the responsibilities we perceive as arising out of special relationships actually arise out of discrete interactions that occur in the context of those relationships. Thus, for example, some special responsibilities, like the mutual responsibilities of spouses, may be said to arise out of promises or commitments that the participants have made to each other. Others, like the responsibilities of children to their parents, may be seen as arising from the provision of benefits to one party by the other. And in cases like those mentioned earlier, in which two people are both members of some group but have not themselves interacted in any way, it may be denied that the people do in fact have any special responsibilities to each other. As already noted, claims of special responsibility tend to be controversial in such cases anyway, and it may be thought an advantage of this position that it sees grounds for skepticism precisely in the cases that are most controversial.

Clearly, the view that duties arising out of special relationships can always be reduced to duties arising out of discrete interactions is compatible with the view that the relevant interactions, and hence the relevant duties, may be of fundamentally different kinds. Indeed, to some philosophers it seems clear that the relationships that have been seen as generating special responsibilities are so heterogeneous that the responsibilities in question cannot possibly have but a single ground. Nevertheless, one of the greatest pressures toward a reductionist position has come from those who believe that all genuine special responsibilities must be based on consent or on some other voluntary act. These voluntarists, as we may call them, are not hostile to the idea of special responsibilities as such. However, they reject the notion that one can find oneself with such responsibilities without having done anything at all to incur them. Different voluntarists disagree about the types of voluntary act that are capable of generating special responsibilities. Some insist that such responsibilities can only arise from explicit agreements or undertakings. Others believe that one can incur special responsibilities just by voluntarily entering into a relationship with someone, and that no explicit agreement to bear the responsibilities is required. Still others believe that one's acceptance of the benefits of participation in a relationship can generate responsibilities even if one's entry into the relationship was not itself voluntary. Obviously, then, voluntarists will sometimes disagree among themselves about the specific responsibilities of particular people. And different versions of voluntarism will be more or less revisionist with respect to our ordinary moral beliefs, depending on which types of voluntary act they deem capable of generating special responsibilities. For example, voluntarists who believe that special responsibilities can only be incurred through an explicit undertaking or the voluntary establishment of a relationship may deny that children have such responsibilities to their parents. But those who think that the voluntary acceptance of benefits can also generate special responsibilities may disagree, at least insofar as they think it makes sense to regard children as voluntarily accepting benefits from their parents. What all voluntarists do agree about, however, is that the mere fact that one stands in a certain relationship to another person cannot by itself give one a special responsibility to that person. In order to have such a responsibility, one must have performed some voluntary act that constitutes the ground of the responsibility.

Voluntarists are sensitive to the fact that special responsibilities can be costly and difficult to discharge, and thus quite burdensome for those who bear them. It would be unfair, they believe, if people could be saddled with such burdens against their wills, and so it would be unfair if special responsibilities could be ascribed to people who had done nothing voluntarily to incur them. In effect, then, voluntarists see a form of reductionism about special responsibilities as necessary if our assignments of such responsibilities are to be fair to those who bear them. Voluntarism is an influential view, and many people find the voluntarist objection to unreduced special responsibilities quite congenial. At the same time, however, there is another objection that may also be directed against such responsibilities. According to this objection, the problem with special responsibilities is not that they may be unfairly burdensome for those who bear them, but rather that they may confer unfair advantages on their bearers. And for the purposes of this objection, it does not matter whether the source of those responsibilities is understood voluntaristically or not.

Suppose that you have recently become my friend and that I have therefore acquired special responsibilities to you. Clearly, these responsibilities work to your advantage, inasmuch as I now have a duty to do things for you that I would not previously have been required to do. At the same time, there are at least two different ways in which my responsibilities to you work to the disadvantage of those people with whom I have no special relationship. First, in the absence of my responsibilities to you, I might have done certain things for them even though I had no duty to do so. Now, however, discharging my responsibilities to you must take priority over doing any of those things for them. Second, there may also be situations in which my responsibilities to you take priority over the responsibilities that I have to them simply as human beings. For example, there may be times when I must help you rather than helping them, if I cannot do both, even though I would have been required to help them but for the fact that you too need help. Thus, in both of these ways, my special responsibilities to you may work to the disadvantage of other people. In one respect, moreover, they may also work to my own disadvantage, since, as the voluntarist objection points out, such responsibilities can be quite burdensome. At the same time, however, my responsibilities to you may also confer some very important advantages on me. For, insofar as I am required to give your interests priority over the interests of other people, I am, in effect, called upon to act in ways that will contribute to the flourishing of our friendship rather than attending to the needs of other people. So my responsibilities to you may work to my net advantage as well as to yours, while working to the disadvantage of people with whom I have no special relationship. Furthermore, if you and I have become friends, then, presumably, not only have I acquired special responsibilities to you but you have acquired such responsibilities to me. And, just as my responsibilities to you may work both to your advantage and to mine, while working to the disadvantage of other people, so too your responsibilities to me may work both to my advantage and to yours, while working to the disadvantage of others.

Now the objection that I have in mind challenges this entire way of allocating benefits and burdens, on the ground that it provides you and me with unfair advantages while unfairly disadvantaging other people. Why exactly, this "distributive objection" asks, should our friendship give rise to a distribution of responsibility that is favorable to us and unfavorable to other people? After all, it may be said, the effect of such a distribution is to reward the very people who have already achieved a rewarding personal relationship, while penalizing those who have not. In addition to enjoying the benefits of our friendship itself, in other words, you and I receive increased claims to each other's assistance, while other people, who never received the original benefits, find that their claims to assistance from us have now become weaker.[12] The distributive objection urges that the fairness of this allocation must be judged against the background of the existing distribution of benefits and burdens of all kinds. Providing additional advantages to people who have already benefited from participation in rewarding relationships will be unjustifiable, according to the distributive objection, whenever the provision of these advantages works to the detriment of people who are needier, whether they are needier because they are not themselves participants in rewarding relationships or because they are significantly worse off in other ways. And it makes no difference, so far as this objection is concerned, whether special responsibilities are thought of as voluntarily incurred or not. Either way, the distributive objection insists that unless the benefits and burdens of special responsibilities are integrated into an overall distribution that is fair, such responsibilities will amount to little more than what one writer has called a "pernicious"[13] form of "prejudice in favor of people who stand in some special relation to us."[14]

It may be protested that it is misleading to represent special responsibilities as providing additional rewards to people who have already secured the advantages of participation in a rewarding relationship. Part of what makes a relationship rewarding, it may be said, is that there are special responsibilities associated with it. So any rewards that special responsibilities may confer on the participants in such relationships are inseparable from the other rewards of participation. This reply raises a variety of issues that I have discussed elsewhere[15] but which cannot be dealt with adequately here. For present purposes, suffice it to say that the reply is unlikely, by itself, to persuade proponents of the distributive objection. They are likely to question whether special responsibilities as opposed, say, to the *de facto* willingness of the participants to give special weight to each other's interests—are genuinely necessary for the achievement of a rewarding relationship. They are also likely to argue that, even if it is true that special responsibilities help to make rewarding relationships possible, this only confirms the fundamental point of the objection, which is that such responsibilities work to the advantage of the participants in rewarding relationships and to the disadvantage of nonparticipants. Thus, they are likely to conclude, it remains important that, so far as possible, these advantages and disadvantages should be integrated into an overall distribution of benefits and burdens that is fair.

As we have seen, the voluntarist objection asserts that the source of our special responsibilities must lie in our own voluntary acts. Otherwise, it claims, such responsibilities would be unfairly burdensome for those who bear them. Thus, according to this objection, fairness to the bearers of special responsibilities requires a version of reductionism with respect to such responsibilities. The distributive objection, on the other hand, challenges the fairness of special responsibilities whether or not their source is thought of as lying in the voluntary acts of those who bear them. And its claim is that such responsibilities, far from imposing unfair burdens on the people who bear them, may instead provide those people with unfair advantages. If a nonreductionist account of special responsibilities is to be convincing, it will need to address both of these objections.[16]

In this essay, I will sketch the rudiments of a nonreductionist account. My discussion will remain schematic, inasmuch as I will be concerned with the abstract structure of a nonreductionist position rather than with a detailed accounting of the specific responsibilities that such a position would assign people. Nevertheless, I hope that my sketch may suggest a new way of understanding nonreductionist claims of special responsibility and that, in so doing, it may make nonreductionism seem less implausible than it is often thought to be. In any event, I believe that the type of position I will describe merits careful consideration. As is no doubt evident, questions about the status of special responsibilities bear directly on a number of the liveliest controversies in contemporary moral and political philosophy. For example, such questions are central to the debate within moral philosophy between consequentialism and deontology. They are equally central to the debates within political philosophy between liberalism and communitarianism, and between nationalism and cosmopolitanism. Thus the way that we think about special responsibilities may have far-reaching implications, and it would be a mistake to dismiss nonreductionism without attempting to understand it sympathetically.

Nonreductionists are impressed by the fact that we often cite our relationships to people rather than particular interactions with them as the source of our special responsibilities. They believe that our perception of things is basically correct; the source of such responsibilities often does lie in the relationships themselves rather than in particular interactions between the participants. A nonreductionist might begin to elaborate this position as follows. Other people can make claims on me, and their needs can provide me with reasons for action, whether or not I have any special relationship to them. If a stranger is suffering and I am in a position to help, without undue cost to myself, then I may well have a reason to do so. This much is true simply in virtue of our common humanity. However, if I have a special, valued relationship with someone, and if the value I attach to the relationship is not purely instrumental in character—if, in other words, I do not value it solely as a means to some independently specified end—then I regard the person with whom I have the relationship as capable of making additional claims on me, beyond those that people in general can make. For to attach noninstrumental value to my relationship with a particular person just is, in part, to see that person as a source of special claims in virtue of the relationship between us. It is, in other words, to be disposed, in contexts which vary depending on the nature of the relationship, to see that person's needs, interests, and desires as, in themselves, providing me with presumptively decisive reasons for action, reasons that I would not have had in the absence of the relationship. By "presumptively decisive reasons" I mean reasons which, although they are capable in principle of being outweighed or overridden, nevertheless present themselves as considerations upon which I must act. If there are no circumstances in which I would see a person's needs or interests as giving me such reasons, then, according to the nonreductionist, it makes no sense to assert that I attach (noninstrumental) value to my relationship with that person. But this is tantamount to saying that I cannot value my relationships (noninstrumentally) without seeing them as sources of special responsibilities.[17]

If it is true that one cannot value one's relationship to another person (noninstrumentally) without seeing it, in effect, as a source of special responsibilities, then it hardly seems mysterious that such a wide and apparently heterogeneous assortment of relationships have been seen as giving rise to such responsibilities. Nor, given that different people value relationships of different kinds, does it seem mysterious that some claims of special responsibility remain highly controversial. For if one disapproves of a certain kind of relationship, or of the tendency to invest relationships of that kind with significance, then one is likely to greet claims of special responsibility arising out of such relationships with skepticism. Thus, to take three very different examples, although the members of street gangs, fraternities, and nations often attach considerable importance to their membership in those groups, and although, in consequence, they often have a strong sense of responsibility to their fellow members, someone who disapproves of such groups, or of the tendency to invest them with significance, may be unwilling to accept these claims of responsibility. On the other hand, someone who values his own participation in a relationship of a certain kind is likely to ascribe special responsibilities to the other participants in such relationships, even when they themselves do not value those relationships or acknowledge responsibilities arising out of them. Thus, on the nonreductionist view, differences in the kinds of relationships that people value lead naturally to disagreements about the assignment of special responsibility.

The nonreductionist position as thus far described takes us only so far. It asserts that relationships and not merely interactions are among the sources of special responsibilities, and it claims that people who value their relationships invariably see them as giving rise to such responsibilities. As so far described, however, the position says nothing about the conditions under which relationships actually do give rise to special responsibilities. Now there is, of course, no reason to expect that all nonreductionists will give the same answer to this question, any more than there is reason to expect that all reductionists will identify the same types of interactions as the sources of special responsibilities. In this essay, however, I wish to explore the specific suggestion that one's relationships to other people give rise to special responsibilities to those people when they are relationships that one has reason to value.[18] For ease of exposition, I will refer to this view simply as "nonreductionism," but we should remember that this is just an expository device, and that other versions of nonreductionism are possible.

Several features of the formulation I have given require comment and clarification. First, the term "value," as it occurs in that formulation and in subsequent discussion, should be taken to mean "value noninstrumentally," and the term "reason" should be taken to mean "net reason." In other words, if a person only has reason to value a relationship instrumentally, then the principle I have stated does not treat that relationship as a source of special responsibilities. And if a person has some reason to value a relationship but more reason not to, then again the principle does not treat it as generating such responsibilities. Furthermore, although the formulation I have given does not presuppose any particular conception of the kinds of reasons that people can have for valuing their relationships, reasons that are *reflexively instrumental, in the sense that they derive from the instrumental advantages of valuing a relationship noninstrumentally, are to be understood as excluded. In other words, if attaching noninstrumental value to a certain relationship would itself be an effective means of achieving some independently desirable goal, the principle I have stated does not treat that as a reason of the responsibility-generating kind.*

Second, there is a perfectly good sense of "relationship" in which every human being stands in some relationship to every other human being. However, as far as the view that I am presenting is concerned, only socially salient connections among people count as "relations" or "relationships"—two terms that I use interchangeably. Thus, for example, if you happen to have the same number of letters in your last name as John Travolta does, that does not mean that you have a relationship with him. Nor does the fact that you admire Travolta suffice to establish the existence of a relationship in the relevant sense, for the fact that one person has a belief about or attitude toward another does not constitute a social tie between them. On the other hand, two members of a socially recognized group do have a relationship in the relevant sense, even if they have never met, and if they value their membership in that group they may also value their relations to the other members. Thus, the fact that you are a member of the John Travolta Fan Club means that you have a relation to each of the other club members, and if you value your membership you may also value those relations.

Third, valuing my relationship with another person, in the sense that matters for nonreductionism, means valuing the relation of each of us to the other. So if, for example, I value my status as the Brutal Tyrant's leading opponent but not his status as my despised adversary, then I do not value our relationship in the sense that the nonreductionist principle treats as relevant. Similar remarks apply, mutatis mutandis, to having reason to value a relationship.

Fourth, nonreductionism as I have formulated it is not committed to a fixed view either of the strength or of the content of special responsibilities. It is compatible with the view that such responsibilities can be outweighed by other considerations. It is also compatible with the view that the strength of one's responsibilities depends on the nature of the relationships that give rise to them, and on the degree of value that one has reason to attach to those relationships. As far as the content of the responsibilities is concerned, we may assume that this too depends on the nature of the relationships in question, but that, at the most abstract level, it always involves a duty to give priority of various kinds, in suitable contexts, to certain of the interests of those to whom the responsibilities are owed.

Fifth, the nonreductionist principle states a sufficient condition for special responsibilities, not a necessary condition. Thus the principle does not purport to identify the source of all such responsibilities. In particular, it does not deny that promises and other kinds of discrete interactions can also give rise to special responsibilities. It merely claims to identify conditions under which interpersonal relations give rise to responsibilities that need not be fully accounted for in reductionist terms.

Sixth, nonreductionism makes it possible to claim both that people sometimes have special responsibilities that they think they lack, and that they sometimes lack special responsibilities that they think they have. For it is possible to think both that people can fail to value relationships that they have reason to value, and that they can succeed in valuing relationships that they have no reason to value. We may think, for example, that a neglectful father has reason to value his relations to the children he ignores, or that an abused wife lacks any reason to value her relation to the husband she cannot bring herself to leave. Similarly, we may feel that an ambitious young woman has good reasons to value her relationship with the devoted immigrant parents of whom she is ashamed, and little reason to value her relationship with the vain and self-absorbed classmate whose attention she prizes and whose approval she craves.[19]

Finally, however, our ability to sustain claims of this kind is clearly dependent on a conception of reasons, and, more specifically, on a conception of the conditions under which people may be said to have reasons to value their relations to others. The more closely a person's reasons are seen as linked to his existing desires and motivations, the less scope there will be for distinguishing between the relationships that he has reason to value and the relationships that he actually does value. On the other hand, the less closely reasons are thought of as tied to existing desires, the more room there will be to draw such distinctions. As I have indicated, nonreductionism does not itself put forward a conception of reasons. Its claim, rather, is that many judgments of special responsibility are dependent on the ascription to people of reasons for valuing their relations to others, so that any substantive conception of such responsibilities is hostage to some conception of reasons.[20]

Nonreductionism of the kind I have described makes possible the following simple defense of unreduced special responsibilities. We human beings are social creatures, and creatures with values. Among the things that we value are our relations with each other. But to value one's relationship with another person is to see it as a source of reasons for action of a distinctive kind. It is, in effect, to see oneself as having special responsibilities to the person with whom one has the relationship. Thus, insofar as we have good reasons to value our interpersonal relations, we have good reasons to see ourselves as having special responsibilities. And, accordingly, skepticism about such responsibilities will be justified only if we are prepared to deny that we have good reasons to value our relationships.

It may seem that this argument is fallacious. For consider: even if I have reason to promise that I will meet you for lunch on Tuesday, and even though I would be obligated to meet you if I were so to promise, it does not follow that, here and now, I actually have such an obligation. On the contrary, I acquire the obligation only if I make the promise. Similarly, it may seem, even if I have reason to value my relationship with you, and even if I would acquire special responsibilities to you if I did value our relationship, it does not follow that, here and now, I actually have such responsibilities. On the contrary, I acquire the responsibilities only if I value the relationship. However, the nonreductionist will resist this analogy. In the promising case, I have reason to perform an act which, if performed, will generate an obligation. But the nonreductionist's claim about special responsibilities is different. The claim is not that, in having reason to value our relationship, I have reason to perform an act which, if performed, will generate responsibilities. The claim is rather that, to value our relationship is, in part, to see myself as having such responsibilities, so that if, here and now, I have reason to value our relationship, then what I have reason to do, here and now, is to see myself as having such responsibilities. In the promising case, the promise generates the obligation, and no obligation arises in the absence of the promise. But the existence of a relationship that one has reason to value is itself the source of special responsibilities, and those responsibilities arise whether or not the participants actually value the relationship. Or so the nonreductionist claims.

Even if the disanalogy with the promising case is conceded, it may nevertheless be said that the nonreductionist argument stops short of establishing that we
really do have special responsibilities. As we have seen, the nonreductionist
claims that, insofar as we have reason to value our interpersonal relationships,
we also have reason to see ourselves as having such responsibilities. But, it may
be said, even if we have reason to see ourselves as having such responsibilities,
that is compatible with our not actually having them. This seems to me misleading, however. If the nonreductionist argument establishes that we have good
reason to see ourselves as having special responsibilities, then that is how we
should see ourselves. There is no substantive difference, in this context, between
the conclusion that we do have special responsibilities and the conclusion that,
all things considered, we have good reasons for thinking that we do.

Some may worry that the nonreductionist principle as I have formulated it focuses too much attention on the bearers of special responsibilities and too little
on the beneficiaries. Sometimes, it may be said, the source of a special responsibility does not lie in the fact that the relationship is one that the bearer has reason to value, but rather in the vulnerability created by the beneficiary's trust in
or dependence on the bearer. However, this suggestion is not incompatible with
the principle I have articulated. For that principle purports to identify only a sufficient condition, and not a necessary condition, for a relationship to give rise
to special responsibilities. Thus it no more precludes the possibility that relations
of trust and vulnerability may also give rise to such responsibilities than the
principle that one ought to keep one's promises precludes the possibility that
there are other kinds of obligations as well.

How, then, might a nonreductionist respond to the voluntarist and distributive
objections? The voluntarist objection, we may recall, points out that special responsibilities may constitute significant burdens for those who bear them, and
asserts that it would be unfair if such responsibilities could be ascribed to individuals who had done nothing voluntarily to incur them. The first thing that
nonreductionists may say in response to this objection is that, in addition to our
special responsibilities, there are other moral norms that govern our treatment
of people in general. These moral norms, they may point out, apply to us
whether or not we have agreed to them. For example, one cannot justify one's
infliction of harm on a person by saying that one never agreed not to harm people. There are, in other words, general moral responsibilities that can be ascribed to us without our having voluntarily incurred them. And although these
general responsibilities, like special responsibilities, may be costly or burdensome, we do not ordinarily regard their imposition as unfair. So why, nonreductionists may ask, should special responsibilities be any different? If voluntarists do not require that general responsibilities be voluntarily incurred, how
can they insist that special responsibilities must be? The voluntarist may reply
that special responsibilities, unless voluntarily incurred, give other people undue control over one's life. If certain people can make claims on you without
your having done anything to legitimate those claims, then, the voluntarist may
argue, those people enjoy an unreasonable degree of authority over the way you

live. However, since general moral norms also enable people to make claims on individuals who have done nothing to legitimate those claims, nonreductionists will again want to know why special responsibilities that have not been voluntarily incurred should be objectionable in a way that general responsibilities are not.

One reason for the voluntarist's concern about special responsibilities may be as follows. Our most significant social roles and relations determine, to a considerable extent, the ways that we are seen by others and the ways that we see ourselves. They help to determine what might be called our social identities. To the extent that we choose our roles and relations, and decide how much significance they shall have in our lives, we shape our own identities. But to the extent that these things are fixed independently of our choices, our identities are beyond our control. What disturbs the voluntarist about special responsibilities may be this: if our relations to other people can generate responsibilities to those people independently of our choices, then, to that extent, the significance of our social relations is not up to us to determine. And if the significance of such relations is not up to us to determine, then we may be locked into a social identity we did not choose. This suggests that special responsibilities may be troubling to the voluntarist, in a way that general responsibilities are not, because special responsibilities may seem to threaten our capacity for self determination—our capacity to determine who, in social terms, we are. On this interpretation, it is not wrong to suggest that the voluntarist views special responsibilities, unless voluntarily incurred, as giving other people undue control over our lives. However, the problem is not simply that others may be able to make unwelcome claims on our time and resources. That much would be true even if we had only general responsibilities. The more fundamental problem is that other people may be able to shape our identities in ways that run counter to our wishes.

Seen in this light, the voluntarist's position has obvious appeal. The ability to have our social identities influenced by our choices is something about which most of us care deeply, and which seems to us an important prerequisite for the forms of human flourishing to which we aspire. We regard societies in which one's social identity is rigidly fixed, as a matter of law or social practice, by features of one's birth or breeding over which one has no control, as societies that are inhospitable to human freedom. This does not mean that we are committed to repudiating whatever communal or traditional affiliations may have been conferred upon us at birth. It only means that we want the salience in our lives of such affiliations to be influenced by our own wishes and decisions, rather than being determined by the dictates of the society at large. This is, of course, one reason why liberals insist that the legal status of citizens should be insensitive to facts about their race or religion or social class.

And yet, despite the value that we attach to having our social identities influenced by our choices, and despite the particular importance of protecting this value against political interference, it is clear that the capacity to determine one's identity has its limits. Each of us is born into a web of social relations, and our social world lays claim to us long before we can attain reflective distance from it or begin making choices about our place in it. We acquire personal relations and social affiliations of a formative kind before we are able to conceive of them as such or to contemplate altering them. Thus there is obviously no question, nor can the voluntarist seriously think that there is, of our being able actually to choose all of the relations in which we stand to other people. What the voluntarist can hope to claim is only that the significance of those relations is entirely up to us. However, this claim too is unsustainable. For better or worse, the influence on our personal histories of unchosen social relations—to parents and siblings, families and communities, nations and peoples—is not something that we determine by ourselves. Whether we like it or not, such relations help to define the contours of our lives, and influence the ways that we are seen both by ourselves and by others. Even those who sever or repudiate such ties insofar as it is possible to do so can never escape their influence or deprive them of all significance, for to have repudiated a personal tie is not the same as never having had it, and one does not nullify social bonds by rejecting them. One is, in other words, forever the person who has rejected or repudiated those bonds; one cannot make oneself into a person who lacked them from the outset. Thus, while some people travel enormous social distances in their lives, and while the possibility of so doing is something that we have every reason to cherish, the idea that the significance of our personal ties and social affiliations is wholly dependent on our wills—that we are the supreme gatekeepers of our own identities—can only be regarded as a fantasy. So if, as the nonreductionist believes, our relations to other people can generate responsibilities to them independently of our choices, then it is true that, in an important respect, the significance of our social relations is not fully under our control; but since the significance of those relations is in any case not fully under our control, this by itself does not rob us of any form of self-determination to which we may reasonably aspire.

In the end, then, the nonreductionist's response to the voluntarist objection is to insist that, although the significance of choice and consent in moral contexts is undeniable, nevertheless, the moral import of our relationships to other people does not derive solely from our own decisions. Nor, the nonreductionist may add, need we fear that this is tantamount to conceding the legitimacy of systems of caste or hierarchy, or that it leaves the individual at the mercy of oppressive social arrangements. For the relationships that generate responsibilities for an individual are those relationships that the individual has reason to value. No claims at all arise from relations that are degrading or demeaning, or which serve to undermine rather than to enhance human flourishing. In other words, the alternative to an exaggerated voluntarism is not an exaggerated communitarianism or historicism. In recognizing that the significance of our social relationships does not stem exclusively from our choices, we do not consign ourselves to a form of social bondage. In surrendering the fantasy that our own wills are the source of all our special responsibilities, we do not leave ourselves defenseless against the contingencies of the social world.

Yet even if these remarks constitute an effective response to the voluntarist objection, they may seem only to highlight the nonreductionist's vulnerability to the distributive objection. For, if relationships that are destructive of an individual's well-being do not, in general, give that individual special responsibilities, then presumably the relationships that do give him special responsibilities either enhance or at least do not erode his well-being. But, as we have seen, special responsibilities may themselves work to the advantage of the participants in special relationships, and to the disadvantage of nonparticipants. And, it may be asked, why should a relationship that enhances the well-being of the participants give rise to a distribution of moral responsibility that further advances their interests, while working against the interests of nonparticipants? How can the nonreductionist respond to the charge that, unless the benefits and burdens of special responsibilities are integrated into an overall distribution that is fair, such responsibilities will themselves provide unfair advantages to the participants in interpersonal relations, while unfairly penalizing nonparticipants?

The nonreductionist may begin by reiterating that, as long as people attach value to their interpersonal relations, they will inevitably see themselves as having special responsibilities. And as long as they have good reasons for attaching value to those relations, we must allow that they also have good reasons to see themselves as having such responsibilities. There may, of course, be room for general skepticism about people's reasons for valuing their interpersonal relations. But it seems unlikely that proponents of the distributive objection can afford to be skeptics of this sort. For the distributive objection is animated by a concern for fairness in the allocation of benefits and burdens, and if, as the skeptic asserts, people never have reason to value their social relations, then it is unclear why considerations of fairness should weigh with them at all. Rather than providing grounds for the rejection of special responsibilities in particular, general skepticism about our reasons for valuing personal relations seems potentially subversive of morality as a whole.

Provided that the distributive objection is not taken to support a wholesale repudiation of special responsibilities, however, nonreductionists may concede that it makes a legitimate point. There are important respects in which special responsibilities may work to the advantage of the participants in personal relationships, and to the disadvantage of other people. These facts seem undeniable once they are called to our attention. That we sometimes lose sight of them is due in large measure to the influence of voluntarism, which focuses exclusively on the respects in which special responsibilities can be burdensome for the people who bear them, and sees the task of legitimating such responsibilities solely as a matter of justifying those burdens. Once we face the facts to which the distributive objection calls attention, however, we must agree that there is another side to special responsibilities: that they may also provide significant advantages for the participants in interpersonal relations and significant disadvantages for nonparticipants. Insofar as the distributive objection insists only on the desirability of integrating these advantages and disadvantages into an overall distribution of benefits and burdens that is fair, nonreductionists have no reason to disagree.

Indeed, once the distributive objection is understood in this way, it may be seen as illustrating a more general point, with which nonreductionists also have no reason to disagree. The general point is that special responsibilities need to be set within the context of our overall moral outlook and constrained in suitable ways by other pertinent values. On a nonreductionist view, such constraints may, in principle, operate in at least three different ways. Some may affect the content of special responsibilities, by setting limits to the circumstances in which, and the extent to which, people are required to give priority to the interests of those to whom they have such responsibilities. Other constraints may affect the strength of special responsibilities, by supplying countervailing considerations that are capable of outweighing or overriding those responsibilities in various contexts. Still other constraints may affect people's reasons for valuing their relationships. Perhaps, for example, people have no (net) reason to value relationships which themselves offend against important moral values or principles, so that such relationships do not generate special responsibilities even if people do in fact value them.[21]

The upshot is that, although nonreductionism insists that unreduced special responsibilities must be part of any adequate moral scheme, it is not hostile to the idea that there are a variety of other moral values including the values underlying the distributive objection—by which such responsibilities must be constrained and with which they must be integrated if they are to be fully satisfactory. For example, there is nothing to prevent the nonreductionist from agreeing that considerations of distributive fairness serve to limit both the strength and the content of people's special responsibilities. Of course, the mere fact that nonreductionism is open to such possibilities does not suffice to show that a single moral outlook will be capable of accommodating special responsibilities while fully satisfying the values underlying the distributive objection. In fact, I believe that there is a deep and persistent tension between these two features of our moral thought, and nothing in the nonreductionist position guarantees that we will be able simultaneously to accommodate both features to our own satisfaction.[22]

Although this is a serious problem, however, it is no more of a problem for nonreductionist accounts of special responsibilities than it is for reductionist accounts. In fact, it is a problem for any view that takes special responsibilities seriously, while remaining sensitive to the values underlying the distributive objection. Any such view, and indeed any view that recognizes a diversity of moral values and principles, needs to ask how far that diversity can be accommodated within a unified moral outlook. Too often it is simply taken for granted either that a unified outlook must in principle be available or that any tension at all among our values means that there is no possibility of jointly accommodating them. Neither assumption seems to me to be warranted. Instead, it seems to me a substantive question, the answer to which remains open, to what extent the diverse moral values that we recognize can be jointly accommodated within a unified scheme of thought and practice.

Pending an answer to that question, nonreductionism appears to have the following advantages as an account of special responsibilities. To begin with, it has the virtue of cohering better than do reductionist accounts with our actual practice, which is to cite relationships as well as interactions as sources of special responsibilities. It also has the advantage of being able to explain, in simple and straightforward terms, why it is that people have seen such a diverse and apparently heterogeneous assortment of relationships as giving rise to such responsibilities. Furthermore, nonreductionism makes it possible to agree that our ordinary practices of ascribing special responsibilities to the participants in significant relationships are broadly correct. Like those ordinary practices themselves, however, it also leaves room for the criticism of particular ascriptions of responsibility. Admittedly, the content of the nonreductionist principle depends on some conception of the kinds of reasons people have for valuing their relations to others. Thus, given this principle, disagreements about reasons will inevitably lead to disagreements about the circumstances under which special responsibilities should be ascribed to people. Even this may seem like an advantage, however. For there are many disagreements about the ascription of such responsibilities that do seem plausibly understood as reflecting a more fundamental disagreement about the reasons people have for valuing their relationships. To the extent that this is so, nonreductionism locates controversies about the ascription of special responsibilities in the right place, and provides an illuminating explanation of them. Finally, nonreductionism is sensitive to the concerns underlying the voluntarist and distributive objections, yet it provides reasons for insisting that neither objection supports the complete repudiation of unreduced special responsibilities.

Let me close by returning to a point that I made earlier. The nonreductionist position I have outlined, if it can be persuasively developed, may have implications for a number of important controversies in moral and political philosophy. Inasmuch as it offers a defense of special responsibilities that is non-consequentialist in character, for example, it points to a possible defense of at least some sorts of "agent-centered restrictions."[23] Similarly, I believe, it suggests some constraints that any adequate formulation of cosmopolitanism may need to respect. Detailed discussion of these implications, however, must await another occasion.

NOTES

1. Nicholas Rescher, "Collective Responsibility," *Journal of Social Philosophy* 29 (1998): 46–58.

2. Legal or institutional responsibility is something else again—something rather different from the moral. The captain is "responsible" for what happens on the ship, the officer is "responsible" for the acts of subordinates. But what is at issue here involves rather a different use of the term.

3. Compare G. J. Massey, "Tom, Dick, and Harry, and all the King's Men," *American Philosphical Quarterly* 13 (1976): 89–107.

4. On this feature of "moral luck" see the author's treatment in *Luck* (New York: Farrar Straus & Giroux, 1995).

5. On these issues see Nicholas Rescher and Carey B. Joint, "Evidence in History and the Law," *The Journal of Philosophy* 56 (1959): 561–78.

6. Note that as long as we refuse to project group responsibility unto the constituent individuals, then—even in the "Hebraic" case—we are confronted with the anomalous upshot that a group can, through the deliberate actions of the individuals involved, produce a terrible result for which as regards individuals "no one is to blame" through lack of the right sort of intent on the part of individuals.

7. I am grateful to my colleague David Gauthier for helpful commentary on this issue.

8. To be sure, the presence of some degree of active participation is a crucial factor. Mere membership—wholly passive and inert—in a group that is collectively responsible does not as such contribute to the individual's moral blame or credit. And so the terrible things done by the Nazis at large detract nothing from the credit of Schindler, the Nazi.

9. Samuel Scheffler, "Relationships and Responsibilities," *Philosophy and Public Affairs* 26 (3): 189–209.

10. This is a much-revised version of the paper that I delivered at the Eleventh Jerusalem Philosophical Encounter in December 1995. Versions of the paper were also presented to the NYU Colloquium in Law, Philosophy, and Political Theory; the Columbia Legal Theory Workshop; philosophy department colloquia at Arizona State, Stanford, the University of Miami, and the University of Michigan; and my fall 1995 graduate seminar at Berkeley. I am very grateful to all of these audiences for extremely helpful discussion. Special thanks also to Yael Tamir, who was my commentator in Jerusalem, and to Christopher Kutz, Jeff McMahan, Daniel Statman, Wai-hung Wong, and a reader for *Philosophy & Public Affairs* for providing me with valuable written comments.

11. In this paragraph and at other points in the next few pages, I draw on my discussions of special responsibilities in the following papers: "Individual Responsibility in a Global Age," *Social Philosophy and Policy* 12 (1995): 219–36; "Families, Nations, and Strangers," in *The Lindley Lecture* series (Lawrence: University of Kansas, 1995); "Liberalism, Nationalism, and Egalitarianism," in Robert McKim and Jeff McMahan eds., *The Morality of Nationalism* (New York: Oxford University Press, 1997).

12. If it is ultimately to be convincing, the distributive objection will need to provide a fuller accounting of the various advantages and disadvantages that special responsibilities may confer both on the participants in interpersonal relationships and on nonparticipants. I consider the implications of such an accounting in "The Conflict Between Justice and Responsibility," in *NOMOS XLI: Global Justice* (forthcoming), eds. L. Brilmayer and I. Shapiro.

13. Robert Goodin, *Protecting the Vulnerable* (Chicago: University of Chicago Press, 1985), 1.

14. Goodin, *Protecting the Vulnerable*, 6.

15. In my "Families, Nations, and Strangers," sec. 4.

16. 1 have discussed both objections at greater length in "Families, Nations, and Strangers" and in "Liberalism, Nationalism, and Egalitarianism." I have discussed the

distributive objection most extensively in "The Conflict between Justice and Responsibility."

17. The nonreductionist recognizes, of course, that it is possible for me to regard relationships in which I am not a participant as valuable. The nonreductionist's claim, however, is that valuing one's own relationship to another person is different, not because one is bound to see such a relationship as more valuable than other relationships of the same type, but rather because one is bound to see it as a source of reasons for action of a distinctive kind.

18. On some views, membership in a group may give one special responsibilities *to the* group that transcend any responsibilities one has to the individual members. The view I am exploring is agnostic on this question.

19. Of course, since the nonreductionist principle does articulate only a sufficient and not a necessary condition for special responsibilities, the fact that one has no reason to value one's relationship to a particular person does not by itself show that one has no special responsibilities whatsoever to that person—only that one has no responsibilities arising under the nonreductionist principle.

20. This means that it would be possible for a reductionist to argue that people's reasons for valuing their relations to others derive exclusively from discrete interactions that occur in the context of those relations. Even if this argument were accepted, however, it would remain the case that, according to the principle under consideration, the source of the relevant responsibilities lies in the relationships rather than the interactions. Furthermore, it may not be possible without loss of plausibility to translate reductionism about special responsibilities into reductionism about people's reasons for valuing their relationships. For some of the types of interaction that have been seen as generating such responsibilities do not seem plausibly construed as generating reasons for valuing relationships.

21. Might it be said, by someone sympathetic to the distributive objection, that relationships that run afoul of that objection violate this last type of constraint, and thus do not give rise to special responsibilities after all? This is unpersuasive because the distributive objection is not an objection to a class of relationships. In other words, it does not allege that certain relationships offend against important moral values. Instead, it claims only that considerations of distributive fairness prevent some relationships, which may be entirely unobjectionable in themselves, from giving rise to special responsibilities. But the constraint in question applies only to relationships that themselves offend against important moral values.

22. See, generally, Thomas Nagel, *Equality and Partiality* (New York: Oxford University Press, 1991).

23. See *The Rejection of Consequentialism* (Oxford: Clarendon Press, 1994 [rev. ed. 1), esp. chap. 4.

10

Historical Responsibility: Are the Sins of the Fathers to Be Visited on Their Great-Great-Grandchildren?

George Sher: "Ancient Wrongs and Modern Rights"[1,2]

It is widely acknowledged that persons may deserve compensation for the effects of wrong acts performed before they were born. It is such acts that are in question when we say that blacks deserve compensation because their forebears were originally brought to this country as slaves, or that American Indians deserve compensation for the unjust appropriation of their ancestors' land. But although some principle of compensation for the lasting effects of past wrongs seems appropriate, the proper temporal scope of that principle is not clear. We may award compensation for the effects of wrongs done as many as ten or twenty generations ago; but what of wrongs done a hundred generations ago? Or five hundred or a thousand? Are there any temporal limits at all to the wrong acts whose enduring effects may call for compensation? In the first section of this paper, I shall discuss several reasons for addressing these neglected questions. In subsequent sections, I shall discuss some possible ways of resolving them.

I. A natural initial reaction to questions about compensation for the effects of ancient wrongs is that these questions are, in the main, hopelessly unrealistic. In the case of blacks, Indians, and a few analogous groups, we may indeed have enough information to suggest that most current group members are worse off than they would be in the absence of some initial wrong. But if the wrong act was performed even longer ago, or if the persons currently suffering its effects do not belong to a coherent and easily identified group, then such information will not be available to us. There are surely some persons alive today who would be better off if the Spanish Inquisition had not taken place, or if the Jews had never been originally expelled from the land of Canaan. However, to discover who these persons are and how much better off they would be, we would have to draw on far more genealogical, causal, and counterfactual knowledge than

197

anyone can reasonably be expected to possess. Because this information is not and never will be completely available, the question of who, if anyone, deserves compensation for the current effects of these wrongs will never be answered. But if so, why bother asking it?

This relaxed approach to compensation has the virtue of realism. The suggestion that we might arrive at a complete understanding of the effects of ancient wrongs is a philosopher's fantasy and nothing more. Nevertheless, despite its appeal, I think we cannot rest content with a totally pragmatic dismissal of the issue of compensating for ancient wrongs. For one thing, even if compensatory justice is a partially unrealizable ideal, its theoretical limits will retain an intrinsic interest. For another, even if we cannot now ascertain which persons deserve compensation for the effects of ancient wrongs, the insight that such persons exist might itself suggest new obligations to us. In particular, if the victims of even the most ancient of wrongs can qualify for compensation, and if our current compensatory efforts are therefore aimed at only a small subset of those who deserve it, then we will at least be obligated to enlarge the subset by extending our knowledge of the effects of ancient wrongs as far as possible. Alternatively, the discovery that desert of compensation is not invariant with respect to temporal distance might force us to reduce our compensatory efforts in certain areas.

These considerations suggest that clarifying the theoretical status of ancient wrongs may dictate certain (rather marginal) changes in our actual compensatory policies. But there is also another, far more significant implication which such clarification might have. Given the vastness of historical injustice, and given the ramification of every event over time, it seems reasonable to assume that most or all current individuals have been both benefited and harmed by numerous ancient wrongs. For (just about) every current person P, there are likely to be some ancient wrongs which have benefited P but harmed others, and other ancient wrongs which have benefited others but harmed P. In light of this, neither the distribution of goods which actually prevails nor that which would prevail in the absence of all recent wrongs is likely to resemble the distribution which would prevail in the absence of all historical wrongs. But if so, and if the effects of ancient wrongs do call as strongly for compensation as the effects of recent ones, then it seems that neither compensating nor not compensating for the known effects of recent wrongs will be just. On the one hand, since the point of compensating for the effects of wrong acts is to restore a just distribution of goods among the affected parties, the injustice of the distribution that would prevail in the absence of recent wrongs will undermine our rationale for restoring it. However, on the other hand, even if that distribution is unjust, the distribution that actually prevails is no better; and so a failure to compensate for recent wrongs will be every bit as unpalatable. The only strategy that is just that of restoring the distribution that would have prevailed in the absence of all historical wrongs. But, as we have seen, we will never have the information to do this.

How to respond to this combination of pervasive injustice and indefeasible ignorance is a complicated and difficult question. One possible strategy is to argue that even if compensating for recent wrongs would not restore full justice, it would at least bring us substantially closer to a totally just distribution than we are now. A second alternative is to revise our account of the aim of compensating for recent wrongs—to say that the point of doing this is not to restore a fully just distribution among the affected parties, but rather only to nullify the effects of one particular set of injustices. A third is to accept Nozick's suggestion that we "view some patterned principles of distributive justice [e.g. egalitarianism or Rawls' difference principle] as rough rules of thumb meant to approximate the general results of applying the principle of rectification of injustice."[3] A fourth is to abandon hope of achieving justice by either compensating or not compensating, and simply start afresh by redistributing goods along egalitarian or Rawlsian lines. If their positions can be grounded in either of the latter ways, egalitarians and Rawlsians may hope to rebut the charge that they ignore such historical considerations as entitlement and desert.[4] But as interesting as these issues are, it would be premature for us to consider them further here. The choice among the suggested options arises only if ancient wrongs do call for compensation as strongly as recent ones; and so that claim must be investigated first. The discussion so far has been merely to establish the claim's importance. Having done that, we may now turn to the question of its truth.

II. Intuitively, the effects of ancient wrongs do not seem to call as strongly for compensation as the effects of recent ones. Indeed, the claim that persons deserve compensation even for the effects of wrongs done in biblical times appears to be a reductio of the ideal of compensatory justice. But we should be wary of intuitions of this sort. It is perfectly possible that they reflect only an awareness of the epistemological difficulty of establishing desert of compensation for ancient wrongs; and if they do, then all the problems limned above will remain untouched. To clarify the force of our intuitions, we must ask whether they can be traced to any deeper source in the notion of compensation itself. Is there anything *about* compensation which reduces the likelihood that ancient wrongs may call for it? More precisely, are there any necessary conditions for desert of compensation which become progressively harder to satisfy over time?

Prima facie, the answer to this question is clearly yes. On its standard interpretation, compensation is the restoration of a good or level of well-being which someone would have enjoyed if he had not been adversely affected by another's wrong act. To enjoy (almost) any good, a person must exist. Hence, it seems to be a necessary condition for *X*'s deserving compensation for the effect of *Y*'s doing *A* that *X* would have existed in *A*'s absence. Where *A* is an act performed during *X*'s lifetime, this requirement presents few problems. However, as *A* recedes into the past, it becomes progressively more likely that the effects of the non-performance of *A* will include *X*'s non-existence. If *X*'s currently low level of well-being is due to the defrauding of his great-grandfather in Europe, the very same fraudulent act which reduced *X*'s great-grandfather to poverty may be what caused him to emigrate to America, and so to meet *X*'s great-great-grandmother. Because the prevalence of such stories increases as the relevant wrong act recedes into the past, the probability that the effects of the wrong act will call for compensation must decrease accordingly. And where the wrong act is an ancient one, that probability may approach zero.

This way of explaining our intuitions about ancient wrongs may at first seem quite compelling. But once we scrutinize it more closely, I think doubts must arise. If X cannot deserve compensation for the effects of A unless X would have existed in the absence of A, then not only ancient wrongs, but also the slave trade, the theft of the Indians' land, and many other acts whose effects are often deemed worthy of compensation will turn out to be largely non-compensable. As Lawrence Davis notes, "were we to project the 200 years of our country's history in a rectified movie, the cast of characters would surely differ significantly from the existing cast."[5] Moreover, even if we were to accept this conclusion, as Michael Levin has urged that we do,[6] further problems would remain. Even in the case of some wrong acts performed very shortly before their victims' existence (for example, acts of environmental pollution causing massive genetic damage), it seems reasonable to suppose that it is not the victim, but rather some other person, who would exist in the absence of the wrong act. And there are also cases in which wrong acts do not produce but rather preserve the lives of their victims, as when a kidnapping accidentally prevents a child from perishing in the fire that subsequently destroys his home. Since compensation may clearly be deserved in all such cases, it seems that the proposed necessary condition for deserving it will have to be rejected.

If we do wish to reject that necessary condition, there are at least two alternatives available to us. One is to alter our interpretation of the counterfactual presupposed by the standard account of compensation—to read that counterfactual as requiring not simply that X be better off in the closest possible world in which A is absent, but rather that X be better off in the closest possible world in which A is absent *and X exists.* A more drastic alternative, for which I have argued elsewhere, is to modify the standard view of compensation itself—to say that compensating X is not necessarily restoring X to the level of well-being which *he* would have occupied in the absence of A, but rather that it is restoring X to the level of well-being that some *related* person or group of persons would have occupied in the absence of A.[7] Although both suggestions obviously require further work,[8] it is clear that neither yields the unacceptable consequences of the simpler account. However, it is also true that neither implies that the probability of desert of compensation will decrease over time. Hence, the shift to either of them will call for a different explanation of our intuitions about compensation for ancient wrongs.

III. A more promising way of explaining these intuitions can be extracted from a recent article by David Lyons. In an important discussion of the American Indian claims to land,[9] Lyons argues that property rights are unlikely to be so stable as to persist intact through all sorts of social changes. Even on Nozick's extremely strong conception of property rights, the "Lockean Proviso" implies that such rights must give way when changing conditions bring it about that some individuals are made worse off by (originally legitimate) past acts of acquisition. In particular, this may happen when new arrivals are disadvantaged by their lack of access to established holdings. Because property rights do thus change over time, Lyons argues that today's Indians would probably not have a right to their ancestors' land even if it had *not* been illegitimately taken. Hence, restoring the land or its equivalent to them is unlikely to be warranted as compensation. But if this is true of America's Indians, then it must be true to an even greater degree of the victims of ancient wrongs. If property rights are so unstable, then rights held thousands of years ago would surely not have survived the world's drastic population growth, the industrial revolution, or other massive social changes. Hence, their violation in the distant past may appear to call for no compensation now.

Because wrongful harm and deprivation of property are so closely connected, this approach initially seems to offer a comprehensive solution to our problem. However, here again, a closer examination reveals difficulties. First, even if we grant Lyons' point that changing conditions can alter people's entitlements, and that new arrivals may be entitled to fair shares of goods already held, it remains controversial to suppose that these fair shares must be equal ones. If the shares need not be equal, then the instability of property rights may well permit the preservation of substantial legitimate inequalities through both time and inheritance. Moreover, second, even if property rights do fade completely over time, there will still be many current persons whom ancient wrongs have in one way or another prevented from acquiring *new* property rights. Because these new rights would ex hypothesi not have been continuations of any earlier rights, they would not have been affected by the instability of those earlier rights. Hence, the persons who would have held them will apparently still deserve to be compensated. Finally, despite the close connection between property and well-being, there are surely many ways of being harmed which do not involve violations of property rights at all. As many writers on preferential treatment have suggested, a person can also be harmed by being deprived of self-respect, by being rendered less able to compete for opportunities when they arise, and in other related ways. Although these claims must be scrutinized with considerable care, at least some appear clearly true. Moreover, there is no reason to believe that the psychological effects of a wrong act are any less long-lived, or any less likely to be transmitted from generation to generation, than their economic counterparts. It is true that the psychological effects of wrong acts are often themselves the result of property violations; but the case for compensating for them does not appear to rest on this. Because it does not, that case seems compatible with any view of the stability of property rights.

IV. Given these difficulties, Lyons' insight about property does not itself resolve our problem. However, it suggests a further line of inquiry which may. We have seen that because property rights are not necessarily stable, we cannot assume that anyone who retains his property in a world without the initial wrong is entitled to all (or even any) of it in that world. A world in which that particular wrong is rectified may still be morally deficient in other respects. Because of this, the real question is not how much property the victim *does* have in the rectified world, but rather how much he *should* have in it. Moreover, to avoid arbitrariness, we must say something similar about persons whose losses do not involve property as well. If this is not generally recognized, it is probably because deleting the initial wrong act, which is properly only necessary for establishing what the victim should have had, is easily taken to be sufficient for it. But whatever the source of the oversight, the fact that the operative judgments about rectified worlds are themselves normative is a major complication in the theory of compensation; for normative judgments do not always transfer smoothly to the actual world. By spelling out the conditions under which they do not, we may hope finally to clarify the status of ancient wrongs.

Let us begin by considering a normative judgment which plainly does not carry over from a rectified world to our own. Suppose that *X*, a very promising student, has been discriminatorily barred from entering law school; and suppose further that although *X* knows he will be able to gain entry in another year, he becomes discouraged and so does not reapply. In a rectified world *Wr* which lacks the initial discrimination, *X* studies diligently and eventually becomes a prominent lawyer who enjoys great prestige and a high salary. In that world, we may suppose, *X* is fully entitled to these goods. However, in the actual world, *Wa*, the compensation to which *X* is entitled appears to fall far short of them or their equivalent. Hence, our normative judgment does not fully carry over from *Wr* to *Wa*.

Why does our normative judgment about *Wr* not fully carry over? In part, the answer to this question seems to lie in *X*'s own contribution to the actual course of events. Given more perseverance, *X* could have avoided most of the effects of the initial wrong act; and this certainly seems relevant to what he should now have. However, quite apart from what *X* does or does not do in *Wa*, there is also another factor to consider here. Insofar as *X*'s entitlements in *Wr* stem from what *X* does in law school and thereafter, they arise through a sequence of actions which *X* does not perform in *Wr* until well after the original wrong, and which he does not perform in *Wa* at all. These entitlements are not merely inherited by *X* in *Wr*, but rather are created anew by his actions in that world. But if *X*'s actions in *Wr* are themselves the source of some of his entitlements in that world, then it will make little sense to suppose that those entitlements can exist in an alternative world (that is, the actual one) which lacks the generating actions. To say this would be to hold that what a person should have may be determined by certain actions which neither he nor anyone else has actually performed.[10] We are plainly unwilling to say things like this in other contexts (nobody would say that a person deserves to be punished simply because he would have committed a crime if given the opportunity),[11] and they seem to be no more supportable here.

In view of these considerations, it seems that the transferability of a person's entitlements from a rectified world to the actual one is limited by two distinct factors. It is limited first by the degree to which one's actual entitlements have been diminished by one's own omissions in this world, and second by the degree to which one's entitlements in a rectified world are generated anew by one's own actions there. In the case of *X*, this means that what transfers is not all of his entitlements in *Wr*, but at best his entitlement to the basic opportunity to *acquire* these entitlements—in this instance, the entitlement to (the value of) the lost opportunity to attend law school. Of course, the value of this opportunity is itself determined by the value of the further goods whose acquisition it makes possible. But the opportunity is clearly not worth as much as the goods themselves.

This reasoning, if sound, sheds considerable light on the general concept of compensation. But because the reasoning applies equally to compensation for ancient *and* recent wrongs, its connection with our special problem about ancient wrongs is not yet clear. To bring out this connection, we must explore its implications over time. So let us now suppose that not just *X*, but also *X*'s son *Z*, has benefited from *X*'s admission to law school in *Wr*. As a result of *X*'s wealth and status, *Z* enjoys certain advantages in *Wr* that he does not enjoy in *Wa*. Assuming that *X* is fully entitled to his advantages in *Wr*, and assuming also that *X* only confers advantages upon *Z* in morally legitimate ways (whatever these are), it follows that *Z* too is fully entitled to his advantages in *Wr*. Under these circumstances, *Z* may well deserve some compensation in *Wa*. However, because *Z*'s entitlement to his advantages in *Wr* stems directly from *X*'s exercise of his own entitlements in that world, it would be anomalous to suppose that the former entitlements could transfer in greater proportion than the latter. Moreover, and crucially, given the principles already adduced, it seems that *Z*'s entitlements in *Wr will* have to transfer to *Wa* in even *smaller* proportion than *X*'s.

The reason for this diminution in transferability is easy to see. Just as the transferability of *X*'s entitlements is limited by certain facts about *X*'s omissions in *Wa* and *X*'s actions in *Wr*, so too is the transferability of *Z*'s entitlements limited by similar facts about *Z*'s omissions in *Wa* and *Z*'s actions in *Wr*. More specifically, the transferability of *Z*'s entitlements is also limited by *Z*'s own failure to make the most of his opportunities in *Wa*, and by the degree to which *Z*'s entitlements in *Wr* have arisen through his use of his own special opportunities there. Of course, the opportunities available to *Z* in *Wr* and *Wa* may be very different from the opportunity to attend law school; but this difference is hardly a relevant one. Whether *Z*'s advantages in *Wr* and *Wa* take the form of wealth, political power, special skills or abilities, or simply self-confidence, the fact remains that they are, inter alia, potential opportunities for him to acquire further entitlements. Because of this, the way they contribute to his total entitlements in these worlds must continue to affect the degree to which his entitlements in *Wr* can transfer to *Wa*.

Once all of this is made clear, the outline of a general solution to our problem about ancient wrongs should begin to emerge. Because the transferability of *Z*'s entitlements is diminished twice over by the contribution of actions performed in *Wr* and omitted in *Wa*, while that of *Y*'s entitlements is diminished only once by this contribution, it follows that *Z* is likely to deserve proportionately less compensation for the effects of the original wrong than *X*; and *Z*'s offspring, if any, will deserve proportionately less compensation still. Moreover, since few original entitlements are preserved intact over succeeding generations (quite apart from any instability of property rights, the consumption of goods and the natural non-inheritability of many entitlements must each take a large toll), the progressive diminution in the transferability of entitlements from *Wr* to *Wa* must be absolute, not just proportional. But if the transferability of entitlements from rectified worlds does decrease with every generation, then over the course of very many generations, any such transferability can be expected to become vanishingly small. Where the initial wrong was done many hundreds of years ago, almost all of the difference between the victim's entitlements in the actual world and his entitlements in a rectified world can be expected to stem from the actions of various intervening agents in the two alternative worlds. Little or none of it will be the automatic effect of the initial wrong act itself. Since compensation is warranted only for disparities in entitlements which are the automatic effect of the initial wrong act, this means that there will be little or nothing left to compensate for.

V. This approach to the problem posed by ancient wrongs is not dissimilar to the one extracted from Lyons' discussion. Like Lyons, we have argued that a proper appreciation of the entitlements upon which claims to compensation are based suggest that these claims must fade with time. However, whereas Lyons argued that the entitlement to property itself fades with time, we have held instead that it is the transferability of that and other entitlements from rectified worlds to the actual one which becomes progressively weaker. By thus relocating the basic instability, we avoid the objections that the analysis of property rights is controversial, that some claims to compensation do not view the right to the lost property as continually held in a rectified world, and that other claims to compensation do not involve property at all. . . .

A final difficulty remains. Our argument has been that desert of compensation fades gradually over time, and that ancient wrongs therefore call for no significant amounts of compensation. But even if this is correct, it does not dispose of the vast intermediate class of wrongs which are not ancient, but were still done one or more generations ago. Since the process we have described is gradual, our account suggests that such wrongs do call for some compensation, although not as much as comparable recent ones. But if this is so, then our account may seem at once too strong and too weak. The account may seem too strong because it will classify as intermediate even the wrongs done to blacks and Indians—wrongs which appear to be among our paradigms of full compensability. However, the account may also seem too weak, since it implies that very many partially compensable wrongs remain undiscovered, and that our problem of how to act justly in the face of incurable ignorance is therefore unresolved. Because any response to one aspect of this objection will only aggravate the other, the difficulty seems intractable.

But this dilemma is surely overdrawn. On the side of the claims of blacks and Indians, it may first be said that even if the initial wrongs to these persons do go back several centuries, the real source of their claims to compensation may lie elsewhere. As Lyons notes, the truly compensable wrong done to the Indians may be not the initial appropriation of their land, but rather the more recent acts of discrimination and neglect which grew out of this; and the same may hold, mutatis mutandis, for the truly compensable wrongs done to blacks.[12] Moreover, even if the compensable wrongs to blacks and Indians do go back a number of generations, they may be highly atypical of other wrongs of that period. We have seen that one reason that compensability fades over time is that victims neglect reasonable opportunities to acquire equivalent entitlements; and so if slavery or the appropriation of Indian lands have made it specially difficult for their victims to recoup their lost entitlements, then these wrongs may call for far more compensation than others of similar vintage. Here our earlier results provide a natural framework for further inquiry. Finally, even if these suggestions do not establish full compensability for blacks and Indians, they do at least promise very substantial compensation for them; and this is perhaps all that is needed to satisfy our intuitions on the matter.

The other horn of the dilemma, that this account leaves untouched, our incurable ignorance about past compensable wrongs, is also overstated. The account does leave us unable to diagnose more than a small fraction of the past wrongs requiring compensation; but by itself, this only implies that we cannot right all of history's wrongs. The deeper worry, that in rectifying one injustice we may only be reverting to another, is at least mitigated by the fact that the most significant period of history from the standpoint of compensation is also the best known. Given this fact, the likelihood that our compensatory efforts will make things better rather than worse is greatly increased. If this solution is less precise than we might wish, it is perhaps the best that we have a right to expect.

Jeremy Waldron: "Superseding Historic Injustice"[13,14]

1. Injustice and History

The history of white settlers' dealings with the aboriginal peoples of Australia, New Zealand, and North America is largely a history of injustice. People, or whole peoples, were attacked, defrauded, and expropriated; their lands were stolen and their lives were ruined. What are we to do about these injustices? We know what we should think about them: they are to be studied and condemned, remembered and lamented. But morality is a practical matter, and judgments of "just" and "unjust" like all moral judgments have implications for action. To say that a future act open to us now would be unjust is to commit ourselves to avoiding it. But what of past injustice? What is the practical importance now of a judgment that injustice occurred in the past?

In the first instance the question is one of metaethics. Moral judgments are prescriptive in their illocutionary force; they purport to guide choices.[15] But since the only choices we can guide are choices in front of us, judgments about the past must look beyond the particular events that are their ostensible subject matter. The best explanation of this relies on universalizability. When I make a moral judgment about an event *E*, I do so not in terms of the irreducible particularity of *E* but on the basis of some feature of *E* that other events might share.

In saying, for example, "*E* was unjust," I am saying, "There is something about *E* and the circumstances in which it is performed, such that any act of that kind performed in such circumstances would be unjust." I am not so much prescribing the avoidance of *E* itself (a prescription that makes no sense if E is in the past), but prescribing the avoidance of *E*-type events. If *E* involved breaking a promise, or taking advantage of someone's credulity, then our condemnation of it commits us to a similar condemnation of breaches of faith or exploitation in the present. Though *E* occurred 150 years ago, to condemn it is to express a determination now that in the choices we face, we will avoid actions of this kind.[16]

The point of doing this is not that we learn new and better standards for our lives from the judgments we make about the past. Unless we had those standards already, we would not make those judgments. But our moral understanding of the past is often a way of bringing to imaginative life the full implications of principles to which we are already in theory committed. To be disposed to act morally, it is not enough to be equipped with a list of appropriate principles. One also needs a sense of the type of situation in which these things may suddenly be at stake, the temptations that might lead one to betray them, and the circumstances and entanglements that make otherwise virtuous people start acting viciously. That is what history provides: a lesson about what it is like for people just like us—human, all too human—to face real moral danger.

Beyond that, there is an importance to the historical recollection of injustice that has to do with identity and contingency. It is a well-known characteristic of great injustice that those who suffer it go to their deaths with the conviction that these things must not be forgotten. It is easy to misread that as vain desire for vindication, a futile threat of infamy upon the perpetrators of an atrocity. But perhaps the determination to remember is bound up with the desire to sustain a specific character as a person or community against a background of infinite possibility. That this happened rather that that—that people were massacred (though they need not have been), that lands were taken (though they might have been bought fairly), that promises were broken (though they might have been kept)—the historic record has a fragility that consists, for large part, in the sheer contingency of what happened in the past. What happened might have been otherwise, and, just because of that, it is not something one can reason back to if what actually took place has been forgotten or concealed.[17]

Each person establishes a sense of herself in terms of her ability to identify the subject or agency of her present thinking with that of certain acts and events that took place in the past, and in terms of her ability to hold fast to a distinction between memory so understood and wishes, fantasies, or various other ideas of things that might have happened but did not.[18] But remembrance in this sense is equally important to communities—families, tribes, nations, parties—that is, to human entities that exist often for much longer than individual men and women. To neglect the historical record is to do violence to this identity and thus to the community that it sustains. And since communities help generate a deeper sense of identity for the individuals they comprise, neglecting or expunging the historical record is a way of undermining and insulting individuals as well.

When we are told to let bygones be bygones, we need to bear in mind also that the forgetfulness being urged on us is seldom the blank slate of historical oblivion. Thinking quickly fills up the vacuum with plausible tales of self-satisfaction, on the one side, and self-deprecation on the other. Those who as a matter of fact benefited from their ancestors' injustice will persuade themselves readily enough that their good fortune is due to the virtue of their race, while the descendants of their victims may too easily accept the story that they and their kind were always good for nothing. In the face of all this, only the deliberate enterprise of recollection (the enterprise we call "history"), coupled with the most determined sense that there is a difference between what happened and what we would like to think happened, can sustain the moral and cultural reality of self and community.

The topic of this article is reparation. But before I embark on my main discussion, I want to mention the role that the payment of money (or the return of lands or artifacts) may play in the embodiment of communal remembrance. Quite apart from any attempt genuinely to compensate victims or offset their losses, reparations may symbolize a society's undertaking not to forget or deny that a particular injustice took place, and to respect and help sustain a dignified sense of identity-in-memory for the people affected. A prominent recent example of this is the payment of token sums of compensation by the American government to the survivors of Japanese-American families uprooted, interned, and concentrated in 1942. The point of these payments was not to make up for the loss of home, business, opportunity, and standing in the community which these people suffered at the hands of their fellow citizens, nor was it to make up for the discomfort and degradation of their internment. If that were the aim, much more would be necessary. The point was to mark—with something that counts in the United States—a clear public recognition that this injustice did happen, that it was the American people and their government that inflicted it, and that these people were among its victims. The payments give an earnest of good faith and sincerity to that acknowledgment. Like the gift I buy for someone I have stood up, the payment is a method of putting oneself out, or going out of one's way, to apologize. It is no objection to this that the payments are purely symbolic. Since identity is bound up with symbolism, a symbolic gesture may be as important to people as any material compensation.

II. The Counterfactual Approach to Reparation

I turn now to the view that a judgment about past injustice generates a demand for full and not merely symbolic reparation—a demand not just for remembrance but for substantial transfers of land, wealth, and resources in an effort actually to rectify past wrongs. I want to examine the difficulties that these demands give rise to, particularly when they conflict with other claims that may be made in the name of justice on the land, wealth, and resources in question.

It may seem as though the demand is hopeless from the start. What is it to correct an injustice? How can we reverse the past? If we are talking about injustice that took place several generations ago, surely there is nothing we can do now to heal the lives of the actual victims, to make them less miserable or to reduce their suffering. The only experiences we can affect are those of people living now and those who will live in the future.

But though these are obvious truths, we may miss something if we repeat them too often. To stand on the premise that the past cannot be changed is to ignore the fact that people and communities live whole lives, not just series of momentary events, and that an injustice may blight, not just hurt, such a life. Individuals make plans and they see themselves as living partly for the sake of their posterity; they build not only for themselves but for future generations. Whole communities may subsist for periods much longer than individual lifetimes. How they fare at a given stage and what they can offer in the way of culture, aspiration, and morale may depend very much on the present effect of events that took place several generations earlier. Thus, part of the moral significance of a past event has to do with the difference it makes to the present.

But then there is a sense in which we can affect the moral significance of past action. Even if we cannot alter the action itself we may be able to interfere with the normal course of its consequences. The present surely looks different now from the way the present would look if a given injustice of the past had not occurred. Why not therefore change the present so that it looks more like the present that would have obtained in the absence of the injustice? Why not make it now as though the injustice had not happened, for all that its occurrence in the past is immutable and undeniable?

This is the approach taken by Robert Nozick in his account of the role played by a principle of rectification in a theory of historic entitlement:

This principle uses historical information about previous situations and injustices done in them (as defined by the first two principles of justice [namely, justice in acquisition and justice in transfer] and rights against interference), and information about the actual course of events that flowed from these injustices, until the present, and it yields a description (or descriptions) of holdings in the society. The principle of rectification presumably will make use of its best estimate of subjunctive information about what would have occurred (or a probability distribution over what might have occurred, using the expected value) if the injustice had not taken place. If the actual description of holdings turns out to be one of the descriptions yielded by the principle, then one of the descriptions yielded must be realized.[19]

The trouble with this approach is the difficulty we have in saying what would have happened if some event (which did occur) had not taken place. To a certain extent we can appeal to causal laws or, more crudely, the normal course of events. We take a description of the actual world, with its history and natural laws intact, up until the problematic event of injustice (which we shall call event "E"). In the actual course of events, what followed E (events F, G, and H) is simply what results from applying natural laws to E as an initial condition. For example, if E was your seizure of the only water hole in the desert just as I was about to slake my thirst, then F—the event that follows E—would be what happens normally when one person is deprived of water and another is not: you live and I die. So, in our counterfactual reasoning, we replace E with its closest just counterpart, $E+$ (say, we share the water hole), and we apply the laws of nature to that to see what would have happened next. Presumably what would have happened next is that we both slake our thirst and both survive. The same laws of nature that yield F given E, yield a different sequel $F+$ given the just alternative $E+$ *and* further sequels $G+$ and $H+$ on the basis of that.[20] The task of rectification then is to take some present event or situation over which we do have control (e.g., H, a distribution of resources obtaining now) and alter it so that it conforms as closely as possible to its counterpart $H+$—the situation that would obtain now if $E+$ rather than E had occurred.

But what if some of the events in the sequel to $E+$ are exercises of human choice rather than the inexorable working out of natural laws? Is it possible to say counterfactually how choices subsequent to $E+$ would have been made, so that we can determine what state of affairs ($H+$) would obtain now in a society of autonomous choosers, but for the problematic injustice? Suppose that if E had not occurred, would you have made me a fair offer to form a partnership to cultivate land near the oasis? How are we to know whether I would have accepted the offer? Had I accepted it, I might have acquired wealth that I would not otherwise have had and with it the opportunity to engage in other transactions. How are we to know which transactions I would have chosen to engage in? The problem quickly becomes intractable particularly where the counterfactual sequence $\{E+, F+, G+, H+\}$ *is* imagined to extend over several generations, and where the range of choices available at a given stage depends on the choices that would have been taken at some earlier stage.

This is not a mere academic difficulty. Suppose (counterfactually) that a certain piece of land had not been wrongfully appropriated from some Maori group in New Zealand in 1865. Then we must ask ourselves, What would the tribal owners of that land have done with it, if wrongful appropriation had not taken place? To ask this question is to ask how people would have exercised their freedom if they had had a real choice. Would they have hung on to the land and passed it on to future generations of the tribe? Or would they have sold it—but this time for a fair price—to the first honest settler who came along?[21] And, if the latter, what would he have done with it? Sold it again? Passed it on to his children? Lost it in a poker game?

Part of our difficulty in answering these questions is our uncertainty about what we are doing when we try to make guesses about the way in which free will would have been exercised. The status of counterfactual reasoning about the exercise of human freedom is unclear. I do not mean that the exercise of human choice is necessarily unpredictable. We make predictions all the time about how people will exercise their freedom. But it is not clear why our best prediction on such a matter should have moral authority in the sort of speculations we are considering.

Suppose that I am attempting to predict how my aunt will dispose of her estate. My best guess, based on all the evidence, is that having no dependents she will leave it to Amnesty International, well known as her one cherished cause. In fact, my aunt surprises everyone by leaving everything to an obscure home for stray dogs that she has only just heard of. My prediction is confounded. But the important point is the following. Even though my prediction was reasonable, even though it was based on the best available evidence, it is her whimsical decision that carries the day. My guess has no normative authority whatever with regard to the disposition of her estate. All that matters is what she eventually chooses.

If this is true of decision making in the real world, then I think it plays havoc with the idea that, normatively, the appropriate thing to do in the rectification of injustice is to make rational and informed guesses about how people would have exercised their freedom in a hypothetical world. For if such guesses carry no moral weight in the real world, why should any moral weight be associated with their use in counterfactual speculation?

This is not an epistemic difficulty. It is not that there is some fact of the matter (what this person would have chosen to do with her goods if things had been different) and our difficulty lies in discovering what that is. The thing about freedom is that there is no fact of the matter anywhere until the choice has been made. It is the act of choosing that has authority, not the existence as such of the chosen option.

Of course there are situations in which we do think it acceptable to substitute our best guess about what a person would have done for that person's actual choice. If my aunt's investments have been entrusted to me, and there is a crisis in the stock market while she is abroad and incommunicado, I must do what I figure she would have done: hold the stocks in the companies to which she has a sentimental attachment and sell the rest. Maybe she would have acted whimsically and done the opposite, but as her trustee this is morally the best I can do. By doing this I adopt in effect a rational choice approach to the decision: given what I know about her preferences, I act in a way that will maximize her utility. She might have acted perversely or she might not. But given that her hypothetical consent is my only warrant to act in this matter at all, I can do nothing except choose rationally to give content to the hypothesis.

Now we are unlikely to be able to reach conclusions this determinate in applying the rational choice approach to aboriginal land claims. We will probably not be in a position to say that selling to Q rather than to R would have been the rational thing for P to do if he had not been forcibly dispossessed, and that selling to S rather than T would have been the rational thing for Q to do if P had sold the land to him rather than to R, and so on down a reconstructed chain of entitlement. But broader conclusions may be available. Suppose P enjoyed a certain level of utility derived from his holdings, U_E, just before the events complained of took place. Then any rational choice reconstruction about what would have happened but for the injustice will maintain P's utility at that level at least. No rational chooser enters a voluntary transaction to make himself worse off. So any account of what would have happened had all transactions been voluntary will require P to emerge at least as well off as he was at the beginning of the story. If in actual reality he is worse off, the counterfactual approach will require that he be restored to a level at or above *UE*. By making our rational choice assumptions airy enough, we can reach similar conclusions about the well-being of *P*'s descendants and the well-being of the person who dispossessed *P* and of his descendants as well. And these conclusions are likely to match our intuitions: if the injustice had not taken place, the descendants of those who suffered it would be better off than they are and descendants of those who perpetrated it would be somewhat worse off than they are. So a transfer from the latter to the former seems justified.

However, several difficulties remain. One concerns what might be called the contagion of injustice. Suppose I possess a piece of land which I inherited from my father who bought it from his sister-in-law who bought it from a settler who obtained it in the mid-nineteenth century from a fraudulent transaction with a member of the Maori tribe. The counterfactual approach to reparation suggests that some transfer from me to the surviving members of the tribe may be required in order to bring the present state of affairs closer to the state of affairs that would have obtained if the fraud had not been perpetrated. Unfortunately we cannot leave the matter there. My neighbor may be in possession of a similar piece of land whose pedigree, considered in itself, is impeccable: there is no fraud, no coercion, no expropriation in the history of her holding. Still the price my neighbor (and her predecessors in title) paid for her land is likely to have been affected by the low price that was paid for my land (on account of the original fraud). Thus, rectification of the injustice will involve an adjustment of her holding as well. We cannot assume that rectificatory transfers will be confined to those who have had dealings with tainted holdings. All present holdings are called in question by this business of winding the film back to the injustice, changing that frame (from *E* to *E+),* and then winding the film forward to see what results. If one person behaves unjustly, particularly in the context of a market, the injustice will have an effect not only on her immediate victim, but—via the price mechanism—on all those who trade in the market in question. Some will gain and some will lose as a result of the injustice, and any attempt at rectification—any attempt to implement the state of affairs that would have obtained but for the injustice—will involve interfering with those holdings as well.

Worse still, the events of justice and injustice may make a considerable difference in who exists at a later time. We cannot simply hold the dramatis personae constant in our speculations. Children may be conceived and born, and leave descendants, who would not have existed if the injustice had not occurred. Short of putting them to death for their repugnancy to our counterfactuals, the present approach offers no guidance at all as to how their claims are to be dealt with.

A more general difficulty has to do with our application of rational choice in counterfactual reconstruction. People can and often do act freely to their own disadvantage, and usually when they do, they are held to the result. A man who actually loses his land in a reckless though voluntary wager and who accepts the justice of the outcome may be entitled to wonder why, in the attention we pay to aboriginal reparations, we insulate people from the possibility of similar vicissitudes. He may say, "If we are going to reconstruct a history of rational choice, let us do so for all holdings, giving everyone what they would have had if they had never acted voluntarily to their own disadvantage. Maybe that will lead to a more just world. But if we are not prepared to do that, if we insist that it is alright, from the point of view of justice, to leave a person like me stuck with the results of his actual choices, it may be more consistent to admit that we simply can't say what (by the same token) justice now requires in the case of those whose ancestors were wrongfully dispossessed."

The dilemma is a difficult one. On the one hand, there is nothing normatively conclusive about rational choice predictions. Why should the exaction of specific reparation in the real world be oriented to what the idealized agents of rational choice would have secured for themselves in a hypothetical world? On the other hand, hypothetical rational choice is essential to our normative thinking about justice. Modern contractarian theories consist almost entirely of asking what the people of a society would have agreed to in the way of institutions governing the distribution of resources, had they been consulted.[22] But it is characteristic of such approaches that they are holistic, systemic, and structural rather than local and specific in their conclusions and recommendations. We deploy the counterfactuals of modern contractarianism to evaluate the entire basic structure of a society, not to evaluate some particular distribution among a subset of its members.[23]

The issue is particularly acute because the reparations that these counterfactuals support are likely to have a wide effect on holdings across the board. The case is quite different from the simple situation of my aunt's investments, where I ask only what she would have done with her capital and do not attempt to redistribute a whole array of different people's holdings. Reparation of historic injustice really is redistributive: it moves resources from one person to another. It seems unfair to do this on a basis that reconstructs a profile of holdings by attributing rational choice motivations to only some, and not all, of the parties who are affected.

Ultimately, what is raised here is the question of whether it is possible to rectify particular injustices without undertaking a comprehensive redistribution that addresses all claims of justice that may be made. The counterfactual approach aims to bring the present state of affairs as close as possible to the state of affairs that would have obtained if some specifically identified injustice had not occurred. But why stop there? Why be content merely to bring about the state of affairs that would have ensued if this injustice had not occurred? Why not try to make things even better than they would have been if that particular unjust transaction, or any unjust transaction, had not taken place? Are we so sure that a smooth transition, untainted by particular injustice, from some early nineteenth-century status quo ante would leave us now where we actually want to be? Quite apart from particular frauds and expropriations, things were not marvelous in the nineteenth century. Many people lacked access to any significant resources, and many people had much more than what one might regard as a fair share. Why take all that as the baseline for our present reconstruction?

III. The Perpetuation and Remission of Injustice

So far we have focused on the effects of isolated acts of injustice like event *E*, events that took place firmly in the past. But we are seldom so fortunate as to confront injustice in discrete doses. The world we know is characterized by patterns of injustice, by standing arrangements—rules, laws, regimes, and other institutions—that operate unjustly day after day. Though the establishment of such an arrangement was an unjust event when it took place in the past, its injustice then consisted primarily in the injustice it promised for the future. To judge that establishment unjust is to commit oneself to putting a stop to the ongoing situation; it is a commitment to prevent the perpetuation of the injustice that the law or the institution embodies; it is to commit oneself to its remission.

Suppose someone stole my car yesterday. That is an unjust act that took place at a certain place and at a certain time: at 9:30 A.M. on September 5, my car was stolen from the parking lot. Clearly anyone committed to the prevention of injustice should have tried to stop the theft taking place. But once the car has been driven nefariously out of the parking lot, the matter does not end there. For now there is a continuing injustice: I lack possession of an automobile to which I am entitled, and the thief possesses an automobile to which she is not entitled. Taking the car away from the thief and returning it to me, the rightful owner, is not a way of compensating me for an injustice that took place in the past; it is a way of remitting an injustice that is ongoing into the present. Phrases like "Let bygones be bygones" are inappropriate here. The loss of my car is not a bygone: it is a continuing state of affairs.

The implications of this example are clear for the historic cases we are considering. Instead of regarding the expropriation of aboriginal lands as an isolated act of injustice that took place at a certain time now relegated firmly to the past, we may think of it as a persisting injustice. The injustice persists, and it is perpetuated by the legal system as long as the land that was expropriated is not returned to those from whom it was taken. On this model, the rectification of injustice is a much simpler matter than the approach we discussed in the previous section. We do not have to engage in any counterfactual speculation. We simply give the property back to the person or group from whom it was taken and thus put an end to what would otherwise be its continued expropriation.

Difficulties arise of course if the original owner has died, for then there is no one to whom the property can be restored. We could give it to her heirs and successors, but in doing so we are already setting off down the counterfactual road, reckoning that this is what the proprietor's wish would have been had she had control of her property. Fortunately, that difficulty is obviated in the case of many aboriginal claims: usually the property is owned by a tribe, a nation, or a community—some entity that endures over time in spite of mortality of its individual members. It is this enduring entity that has been dispossessed, and the same entity is on hand now more than a hundred years later to claim its heritage.

What, if any, are the difficulties with this approach? It does not involve any of the problems of counterfactual reasoning that we identified earlier, but does it face any other problems? As I see it, the main difficulty is the following. Are we sure that the entitlement that was originally violated all those years ago is an entitlement that survives into the present? The approach we are considering depends on the claim that the right that was violated when white settlers first seized the land can be identified as a right that is still being violated today by settlers' successors in title. Their possession of the land today is said to be as wrongful vis-à-vis the present tribal owners as the original expropriation. Can this view be justified?

It is widely believed that some rights are capable of "fading" in their moral importance by virtue of the passage of time and by the sheer persistence of what was originally a wrongful infringement. In the law of property, we recognize doctrines of prescription and adverse possession. In criminal procedure and in torts, we think it important to have statutes of limitations. The familiarity of these doctrines no doubt contributes to the widespread belief that, after several generations have passed, certain wrongs are simply not worth correcting. Think of the earlier example of the theft of my automobile. Certainly, the car should be returned if the thief is discovered within weeks or months of the incident. But what if she is never caught? What if the stolen car remains in her family for decades and is eventually passed down as an heirloom to her children and grandchildren? Are we so sure that when the circumstances of its acquisition eventually come to light, it should be returned without further ado to me or my estate?

The view that a violated entitlement can "fade" with time may seem unfair. The injustice complained of is precisely that the rightful owner has been dispossessed. It seems harsh if the fact of her dispossession is used as a way of weakening her claim. It may also seem to involve some moral hazard by providing an incentive for wrongdoers to cling to their ill-gotten gains, in the hope that the entitlement they violated will fade away because of their adverse possession.

Still, the view that certain rights are prescriptable has a number of things to be said in its favor. Some are simply pragmatic. Statutes of limitations are inspired as much by procedural difficulties about evidence and memory, as by any doctrine about rights. It is hard to establish what happened if we are enquiring into the events that occurred decades or generations ago. There are nonprocedural pragmatic arguments also. For better or worse, people build up structures of expectation around the resources that are actually under their control. If a person controls a resource over a long enough period, then she and others may organize their lives and their economic activity around the premise that that resource is "hers," without much regard to the distant provenance of her entitlement. Upsetting these expectations in the name of restitutive justice is bound to be costly and disruptive.[24]

There may be reasons of principle as well. One set of reasons has to do with changes in background social and economic circumstances. If the requirements of justice are sensitive to circumstances such as the size of the population or the incidence of scarcity, then there is no guarantee that those requirements (and the rights that they constitute) will remain constant in relation to a given resource or piece of land as the decades and generations go by. I shall deal with this in detail in the next section of this article.

The other reason entitlements may fade has to do with the basis of the rights themselves. Theories of historic entitlement, like the theory of John Locke or the theory sketched more recently by Robert Nozick, focus on the establishment of an intimate relation between a person and a resource as the basis of property rights.[25] A person works with an object, shaping and modifying it, so that it becomes imbued with part of her personality; it comes to contain a part of herself. But if the right is taken out of her hands for a long period, the intimacy of that relation may evaporate.

Whether this happens depends partly on what we take to be the morally important relation between the person and the thing. In John Locke's theory, the relation is described as mixing one's labor.[26] A person mixes her labor with a piece of land, and the land comes to embody her efforts; that labor is now like a jewel embedded in the land for all time. So anyone who takes hold of the land is necessarily taking hold of the jewel. And no one can doubt that the jewel— the labor—continues to belong to the original person who invested it. So even if a hundred years of adverse possession go by, the land still contains the labor— and thus part of the personality—of that individual. The labor is intrinsically and essentially hers, though embedded in an object that has been out of her possession for all that time. As long as the personality of this individual commands our moral respect, she is always entitled to demand this part of it back.[27]

Unfortunately, as I have argued elsewhere, the Lockean image of labor (whether it is individual or cooperative) being literally embedded or mixed in an object is incoherent.[28] Even if it did make sense, the idea would be far too strong to do the work its proponents want it to do. For it would it be impossible to explain how property rights thus acquired could be alienable—how they could be transferred, through sale or gift, from one person to another—without offense to the personality of the original acquirer. If a resource, once labored on, contains for all time a fragment of the laborer's personality, how can that same resource be held legitimately by someone to whom that laborer has chosen to transfer it? Not only that, but how can that second entitlement (the entitlement of the transferee) have anything like the moral force of the original entitlement? Does a fragment of the transferee's personality replace the original nugget of labor in the object? If it does (and if we can make sense of the idea that this is possible), then surely we cannot dismiss out of hand the possibility that an expropriator may also in time replace the original embedded labor of the person she expropriated with something of her own.

In recent years, historical entitlement has been found its most able and consistent defender in Robert Nozick, and some reliance on Nozick's approach is almost inevitable for any defender of historic reparations.[29] But Nozick also dismissed the conundrums of Locke's theory about the "mixing of labor." He retained the form of a Lockean approach—insisting that an adequate theory of justice must be founded on some principle of unilateral acquisition—without telling us much about the content of that principle or how it might be justified.[30] However, the task of filling in the content cannot be indefinitely postponed because the substance and justification of a principle of acquisition will partly determine what we can do with it. Do entitlements based on acquisition fade over time, or can we appeal to them generations later as a basis for reparation? We cannot answer this question until we know what the entitlement theorist proposes to put in the place of the incoherent Lockean idea.

If we abandon Locke's image of the mixing of labor, the most plausible account of initial acquisition goes like this. An individual, *P*, who takes possession of an object or a piece of land and who works on it, alters it, and uses it, makes it in effect a part of her life, a pivotal point in her thinking, planning, and action. She shapes it in a certain way—ploughing it, for example, or practicing good husbandry in her hunting over it—so as to allow it to perform a certain role in her life and activity not only now but in the future. If someone else, *Q*, comes along and seizes the land, taking it from *P* without her consent, then the whole structure of action is disrupted. *P*'s planning and the structure of *P*'s action are destroyed and replaced by that of *Q*. Moreover, *P* did not have to do anything equivalent to this disruption in order to establish the resource as the center of her life. Before *P* took it, shaped it, etc., the resource was the center of nobody's life. But when *Q* took it, it was already the center of *P*'s. This asymmetry between the first and subsequent appropriator is the basis of *P*'s historical entitlement and the basis of its moral priority. It is the reason why we say that *Q*'s taking is wrong in a way that *P*'s original appropriation was not, despite the fact that both parties are seeking to realize their autonomous purposes in the resource.

If any defense of historical entitlement is possible, it is going to be something along those lines. But unfortunately, if this sort of line is taken, then we have a justification for historical entitlement that is vulnerable to prescription, a justification that is weakened by the historic persistence of dispossession, a justification that does fade over time. If something was taken from me decades ago, the claim that it now forms the center of my life and that it is still indispensable to the exercise of my autonomy is much less credible. For I must have developed some structure of subsistence. And that will be where my efforts have gone and where my planning and my practical thinking have been focused. I may of course yearn for the lost resource and spend a lot of time wishing that I had it back. I may even organize my life around the campaign for its restoration. But that is not the same thing as the basis of the original claim. The original entitlement[31] [was] based on the idea that I have organized my life around the use of this object, not that I have organized my life around the specific project of hanging on to it or getting it back.

It may be objected that this argument furnishes an incentive to anyone who is inclined to violate another's rights. She knows that if she steals resources and hangs on to the proceeds, her victim will have to reorder his life and, once he does, he will no longer be in a position to claim that the stolen resources should be restored because of their centrality to his plans. But I do not see how this difficulty can be avoided, unless we introduce a different theory of the basis of property entitlements. We cannot pretend that a long-stolen resource continues to play a part in the original owner's life when in fact it does not, merely in order to avoid the moral hazard of this incentive effect. What the objection shows, I think, is that the normal line of argument for property entitlements based on autonomy is simply insufficient to establish imprescriptible rights. And what the failure of Locke's argument shows is that any case for making property rights fully imprescriptible is likely to run into other serious difficulties.

Historical entitlement theories are most impressive when moral entitlement is conjoined with present possession. Then it seems plausible to suggest that continued possession of the object might be indispensable to the possessor's autonomy and that an attack on possession is an attack on autonomy. But when the conjunction is disrupted, particularly when, as in the cases we are considering, it is disrupted for a considerable period of time, the claim looks much shakier.

I think this argument is important, by the way, but not always conclusive. It may not apply so clearly to cases where the dispossessed subject is a tribe or community, rather than an individual, and where the holding of which it has been dispossessed is particularly important for its sense of identity as a community. Many of the aboriginal claims, in New Zealand, Australia, and North America, have to do with burial grounds or lands which have some other symbolic or religious significance. Religions and cultural traditions we know are very resilient, and the claim that the lost lands form the center of a present way of life—and remain sacred objects despite their loss—may be as credible a hundred years on as it was at the time of the dispossession. In this regard, claims that land of religious significance should be returned to its original owners may have an edge over claims for the return of lands whose significance for them is mainly material or economic. Over the decades people are likely to have developed new modes of subsistence, making the claim that the land is crucial to their present way of life less credible in the economic case than in the religious case.

IV. Circumstances and Supersession

I mentioned two ways in which an entitlement might be vulnerable to the passage of time. As well as the one we have just considered, there is also an important point to be made about changes in background circumstances that occur in the period after the original violation. I have in mind changes in population, changes in resource availability, occurrence of famine or ecological disaster, and so on. To assess these cases we have to ask questions about the relation between justice and background circumstances. Is justice relative to circumstances? Do entitlements change as circumstances change? If so, does the significance of past injustice change also? Or should we simply say that once something becomes mine it remains mine (and so it remains wrong for you to keep it), no matter what else happens in the world?

It is difficult to resist the conclusion that entitlements are sensitive to circumstances. Certainly, the level of our concern for various human predicaments is sensitive to the circumstances that constitute those predicaments. One's concern about poverty, for example, varies depending on the extent of the opportunities available to the poor: to be poor but to have some opportunity for amelioration is to be in a better predicament than to be poor with no opportunities at all. Similarly, our concern for the homeless may vary with the season of the year or the climate of the state in which they live. And these are not just fluctuations in subjective response: they are circumstantially sensitive variations in what we would take to be the appropriate level of concern. Now, the (appropriate) level of our concern about such predicaments is directly related to the burden of justification that must be shouldered by those who defend property rights. If an individual makes a claim to the exclusive use or possession of some resources in our territory, then the difficulty of sustaining that claim will clearly have some relation to the level of our concern about the plight of other persons who will have to be excluded from the resources if the claim is recognized. The only theory of property entitlement that would be totally immune to variations in background circumstances would be one that did not accept any burden of justification in relation to our real concerns.

We can express this claim about sensitivity to circumstances as follows. In the case of almost every putative entitlement, it is possible to imagine a pair of different circumstances, C, and $C2$, such that the entitlement can only barely be justified in C, and cannot be justified at all in $C2$. The shift from C to $C2$ represents a tipping point so far as the justification of the entitlement is concerned. If this is accepted it clearly makes a difference to the original acquisition of property rights. A scale of acquisition that might be appropriate in a plentiful environment with a small population may be quite inappropriate in the same environment with a large population, or with the same population once natural resources have become depleted. In a plentiful environment with a small population, an individual appropriation of land makes no one worse off. As John Locke put it, "He that leaves as much as another can make use of, does as good as take nothing at all. No Body could think himself injur'd by the drinking of another Man, though he took a good Draught, who had a whole River of the same Water left him to quench his thirst. And the case of Land and Water, where there is enough of both, is perfectly the same."[32] But as Locke also recognized, the picture changed once the population increased to the point where scarcity was felt. If one person's appropriation cast a shadow on the survival prospects of others, then it evidently raised questions of a moral character that were not raised when resources were as plentiful as water in a river.[33] One does not need the exact formulation of a "Lockean proviso" to see this. It is simply that there are real and felt moral concerns in the one case that have to be addressed which are not present in the other.

The same point is recognized by Robert Nozick. The principle of acquisition that forms the linchpin of his theory depends for its acceptability on the claim that individual appropriations of previously unowned goods do not worsen anybody's situation.[34] (Nozick wishes, as far as possible, to present initial acquisition in the same light of Pareto improvement as consensual transfer.) We need not worry about the exact details of this proviso or of the various Lockean and Nozickian formulations of it.[35] What is clear is that in any plausible theory of historic entitlement, there is some spectrum of social circumstances, relating to the effect a putative acquisition would have on the prospects and life chances of other people, such that the further one goes along this spectrum the less inclined we are to say that the acquisition in question generates legitimate rights.

So far I have talked about one acquisitive act, A, taking place in one set of circumstances, $C1$, and another acquisitive act, $A2$, taking place in different circumstances, $C2$. I have said that circumstances may make a difference so that the conditions for the moral legitimacy of $A2$ may be different from the conditions for the moral legitimacy of $A1$ (even though, considered in themselves, $A1$ and $A2$ are the same type of act). However, we know that acquisition is not an isolated act. By laboring on a resource, the would-be acquirer not only takes it now but also purports to appropriate it permanently. The effect of her acquisition continues to be felt long after the acquisitive action has taken place. What happens, then, if circumstances change after the moment of the acquisitive act but during the time that the act has effect, that is, during the period of ownership to which the acquisitive action gives rise? A person performs acquisitive act A, in circumstances $C1$ that make it legitimate. She establishes a title for herself (and her successors) that endures through time. During that time circumstances change, so that conditions $C2$ now obtain, and conditions $C2$ are such that an equivalent act of appropriation would not be legitimate. What effect does this change have on the legitimacy of the title founded by action $A1$?

The answer has to be that it calls the legitimacy of that title into question. We can reach this conclusion by two routes.

The first and most straightforward argument is that property entitlements constrain us over a period of time, and they do so continually in the sense that they constantly call for action in support of them or they constantly involve action undertaken in their exercise. Day after day, an owner performs acts whose legitimacy is based on her entitlement; if she did not have the entitlement, she would have no right to perform these acts. Also, day after day, the owner faces explicit or implicit challenges from others, wanting to use her resource; if she did not have the entitlement to rely on she would not be in a moral position to rebut or resist these challenges. So each time she exercises her right and each time she resists an encroachment, she relies on the entitlement founded by $A1$. At each of those times, the legitimacy of what she does depends on the appropriateness of her entitlement as a moral right at that time. So long as circumstances remain unchanged or so long as any changes are broadly consonant with the necessary conditions for the legitimacy of her entitlement, the fact that her claim is, so to speak, renewed day after day is not a worry. Its renewal is automatic. But if circumstances change radically in the way we have been envisaging, the continued application of her entitlement cannot be taken for granted.

The second line of argument is a response to an objection that might be made. Someone might object as follows: Surely if the original appropriation were legitimate, the conditions of its legitimacy would take into account the normal vicissitudes of human life including the prospect that things might change, goods become scarce, etc. To say that *P* acquires an entitlement by *A*, is surely to say that she acquires an entitlement that endures even in the face of changing circumstances. That is why we subject *A* to such strict scrutiny, for it purports to found an enduring entitlement, not a temporary and circumstantially vulnerable one. The test for initial appropriation should be severe and morally rigorous, but if *A1* passes this test, it should not have to face further scrutiny later simply because conditions are not the same.

Here is the response to this objection. Maybe it is a good thing for the test of the initial acquisition, *A1*, to take into account the possibility that conditions may change and therefore only to certify entitlements that survive that consideration. But it surely cannot be the upshot of this that, in circumstances *C1*, only those acquisitions are certified that would be valid in all circumstances including *C2*. That would be wasteful and pointless: why shouldn't people act as though goods are plentiful, at least when they are plentiful?

No. If a rigorous test of initial acquisition does take future vicissitudes into account, it will do so in a more subtle way. What it will do is provide ab initio, in the terms of the entitlement, that the exact array of rights, liberties, and powers is to be circumstantially sensitive. Thus, what *P* acquires through *A1* are rights that entitle her to do one set of things in *C1*, and another, perhaps more restricted, set of things in *C2*. So, as before, the net effect of *P*'s entitlement does vary, depending on the circumstances. If, for example, *P* acquires an oasis in conditions of plenty, she acquires (i) a right to use it freely and exclude others from its use so long as water remains plentiful in the territory, and (ii) a duty to share it with others on some fair basis if ever water becomes scarce. The right that is (permanently) acquired through *A* is thus circumstantially sensitive in the actions it licenses.

If all this is accepted so far as justice in acquisition is concerned, it must also apply to issues and allegations of injustice. Suppose a person has legitimately acquired an object in circumstances of plenty, *C1*, and another person comes along and snatches it from her. That act of snatching, we may say, is an injustice. But the very same action of snatching an already appropriated object may not be wrong in a different set of circumstances, *C2*, where desperate scarcity has set in and the snatcher has no other means of staying alive. One and the same type of action may be injustice in one set of circumstances and not injustice in another.[36]

I hope it is clear where the argument is going. I said that the burden of justifying an exclusive entitlement depends (in part) on the impact of others' interests of being excluded from the resources in question and that that impact is likely to vary as circumstances change. Similarly an acquisition which is legitimate in one set of circumstances may not be legitimate in another set of circumstances. From this I inferred that an initially legitimate acquisition may become illegitimate or have its legitimacy restricted (as the basis of an ongoing entitlement) at a later time on account of a change in circumstances. By exactly similar reasoning, it seems possible that an act which counted as an injustice when it was committed in circumstances *C*, may be transformed, so far as its ongoing effect is concerned, into a just situation if circumstances change in the meantime from *C* to *C2*. When this happens, I shall say the injustice has been *superseded*.

Consider the following example.[37] On the savanna, a number of groups appropriate water holes, in conditions where it is known that there are enough water holes for each group. So long as these conditions obtain, it seems reasonable for the members of given group, *P*, to use the water hole they have appropriated without asking permission of other groups with whom they share the plains; and it may even seem reasonable for them to exclude members of other groups from the casual use of their water holes, saying to them, "You have your own water hole. Go off and use that, and leave ours alone." But suppose there is an ecological disaster, and all the water holes dry up except the one that the members of *P* are using. Then in these changed circumstances, notwithstanding the legitimacy of their original appropriation, it is no longer in order for *P* to exclude others from their water hole. Indeed it may no longer be in order for members of *P* to casually use "their own" water hole in the way they did before. In the new circumstances, it may be incumbent on them to draw up a rationing scheme that allows for the needs of everyone in the territory to be satisfied from this one resource. Changing circumstances can have an effect on ownership rights notwithstanding the moral legitimacy of the original appropriation.

Next, suppose as before that in circumstances of plenty various groups on the savanna are legitimately in possession of their respective water holes. One day, motivated purely by greed, members of group *Q* descend on the water hole possessed by group *P* and insist on sharing that with them. (What's more they do not allow reciprocity; they do not allow members of *P* to share any water hole that was legitimately in the possession of *Q*.) That is an injustice. But then circumstances change, and all the water holes of the territory dry up except the one that originally belonged to *P*. The members of group *Q* are already sharing that water hole on the basis of their earlier incursion. But now that circumstances have changed, they are entitled to share that water hole; it no longer counts as an injustice. It is in fact part of what justice now requires. The initial injustice by *Q* against *P* has been superseded by circumstances.

Once again, it may be objected that this reasoning generates a moral hazard—an incentive for wrongdoers to seize others' lands confident in the knowledge that if they hang on to them wrongfully for long enough their possession may eventually become rightful.[38] But the argument of this section is not that the passage of time per se supersedes all claims of injustice. Rather, the argument is that claims about justice and injustice must be responsive to changes in circumstances. Suppose there had been no injustice: still, a change in circumstances (such as a great increase in world population) might justify our forcing the aboriginal inhabitants of some territory to share their land with others. If this is so, then the same change in circumstances in the real world can justify our saying that the others' occupation of some of their lands, which was previously wrongful, may become morally permissible. There is no moral hazard in this supersession because the aboriginal inhabitants would have had to share their lands, whether the original injustice had taken place or not.

I do not think this possibility—of the supersession of past injustice—can be denied, except at the cost of making one's theory of historical entitlement utterly impervious to variations in the circumstance in which holdings are acquired and withheld from others. If circumstances make a difference to what counts as a just acquisition, then they must make a difference also to what counts as an unjust incursion. And if they make a difference to that, then in principle we must concede that a change in circumstances can affect whether a particular continuation of adverse possession remains an injustice or not.

Of course, from the fact that supersession is a possibility, it does not follow that it always happens. Everything depends on which circumstances are taken to be morally significant and how as matter of fact circumstances have changed. It may be that some of the historic injustices that concern us have not been superseded and that, even under modern circumstances, the possession of certain aboriginal lands by the descendants of those who expropriated their original owners remains a crying injustice. My argument is not intended to rule that out. But there have been huge changes since North America and Australasia were settled by white colonists. The population has increased manyfold, and most of the descendants of the colonists, unlike their ancestors, have nowhere else to go. We cannot be sure that these changes in circumstances supersede the injustice of their continued possession of aboriginal lands, but it would not be surprising if they did. The facts that have changed are exactly the sort of facts one would expect to make a difference to the justice of a set of entitlements over resources.

V. Conclusion

It is important that defenders of aboriginal claims face up to the possibility of the supersession of historic injustice. Even if this particular thesis about supersession is mistaken, some account has to be given of the impact on aboriginal claims and on the reparation of generations old injustices of the demographic and ecological changes that have taken place.

Apart from anything else, the changes that have taken place over the past two hundred years mean that the costs of respecting primeval entitlements are much greater now than they were in 1800. Two hundred years ago, a small aboriginal group could have exclusive domination of "a large and fruitful Territory,"[39] without much prejudice to the needs and interests of very many other human beings. Today, such exclusive rights would mean many people going hungry who might otherwise be fed and many people living in poverty who might otherwise have an opportunity to make a decent life. Irrespective of the occurrence of past injustice, this imbalance would have to be rectified sooner or later. That is the basis for my argument that claims about historic injustice predicated on the status quo ante may be superseded by our determination to distribute the resources of the world in a way that is fair to all of its existing inhabitants.

Behind the thesis of supersession lies a determination to focus upon present and prospective costs—the suffering and the deprivation over which we still have some control. The idea is that any conception of justice which is to be made practically relevant for the way we act now must be a scheme that takes into account modern circumstances and the way those affect the conditions under which people presently live their lives. Arguments for reparation take as conclusive claims of entitlement oriented toward circumstances that are radically different from those we actually face: claims of entitlement based on the habitation of a territory by a small fraction of its present population, and claims of entitlement based on the determination to ignore the present dispersal of persons and peoples on the face of the earth, simply because the historic mechanisms of such dispersal were savagely implicated in injustice. And yet, here we all are. The present circumstances are the ones that are real: it is in the actual world that people starve or are hurt or degraded if the demands of justice in relation to their circumstances are not met. Justice, we say, is a matter of the greatest importance. But the importance to be accorded it is relative to what may actually happen if justice is not done, not to what might have happened if injustice in the past had been avoided.

I want to end by emphasizing two points that qualify or clarify this thesis of the supersession of historic injustice. First, what I have said applies only if an honest attempt is being made to arrange things justly for the future. If no such attempt is being made, there is nothing to overwhelm or supersede the enterprise of reparation. My thesis is not intended as a defense of complacency or inactivity, and to the extent that opponents of reparation are complacent about the injustice of the status quo, their resistance is rightly condemned. Repairing historic injustice is, as we have seen, a difficult business and, as a matter of fact, it is almost always undertaken by people of good will. The only thing that can trump that enterprise is an honest and committed resolve to do justice for the future, a resolve to address present circumstances in a way that respects the claims and needs of everyone.

Second, my thesis is not that such resolve has priority over all rectificatory actions. I claim only that it has priority over reparation which might carry us in a direction contrary to that which is indicated by a prospective theory of justice. Often and understandably, claims based on reparation and claims based on forward-looking principles will coincide, for, as we saw in Section III above, past injustice is not without its present effects. It is a fact that many of the descendants of those who were defrauded and expropriated live demoralized in lives of relative poverty—relative, that is, to the descendants of those who defrauded them. If the relief of poverty and the more equal distribution of resources is the aim of a prospective theory of justice, it is likely that the effect of rectifying past wrongs will carry us some distance in this direction. All the same, it is worth stressing that it is the impulse to justice now that should lead the way in this process, not the reparation of something whose wrongness is understood primarily in relation to conditions that no longer obtain.

Entitlements that fade with time, counterfactuals that are impossible to verify, injustices that are overtaken by circumstances—all this is a bit distant, I am afraid, from the simple conviction that, if something was wrongly taken, it must be right to give it back. The arguments I have made may seem to deflate a lot of the honest enthusiasm that surrounds aboriginal claims and the hope that now for the first time in centuries we may be ready to do justice to people and peoples whom we have perennially maltreated. The arguments may also seem to compromise justice unnecessarily, as they shift from the straightforward logic of compensation to an arcane and calculative casuistry that tries to balance incommensurable claims.

But societies are not simple circumstances, and it does not detract one bit from the importance of justice nor from the force of the duties it generates to insist that its requirements are complex and that they may be sensitive to differences in circumstance. Even the members of a modern society not afflicted by a history like ours would find the demands of justice difficult to discern and hard to weigh: the modern discussion of the subject, with the utopian cast of its "perfect compliance" assumptions, has made that at least clear.[40] It is true that in many cases the complexity of these issues does not diminish our ability to recognize acts of injustice—stark and awful—like direct expropriation and genocide. The fallacy lies in thinking that the directness of such perception and the outrage that attends it translate into simple and straightforward certainty about what is to be done once such injustices have occurred.

"First come, first served." "We were here first." These simplicities have always been unpleasant ways of denying present aspirations or resisting current claims of need. They become no more pleasant, and in the end no more persuasive, by being associated with respect for aboriginal peoples or revulsion from the violence and expropriation that have disfigured our history.

Janna Thompson: "Historical Obligations"[41]

I. A historical obligation is a moral responsibility belonging to citizens of a state, members of a family, or some other inter-generational group, in respect to commitments made, deeds done, or obligations incurred by their predecessors. The relation between past actions and what individuals are now required to do is a moral/logical one. "We ought to make recompense for the injustices of our predecessors because injustices require restitution." "We ought to keep their promises and fulfill their contracts because promises ought to be kept and contracts ought to be honoured." Historical obligations invoke the past as a source of obligation or right. History is important not merely because what happened in the past is often causally responsible for present inequities, but because it defines some of our present duties and rights.

Do we have historical obligations? Some people think so. Tichy and Oddie suggest that the Treaty of Waitangi could be understood as New Zealand's so-

cial contract, as the basis for cooperation among the peoples making up this society. If it is so understood, they say, then we are required to restore the course
of justice by returning to the terms of the treaty.[42] Maoris themselves have demanded that some of their traditional hunting, fishing, and territorial rights guaranteed by this treaty be restored to them.[43] In America and Canada claims have
been made by indigenous people for restoration of treaty rights or compensation for treaty violations. Australian Aborigines have made claims for the restoration of land rights, and are demanding apology and compensation for past injustices to their communities.[44]

In debates about the moral legitimacy of such demands two major issues
arise. The first is the question of whether it is fair to burden presently existing
people with the task of making recompense for injustices committed in the past.
The Australian Prime Minister John Howard persistently responds to requests for
an official apology or compensation for harms done by past Australian governments to Aborigines by maintaining that Australians of this generation should
not be required to accept guilt and blame for past actions and policies over
which they had no control.[45] Some New Zealand politicians have responded in
a similar way to Maori claims for reparations for violations of the Treaty of Waitangi.[46] Citizens who reject historical obligations for this reason would probably
be prepared to take responsibility for their own injustices. They may acknowledge some responsibility for injustices committed by their present government.
What they object to is the idea that they have an obligation to make recompense
for deeds done before they were born, came of age, or arrived in the country.

The second issue is how historical obligations are related to other obligations
of justice—in particular requirements of equity. "Why should not governments
do what principles of equality require now rather than what outdated and often
unprincipled agreements require?" asks Will Kymlicka about treaties made with
indigenous people.[47] Even if an agreement is not out of date or unprincipled its
provisions may be outweighed by entitlements of existing and future people or
by the duty to remedy present inequities. It might be argued that historical obligations are trumped by more pressing moral requirements, or that they simply
fade away over time.

This is a defence of historical obligation. I will argue that we do have historical obligations of a moral kind and I will present reasons for thinking that they
persist through time and change and are not likely to be overridden by other duties of justice. The defence I will offer does not encompass all of the demands that
could be called historical obligations. Its concern is to provide an account of obligations that we have as citizens or as citizens of a certain kind, for example, as
Pakeha New Zealanders or non-Aboriginal Australians, for commitments made
and injustices done by representatives or officials of our society in the past. It
concentrates on obligations that arise from commitments made and injustices
done to people as members of inter-generational communities—injustices such
as breaking treaties, seizing communal land, or undermining cultural life.

II. From the mere fact that injustice was done in the past it does not follow
that anyone now has an obligation to make restitution or that anyone is entitled

to receive it. Right of possession does not by itself require that those who did no wrong make restitution for unjust dispossession. Even "right of inheritance" does not imply that the descendants of those who did the wrong are obliged to make restitution to the descendants of those who were wronged. Historical obligation and entitlement need an independent justification.

Historical obligations and entitlements are often justified by an appeal to "moral collectivism"—to the idea that responsibility and entitlement in these cases belongs not to individuals but to states and other inter-generational communities. States, nations, tribes, and other such communities are regarded by moral collectivists as the agents who make and break treaties, incur moral debts, and have the obligation to make restitution, and they are assumed to be responsible to the community to whom the commitment was made or to whom the injustice was done, not to particular individuals or governments.[48] Historical obligations, say moral collectivists, are morally analogous to the obligations individuals incur through their past actions and commitments. Just as individuals are required to keep their promises and pay their debts, so too are states, tribes, and corporations.

The problem with moral collectivism is that it simply assumes that it is morally legitimate to pass on obligations and entitlements from members of one generation to their successors. To answer those who wonder why they should be burdened with obligations from the past we require a justification for imposing and accepting these responsibilities. It should be noted that the problem of justification is more severe than the familiar one of justifying the obligation to obey laws made by our predecessors. Through democratic processes we can repeal or change laws, even constitutional provisions, but historical obligations cannot be abrogated by the combined will of the people.

Standard theories of collective responsibility do not provide this justification. They assume that individuals can only be held responsible for what their group did if they were able to influence its behaviour. Joel Feinberg, for example, lists "opportunity for control" as one of the necessary conditions for liability for an action or practice of a group.[49] Since we have no opportunity to control our political predecessors, this account cannot justify collective responsibilities from the past. Those who identify with their state or nation, or with past as well as present citizens, may be predisposed to accept historical obligations. But the fact that some people do not think that they have them suggests that not every citizen has such an identity, or that having it does not necessarily lead to acceptance of the responsibility. My defence of historical obligations does not deny that we can speak of states and other groups as having moral responsibilities. It explains why we should accept responsibilities incurred by our political predecessors—and why it is therefore possible for states to make inter-generational moral commitments that future people are obliged to honour. It reveals the moral machinery on which moral collectivism depends.

Let us assume that citizens of a political society accept some responsibility for the commitments and deeds of their representatives and officials. The acts that these representatives may perform include making treaties with representatives of other societies or commitments to particular communities within the society. Acts of these kinds are "posterity-binding:" they are supposed to impose moral obligations on future members of a society. A treaty is meant to bind not only present citizens but also their successors. Those with whom it is made are entitled to assume this. An act of reconciliation between communities is supposed to be a historically significant event that commits future as well as present members to maintaining relations of mutual respect. It is meant to be a watershed that separates citizens now and forever from the injustices and animosities of the past.

In performing such acts or going through such processes citizens through their representatives intend to impose upon their successors whatever obligations, moral and legal, follow from the commitment. They intend that present and future members of the community with whom they have made an agreement should be entitled to trust that the commitment will be fulfilled. But what makes such a posterity-binding commitment possible? Sincerity of the participants is not enough, nor their exemplary moral character. It is not only the willingness of participants to fulfil the undertaking that is in question but its acceptance as an obligation by their successors. Why should future people regard themselves as bound by it? We must explain both how citizens can be justified in making commitments that bind their successors and why these future citizens should accept that they are bound by the acts of their predecessors.

Having the moral entitlement to make a "posterity-binding" commitment, I suggest, depends upon this act taking place within the framework of a moral practice or understanding that requires citizens to take responsibility for fulfilling posterity-binding commitments of their political predecessors. This responsibility is, to be sure, hedged around by conditions. If the community to which the commitment was made has ceased to exist or if the terms of the commitment are no longer relevant or are not morally acceptable then the responsibility will either no longer exist or it will become a duty of a different kind. Nevertheless, the fact that the agreement was made by their predecessors and not themselves cannot be used as a reason for abrogating responsibility for its fulfillment.

It might be protested that making a posterity-binding commitment requires only that citizens take steps to ensure that their successors will honour it. They might make a law to that effect or even enshrine the agreement in their political constitution. They might educate their children in the importance of honouring commitments. What is at issue, however, is not the means that citizens might use to induce or encourage their successors to do what they want them to do. The fundamental question is what gives citizens an entitlement to impose a moral obligation on their successors. We think that our political successors ought to fulfil commitments we have made. It is a basic meta-ethical principle that like cases ought to be treated alike: that if we assign duties to others then we have to be prepared to accept relevantly similar obligations. Since we think that our successors ought to fulfil our commitments this means that we have an obligation to fulfil the commitments of our predecessors.

If we are honest and morally responsible we will be prepared to honour the terms of agreements we make and will believe that our successors ought to honour

them too. However, our predecessors were not always so honest or responsible—
particularly in their dealings with indigenous communities. They did not always intend to honour the agreements they made; nor did they intend that we do so. Does
this mean that we are not obliged to honour insincere agreements? The answer requires a more careful consideration of what we think our successors ought to do.
What we want is that our successors accept a duty to maintain relations with other
communities as required by the terms of our agreements. We want them to honour
our agreements not because we intend them to do so, but because we think the
terms of our agreements should be fulfilled. In other words, they have a duty to honour our commitments, not a duty to fulfil our intentions. This means that the appropriate and relevant description of our duty is to fulfil the commitments made by
our predecessors. Their intentions are not relevant—at least not to determining
what it means to treat like cases alike.

Let us assume that we are entitled to make posterity-binding commitments.
Why should our political successors think that they are obliged to keep them?
The answer is simply that these successors, like us, will have reason to make
commitments that they think that their successors should honour. They will want
to maintain into the future some of the commitments and understandings that
they have inherited. They too need an entitlement to make posterity-binding
commitments. They too have reason to sustain the moral practice of honouring
the commitments of their predecessors.

My account of why we have historical obligations is forward-looking in the
sense that the moral motivation for honouring the commitments of our predecessors depends upon our concern that the commitments we make be honoured. It might be thought that this account allows us to avoid inheriting responsibilities by refraining from making any posterity-binding commitments,
formal or informal. But abstinence is not only likely to be impractical but immoral. We often have prudential reasons to make posterity-binding agreements.
We want our successors as well as ourselves to live in peace and have benefits
that come from cooperation with other communities. But we also have moral
reasons for making such commitments. A respect for persons includes a respect
for their desire to establish and maintain communities that enable them to exercise control over their lives, protect their culture and traditions and pass them
on to their children. Respectful relations between inter-generational communities require commitments that are understood to hold for future as well as present members. Even an informal understanding based on customary relations that
each party has come to depend upon, sets up expectations and obligations concerning the future. Though members of a society can disagree about what their
relations with another community require, they must commit themselves, or
regard themselves as committed, to maintaining ongoing relations of ongoing
respect.

The duty to honour the commitments of our predecessors is inescapable, at
least for morally responsible people. But are citizens also committed to making
recompense for the failure of their predecessors to honour commitments? It might
be thought that if governments over which they have some control can be de-

pended upon to act justly—at least to keep agreements—then they will not have to ask their successors to make recompense for their violations, and thus will be relieved from the obligation to make recompense for the violations of their predecessors. However this is not so. We approach our historical obligations from the perspective of those who want to maintain or establish posterity-binding commitments. Commitments of this kind presuppose a moral practice that also requires us to take responsibility for past violations.

To be entitled to make a commitment agents have to accept certain moral duties. They are responsible for fulfilling the commitment and also responsible for making appropriate recompense for a failure to do so (unless they have a legitimate reason for nonperformance). An agent who refuses to acknowledge these duties would not be entitled to make commitments in the first place. Accepting these responsibilities is intrinsic to the practice of making commitments. It is in the nature of posterity-binding commitments that the duties associated with them have to be accepted by the successors of those who make them. Our successors would have a duty to make recompense for violations (including our violations) of our posterity-binding commitments should they occur. This means that we have a duty to make recompense for the violations of our predecessors.

Violations of commitments are only one kind of injustice done by our political predecessors to indigenous communities. Notoriously, British officials and colonial governments in Australia refused to make any kind of agreement with Aboriginal communities. They refused to recognise the entitlement of these communities to the land that they occupied, and even in many cases their right to exist.[50] These injustices seem to be at least as serious as the injustice involved in the breaking of a commitment. Many people would regard them as more serious. So it would be a significant failing of my account of historical obligations if it could not explain why citizens have a duty to acknowledge and make recompense for past injustices of these kinds.

One way of meeting this difficulty is to argue that there was a commitment between Australian governments and Aboriginal communities. A formal agreement is not the only form that a commitment can take, and by assuming responsibility for sovereignty over Australia predecessors of non-Aboriginal Australians were in effect making a commitment to protect Aborigines and their communities—a responsibility they failed to fulfill. Even by living alongside Aboriginal communities, interacting with them, or making use of their local knowledge or labour, non-Aboriginal Australians and their governments could be said to have established a relationship that brought with it obligations and entitlements. However, the claim that presently existing non-Aboriginal Australians have a historical obligation to make restitution for past injustices to Aboriginal communities does not depend on the existence of a commitment, formal or informal.

Once again let us consider the matter from the point of view of morally responsible citizens who want to reach an understanding with communities that have been treated unjustly in the past. One problem they face is demonstrating that their act means what they intend it to mean—that the unjustly treated community is entitled to believe that the commitment will be honoured by them and their successors. Their being trustworthy is not sufficient to justify this entitlement. What they have to demonstrate is that they are giving an undertaking on behalf of their political successors as well as themselves. They have to show that they are participating in a moral practice that requires successors to act as the moral heirs of their predecessors.[51] The appropriate demonstration in such a case is to acknowledge and make recompense for the injustices done by their predecessors.

Making recompense for past injustices is not merely an appropriate thing to do. Intrinsic to the making of a promise or commitment is the requirement that agents respect each other's existence and interests. Having and maintaining this respect can be more important than the actual terms of the commitment for terms may have to be altered or renegotiated as conditions change. Upholding the spirit of the agreement when the terms are unclear or difficult to apply, being willing to re-negotiate in good faith are part of what it means to maintain relations of respect. Those who make commitments not only have a duty of respect but, as a corollary, the duty to acknowledge and make appropriate recompense for, the failure to fulfil the duty of respect. When we reach a posterity-binding understanding with people of a community we intend to commit our successors, above all, to maintaining relations of respect with future members of that community, and this duty requires these successors to make recompense for any acts of disrespect that have been committed. This means that we have to be prepared to make recompense for acts of disrespect committed by our political predecessors. The injustices done to Aboriginal communities by government officials were gross acts of disrespect and thus wrongs for which non-Aboriginal Australians should make recompense.

A defence of historical obligation that appeals to the moral pre-requisites of posterity-binding commitments may seem counter-intuitive. Some people think that our obligations arise out of a more direct response to the injustices of the past: remorse for what our predecessors did, a sense of duty to the dead, or from a duty of restitution for the benefits we have received as the result of the injustices, I do not rule out other ways of justifying historical obligations. Nevertheless, my account has some important advantages.

It does not require us to think that we have a duty to the dead or a duty to fulfil the intentions of our predecessors. This is obviously an advantage in dealing with those who argue that it makes no sense to suppose that we are obliged to people whom we cannot harm or benefit. More important, it relieves us of problems associated with intentions of past people. We may not know what the intentions of our political predecessors were, whether they were sincere in the agreements they made with other communities. We have good reason to think that in many cases they were not sincere, or at least that many of those engaged in making treaties and other agreements with indigenous people had no intention that they be kept. According to my account this is irrelevant. We have a moral concern that the commitments we make be honoured, and we earn the right to bind our successors by participating in a moral practice that requires us to acknowledge responsibilities for honouring the commitments of our predecessors and making recompense for injustices related to these commitments. What is important is that the commitments were made—not the state of mind of those who made them.

However, my account does not require that we honour commitments we believe to be unfair. Nor does it confine us to making recompense for deeds that our predecessors would have recognised as unjust. In determining our duties in respect to the past we are entitled, indeed obliged, to judge the acts of our predecessors from our own moral point of view. This is a consequence of having to determine our historical obligations by considering what we think our successors ought to do in respect to our commitments and deeds. We judge what our successors ought to do from our moral perspective and are thus required by the 'treat like cases alike rule' to use the same moral perspective when we interpret and evaluate the past. We want our successors to keep our commitments not simply because we made them but because we judge that the terms of our agreements are fair and honourable. We are required to make judgments about the agreements of our predecessors using the same criteria of fairness—despite knowing that in some cases our predecessors would have judged differently.[52] We also know that our successors will judge our deeds from their moral perspective and may not think that they are morally obliged to do what we think they ought to do. Knowing this cannot affect our reasoning. Our objective is not to anticipate how they will judge (even if this were possible). Reasoning about our historical obligations must begin from a consideration of what we think our successors ought to do.

My account does not preclude our feeling remorse for what our predecessors did. But it does not require that we do so. This is an advantage when dealing with those who do not think that it makes sense to feel remorse for what our predecessors did or who as a matter of fact do not feel remorse. Such people are often resentful of attempts to make them feel remorseful and reject for this reason the very idea of historical obligation. My account explains why they are wrong. My defence of historical obligation does not reject the notion that we owe restitution for the benefits we have received from past injustices. But it avoids the objection often advanced against this idea—that we cannot owe anything for benefits that we have not consented to receive (and cannot easily reject).

Finally, it is a positive aspect of my defence that historical obligations of citizens in a political society have nothing to do with ancestry. To inherit a historical obligation it is not necessary that a citizen be a descendant of those who made or violated an agreement. Bloodlines are as irrelevant to the historical obligations of citizens as they are to other duties of citizenship. You assume the responsibility when you become a citizen—however that occurs. This means that my account is not subject to the common objection that citizens by immigration cannot have a responsibility for making recompense for past injustices of their new political society. Immigrants may not feel remorse for such misdeeds: people are perhaps more likely to be ashamed of the deeds of those they count as their ancestors. But this has nothing to do with their responsibilities as citizens.

III. Historical obligations exist—in particular obligations to keep commitments made by our political predecessors and to make recompense for their injustices to other communities. However, people may yet deny that they have a duty all things considered to fulfil such historical obligations—either because the agreements or injustices took place too long ago or because they think that other duties of justice take precedence.

Jeremy Waldron in "Superseding Historical Injustice" offers two reasons why passage of time can undermine claims for recompense for historical injustice. The first has to do with the contingencies that separate a past act of injustice from the present. If we think, as Nozick does, that injustice requires that the situation of those who were dispossessed ought to be returned to what it would have been if the injustice had not done, then we are faced with the impossible task of making a judgment about what victims of injustice would have done under counterfactual circumstances. If Maori land had not been wrongly appropriated in 1865, what would successive generations of tribal owners have done with it? Would they have passed it on to future generations? Sold it to settlers? Would they have lost in it in some other way? Waldron wants to stress that the problem is not merely epistemological.[53] Given the nature of human freedom, there is no fact of the matter, and the more time passes and the more choices that could have been made, the less viable are reparative claims.

If uncertainty created by possibilities of choice is the reason for doubting that there is a fact of the matter that makes a counterfactual claim true, then this is so for every counterfactual statement about human action. We do, however, believe that we are sometimes justified in making counterfactual assertions on the basis of evidence. The issue is where we put the onus of proof. Waldron is suggesting that those who make a historical claim have to prove that they would have inherited their tribal land if their ancestors had not been dispossessed—an impossible task given the contingencies of history. But this view of the matter is mistaken. In most cases the burden of proof should be on those who deny the claims of indigenous people.

We have intuitive grounds for thinking that this is so. If a woman who has no surviving friends or family dies without making a will and her neighbour claims that she intended to leave him her money, the burden of proof clearly rests on him. If, on the other hand, she had grandchildren to whom she was very close, if she continually stated her intention of leaving them her money, indeed regarded it as her family duty to do so, the burden of proof would lie on those who dispute the claim of the grandchildren. The historical claims of indigenous people are more like the second case than the first. The Maori leaders who signed the Treaty of Waitangi regarded the land of their community as something held in trust on behalf of past and future as well as present members. It is true that they might have later sold some of their land to settlers if they had not been unjustly dispossessed (as some Maoris did), but it is not likely that the leaders would have sold land essential to the traditions and economic well-being of the community—or that other members of the community would have acquiesced.[54] Since Maori communities, traditions, culture, and attitude to land have survived down through the generations, it is also reasonable to suppose that none of the leaders in intervening generations would have sold or gambled away land essential to culture and economic practices. The onus of proof lies on those who assert the contrary.

The correctness of this intuitive judgment is confirmed by the forward-looking considerations that motivate our moral response to historical injustices. When we make a treaty we wish to impose on our successors an obligation to respect the rights and possessions that those party to the agreement regard as important enough to protect through this means. We commit ourselves and our successors to respect the desire of community members to pass these things on to future generations. So long as these interests persist we think that they should be respected and a failure to respect them requires compensation. We would not think it legitimate for our successors to deny the duty to make recompense merely because it was possible that people in the wronged community might have done something detrimental to their interests if the injustice hadn't occurred. Waldron's concern about counterfactuals is not likely to undermine the reparative claims of indigenous people.

Waldron has a second reason for claiming that historical injustices fade with time. If land or some other possession comes to perform a certain role in the life and activity of a group or individual and if someone else seizes it, then the plans and way of life of those who are dispossessed are undermined. Justice demands that the possession be returned to its original owners. However, as time passes the strength of the justification fades. "If something was taken from me decades ago, the claim that it now forms the center of my life and that it is still indispensable to the exercise of my autonomy is much less credible."[55] It would be even less credible for my descendants to claim that it is indispensable to the exercise of their autonomy.

Waldron allows exceptions. If a community has been dispossessed of something that has religious significance he thinks that it may retain its entitlement over time. "Religions and cultural traditions we know are very resilient, and the claim that the lost lands form the center of a present way of life—and remain sacred objects despite their loss—may be as credible a hundred years on as it was at the time of the dispossession."[56] This exception may justify many, if not all, of the land claims made by indigenous people. For in many cases there is no clear distinction between economic and religious or cultural reasons for land claims. A community may have a tradition that depends upon economic activities being carried on in the land of their ancestors: fishing in a particular river, or hunting in a particular territory. Moreover, it is a weakness of Waldron's position that it concentrates merely on unjust possession. The seizure of land of indigenous people was associated with injustices of other kinds. Maoris did not merely have their land and rights over resources taken from them. A promise made to their communities was broken. Australian Aborigines were not only slaughtered, robbed, and treated as less than human. Their communities were not recognised as having entitlements.

Injustices such as these do not fade away with time. Treaties are assumed to be lasting. "A treaty is intended to be of perpetual duration and incapable of unilateral termination." [57] Agreements reached with indigenous people have the same binding force—morally, if not legally. Commitments whether formal or informal are supposed to be based upon mutual respect, and the duty of respect is something that also persists. If commitments and the duties they presuppose are of perpetual duration then injustices that result from their violation resist being superseded by time.

However, even if historical injustices do not fade away, they may be superseded by circumstances. Changing conditions can cause agreements to become unjust or put injustices beyond remedy. They can do this, Waldron claims, because of overall changes that have occurred in the world or in a country since the agreement was made or the injustice done—such things as immigration of large numbers of people into territory once held by indigenous people or growth in world population. The needs of existing and future people may make it unjust as well as impractical to return all lands unjustly taken or to recognise rights over resources once guaranteed to indigenous people. Or injustices may be beyond remedy because innocent people are now the legitimate possessors of land unjustly taken.[58]

Changes of circumstance are not by themselves reasons for denying the obligation to make restitution for historical injustices. At best they are reasons for re-negotiating agreements, or compensating for what cannot justly be returned, or for denying that those wronged are entitled to demand back all of what they once possessed.[59] Changed circumstances are not generally going to mean that wronged communities have no entitlements, or that members of a political society have no historical obligations. Nor does the fact that land once possessed by indigenous people is now owned by others mean that indigenous communities cannot make any just claims for its use or return. It is not necessarily unjust for a political society to appropriate privately owned land, or require present possessors to share it with others, and the remedying of past injustices could be a good reason for doing this.[60]

However, changed circumstances clearly do affect historical duties and entitlements. They mean that the popular idea of restitution—that those who were wronged should get back what was taken from them—will sometimes have to be rejected in the interests of justice. In practice what counts as just recompense is likely to be settled by negotiation and precedent, and those making the decisions will be concerned with the existing needs of the parties to reconciliation.

It might be argued that our primary duty of justice as citizens is to promote equity among existing and future people of our society and that indigenous people are owed no more or less than their fair share. Giving them their fair share is simply a matter of equity; to give them more would be unjust to others. This position implies that reparative claims are either irrelevant or unjust. They are irrelevant if what is claimed in restitution could be claimed on grounds of equity; unjust if what is being claimed would give members of a community privileges or special treatment that cannot be justified on the grounds of equity. David Lyons seems to support this position when he suggests that Native American land claims should be viewed "not as invoking an original right to the land, a right that has been passed down to current Native Americans and that now needs to be enforced, but rather as an occasion for rectifying current inequities (some of which, of course, may trace back causally to the dispossession of Native Americans and the aftermath)."[61] Waldron seems to be making a similar point when he says that "Behind the thesis of supersession lies a determination to focus on present and prospective costs—the suffering and the deprivation over which we still have some control."[62]

Neither Lyons nor Waldron want to deny that promises should be kept, debts should be paid, and compensation should be made for injustice. Such "backward-looking" duties are bound to play an important role in any theory of justice. It is not plausible to suppose that principles of equity prevail whenever promises, entitlements, or injustices become historical. Indeed Lyons insists that the American government should live up to its past commitments to Native Americans.[63] This presumably means that governments should keep their word even when doing so results in special benefits for some communities. Changing conditions and the inequities that result may be a reason for re-negotiating an agreement, but it would be wrong for a community to unilaterally break a promise every time doing so would further its commitment to equity. Making a commitment to a community means that we intend our successors to continue to respect interests that are important to it. We can allow that change of interests or circumstances might make a commitment invalid or in need of alteration, but the very nature of the act, and the duty of respect it entails, creates legitimate expectations that our successors should normally fulfil. We have the same obligation in respect to the commitments of our predecessors. Since the moral practice of making restitution for past injustices is bound up with acts of commitment and reconciliation, our duties of recompense resist for similar reasons being superseded by demands of equity.

Behind Lyons' and Waldron's inclination to suppose that historical claims give way to demands of equity is the commonsense idea that only present and future people—those who can be harmed or benefited by what we do—are morally considerable. Injustices to the dead are beyond remedy. The past, it seems, is relevant only as a cause of present conditions, or (as Waldron allows) because it exists in the memories of individuals. This is why it seems so plausible to insist that our primary duty of justice is to establish relations of equity.

Because it derives historical obligations from forward-looking considerations my thesis provides a way of challenging this idea. We have obligations in respect to the deeds and commitments of our predecessors because we participate in the moral practice of making commitments that we think our successors ought to fulfil. Our historical obligations are bound up with a concern for establishing and maintaining inter-generational relations between communities. They are not duties to the dead or attempts to impose on the living burdens irrelevant or detrimental to the interests of present and future citizens.

My account of historical obligations is incomplete. It does not explain where they fit within a comprehensive theory of justice—how exactly they are related to demands of equity. It does not say very much about how demands for restitution should be assessed, or anything at all about how the burdens of restitution might be shared by several generations of citizens. It does not say very much about how vague or unfair agreements should be treated and nothing at all about how problem cases concerning community membership or the identity of a community over time should be solved. These are matters that a theory of historical obligations must encompass. My defence does at least establish that we have historical obligations, especially in respect to indigenous people, and it provides reasons for thinking that they have not faded away and are not superseded by other moral considerations.

Janna Thompson: "Historical Injustice and Reparations: Justifying Claims of Descendants"[64,65]

I. The history of humankind is a tale of unrequited injustice. People have been killed, tortured, cheated, enslaved, exploited, and dispossessed, and no reparation has ever been made either to them or their descendants. The fact that there has been no redress for so many historical injustices is a disturbing or even terrible fact about our world. But what, if anything, is owed to those now living for wrongs committed long ago?

Claims for reparation for historical injustices can be put into three main categories. The first consists of claims of individuals who were victims of an injustice committed many years ago. The compensation claims now being made by Aboriginal Australians who were abducted from their families when they were children come into this category. So do requests for compensation of American and Canadian Japanese who were interned during World War II and the demands for the return of their possessions of those dispossessed by communist regimes in Eastern Europe.[66] That individuals ought to be recompensed for the injustices they have suffered is a basic moral and legal idea. If an injustice was done long ago then it may be difficult to find an appropriate remedy or to determine who is responsible for reparation. Nevertheless, it seems reasonable that individuals should be able to make reparative claims for injustices done to them long ago, particularly if political or social circumstances have prevented them from doing so at an earlier time.

In the second category are reparative claims made by members of communities—tribes nations, states, corporations, and other intergenerational associations—for injustices done to the community itself, such as seizing communal lands, breaking agreements, or undermining communal life. The land claims of indigenous communities in Australia, New Zealand, Canada, and the United States belong to this category as do the historical grievances of nations, or the claims made by states for territory that was taken from them by an act of aggression.[67] Particular demands made by communities may be disputed, and we may be uncertain what compensation would be appropriate. Nevertheless, claims of this kind seem to be perfectly legitimate so long as we accept that states, tribes, and corporations should, like individuals, be able to demand reparation for wrongs done to them.[68]

In the third category are claims for restitution or compensation made by individuals who are the descendants of victims of injustice. In law these claims may take the form of a class action of people whose forebears were done a similar injustice. But people in this class are not representing a community or making demands on behalf of a community. They are making demands on their own behalf as people whose forebears suffered injustice. Bernard Boxill argues that descendants of slaves are entitled to receive reparation for the exploitation of their ancestors.[69] Boris Bittker's consideration of Black reparations begins with the question of what is now owed to African Americans for the unpaid labor of their ancestors.[70] Anthony Gifford argues that continental Africans, as well as the descendants of African slaves, can make a good case for reparations for the injuries flowing from "the 400-years-long atrocity of the slave system."[71] Heirs as well as victims are making claims against institutions which benefited from Nazi persecution.[72]

The problem with claims of this third kind is that the individuals to whom injustice was done are different from those who are now demanding reparation. It is a principle basic to reparative justice—one that I will call the "Exclusion Principle"—that individuals or collectives are entitled to reparation only if they were the ones to whom the injustice was done.[73] Sarah cannot be recompensed for an injury done to Sam. If Sam is beyond the reach of reparation then no one is entitled to demand reparation for the wrong done to him. So if descendants are to make a legitimate claim for reparation for a historical injustice then they must demonstrate that it has violated their rights or harmed their interests. There are two ways in which they might do this. The first is to claim that they have themselves been injured by the injustice—that they suffer from its effects. The second is to argue that their status as heirs of the victims gives them an entitlement to claim possessions that were wrongly expropriated from their forebears. In the next section I will examine these strategies showing that common defenses of historical entitlements of descendants are weak or unsatisfactory. This does not mean that claims of descendants should be rejected. I will introduce in the remaining sections a perspective from which these strategies can be more successfully pursued.

II. Injustice can cast a long shadow. It injures not only the victims. Descendants of victims are likely to lack resources or opportunities that they probably would have had if the injustice had not been done or they are adversely affected in other ways by the suffering of their parents or grandparents. Justice as equity might require that they be compensated for being born into a disadvantageous social position. Humanitarian feelings may motivate us to try to alleviate their suffering. The issue is whether they are owed reparation.

Reparative claims that hinge upon a causal relation between an injustice and injuries to descendants face serious difficulties. One of these is that injustice not only affects how people fare. It can also determine what people there are. African Americans who presently exist would never have been born if their ancestors had not been abducted and forced into slavery. But it doesn't seem to make sense for a person to demand what she would have obtained if the injustice had not been done if, in this contrary to fact circumstance, she would not have existed at all. George Sher deals with the problem by saying that descendants of victims of injustice ought to be restored to the level of well-being that a related group of persons would have had if the injustice had not been done.[74] The descendants of slaves would presumably be compared with those who would have been the present descendants of these ancestors in a world where they had not been enslaved. The problem is not merely that it is impossible to determine the level of well-being of these possible descendants. Since many things would have happened to these alternative family lines between then and now, it is difficult to understand how these possible people could be related in a relevant way to actual descendants.

Even if this difficulty is resolved, or simply put aside, further problems await those who appeal to the causal relation between a past injustice and present harms to justify claims of descendants. The disadvantages that descendants presently suffer are the result of a long chain of causes reaching back to, and through, more than one historical injustice. The causes include the choices and deeds of existing individuals and those of people who existed between the time of the injustice and the present. Sher thinks for this reason that the claims of descendants of victims of more recent historical injustices have more validity than claims based upon ancient injustices [and] become more plausible the more that present disadvantages can be seen to be the "automatic effect of the initial wrong act."[75] This criterion, when more closely examined, threatens to undermine many of the reparative claims of descendants of victims of injustice.

Sher does not tell us what counts as an "automatic effect," but two conditions seem necessary and jointly sufficient. An automatic effect of an injustice is, first of all, a causal effect for which the perpetrator can reasonably be held responsible. It is an inevitable, natural, or difficult to avoid result of the injustice. Either the perpetrator intended his or her act to have this effect or he should have been able to foresee that the effect would result from his act or failure to act. The second condition is that there is no independent action or failure to act to which the effect should be attributed. An act fails to be independent when its intent or meaning cannot be understood without reference to the injustice. The scope of an injustice consists of those harms and disadvantages that are its "automatic effects." If a factory worker is killed as the result of the negligence of his employer the grief and the economic disadvantages the death causes to his wife and children are within the scope of the injustice. These injuries, though not something the employer intended, are the foreseeable effects of the death. The family's economic loss is made inevitable by the death. The widow's grief is a natural response to the tragedy. The harms are not attributable to the independent actions or omissions of any other agent. The action of the person who told the widow that her husband had been killed was the more immediate cause of her grief, but her grief cannot be attributed to it. Bringing this message was not an independent action. Its intent was to tell her about the killing, and it had its effect because that's what it did.

Not all of the harms caused by the injustice are within its scope. Suppose that the son of the family, angered by his father's death, rebels against authority, joins a gang and cripples a shopkeeper while robbing a liquor store. This harm is an effect of the unjust killing of his father—and it probably wouldn't have happened if the injustice had not been done—but it is not within its scope. It is not an effect that the employer or anyone else could have foreseen. Even if it had been predicted that the son would commit some antisocial action, the harm he did is more plausibly attributed to his choices and actions, or perhaps to the failure of teachers or family members to curb his destructive behavior.

Demands for reparation for an injustice become less plausible when injuries are outside its scope. The problem is illustrated by Bittker's case for Black reparations. Bittker thinks that it is not plausible for African Americans to demand reparation for slavery because slavery, he says, is not the injustice responsible for the present disadvantages suffered by African Americans. After the Civil War, reforms in the Southern states, he thinks, were starting to bring about a society in which former slaves could take their place as free and equal citizens. If these reforms had been allowed to continue the harms caused by slavery would eventually have been undone and there would not now be any case for reparation. However, history did not follow this course. White supremacists and contriving governments brought the reforms to an end and introduced a system of oppression and segregation. It is this system, Bittker argues, to which present (for him, the early 1970s) disadvantages suffered by African Americans should be attributed.

However, driven by this reasoning, he cannot stop short of assigning the blame to present or recently discontinued policies of discrimination or segregation. The system of oppression adopted by Southern states after the Civil War could have been discontinued by later generations or by earlier actions of the federal government. If this is so, then the harm caused by the continuation of policies that suppressed Black Americans in the 1950s and 1960s cannot be regarded as an automatic effect of their introduction. The injustice for which African Americans deserve reparation is the persistence of segregation policies into recent times. Bittker ends by advocating compensation for individuals who themselves have been harmed by segregation. Historical injustices like slavery or the actions of Southern white politicians after the Civil War have dropped out of the picture as far as his defense of reparative claims is concerned, and with it the idea that people are owed reparation as descendants of victims of injustice.

The collapse of demands for reparation for harm done by historical injustices to demands for reparation for present or recent injustices seems inevitable. For once we recognize that present harms are outside the scope of more ancient injustices then it seems that only later links in the chain of injustices are going to be a suitable focus for reparative demands—those wrongs to which present injuries can be attributed. Almost inevitably those will be the injustices that were done by and to existing people. It is true that a person may be deeply affected by the unjust treatment of her forebears. Thinking about what they suffered may cause her to suffer. But the connection between the injustice and her suffering seems more like the relation between the employer's negligence and the son's angry actions than between the unjust killing and the widow's grief. If we are to attribute such psychological suffering to a historical injustice then we have to explain how it can be regarded as the automatic effect of this injustice—rather than the result of an individual's psychological susceptibilities or her particular upbringing.

The second strategy for justifying reparative claims of descendants of victims of injustice looks more promising because it makes entitlement depend on inheritance rather than causation of harm. What I have called the Exclusion Principle prevents individuals from inheriting an entitlement to reparation from their forebears. However, they can have an entitlement by virtue of being heirs to possessions that would have been theirs if the injustice had not been done. By being deprived of their inheritance the injustice has violated their right to possession. This approach not only allows individuals to make claims for reparation for historical injustices. It allows them to do so even if they have not been harmed in any other way than by being deprived of their inheritance. Moreover, it provides a simple way of solving the problem of existence. Their claims depend on their being the heirs of their forebears—not on being the particular individuals that they are. The fact that they might not have existed if the injustice had not been done does not seem to undermine their claim.[76]

However, the approach puts limits on what kinds of injustice can be the subject of claims and on what can be demanded. Claims have to be confined to demands for what Robert Nozick calls "rectification"—the restoration of expropriated possessions or the provision of an equivalent for these possessions. Descendants can claim nothing in reparation for the murder, torture, abduction, or maltreatment of their forebears, for the disrespect shown to them as persons, however large these injustices may loom in their thoughts about the past. Indeed reparation as rectification makes no distinction between dispossession caused by injustice and dispossession that results from a mistake—a belief that something was unowned when this was not so. Rectification misses what Boxill claims is an important part of reparation—"an acknowledgment on the part of the transgressor that what he is doing is required of him because of his prior error."[77] The demand for acknowledgment of injustice or apology that is so central to many demands for reparation cannot be justified by an appeal to rectification.

Nevertheless, many reparative claims do involve a demand for the return of possessions expropriated from forebears or compensation for expropriation. As Bittker suggests, the demand for reparation for slavery can be interpreted as a demand for compensation for wrongful expropriation of the fruits of labor. So if descendants can obtain rectification for past injustices most would regard this as a good, if not ideal, result. The difficulty is establishing that they do have a right to rectification. To do this we not only have to defend rights of possession and inheritance but also establish in particular cases that the forebears rightly possessed the property being claimed and that the descendants would have inherited it if the injustice had not been done.

Let us assume for the sake of argument that individuals have a right of possession over goods rightly acquired, a right to transfer their possessions to others, and a right of rectification for unjust expropriation. We need not suppose that right of possession gives an individual unlimited right to use his or her property as she pleases, excluding all others, or that it makes her immune to re-distributive requirements. We need not suppose that right of transfer exists for everything she possesses or that it cannot be constrained by other, moral considerations, or that the right of rectification requires that her heirs receive, or be compensated for, everything that she would have given them. We do need to suppose that these entitlements, whatever they turn out to be, resist extinction—in particular that heirs retain a right to at least some part of what they would have received if the injustice had not been done, despite the passage of time, changes of circumstance, and requirements of distributive justice.

The problem is that if these rights are completely resistant to extinction then many of the claims of descendants of victims of injustice will be undermined. For in many cases forebears possessed what they did only because of a previous injustice—the dispossession of earlier owners and the developments that occurred because these owners were dispossessed. Nozick, who makes right of possession and transfer relatively immune from extinction, throws up his hands at this problem and suggests cleaning the slate by organizing society to provide benefits to the least well off.[78] This is no help to descendants of victims who are not among the least well off or who think that they ought to receive reparation for injustices done to their forebears and not merely compensation for their poverty. On the other hand, if entitlements are not all that immune to extinction, if we allow that they can be extinguished by time or change, then this may also undermine reparative claims.

Jeremy Waldron argues that historical injustices are indeed superseded by time and change and that reparative entitlements are liable to wither away. This contention is supported, first of all, by what he thinks is the reason for recognizing a right of possession in the first place. The most plausible basis for a right of property, he says, is the role possessions play in an individual's life—the way in which our projects and plans depend upon them. Expropriation is unjust because it undermines our activities and plans. But descendants of victims cannot have built their life or plans around a possession that they don't have.[79] Their claim seems inherently more tenuous.

However, Waldron's primary reason for thinking that historical injustices are superseded by time is that descendants who demand what they would have received from their forebears if the injustice had not been done have no way of establishing what this is—if anything at all. The difficulty, he thinks, is not merely epistemological. Where human choice is involved there is no fact of the matter. If victims of injustice had not been dispossessed they may have disposed of their possessions in some other way. They may have gambled them away, given them to someone else, or used them for their own projects. The more time passes, the more choices that could have been made, the greater the uncertainty.[80]

There are two ways of interpreting Waldron's indeterminacy thesis. According to the first, there is no answer to the question of what descendants would have got if the injustice had not been done, and thus nothing on which they can base their claims. Guesses, he says, have no moral authority.[81] The thesis would apply as much to claims for rectification of more recent historical injustices as to more ancient ones—indeed it is likely to apply to the demands of an individual for rectification for injustices done to him in an earlier part of his life. The second more plausible interpretation allows that we can assert counterfactuals about human actions and choices on the basis of evidence but insists that as time passes and possibilities for choice multiply, our evidence becomes less conclusive.[82] The issue then becomes one of onus of proof. Does it rest on those who make a claim for rectification or those who oppose the claim? Waldron seems to accept that it rests on those who make the claim—perhaps because of what he calls the "contagion of injustice"—the ramifications over time of the effect of an injustice on people's lives, especially the lives of innocent third parties. His reasons for supporting a right of possession count against claims that threaten to undermine the projects and plans of those who are not to blame for historical injustice.

These difficulties encountered by claims for rectification by descendants of victims of injustice do not necessarily defeat all of them. However, they put substantial barriers in the way of reparation for historical injustices of the third kind. Those who want to support the claims of descendants need to find a way in which this can be done. The position that I will present and defend interprets the reparative claims of descendants as being more like claims of the second kind—the claims of communities—than they first appear.

Those who claim reparations for historical injustice are not merely individuals who happened to have been harmed or who might have been the recipients of possessions or benefits. They are the descendants of the victims of injustice. They are in a special relation to those to whom the wrong was done. Highlighting this relationship I suggest, will enable us to understand why they have a right to an inheritance and, in so doing, will justify some of their reparative claims. By emphasizing the relation between individuals—in this case, descendants and their forebears—rather than the relation between individuals and their property, it may also be able to take us beyond the limits of a theory of reparation as rectification.

John Rawls, in *A Theory of Justice,* adopts a perspective that can, with some modifications, provide a starting point for such a theory. He says that those in the original position who are determining principles of justice for their society could be thought of not simply as individuals but as representatives of "family lines": "The parties are thought of as representing continuing lines of claims, as being so to speak deputies for a kind of everlasting moral agent or institution. They need not take into account its entire life span in perpetuity, but their goodwill stretches over at least two generations."[83]

Establishing from the perspective of representatives of the family lines that inheritance should be accepted seems like a straightforward task. Consider the impassioned declaration of Loren Lomasky: "Confiscatory inheritance taxation runs roughshod over the deceased's interest in the ends his property will serve. . . . It is an especially cruel injury because it deprives the dead of one of their last opportunities for securing the goods that they value. The dead can no longer offer loved ones their advice, their encouragement, sympathy in times of hardship, and joy when things go well; all they can do is pass on worldly goods to intended beneficiaries. To be robbed of that opportunity is to have one's ability to exercise agency sharply curtailed."[84] Lomasky is concerned with individuals as project pursuers. But the interests of these agents are likely to overlap with the interests of representatives of family lines who would surely make the same kind of case for being allowed to benefit their descendants.

However, [there is other] reasoning: Why should *someone who* thinks that she and her family may be among the least well off support the ability of the wealthy to keep their resources in the family? There are several ways of answering this question.

"The unequal inheritance of wealth is no more inherently unjust than the unequal inheritance of intelligence," says Rawls. The important thing is that these inequalities satisfy the Difference Principle—that they are to the advantage of the least well off.[85] Allowing people to provide some benefits for their descendants seems likely to satisfy this principle. For the sake of their families people work hard, save, invest and protect their assets, and thus benefit others in their society. If they were not allowed to provide any inheritance to their descendants they would have less reason for doing these things. A society might adopt other means of achieving socially desirable results—tax incentives to encourage investment, for example. But as a general rule it is likely to be more efficient, and less restrictive of individual liberty, for a society to make use of motivations that most people already possess—especially since inequalities that go beyond what can be justified by the Difference Principle could be remedied by inheritance (or other) taxes.

This familiar reason for favoring inheritance is not, it seems to me, the most important. The perspective of representatives of family lines resists treating individuals as units of production who just happen to have particular motivations (and might be induced to have different ones). It takes family relations as central to the reproduction of relations of justice and requires that a just state maintains, or at least does not undermine, arrangements that enable family members to carry out their responsibilities to express their love and concern for each other. For this reason it is important to consider why family relations are so valuable to family members and thus able to play the role that Rawls and others assign to them.

Family relations are, first of all, personal relations of love and care—they embody the special regard that members are supposed to have for each other and their willingness to benefit each other. Family relations are in this respect like friendships. A just state should allow participants in personal relationships to provide benefits to each other that they don't provide to others. Family relations are special in that parents are likely to regard themselves as having responsibilities that go beyond friendship—even to their grown children. They have had a significant influence on their children's character, on the particular needs and interests that they now possess. Moreover, their concern is not merely for their children as individuals. They also want their children to be capable of providing a good life for children of their own. Being able to provide their children and grandchildren with benefits, particularly lasting benefits, is a way of expressing the love and concern that is supposed to be central to family relations. In a just state where Rawlsian requirements of distributive justice apply, children and grandchildren will not need an inheritance in order to have good lives. Such a society is justified in putting limits on the value of what can be transferred as a gift from parents to children. But it would be a gross interference with family relations to prevent parents from giving gifts to their children and grandchildren. Inheritance taxes are justifiable, but not taxes so high as to negate the value, and thus the point, of the gift.

Families are, second, associations that provide individuals with recognition. Family members are predisposed to understand and value each other's activities. The memory of individuals and their accomplishments is often preserved by families, and in many cases children and grandchildren are the ones most likely to carry on the projects and maintain the values of their forebears. Moreover, the projects of individuals are often inseparably connected with their family life and their hopes for their children. A person who builds up a family business is likely to regard himself as laboring for the sake of his descendants as well as himself. An art lover may regard it as of central importance that her children will be able to maintain the collection of paintings that she taught them to appreciate. Such "life-time transcending interests" are of great importance to many individuals, and a just society ought to respect them (other things being equal). As Lomasky says, it seems a cruelty to deny people the possibility of passing on things that have a personal significance to those for whom they have labored or who are most likely to appreciate, value, and keep alive what they have done. It would not be unjust to impose taxes on those who benefit from inheritance, but it would be wrong to impose confiscatory taxes or other measures that have the effect of preventing individuals from passing on to their heirs goods so intimately connected to themselves and their lifetime activities.

The values of family membership considered above provide a defense, though a limited one, of the right of bequest—the entitlement of individuals to leave their possessions to whomever they choose. The right to inherit is the entitlement of those chosen as heirs to receive these possessions. These heirs are usually, but not necessarily, family members. The right of bequest is a liberty right possessed by the person who makes the bequest. It does not entitle family members to claim an inheritance as their right. A. J. Simmons, criticizing the idea that entitlement to inherit can be superseded by time, notes that if individuals have an obligation to provide their descendants with certain resources, then these heirs have a right to inherit that cannot be thrown into doubt by the possibility that their forebears might have done something else with their possessions.[86] The right of children to inherit is a right to claim an inheritance, and it would exist regardless of whether parents wanted to leave them their possessions, regardless of whether they in fact did so. Are there any reasons why representatives of family lines should support, or at least take seriously, this stronger, unconditional right of inheritance?

Locke insisted that children have a right to a share of their parents' resources and, thus, that parents should not be free to transfer their possessions in any way they please. However, he also believed that the responsibility of parents ends when children reach maturity. The law underwrites this idea of parental responsibility and its limits in those countries influenced by the British Common Law tradition. In countries influenced by Napoleonic Law parental freedom has traditionally been more limited. Even in societies where freedom of bequest is protected few would agree that parents have a moral right to disinherit their children whenever they please, and there are some cases where doing so seems particularly unjust.

A son who has been led by his parents to expect that he will inherit the family business would be wronged if they exercise their freedom of bequest by giving it to someone else. But even in cases where no explicit or implicit promise has been made, children may have a rightful expectation of benefits. There is no consensus about the duties that members of families have to each other, but most parents seem predisposed to think that they retain some kind of responsibility for their grown children—the obligation to come to their aid in times of need, if nothing else. They are also likely to think that they bear some responsibility for ensuring that their grandchildren can live good lives. That is, they accept a duty to share their resources with members of their family that goes beyond the duty they have to their children when dependent. To the extent that these obligations exist, children and grandchildren have a moral right, at least in some circumstances, to their expectations.

Moreover, descendants also have a claim to those objects that count as family heirlooms. This fight arises from the third value associated with families. Family relationships play an important role in determining the identity of individuals. They give individuals a sense of belonging, of being a part of a history that began before their own life and will continue after their death. They provide them with a legacy. This could consist of memories, stories, but also memorabilia: possessions that have historical significance for a family or a meaning to its present members. For reasons discussed above it seems right for a just society to allow parents to pass these heirlooms on to their children. People should be able to give gifts of special significance to those they love or endow them with things that have played a special role in their lives. But there is also reason to insist that the children have an independent claim to those things that can be considered, because of the meaning invested in them, to be possessions of the family. A mother who gives away an heirloom to a friend rather than maintaining the family tradition of passing it on to her eldest daughter may not be doing anything illegal, but the daughter is justified in thinking that her rightful expectations have been disappointed.

A confiscatory inheritance tax would not only interfere with a parental right of bequest. It would also violate the independent right of children or grandchildren to receive something that has a special relation to their family and thus a special meaning to them. It would undermine the ability of families to maintain a heritage. For example, the suggestion of D. W. Haslett that heirs should be required to purchase their family heirlooms at market value or the idea of compensating those who do not have heirlooms with goods of equal value treats family treasures as if their market value is their only significant value.[87] Doing so puts at a relative disadvantage those who think that their family heritage should not be treated as a marketable asset. Families would be able to keep their heirlooms only by using up some of their other resources (if they have them in the first place). Their society would be making it more difficult for them to maintain the values and historical connections that are important to their identity as family members.

Haslett, it could be argued, is merely applying a requirement basic to a theory of justice that treats individuals as equals.[88] If no individual or family is entitled to special treatment because of attachments or tastes, then why should a society subsidize a family that chooses to keep its heirlooms? However, a strict insistence on equality of resources can have results that seem obviously unfair. Suppose your friend, a famous painter, paints your portrait and gives it to you as a mark of his friendship. You treasure it accordingly and know that selling it would violate the spirit behind the gift. However, it is worth hundreds of thousands of dollars, and if you are required to compensate those who do not possess expensive paintings you will either have to sell it or use up money you have saved for other projects. Or suppose that land treasured by an Aboriginal tribe as its spiritual heritage is found by prospectors to contain rich deposits of gold. The Aborigines have no intention of mining the gold. Indeed they regard mining as a desecration. But the equality of resources principle, strictly applied, would require them to compensate those who do not have rich deposits of gold.

To determine how an equality of resources principle should deal with cases like these would require a lengthy discussion. However, it seems obvious that a society should exempt individuals and groups in those cases where its application subverts or does not allow expression of values or attitudes that are intrinsic to relationships that a society ought to protect or even promote. Individuals ought to be able to give each other gifts as gestures of friendship providing the gifts are relatively small (as I argued above) or are not intended or used for economic advantage. Groups ought to be able to protect those things that are important to their spiritual life. And representatives of family lines are likely to insist that members of families ought to be able to maintain and enhance the bonds that unite the generations by passing down heirlooms to their descendants. Those who want to bring about a greater equality of resources (and thus approach what a Rawlsian could accept as just) would want to put restrictions on how valuable heirlooms can be used. They might insist that heirs cannot use them as commodities or capital (without attracting a full rate of taxation). They might require that families with valuable collections of paintings or jewelry put them on public display occasionally so that everyone can enjoy them. They will want restrictions on what can be regarded as a family heirloom. A family with aristocratic forebears is not likely to be allowed to keep its wealth and land however important these things were in the history of the family. But this does not mean that the family is not entitled to keep anything at all. It does not mean that families should never be allowed to treat as heirlooms possessions that have considerable market value—like paintings, jewelry, or even houses.

A just society will stipulate that heirlooms are held in trust, that they cannot be used or disposed of as individuals please. Descendants must be presumed to have an unconditional right to inherit possessions whose status depends on them being an expression of family identity and intergenerational connections. Even if the laws of a society do not directly protect this right, its existence will affect our reasoning about reparation.

IV. Reparative justice only gets on the agenda if injustice has occurred or if people at least believe that it could occur. We have to drop Rawls's assumption that there is strict compliance with principles of justice in order to consider how representatives of family lines would regard claims for reparation for historic injustices. I have argued that these representatives will insist that members of families are entitled to make and receive bequests, and that in those cases where possessions have a special meaning to family members descendants can claim an unconditional right to inheritance. These representatives will think that future members of their society ought to protect these entitlements, and by so insisting they commit themselves to honoring and protecting the entitlements of descendants of past members of their society. Protecting these entitlements means not only trying to prevent violations but also ensuring that the violations that have occurred, in the past as well as the present, are remedied. Representatives of family lines will be moved to support a principle of reparation that makes it possible for descendants of victims of injustice to claim their inheritance—even if their society is now just in all other respects.

The approach I am defending is able to resist Waldron's contention that the reparative claims of descendants are undermined by there being no way of determining what they would have received if the injustice had not been done. His argument, I have contended, is best understood as a view about where the burden of proof belongs. From the perspective of representatives of family lines there is good reason to shift this burden from those who defend reparative claims to those who oppose them. This is most obviously so in those cases where descendants can claim an unconditional right to a family possession. What their forebears might have done with this possession if the injustice had not been done is of little or no relevance. But even when right of inheritance is predicated on the right of bequest, as in the case of gifts, representatives of family lines will want the claims of descendants of victims of injustice to be viewed in a favorable light. Entitlements that result from expressions of love and concern intrinsic to family relationships ought to be regarded with great respect. A society that wants to protect and promote these relations should give the claims of descendants the benefit of the doubt.

Suppose an injustice stripped a man and his wife of a small family property. Circumstances prevented them making a reparative claim, but long after their deaths their children are able to do so. If the parents had retained the property they might not have given it to their children. They may have gambled it away (as Waldron reminds us). But if there is no reason to believe that they were feckless or lacked concern for the well-being of their children, it should be accepted that the children's claim is legitimate. Should we so generously assume that descendants of victims would have been favored by fortune if the injustice had not occurred? Those whose forebears were not done an injustice are forced to accept the results of outrageous fortune—of fires that destroy treasured possessions, of parents who make unwise investments. But giving descendants of victims of injustice the benefit of the doubt is the right way of responding to their claims. It would be mean-minded to question the claims of descendants of the victims of Nazis on the grounds that their parents or grandparents might have lost their possessions in some other way if the Nazis had not stolen them. The perspective of representatives of family lines can explain why we think a generous response is more appropriate. The importance of doing something to alleviate an injustice destructive of family relationships outweighs quibbles about contingencies.

Nor should we think that the entitlements of descendants depend on whether they suffer because of their loss of their inheritance. Children who are prevented from receiving their inheritance must, as Waldron says, learn to live without it. They may not even miss what they never had. But from the perspective of representatives of family lines, this does not make the situation any less unjust. In the case of bequests children are being prevented from enjoying or learning to appreciate something that their parents out of love and concern, or because of their own values and projects, wanted them to possess. If an injustice prevents them from obtaining the heirlooms to which they have a claim then they are not able to enjoy a meaningful connection with a part of their family's heritage. The fact that families are usually able to survive a loss of heritage is not likely to obliterate the requirement of reparation from the point of view of representatives of family lines.[89]

Right to reparation is, however, a right all things being equal. The possibility remains that representatives of family lines will not think that satisfying reparative claims is just, all things considered, when they consider that the possessions of their descendants could be subject to reparation claims. They have, it seems, reasons similar to Waldron's for wanting entitlements to reparation to be superseded by time. What justice requires all things considered needs further discussion, especially when making judgments about actual cases in a world that is far from just. Nevertheless, the importance of inheritance rights of both kinds for maintaining family relations prevents an endorsement of the supersession thesis. Concern for the entitlements of blameless descendants of perpetrators or others who have benefited from injustice may affect views about what form reparation should take and who should be responsible for bearing the burden. In some cases just reparation might take the form of compensation paid by the society as a whole for lost possessions rather than the return of possessions that might now be in the hands of blameless people. Or blameless people might be compensated for being forced to meet claims for reparation.

How far down the generations does the entitlement to reparation extend? Rawls thinks that the just savings principle encompasses two generations—children and grandchildren. The justification I have offered for the entitlements of descendants of victims of injustice suggests that they are similarly limited, at least in the case of bequests. Parents mean to express their love or connection to their children or grandchildren and think that their society ought to ensure that these individuals obtain their inheritance. They are not likely to be so much disturbed by the possibility that their distant descendants may fail to receive these things (at least in a society where individuals are not likely to be disadvantaged by injustices that happened many generations ago). Family heirlooms are another matter. They belong to families, not to particular individuals, so if they have been passed down from one generation to another for a very long time and have become important to family history or tradition, then descendants are likely to have a claim on them even if more than two generations have passed since the injustice was done.[90] However, family relations change, connections between existing people and distant generations become tenuous, ideas about what is meaningful to the family do not stay the same, and so as time passes even these claims will become less plausible.

My defense of the right of reparation is unlikely to support the claims of descendants of slaves for this and other reasons. To claim a lost inheritance descendants must be able to specify what possessions they should have received from their forebears. They must be able to establish that they are the ones entitled to make a claim. In most cases descendants of slaves will not be able to satisfy these conditions either because there is no way of establishing what possessions their forebears had, or would have had if they had not been enslaved, or no way of determining who their slave forebears were.

V. The approach discussed in the last sections leaves many historical injustices beyond the range of reparation. Like other accounts focusing on inheritance, it confines itself to providing a basis for "rectification"—for reparative claims to property. So it can be criticized not only by those who think that more ancient injustices, like slavery, require reparation but also for ignoring injustices that seem to require reparation of another kind. I will argue in this section that the perspective of representatives of family lines can be used to defend reparative claims for harms caused to descendants by historic injustices—that it can escape the difficulties associated with such claims.

Rawls says that the representatives of family lines are deputies for a kind of everlasting moral agent and that their goodwill stretches over at least two generations. There is a tension in this description. How can a deputy for an everlasting agent be concerned only with a few generations of it? Let us allow that our responsibility for providing resources for our descendants is limited. Nevertheless, the concerns of representatives of families for their descendants do not remain within these limitations. Parents not only care about the well-being of their children and grandchildren. They also want their children and children's children to be in the position to care and provide benefits for their own children. They can assume that these children will have the same concern, and so on down through the generations. Though responsibility for the well-being of members of more distant generations may be limited or nonexistent, representatives of families are likely to think it morally important that social relations, institutions, and practices that enable members of families to care for their children and grandchildren and discharge their obligations to them are "everlastingly" maintained. This will motivate them to assign to future members of their society a duty to maintain these institutions and practices and ensure that failures to do so are rectified.

Policies or actions that undermine the ability of individuals to maintain family relations, carry out their obligations and obtain their entitlements as members of families are not merely injustices that harm individuals. They are "injustices against family lines." An injustice is directed against family lines when the perpetrators seek to wipe out family lines, keep them in perpetual slavery or submission, or attempt to prevent individuals of certain kinds from maintaining family relations, carrying out family obligations, or receiving entitlements as members of a family. Perpetrators may not have the objective of persecuting families. Their attacks may be aimed at religious, ethnic, or racial groups. However, the intention to attack such groups necessarily involves an intention to undermine, wipe out, or subjugate families. Slavery, for example, is an injustice directed against family lines. Not only do perpetrators aim to perpetuate slavery down through family lines. They also systematically undermine the ability of individuals to care for their children and maintain family relations.

From the perspective of representatives of family lines such attacks on families count as serious injustices. They will think that their society ought to protect their families from such an attack and that the harm caused by injustices against family lines ought to be repaired or alleviated. This responsibility, it might be thought, is simply a requirement of justice as equity. If past persecution of their families has put individuals among the least well off then they can reasonably expect to receive a fairer share of social resources according to the principles that Rawls supports. To make a case for reparation we have to show that some of the harms suffered by present members of persecuted families are in the scope of the injustice in question—that they are among its automatic effects.

In the case of injustices against family lines the case can be made even when an injustice was committed a long time ago. A family line, as I have indicated, is not merely a succession of generations. A family, like a community, has a history—a narrative that connects past and present members and gives individuals a place and role in an intergenerational story of birth, death, marriage, family relationships, loss, and renewal. The story may be detailed and well documented or vague and based on surmise. Whatever form it takes, it is part of the legacy that is passed on from one generation to another and influences how people think about themselves, their lives, and their place in society. The history of their family or community, says Waldron, is important to its members. Collective remembrance plays an important role in forging individual identity, and what happened in the past thus makes a difference to the well-being of people of the present.[91] It matters to representatives of family lines what their family history contains—injustice and loss, or reconciliation and renewal. Those whose family lines were in the past attacked, exploited, suppressed, or denigrated are likely to suffer from feelings of anger, regret, sadness, or insecurity, as likely in those cases where the damage done has not been alleviated by more recent social developments.[92]

These effects of the injustice are within its scope and should be regarded as its automatic effects. Like the widow's grief they are a natural, appropriate, even proper, response to the injustice, given the kind of injury it is. The long period of time between the injustice and the effects—with its many intervening causes and effects—does not disqualify these responses from counting as automatic effects. For it is the meaning of the injustice to descendants, not the immediacy of the causal relationship, which is crucial. Their sadness and anger are effects that are attributable to the injustice and not to other actions or failures to act. They are not psychological states that some overly sensitive or obsessive people happen to feel when thinking about past injustice. Descendants suffer because what happened to their family is important to their identity as individuals. It is true that this harm would have been alleviated if appropriate reparation had been made in the past. But the failure of past governments to make reparation does not replace the original injustice as the wrong to which present suffering should be attributed, any more than the failure of the employer to offer compensation to the widow replaces the injustice to which her suffering should be attributed. Apologizing and compensating are acts logically tied to what is apologized or compensated for. They are not independent actions. Failure to make repair is an additional cause of suffering.

The harmful effects of injustices against family lines are not merely, or even primarily, such things as loss of property. They are psychological effects that arise from the meaning possessed by a particular history. The most appropriate way for people of a society to make reparation for such injustice may be to acknowledge that the deed or policy was a serious injustice and to make an apology. An approach to reparation which emphasizes the perspective of representatives of family lines thus makes intelligible, and provides a justification for, a common demand made by descendants of victims of injustice. To demonstrate that apology is sincerely meant it may be appropriate to offer symbolic compensation that could take the form of benefits to descendants, a public ceremony, or an appropriate change to the official history of the nation. An injustice to family lines does not entitle disadvantaged descendants to more social resources than members of any other group of disadvantaged people. Nevertheless, it creates a special obligation that should be fulfilled by a society that aims to be just.

NOTES

1. George Sher, "Ancient Wrongs and Modern Rights," *Philosophy and Public Affairs* 10 (1980): 3–17.

2. I am grateful to Patricia Kitcher, Philip Kitcher, and Alan Wertheimer for their helpful comments and suggestions.

3. Robert Nozick, *Anarchy, State, and Utopia* (New York: Basic Books, 1974), 231.

4. For development of this charge as it pertains to entitlement, see Nozick, *Anarchy, State, and Utopia*, chap. 7. For discussion involving desert, see George Sher, "Effort, Ability, and Personal Desert," *Philosophy and Public Affairs* 8, no. 4 (Summer 1979): 361–76.

5. Lawrence Davis. 1976. "Comments on Nozick's Entitlement Theory," *Journal of Philosophy* 73 (21): 842.

6. Michael E. Levin, "Reverse Discrimination, Shackled Runners, and Personal Identity," *Philosophical Studies* 37, no. 2 (1980): 139–49.

7. George Sher, "Compensation and Transworld Personal Identity," *Monist* 62, no. 3 (1979): 378–91.

8. Although I have presented them as alternatives, the two suggestions need not be viewed as mutually exclusive. Indeed, the most promising approach appears to be to combine them. The first suggestion appears the more natural in those cases where there are many close alternative worlds that lack the initial wrong act but contain the victim himself; while the second appears indispensable in those instances where the initial wrong is so intimately associated with the victim's existence that there is no such world.

9. David Lyons, "The New Indian Claims and the Original Rights to Land," *Social Theory and Practice* 4, no. 3 (1977): 249–72.

10. This point is discussed in a more limited context in George Sher, "Justifying Reverse Discrimination in Employment," *Philosophy and Public Affairs* 4, no. 2 (Winter 1975): 166 ff.

11. For discussion, see Thomas Nagel, "Moral Luck," in his *Mortal Questions* (Cambridge: Cambridge University Press, 1979), 24–38.

12. Lyons, "The New Indian Claims," esp. pp. 268–71. See also Boris Bittker, *The Case for Black Reparations* (New York: Random House, 1973).

13. Jeremy Waldron, "Superseding Historical Injustice," *Ethics* 103 (1992): 4–28.

14. An earlier version of this article was presented in 1990 at the annual conference of the New Zealand division of the Australasian Association of Philosophy. I am grateful to Graham Oddie for his invitation to attend that conference and to the Waitangi Foundation for their support. A later version was presented as a public lecture at Boalt Hall, University of California. I am particularly grateful to Robert Cooter, Meir Dan Cohen, Einer Elhauge, Sanford Kadish, David Lewis, Richard Mulgan, Carol Sanger, Joseph Sax, Andrew Sharp, Henry Shue, and the editors and referees of this journal for their criticisms and suggestions.

15. Opinions differ in metaethics about whether this illocutionary function provides a complete explanation of the distinctively moral meaning of the words "right," "wrong," "unjust," etc. For the view that it does, see R. M. Hare, *The Language of Morals* (Oxford: Clarendon, 1952). But most moral philosophers concede that even if it is not the whole story, still it is an essential part of the explanation of the meaning of such words that they have this prescriptive function. The few philosophers who deny this do so purely because of the embarrassment it poses for their realist claims that moral judgments are nothing but judgments about matters of fact. For examples, see Michael Moore, "Moral Reality," *Wisconsin Law Review* (1982), pp. 1061–156); and David Brink, *Moral Realism and the Foundations of Ethics* (Cambridge: Cambridge University Press, 1989), chap. 3.

16. For this understanding of moral judgments made about the past, and for the assumed interaction between prescriptivity and universalizability, see R. M. Hare, *Freedom and Reason* (Oxford: Clarendon, 1963).

17. For a moving discussion, see Hannah Arendt, "Truth and Politics," in her collection *Between Past and Future: Six Exercises in Political Thought* (New York: Viking, 1968).

18. John Locke, *An Essay Concerning Human Understanding*, bk. 2, chap. 27, secs. 9–10, ed. John Yolton (London: Everyman's Library, 1965), vol. 1, pp. 280 ff.; see also Stuart Hampshire, *Thought and Action* (London: Chatto & Windus, 1970).

19. Robert Nozick, *Anarchy, State, and Utopia* (Oxford: Blackwell, 1974), 152–53. To this passage, Nozick appends the following footnote: "If the principle of recodification of violations of the first two principles yields more than one description of holdings, then some choice must be made as to which of these is to be realized. Perhaps the sort of considerations about distributive justice and equality that I argue against play a legitimate role in this subsidary choice" (p. 153n.).

20. We could of course imagine a world in which not only $E+$ occurs instead of E but also in which the laws of nature are different (e.g., living beings can survive and flourish without water). But those worlds are of limited practical interest. The reason why we choose (in David Lewis's terminology) the closest possible world in which $E+$ occurs, and why "closest" includes "same laws of nature" in that that is the world which ought to have been in the contemplation of the agent who faced the choice between E and $E+$. See David Lewis, *Counterfactuals* (Cambridge, Mass.: Harvard University Press, 1973).

21. Often the injustice complained of is that some renegade member of the tribe disposed of tribal land as though it were his own private property. So if a piece of land is indeed tribally owned and its alienation prohibited by tribal custom, is there any point in asking how it would have been disposed of if the injustice of this individual's alienation of it had not occurred? Surely we ought to assume that, if the land had not been wrongfully disposed of, it would have remained the property of the tribe. So, it might be thought, there should be no difficulty in showing that the counterfactual approach requires its present restoration to the tribe. Unfortunately, things are more complicated than that. There are two other things that might have happened if the injustice had not taken place. The members of the tribe might have decided, in the exercise of their powers as communal owners, to sell some of the land. Or the members of the tribe might have decided, in an exercise of sovereignty over their own laws and customs, to abrogate the system of communal property. Both possibilities need to be taken into account in any realistic reconstruction of what would have happened if the injustice had not taken place. The second is particularly important. All societies change their customs and laws, including their property laws, from time to time, and there is every reason to imagine such change as a probable and reasonable response to new circumstances and conditions on the part of such flexible and resourceful polities as Maori tribes, for example. If we are honestly inquiring into what would have happened in a just world, we have to take at least the possibility of such adaptive exercises of sovereignty into account.

22. See John Rawls, *A Theory of Justice* (Oxford: Oxford University Press, 1971); and T. M. Scanlon, "Contractualism and Utilitarianism" in *Utilitarianism and Beyond*, eds. Amartya Sen and Bernard Williams (Cambridge: Cambridge University Press, 1986).

23. See Rawls, *A Theory of Justice*, 7. For the distinction between holistic and piecemeal uses of contractarian models, see Kim Scheppele and Jeremy Waldron, "Contractarian Methods in Political and Legal Evaluation," *Yale Journal of Law and Humanities* 3 (1991): 206–10.

24. Hence the insistence of Jeremy Bentham on absolute security of expectations as the proper basis of a utilitarian theory of property. See the extract from Jeremy Bentham, *Principles of the Civil Code*, in *Property: Mainstream and Critical Positions*, ed. C. B. MacPherson (Oxford: Blackwell, 1978), 42–58.

25. John Locke, *Two Treatises of Government* ed. Peter Laslett (Cambridge: Cambridge University Press, 1988 [1689]), bk. 2, chap. 5; Nozick, *Anarchy, State, and Utopia*, chap. 7. There is a comprehensive discussion of this approach in Jeremy Waldron, *The Right to Private Property* (Oxford: Clarendon, 1988), chaps. 6, 7.

26. Locke, *Two Treatises*, bk. 2, chap. 5, sec. 27.

27. It is not hard to see how this could be adapted to express a conclusion about the labor and the identity or personality of a whole community. A community takes possession of a resource by investing the labor of its members. The resource now contains something of the community's spirit and personality. And this is what the community is claiming back when it demands the restoration of stolen lands.

28. See Jeremy Waldron, "Two Worries about Mixing One's Labor," *Philosophical Quarterly* 33 (1983): 37–44; and Waldron, *Right to Private Property*, 171–94. See also the criticisms of Locke's idea in Nozick, *Anarchy, State, and Utopia*, 174–75.

29. For a full elaboration of this problem, see Waldron, *Right to Private Property*, 259–62.

30. Nozick, *Anarchy, State, and Utopia*, chap. 7.

31. There were good reasons for this reticence: it was worth focusing for a while on the question of what the basic shape of a theory of justice should be. As Nozick put it, "I am as well aware as anyone of how sketchy my discussion of the entitlement theory has been. But I no more believe that we need to have formulated a complete alternative theory in order to reject Rawls's undeniably great advance over utilitarianism, than Rawls needed a complete alternative theory before he could reject utilitarianism. What more does one need or can one have, than a sketch of a plausible alternative view, which from its very different perspective highlights the inadequacies of the best existing well-worked-out theory?" (p. 230).

32. Locke, *Two Treatises*, bk. 2, sec. 33.

33. Locke, *Two Treatises*, bk. 2, secs. 36 ff.

34. Nozick, *Anarchy, State, and Utopia*, 174 ff.

35. But see the discussion in Jeremy Waldron, "Enough and as Good Left for Others," *Philosophical Quarterly* 29 (1979): 319–28.

36. The point can be borne out by comparing the following passages from Locke's *Two Treatises*. The first follows on from the statement about conditions of plenty that was quoted a page or two earlier: "He that has as good left for his Improvement, as was already taken up, needed not complain, ought not to meddle with what was already improved by another's Labour: If he did, 'tis plain he desired the benefit of another's Pains, which he had no right to, and not the Ground which God had given him in common with others to labour on, and whereof there was good left, as that already

possessed." But the second passage raises the specter of scarcity: "God . . . has given no one of his Children such a Property, in his peculiar Portion of the things of this World, but that he has given his needy Brother a Right to the Surplusage of his Goods; so that it cannot justly be denied him, when his pressing Wants call for it." An action which may be condemned in one set of circumstances as the covetous meddling of someone too lazy to fend for herself, becomes in another set of circumstances the exercise of a right, which may not be resisted by the initial appropriator.

37. The example is suggested by David Lyons, "The New Indian Claims and Original Rights to Land," in *Reading Nozick*, ed. J. Paul (Oxford: Blackwell, 1982), 371.

38. I am grateful to Carol Sanger for this formulation of the objection.

39. The phrase is from Locke, *Two Treatises*, bk. 2, sec. 41.

40. For the assumption of "perfect compliance," see Rawls, *A Theory of Justice*, 8–9.

41. Janna Thompson, "Historical Obligations," *Australasian Journal of Philosophy* 78, no. 3 (2000): 334–45.

42. J. Tichy and G. Oddie, "Is the Treaty of Waitangi a Social Contract?" in *Justice, Ethics and New Zealand Society*, eds. Graham Oddie and Roy Perrett (Melbourne/Oxford: Oxford University Press, 1992), 86.

43. For details see Andrew Sharp, *Justice and the Maori: Maori Claims in New Zealand Political Argument in the 1980's* (Oxford/Auckland: Oxford University Press, 1990).

44. For details see Elliott Johnston, ed., *Indigenous Australians and the Law* (Sydney: Cavendish, 1997).

45. John Howard, Speech to the Australian Reconciliation Convention in Melbourne, 26 May 1997. Howard has used the same reasoning on many occasions.

46. Sharp, *Justice and the Maori*, 115.

47. Will Kymlicka, *Multicultural Citizenship* (Oxford: Clarendon Press, 1995), 116.

48. "It cannot be insisted too strongly that the parties to treaties are States not governments," says Lord McNair, *Law of Treaties* (Oxford: Clarendon Press, 1961), 515.

49. Joel Feinberg, "Collective Responsibility," *Journal of Philosophy* 65 (1968): 687. He briefly discusses, but seems to dismiss, a way in which individuals might have responsibility without control (687–88). For an account of collective responsibility that does include historical obligations see Peter Forrest, "Collective Responsibility and Restitution," *Philosophical Papers* 27 (1998): 79–91.

50. Henry Reynolds reveals these injustices in *Law of the Land* (Harmondsworth: Penguin, 1984) and *Aboriginal Sovereignty* (Harmondsworth: Penguin, 1996).

51. The importance of ensuring that an act of reconciliation can be understood in this way is illustrated by the debate in Australia about apologising to Aborigines. The Prime Minister has offered a personal apology for past wrongs, but Aboriginal leaders insist that an official apology, an apology on behalf of the nation, is required.

52. Ross Poole has suggested that this reasoning may commit us to keeping the agreement that we think that our predecessors should have made even when (as in the case of Australia) they failed to make an agreement.

53. Jeremy Waldron, "Superseding Historical Injustice," *Ethics* 103 (1992): 9.

54. In fact these leaders had a duty not to sell land essential for communal purposes. A. J. Simmons makes the point that in such cases heirs should be able to claim

their rightful inheritance even when their forebears did dispose of their possessions in some other way. See "Historical Rights and Fair Shares," *Law and Philosophy* 14 (1995), 178–89.

55. Waldron, "Superseding Historical Injustice," 18–19.

56. Waldron, "Superseding Historical Injustice," 19.

57. Lord Nair, *Law of Treaties*, 493.

58. Waldron, "Superseding Historical Injustice," 26.

59. A. J. Simmons makes the same point in "Historical Rights and Fair Shares," 161ff.

60. The Wik judgment of the Australian High Court allows that both Aboriginal communities and present leaseholders may have rights of different kinds over the same land.

61. David Lyons, "The New Indian Land Claims and Original Rights to Land," *Social Theory and Practice* 4 (1977): 268.

62. Waldron, "Superseding Historical Injustice," 26.

63. Lyons, "The New Indian Land Claims," 267.

64. Janna Thompson, "Historical Injustice and Reparations: Justifying Claims of Descendents," *Ethics* 112, no. 1 (2001): 114–35.

65. I am grateful for the critical comments of philosophers at La Trobe and Melbourne Universities, especially Robert Young and John Campbell, and of the editors and reviewers of *Ethics*.

66. For discussions of claims made by indigenous Australians for compensation for the injuries they received as the result of the governmental policy of removing half caste children from Aboriginal parents, see Elliott Johnston, Martin Hinton, and Daryle Rigney, *Indigenous Australians and the Law* (Sydney: Cavendish, 1997). The case for reparations for Japanese Americans is argued by Shirley Castelnuovo, "With Liberty and Justice for Some: The Case for Compensation to Japanese Americans Imprisoned during World War II," in *Japanese Americans: From Relocation to Redress,* eds. Roger Daniels, Sandra Taylor, and Harry Kitano (Seattle: University of Washington Press, 1991). Both the U.S. and Canadian governments did offer token compensation to those actually interned, but not to their heirs.

67. For particular examples see Elliott Johnston, Martin Hinton, and Daryle Rigney, *Indigenous Australians and the Law* (Sydney: Cavendish, 1997; Andrew Sharp, *Justice and the Maori: The Philosophy and Practice of Maori Claims in New Zealand Since the 1970s,* 2nd ed. (Oxford: Oxford University Press, 1997); Wilcombe E. Washburn, *Red Man's Land / White Man's Law: A Study of the Past and Present Stains of American Indians* (New York: Scribner's, 1971).

68. States and other such associations are not real individuals, and their members sometimes object to being burdened with the responsibility for making recompense for injustices committed by past generations. I discuss this issue in "Historical Obligations," *Australasian Journal of Philosophy* 78 (2000): 334–45.

69. Bernard Boxill, "Morality of Reparation," *Social Theory and Practice* 2 (1972): 113–21. In 1969 James Forman, a Black Panther leader [*sic*], demanded that Christian churches and Jewish synagogues pay $500 million in reparation to African Americans for the historical role these organizations played in exploiting their fore-

bears. This action gave rise to a discussion about black reparations to which a number of philosophers contributed. The black reparations movement has not disappeared. The awarding of damages to Japanese Americans has resulted in renewed demands from African Americans. For an account of these developments and a defense of reparation for slavery, see Rhonda V. Magec, "The Master's Tools, from the Bottom Up: Responses to African-American Reparations Theory in Mainstream and Outsider Remedies Discourse," *Virginia Law Review* 79 (1993): 876–92.

70. Boris Bittker, *The Case for Black Reparations* (New York: Random House, 1973), 8.

71. Lord Anthony Gifford, "African Reparations Movement: The Legal Basis of the Claim for Reparations." A paper presented to the First Pan-African Congress on Reparations, 1993, online at http://the.arc.co.uk/arm/legalBasis.html#3.

72. For example, Swiss banks have agreed to settle legal claims relating to World War II era conduct of Swiss banks, businesses, and government agencies, and heirs as well as victims of Nazi persecution who may have claims are invited to apply for settlement. See http://Nvivw.swissbankclaims.com. For details of the accusations against Swiss banks, see "Court TV Library: Miscellaneous Cases—Survivors of the Nazi Regime Sue Swiss Banks for Seized Assets," 1999, online at www.courttv-com/legaldocs/misc/iiaziswiss.html.

73. It is also part of the Exclusion Principle that only perpetrators, whether these are groups or individuals, should be punished for injustice or required to make recompense. Demands for reparation for historic injustices are often thought to raise the issue of how individuals now living can be made responsible for the acts of their ancestors or predecessors. However, most demands for reparation, including those for reparation for slavery (discussed below) are directed to intergenerational groups like churches or national societies. I will argue in Sec. VI that there is good reason for assigning responsibility for reparation to such groups rather than to individuals who happen to be descendants of perpetrators or beneficiaries of injustice.

74. George Sher, "Compensation and Transworld Personal Identity," *Monist* 62 (1979): 378–91. He has in mind cases where the injustice was done not long before an individual was conceived. It seems plausible to compare the well-being of the child born with that of a child that would have been born to these parents in a world where the injustice had not been done.

75. George Sher, "Ancient Wrongs and Modern Rights," *Philosophy and Public Affairs* 10 (1981): 3–17.

76. Stephen Kershnar makes this point in "Are the Descendants of Slaves Owed Compensation for Slavery?" *Journal of Applied Philosophy* 16 (1999): 95–101.

77. Bernard Boxill, "Morality of Reparation," 118.

78. Nozick, *Anarchy, State, and Utopia*, 231.

79. Waldron, "Superseding Historical Injustice," 18–19.

80. Waldron, "Superseding Historical Injustice," 8–9.

81. Waldron, "Superseding Historical Injustice," 10.

82. A. J. Simmons, "Historical Rights and Fair Shares," *Law and Philosophy* 14: 149–84, at 178, argues that it is reasonable to make conservative judgments about what would have happened if an injustice had not been done.

83. Rawls, *A Theory of Justice,* 128.

84. Loren Lomasky, *Persons, Rights, and the Moral Community* (New York: Oxford University Press, 1987), 270. Lomasky implies that the dead have interests. One of the advantages of the approach to inheritance and reparation that I adopt is that it does not ascribe interests to the dead.

85. Rawls, *A Theory of Justice*, 278.

86. Simmons, "Historical Rights and Fair Shares," 179.

87. D. W. Haslett, "Is Inheritance Justified?" *Philosophy and Public Affairs* 15 (1986): 121–55.

88. Ronald Dworkin, "What Is Equality, Part 2: Equality of Resources," *Philosophy and Public Affairs* 10: 283–345, thinks that an economic market as a device for setting prices for goods and services must be central to any account of what equality of resources means. However, he admits that inheritance is a matter that requires more consideration (p. 334).

89. If an heirloom has been destroyed, then descendants have no right to reparation. Their loss is tragic, but there can be no duty of justice to give them what no longer exists, and monetary compensation is clearly not appropriate.

90. Waldron, "Superseding Historical Injustice," 19–20, makes a similar point about the survival of entitlements in some cases.

91. Waldron, "Superseding Historical Injustice," 6. He also stresses the importance to people of their historical record and suggests that apology and token compensation is a way of acknowledging and dealing with this history. However, it is not clear whether he regards these symbolic actions as required by reparative justice or by considerations of humanity—whether they should be thought of as a form of recompense for historical injustice or as a way of making people feel better about their present.

92. How people feel about a past injustice done to their family will depend on what has happened in the meantime. If their society now treats them fairly and they have as a result been able to better the position of themselves and their family, the past injustice is not so likely to rankle. Anger or sadness is more likely to be the result of a whole history of injustice which continues up to the present time. However, this does not mean that the original injustice is no longer relevant, as I explain below.

IMPORTANT SUBSIDIARY ISSUES

V

SOME DEVILISH DETAILS

The last section of this book—"Important Subsidiary Issues"—is devoted to considerations that, while important, tend to push questions of justice and right into the shadows, where they do not belong.

American political life and discourse is, it could be argued, dominated by legal and economic concerns. Often questions of law and economics are unwittingly substituted for questions of right and of morality. The same is true of the discussion of reparations. So, we have placed legal and economic considerations toward the end of this book, recognizing that while they are subsidiary to moral questions, they are nonetheless important and also affect deliberation about "the right thing to do."

Part 5—"Some Devilish Details"—begins in chapter 11 with a forum originally published in *Harper's Magazine* among prominent class action attorneys who discuss the legal basis and obstacles for making the case for reparations. These legal experts include

WILLIE E. GARY [who] won a $500 million judgment against The Loewen Group Inc., the world's largest funeral-home and cemetery operators, in 1995 and $240 million against The Walt Disney Company. . . . He is an attorney with Gary, Williams, Parenti, Finney, Lewis, McManus, Watson & Sperando, in Stuart, Florida.

ALEXANDER J. PIRES JR. [who] won a $1 billion settlement for black farmers in their discrimination case against the U.S. Department of Agriculture and is currently working on a multibillion-dollar class-action suit on behalf of Native Americans. He is an attorney with Conlon, Frantz, Phelan & Pires, L.L.P., in Washington, D.C.

RICHARD F. SCRUGGS [who] won the historic $368.5 billion settlement for the states in their suit against tobacco companies in 1997 and is currently

building a class-action suit against HMOs. He is an attorney with Scruggs, Mil-
lette, Bozeman & Dent, P.A., in Pascagoula, Mississippi.

DENNIS C. SWEET III [who] won a $400 million settlement in [the] "fen-
phen" diet-drug case against American Home Products Corporation and $145
million against the Ford Motor Company. He is an attorney with Langston
Sweet & Freese, in Jackson, Mississippi.[1]

The next reading, in chapter 12, is excerpted from a 1999 book by sociol-
ogist Dalton Conley, *Being Black, Living in the Red: Race, Wealth and Social
Policy in America.* The study on which this book was based won the 1997
American Sociological Association Award for Best Dissertation.

Dalton Conley is professor of sociology and public policy at New York
University and Director of NYU's Center for Advanced Social Science Research. He is also adjunct associate professor of community medicine at
Mount Sinai School of Medicine and a research associate at the National Bureau of Economic Research (NBER). Conley has taught at Yale and Princeton as well. His research focuses on how socioeconomic status is transmitted
across generations and the public policies that affect that process.

Here Conley argues that African Americans have overcome a number of
the obstacles of discrimination and prejudice, and they have made important
gains in access to opportunity and in income. Nonetheless it is wealth, not income, that matters, and wealth has an historical dimension. The history of
Africans in America, both remote and recent, continues to affect the wealth of
today's African Americans, a fact to be taken into consideration insofar as
reparations are concerned.

NOTE

1. "Making the Case for Racial Reparations: Does America Owe a Debt to the
Descendants of Its Slaves? A Forum." *Harper's Magazine*, vol. 301, November 2000,
pp. 37–41.

11

Legal Matters

Forum: "Making the Case for Racial Reparations," *Harper's Magazine*[1]

Contents

Does America owe a debt to the descendants of its slaves?

Hardly a week goes by that we don't read of another gigantic lawsuit with thousands of plaintiffs and billions in damages. Once an esoteric legal device, the class-action lawsuit has become the dominant form of litigation to resolve bitter disputes over collective guilt and innocence that not so long ago played out in Congress. Indeed, our preening national legislature, besotted with special-interest money, seems rivaled by the big budgets and major issues that now thrive in the class-action courtroom.

At the same time, one hears rumblings among historians and philosophers to consider a lawsuit for slave reparations. After all, class-action lawyers have ridden to the rescue of those forced into slave labor in Germany and prostitution in Korea. The academics discuss such a slavery suit in moral, historical, or metaphysical terms. That's nice. But in this, the land of show-me-the-money, the thinking quickly becomes practical: Who gets sued? For how much? What's the legal argument? How do you get a case into court?

To answer these questions, *Harper's Magazine* invited four of the country's most successful class-action lawyers to strategize about how to bring America's most peculiar sorrow into a court of law.

The following forum is based on a discussion held at the Palm Restaurant in Washington, D.C. Jack Hitt [a contributing editor of *Harper's Magazine*] served as moderator.

Cause of Action

JACK HITT: We're here today to talk about how: how, that is, to repay blacks for what they suffered under slavery and what they've suffered since because of it. But first let's talk about why, because when many people hear the term "slave reparations," they go nuts. "Oh, that was so long ago," they say. "Can't we just leave this alone? Everybody's got gripes. Blacks should just get over it." To a lot of people, the very idea of a lawsuit seems unreasonable.

DENNIS C. SWEET III: That's because people think slavery ended in 1865. And it did, but the aftermath of slavery is still with us.

ALEXANDER J. PIRES JR.: Every great lawsuit tries to tell a story of injustice in a way that will resonate. There's a lot to work with here. Slavery's the most unacknowledged story in America's history.

HITT: Unacknowledged?

SWEET: This is what Randall Robinson says in his new book, *The Debt.*

HITT: What's unacknowledged?

SWEET: Oh, just about everything. Take our nation's capital. Nearly every brick, every dab of mortar, was put there by slaves. There's not a plaque in all of Washington acknowledging that slaves built the Rome of the New World. This is how it is with slavery. We've heard of it, but we don't really know anything about it.

WILLIE E. GARY: Think about this. In 1865 the federal government of this country freed four million blacks. Without a dime, with no property, nearly all illiterate, they were let loose upon the land to wander. That's what begins the aftermath of slavery.

SWEET: How many Americans know that 25 million blacks died in slavery? And how many know that virtual slavery was perpetuated for nearly a century after emancipation? Peonage laws made unpaid workers out of debtors. There were sharecropping schemes. Then Jim Crow laws. And even after that, there were other entrenched policies that have kept African Americans living in ghettos.

HITT: Robinson points out that until 1950 the federal government included in mortgage loans restrictive covenants preventing blacks—and only blacks, no other group—from buying houses in white neighborhoods. So blacks could not make their equity work for them. They couldn't move up.

RICHARD F. SCRUGGS: A house is the largest single investment and asset most people have.

PIRES: And it's how every immigrant first got into the middle class. So that policy effectively delayed the arrival of the black middle class by half a century.

GARY: And banks kept it up—denying loans to blacks, often by redlining, by which they literally would draw lines on a map around a neighborhood and not give loans to even creditworthy people living there. That happened until almost last week.

HITT: These are all compelling examples. And so you wonder: If Koreans can sue the Japanese about heinous acts carried out in the 1930s, and Jews are suing over prewar slave-labor camps, and American POWs imprisoned in Pacific camps are even suing the Japanese for slave-labor wages, why can't blacks also sue for similar recompense?

SWEET: It can be done. In fact, Alex won one of the great reparations lawsuits in the last few decades. He filed on behalf of how many was it, Alex?

PIRES: Twenty-four thousand black families.

SWEET: Until 1997 the United States Department of Agriculture had an almost zero rate of granting black farmers loans. Until 1997, okay?

PIRES: Ninety-five percent of all farm loans went to white farmers. And until the 1960s, the U.S.D.A. had a special section called Negro Loans, which ensured that black applicants were rejected. It's amazing.

SWEET: It's amazing how young this country is and how close in time, when you come to think about it, all our history is. No part of our history is that far off. The effects of slavery are still with us, we all know that: single parents, black men wandering off from their families, a tradition of not going to school, distrust of the future. This is not black culture. It's slave culture.

GARY: My children and I have talked about your case, Alex. They've never been on a farm, but for them and a lot of black people you changed our whole thinking about what we can be in this country. If you're black, I mean, you're thinking, it's not going to happen, the government isn't going to give you a fair shake. Then all of a sudden you see this happen. I mean, the country stepped up to the plate.

PIRES: In the end, it did.

GARY: Man, it was such a big message. You know, as an African American I felt really good about it.

SWEET: So how do we make a case?

Legal Strategy I: Breach of Contract

GARY: I think this could be a tort, a simple lawsuit where one party sues another.

HITT: So a variation of the classic you-done-me-wrong lawsuit. Just really big.

GARY: Specifically, it could be a breach-of-contract suit, too. After the war, former slaves were promised forty acres and a mule, and we never got it. That was a contract. It was a promise. We just have to stand up and tackle this wrong or try to make it right. So it could be a tort, it could be a breach of contract. You almost have to start a lawsuit to see where it can go. And I don't think that the fact that it's 135 years later should be a hindrance to people waking up, realizing that it was a grave injustice. And until America accounts for its actions, this friction is always going to be there.

SCRUGGS: Breach of contract after 135 years? You do have a statute of limitations problem.

GARY: Not if Congress steps in.

HITT: But can you count on that?

PIRES: I don't think the legislature's going to help until the lawsuit goes forward. You have to file that suit, and you have to go forward yourself.

SWEET: Al, it's just like your black farmers' suit. I joined Al on that case. They had studies showing rank discrimination, years and years and years of it, and the courts never did anything about it

PIRES: This is how these lawsuits go. Everybody said the statute of limitations is against you, as well as other legal problems too. But we just kept marching, marching, marching. Getting more folk, going around the country. And there were motions to dismiss. Then motions against class certification, the process by which you define who is suing. But as the facts started getting out, people started to say, "Hey, this argument makes sense. These people were wronged. Something's not right." The judges began to think, are we going to let this great injustice go unanswered because of a technicality? I think this situation is like that.

SWEET: We still have to get specific here. We have to get past *Cato*.

HITT: *Cato?*

PIRES: *Cato v. United States* was a slave-reparations decision issued in 1995 by the Ninth Circuit Court of Appeals. This case was easily dismissed, because the judges said, "We can't find a theory with which to move the case forward." Since the Ninth Circuit is basically liberal, this decision sort of took the wind out of reparations thinking. You either find a theory under statutes or you're going to have to find it under constitutional law.

SCRUGGS: We have to find a legal theory, then.

PIRES: And people have tried. They considered the Thirteenth Amendment—didn't work. They've considered a tort claims act—didn't work. They've considered the civil rights acts—didn't work. The *Cato* case is useful, because the Ninth Circuit said, "We've looked real hard at it. We can't find a way."

GARY: Let's think about the breach of contract: forty acres and a mule.

PIRES: Well, how can you sue?

HITT: The promise of forty acres and a mule was an executive order sanctioned by Congress.

GARY: It's in writing! Breach of contract.

HITT: Well, that contract was voided by President Andrew Johnson in 1865. Not only did he reverse the very first stab at reparations but the few thousand blacks in Florida and South Carolina who actually did get the forty acres and a mule had them taken away.

GARY: Well, that's it right there. The government can take property only under the eminent-domain clause. But they didn't deprive the former slaves of their property for any national purpose. This was theft. If anything, the "takings" clause applies.

HITT: Takings?

GARY: Takings is part of the Fifth Amendment: "nor shall private property be taken for public use without just compensation."

SCRUGGS: But you still have the statute of limitations problem. Look, I've been wrestling with this thing. I mean, I love big stuff. We all do. We love to think of elegant solutions to major national social problems, and this is the biggest one there is.

GARY: I think either way we look at it we're going to need help politically, because we don't have the law squarely on our side. We don't have the statute of limitations on our side. We don't have any of that stuff. So it's going to require more than just a simple, single legal theory.

PIRES: In a federal case you've got six years before the statute of limitations runs out.

SWEET: Unless you can prove fraudulent concealment.

SCRUGGS: But there wasn't any fraudulent concealment here.

PIRES: Wait. In recent cases involving World War II slave-labor victims, the statute of limitations doesn't apply if there is a war crime or if there's a crime upon humanity. So I say: If there ever was a crime upon humanity, what white folks did to black people is the worst that ever happened in this country. We would argue that it's not fair to apply the statute of limitations upon us. But Dickie Scruggs is right. It's the main problem. Well, actually there are two. The second is sovereign immunity—you can't sue the government without its consent.

HITT: But to take Willie's breach of contract argument, no former slave could have sued in, say, 1870 and expected to get a hearing. Is the clock not suspended for the century or so it took us to recognize that the courts should be open to African Americans?

SWEET: If not, you have to ask yourself: Is an injustice no longer an injustice so long as you get away with it for a long period of time?

HITT: Well, that gets us to the next logical question. Who is suing here, who are the plaintiffs?

SWEET: No, no, Jack. That's never the first question.

PIRES: The first question is: Who are the defendants?

SWEET: That's better.

HITT: Who are the defendants—i.e., who pays?

GARY: That's it.

The Defendants

SWEET: I think you have two defendants here. The government and private individuals.

HITT: Private individuals?

SWEET: I mean private companies.

GARY: And private individuals. There are huge, wealthy families in the South today that once owned a lot of slaves. You can trace all their wealth to the free labor of black folks. So when you identify the defendants, there are a vast number of individuals.

HITT: Descendants of former slave owners? You're making me nervous.

GARY: Well, like Dennis said, you've got those families that owned slaves, had the plantations, worked the slaves, and because of the sweat and suffering of the slaves those families are major players now in the United States. I think you just track them down. You have to go into North Carolina, South Carolina.

SWEET: Mississippi, Alabama, all over.

HITT: As the descendant of—I'm not making this up—Martin Van Buren Hitt, slave owner, I think I speak for a lot of people when I ask, "How do you do that?" But you're saying it's possible?

GARY: It's possible. Look, nobody ever said it was going to be easy. You know, if you're not ready to get in the trenches and fight—if you're not ready to get knocked down, kicked out of court, and everything else—then it's not the type of issue you want to pursue, because it will be a struggle.

PIRES: Let's talk about the corporate defendants. You have in America, from the 1830s, 1840s, 1850s, the beginning of the greatest accumulation of our wealth. The early oil industry, for example, predates the Civil War. You've got to look back and find out, because many of those companies still exist, under other names. Standard Oil, a.k.a. Esso, a.k.a. Exxon, is still here. They're all still here.

GARY: Aetna Inc., which has been around since 1853, just apologized to blacks for underwriting slave insurance policies. And the Hartford *Courant,* which is still publishing, also apologized for running ads that assisted in the capture of slaves running away, making a break for freedom.

PINES: You look at a banker like J. P. Morgan and you look at the other trusts, like the railroads. Fleet Bank used to be the Providence Bank, whose original wealth dates back to the family of John Brown, whose descendants underwrote Brown University enough to cover up the embarrassment of where he made his money.

HITT: Embarrassment?

PIRES: The Browns made much of their money as slave traders in the late eighteenth century.

GARY: So we've got the federal government.

PIRES: And we've got the states.

GARY: And we've got the private profiteers.

SWEET: Looking good so far.

The Plaintiffs

PIRES: Since we've agreed that our case would extend beyond the end of slavery, it seems to me that the issue of plaintiffs would be best dealt with if you think of the suit as falling into three time brackets. There's slavery up until 1865. Then you have government-approved segregation for, what, seventy or eighty years? And then we have this kind of fuzzy land we lived in until the 1960s, and I don't even know what you call that.

SWEET: Denial.

PIRES: It's easy to go back to the 1940s, the 1950s, because we have precedent—the Japanese internment, the case of the Jews in Germany, we have lots of cases. So if I say, "We're going to go back to the 1940s, which is sixty years ago, and pick up claims," that's an easy case. But to go back to the second time bracket, which is to the 1860s, is a little tougher, because of sovereign immunity and the statute of limitations.

HITT: Well, that's one of Robinson's points in his book. Why not just sue for the more recent cases, which stem from slavery? Their proximity in time gives us two things: living victims and a quantifiable economic case. As was mentioned, the federal government sanctioned mortgage covenants that essentially restricted blacks from entering the middle class. That is an economic damage. We can measure it and put a numerical figure on it—a precise amount of money. And then you can sue. You have a class of African Americans who were struggling to join the middle class—very appealing. Your average jury would support it, easily.

PIRES: And even a case as good as that one leads us to another problem. Willie, let's suppose you are the lead lawyer. We have a plaintiffs' meeting and people say, "How far back are we going? Are we going to go back 250 years, 150 years, or 50 years?" Isn't that the question?

GARY: Obviously as a lawyer you want to make your job as easy as you can and also put yourself in the best position to win. And to do that, you want to put your hands on those damages that you can quantify so that you can develop them. You've got evidence still available, and you've got people. The only problem with it, though, is that this kind of lawsuit is going to appear in the court of public opinion, and you're going to need the support of the people.

PIRES: The white people.

GARY: And black people.

PIRES: Black people you got, right?

GARY: No, not necessarily.

PIRES: Black people aren't going to be happy with such a suit?

GARY: What about those people who, for whatever reason, maybe were excluded because you started in the 1940s? Would we pick up everybody? One third, two thirds, of all living blacks? I don't know. If you leave a substantial number of people outside . . . I mean, it's got to be like we are not leaving anyone behind. Because if we pick the best, most recent case, some people are going to complain. Then we've got to be prepared to meet the fight within the fight. And that could be a major problem.

PIRES: What's more important, to tell the real story of American slavery or to win specific damages from 1940 onward?

GARY: It's something we'd have to think about. You would have some people saying—

PIRES:—you lawyers didn't do your job.

GARY: No, that we're taking the easiest way out. And that we're leaving people behind. No one should be left behind, and if you're going to do it, you should do it right, and it's not fair just for a few and not for all.

SWEET: Let me say this to you: All black folks are not going to be happy. You can go back 200 years, include every damage in the world, and you still will have blacks who are not happy.

PIRES: Why?

SWEET: I mean, Clarence Thomas'll probably write an opinion saying it stigmatizes black folks to bring any action.

PIRES: Why?

SWEET: You have some self-hating black folks. You'll even have some black folks who feel like they don't want to have the issue brought to the forefront.

SCRUGGS: There are so many different parts here that you have to think about. Let's get to this one. Who are your plaintiffs, first of all?

PIRES: Black people.

SCRUGGS: Well, okay. Does that include Tiger Woods? What are his damages? What are Denzel Washington's damages?

GARY: Well, one thing about a class-action lawsuit, you don't have to try to figure out the damages. You can do that on a grid.

HITT: Do you use some kind of damages formula when you're dealing with a large class like this?

GARY: Yes. But look here, we've got more non-Tiger Woodses than we have Tiger Woodses. For every Tiger Woods, we have 100,000 non-Tigers.

PIRES: That's true.

SWEET: Well, the thing about it is, in a class action, you have people with different degrees of damage. In my fen-phen case, some people were hurt. But some weren't. And, hell, some people even lost weight. I mean, they were better off, I guess. Some people died, of course.

GARY: But they were all still members of the class. They each experienced the risk.

SWEET: They were all members of the class, and their damages vary along with the degree of impact.

SCRUGGS: I think you'd need to really define the class pretty well, so you keep the Tiger Woodses and people like that out. You can't have people say, "Well, damn, you're going to give all this money to Tiger Woods or Denzel Washington?"

SWEET: When you say "the class," you've got to remember that you're still covering a large majority of the black people in the United States of America. Then you have certain representatives who'll be in court with you.

SCRUGGS: Right, but you've got to come up with an appealing plaintiff, just like you would in an individual personal-injury case.

HITT: Who would you want to be representatives?

SWEET: You go and you pick them.

SCRUGGS: You interview a lot of people to pick somebody who's articulate, who's got an appealing personal case, and who is typical of the class that he's going to represent.

HITT: In the Japanese-American case, they brought forward as class representatives only the Japanese Americans who in the 1940s said, "I acquiesced to this because it was my patriotic duty." They did not bring forward the ones who rioted or resisted the draft.

SCRUGGS: Right. You don't want to trot Mike Tyson out there.

HITT: You want to trot out the black guys who fought in World War II and came back to freedom's home only to be told they couldn't sit at a lunch counter.

SCRUGGS: That's right. You carefully pick them.

PINES: All our famous plaintiffs are selected. Rosa Parks was selected.

SCRUGGS: Yeah, Rosa Parks. Perfect example.

PIRES: They're all selected. I mean, the history of American plaintiffs, Jack, is that they are all selected. Remember Darrow's famous case, the Scopes trial? Well, the lawyers found Scopes by taking an ad out in the paper.

Damages

PIRES: I have this theory about big lawsuits. Their chance of success is not really a matter of the plaintiff or the defendant, nor of legal theory, nor of arguments of liability. It is a matter of the damages to the plaintiff. People react to damages in a visceral way. Take Dickie's tobacco case. Why did people warm to it? Because the average person knows what medical costs are and how much he or she is spending on them. Poor folks have no medical insurance, and middle-class folks are gagging on paying for it. Then someone like Dickie Scruggs comes along and says, "We're going to sue on behalf of the attorneys general because the tobacco people are responsible for a lot of our medical costs, and they're not paying their fair share!" The average person says, "That's right, yeah. Screw them! It's hundreds of billions of dollars. Good! GET them!" No one cares about the technicalities.

GARY: That case also changed our whole attitude toward tobacco.

PIRES: In my black farmers' case, people finally said, "Hey, blacks are farming without access to loans? I've had trouble getting loans. Give them a hearing!" People relate to it. They react to those damages, and they say, "We're going to pay these black folks for what we did to them." It wasn't liability-based, it was damages-based. Every decade has its case. In the seventies it was IBM. In the eighties it was AT&T. And in the nineties it was tobacco. People reacted to those damages too. "Break up this big monopoly. Yeah, that's wrong." So how do we make our damages appealing?

SCRUGGS: First, by making it clear that the damages are not just about money. You know that old saying: If you catch a man a fish, you've fed him for a day; if you teach him how to fish, you've fed him for a lifetime. And that's what I'm talking about here. Regardless of whether the defendant is the federal government or a corporate institution that profited from the inhuman treatment of blacks—like German corporations that used Jewish slave labor to make money and are still reaping the benefits—you've got to describe the damages in such a way that makes sense to the public.

GARY: But a lawsuit is also about the money.

SCRUGGS: I worked with a tribal corporation established under the Alaska Native Claims Settlement Act. And the way the federal government settled similar claims was that it vested the Indian tribes with large sums of money and land and resources. And I'm afraid that it gave too much wealth too soon to people who were not sophisticated enough to do anything with it, and they were victimized.

PIRES: They lost it all.

SCRUGGS: Many did. In one generation.

PIRES: People will worry about that.

SCRUGGS: I'm not saying that blacks are less sophisticated than whites. If you gave money to a bunch of WASP Harvard graduates, they'd blow through it, too. It's human nature.

SWEET: But Dickie, the better part of the solution would be the victory itself, the benefit that comes when it's recognized by this country that reparations are in order.

SCRUGGS: That's a different goal.

GARY: But there's got to be money, because it goes a long way toward achieving the very goals you're talking about.

PIRES: Let me put my question this way: Say the government finally admitted, "You're right. It's the worst injustice in the history of our country. We're the most successful nation on Earth—ever. You win! What do you want for damages?"

GARY: That's the big issue. You want healing, because you can change the thinking of generations unborn, the future of race relations in America.

HITT: Let's stick with the law.

GARY: No, this is important. It would say that America stepped up to the plate and acknowledged its wrongdoing and reached out to the people and said there is justice for all. It would change things—the way you and I see each other. It would be nice, you know, sometime to sit down together, and you say "I'm sorry" and I say "I'm sorry," and then we could just break bread together. We can go forward, we can do greater things than we ever anticipated.

HITT: But when I was asking a black woman once about this, I said, "You know, maybe in the end the money should all be directed toward the poorest of African Americans, because they are the real heirs of slavery's worst tragedy, the people in the ghettos. And we'll aim that money at them." And she goes, "No, no. I want some of the money." Wouldn't you want just a little bit of that money, Willie? For the symbolism of it, if nothing else? Just for the satisfaction?

GARY: There is the money.

SCRUGGS: Money is not the solution. It's setting in place institutions and programs.

GARY: Education.

SCRUGGS: Exactly. It's the difference between giving them the fish and teaching them how to fish.

SWEET: I think a small part of it is going to be the money and the remedies. But the message that will be sent is so important. By having the whole country come forward and say, "This situation has gone on too long," that's a huge step.

GARY: And for every dollar paid the government would get a $100 return.

HITT: Charles Krauthammer, a conservative columnist, is very much in favor of black reparations.

GARY: Really?

HITT: He says that black reparations make sense. We've done something wrong, we need to pay for it, right? He sees it in pure economic terms, as if it were the nation's biggest tort claim in history. They were done wrong. Let's figure out an adequate sum of compensation and pay. Then he adds: And affirmative action doesn't make sense, because we're unfairly putting one person ahead of another person. So let's eliminate all the minority-preference programs, and then let's move forward with the pay schedule.

GARY: It makes a lot of sense. No doubt about it.

PIRES: Wait a minute. What fundamentally separates black folks from white folks? Not money, but education?

SWEET: I say if you're forced to go through a trial, and you're forced to stand up there and talk about damages, the only thing to do is quantitatively ask for damages, for money.

PIRES: You can't think that money will be enough. What do you really want, Dennis? Huh?

SWEET: I'm saying that's all you can ask for.

PIRES: Suppose the judge says, "What do you want me to give you? You want money? You want education? You want access to housing? You want health care?" Dennis, what do you want?

SWEET: Al, Al, Al, hold on, hold on a second. Let me tell you this: If you're in a situation with a jury, then you can only ask for monetary relief. If you have a judge, you can say, "Judge, I need you to create these programs," or other more nuanced solutions.

SCRUGGS: That's right. All a jury can do is award money.

PIRES: What's that going to fix when the only major difference between black folks and white folks today is education?

SWEET: Oh, no, no, no, no. Noooo.

PIRES: It's the level of education. That's the biggest difference.

SCRUGGS: Well, that attitude's pretty rough.

SWEET: It's not just education. It's like, you know, Chris Rock, the comedian, said it best. He has a bit in his act where he's talking to just a normal white guy and says, "Despite all the changes in society, you wouldn't switch places with me, a black man." Then he pauses. "And I'm rich!" The thing is, there are a lot of benefits to being white. A lot.

HITT: But that's the nice thing about arguing about damages. You get specific. What do we need to fix this? Alex is right to ask, If the judge said, "Okay, you win," then what would you ask for?

SCRUGGS: That was the very toughest thing we faced in our tobacco case. We asked ourselves hypothetically: If the chairmen of the boards of these major tobacco companies walked in here today and said, "Okay, we're ready to do a deal," what did we want? It took us a year to come to some general consensus among the attorneys general and some of the public-health advocates as to what we really wanted if we had these guys by the throat. What we found out later was once we got what everybody had said he or she wanted, that wasn't enough.

PIRES: Not enough money, $368 billion?

SCRUGGS: No, no. It wasn't enough money. There wasn't enough money in the world to satisfy some people. And it wouldn't have mattered. The problem is that there are people invested in the fight, okay? I mean, like, some people in Palestine or Northern Ireland don't want the wars to end.

GARY: That's the other fight within the fight. Some black people are not going to want you to file this case and then win.

SCRUGGS: Exactly. This was the biggest mistake we made in tobacco. We did not anticipate the self-interest of some of the health groups in perpetuating their existence and their fundraising. Because bashing big tobacco was their fundamental way to raise money.

PIRES: Tobacco-Free Kids?

SCRUGGS: Well, they were on board, strangely enough, but some groups like the American Lung Association saw their fundraising threatened by a tobacco solution.

PIRES: Because when you take away their core issue, people are not happy. If I said to Dennis, "Is education the problem, is that what we're looking for?" and you say, "Let's educate two generations of black folks," people say, "I'm not happy with that. That doesn't do it."

SWEET: I just want you to realize what Chris Rock is saying. It's more complex than one thing.

HITT: If Congress intervened in this case, Dennis, would you be happy—in return for a generous reparations deal—to eliminate all minority preference programs?

SWEET: There's so little left. Sure.

SCRUGGS: What I have envisioned would be a super-affirmative-action program, much more than traditional affirmative-action programs.

HITT: So you agree with Krauthammer?

SCRUGGS: I really have not read this gentleman's work, and I may be doing it a disservice. But if he's just offering money in return for eliminating affirmative action, then no.

HITT: No?

SCRUGGS: I think that's tokenism. Reparations doesn't mean just a bunch of cash payments. The word means "to repair." I'm talking about programs. Straight-out payments will create the excuse for future Congresses to say, "We've done it, and what did they do with the money? They went through it; they blew it like other groups have."

SWEET: I agree with you. But you have to be careful about the remedy. It's like the Ayers case, a higher-education case in Mississippi in which the judge said, "The black schools are not being funded properly. The white schools are being funded more properly." The judge says, "Okay, we can show liability. Now let's do the remedy." Hell, the remedy kicked us in the butts. You know what they've started saying? "Okay, we're going to close this black school, and we're going to close that black school because of improper funding." See, the remedy can be worse than the claim. If the outcome of this suit were to give each black person

$5,000, that would be a disaster. Then we would have eliminated any moral claim to criticizing the causes that have led to widespread African-American poverty, and in return for what?

PIRES: In this case, the money's necessary but the money's not enough.

Legal Strategy II: Multiple Torts

SWEET: I get the feeling that everyone wants to start by suing the United States government. But I'd hate to see the federal government be the only defendant in the case.

PIRES: What about the states? We haven't talked about the states.

SWEET: I'll tell you a claim that's ready to go. It's an idea for a state case that would at least serve as a beginning. In fact, the state of Mississippi is a sitting duck on this. I'm talking about the Sovereignty Commission.

GARY: What was it?

SCRUGGS: It was like a Gestapo organization.

SWEET: Back in the fifties and sixties, white leaders got concerned that black people might gain power, like the right to vote. So elected public officials of the state of Mississippi funded this spy organization whose sole purpose was to keep black people down. They spied on anybody who was supposed to be a leader. They participated in the Byron de la Beckwith trial, the man who killed Medgar Evers, by helping people identify jurors. I mean, there is a library full of material documenting their activities.

GARY: And the state financed that activity?

SWEET: The state financed it. You have a secret state agency that was formed whose only purpose was to keep black folks in place.

GARY: Plus it will be a great place to start if we're going to move forward with the overall issue, including the larger suits dating all the way back.

SCRUGGS: This is a state action. You've got a statute of limitations even under the civil rights acts.

SWEET: Yeah, but you have a fraudulent concealment. So legally, the statute of limitations doesn't kick in until after the fraudulent concealment has been exposed. Well, they said that none of the documents and information conducted in here shall be open to the public; it was fraudulently concealed from the public. And they're still concealing some of the Sovereignty Commission's work. So the statute would start from the time those documents were first opened to the public, which is right now.

GARY: So you'd pick up thousands and thousands of people just with that lawsuit. Then you could branch out and pick up families in every state in the union.

PIRES: No problem.

GARY: Just recently American General Life and Accident Insurance Company paid out more than $200 million for overcharging black Americans for standard insurance premiums over the last decades. We could file a couple of those types of lawsuits as well.

HITT: Willie, are you suggesting a strategy of filing, say, a web of lawsuits—the Aetnas, Fleet banks, on the one hand, and then state and federal governments too?

GARY: I think we could get class representatives from each state in the union. If you're going to go after the government, you do all in one.

PIRES: If we filed a pile of lawsuits, you could put a judge in a position where the statute of limitations would be hard to invoke. If there were a national audience watching, then what judge is going to want to be the man who went down a laundry list of several dozen incredibly powerful and legitimate claims and had to dismiss them on a technicality? It might make it difficult.

GARY: If you've got a public outcry, a political movement behind it, while we're in the process of getting ready to file, I think that can affect the way a judge is going to rule. It can make him not want to rule, it can make him hold and then perhaps Congress will step in and you can talk settlement. There are so many things you'd have to do at once. But you definitely need a massive public-relations program. You'd want your Denzel Washingtons and your Danny Glovers on board. You get the black athletes in the NBA to stand with you, you get the NFL to stand with you. And then you might go to someone high in the ministry, because you want top-flight black people—Reverend Jesse Jackson, NAACP president Kweisi Mfume, all these people—to stand with you. Then it's a different ball game.

PIRES: Just prominent black people?

GARY: No, black and white people. And the same with the lawyers. It should not just be black lawyers. Look, right now I'm fighting for a white client down in Orlando, a very conservative area. There aren't going to be any black people on the jury. But I've got an old white fellow who's shuffling around with a walking cane! And I'm helping him in and out of the court. The two of us. Let me tell you, it neutralizes a whole lot of shit.

PIRES: So it would be important to have both black and white lawyers up front?

GARY: That's right. If you need a lawyer today, the best thing you could do is have a black lawyer fight for you. And for this case, black and white lawyers fighting together. Look, it was a long, long time before people came on board with Stevie Wonder when he was fighting all those years to make Dr. Martin Luther King's birthday a holiday. But after a while Barbra Streisand and other people came on board, saying it's the right damn thing to do. And all of a sudden the issue changed.

SCRUGGS: You're right, you can't do this case without a public-relations strategy.

GARY: This is the type of case where if you bring certain pressure to bear, if you have the right kind of public support for it, both black and white, then nobody's going to say, "Okay, here's another example of the blacks just trying to get something for nothing."

HITT: When the Jews suing in the slave-labor case were preparing their strategy, that was one of their concerns—that the suit would also promote an old ugly stereotype of Jews and money.

GARY: Same thing here. Blacks trying to get something for nothing. But not if we have a public-relations strategy in place when we begin.

HITT: But correct me if I'm wrong. Overall, are you saying that you file numerous cases at the same time so that one has a fighting chance to change the way people think about this issue? For example, if you file the slavery-era case and maybe Willie's breach of contract and they are dismissed, then does that make, say, the more recent, more economically quantifiable case about mortgage covenants seem that much more possible to win?

SCRUGGS: Exactly. You can make us look downright reasonable by filing some outrageous case over here.

HITT: Yeah. So some of those filings would be to your best case what historians say Malcolm X was for Martin Luther King. Malcolm made King's once dicey demands look mainstream.

SCRUGGS: That's not a bad strategy. That's something you have to think about. In other words, get Pat Buchanan in your race so that you'll look—no matter how conservative you are—very reasonable.

GARY: If we file a mess of cases against the states, isn't it also likely that the state would implead the federal government?

HITT: What does that mean?

SWEET: A person charged with a crime can implead other defendants, saying, in effect, "Hey, if I did it, this guy did it, too. We should share the punishment."

GARY: The states could bring in the federal government and say, "Hey, wait, we're not going to pick up this tab. We were doing what you all gave us the right to do, all this shit started in Washington, D.C."

SWEET: Neat. The states would try and prove the liability of the federal government for you.

Pro Bono?

PIRES: I have a question for you all, and you should be as honest as you can be. When we put together the black farmers' case, I thought the only way I could get black folks to trust a white lawyer was to give them a retainer agreement that said we would work for free, that they get 100 percent of their recovery. So I got 21,000 retainer agreements with black folks that said they'd get 100 percent of their recovery and we wouldn't get any money from them. And we have to petition the court for legal fees. My thinking was that many black folks, who aren't used to lawyers, would more likely trust us if we didn't take their money. So would you all work for free?

SWEET: What?

SCRUGGS: Um.

GARY: Clients sometimes try to negotiate me down to 10 percent on a case, and I say, "Why would you want me working unhappy for you? I'll get you 100,000 bucks. If you got me happy, I'll get you 2 million."

PIRES: Maybe I'm wrong.

HITT: I guess that issue's resolved.

Legal Strategy III: Due Process

SCRUGGS: Before we file a pile of lawsuits, I think there's another way be- sides a damages lawsuit under traditional theory.

PIRES: Let's hear it.

SCRUGGS: How about a Fourteenth and Fifth Amendment lawsuit against the federal government for either failure to enact sufficient laws to ensure due process or for passing laws that perpetuated the injustice?

SWEET: So a due-process lawsuit?

SCRUGGS: Just like in the sixties when Congress ordered white legislatures in Mississippi and other southern states to appropriate money for black schools or for school integration. They said no state or local government that discriminated could receive federal aid. They forced the state legislatures to appropriate money.

PIRES: So you're suing for a denial of due process to black people.

SCRUGGS: It would be a case under the laws and the Constitution of the United States, to the effect that under the imprimatur of the United States of America and the protection of the government, black men and women were brought to this country as slaves, against their will and were kept in bondage for a hundred or more years. Remember, slavery existed far longer under the Stars and Stripes than under the Stars and Bars. There were certain half-assed mea- sures taken after the Civil War to try to enfranchise and rectify the injustice that had been done. But they were very ineffectual and incomplete. After the Re- construction era, when whites regained power in the South, where most blacks lived, they went back to an era of repression, keeping blacks uneducated.

PIRES: And segregated.

SCRUGGS:—and disenfranchised. There were parallel societies, mostly in the South, less so in most northern cities. Nevertheless, because the federal government failed to enforce the Fifth, Thirteenth, Fourteenth, and Fifteenth Amendments, the state governments were allowed to continue with this dis- parate treatment of black Americans. And the result is that now blacks are dis- advantaged in comparison with whites and most other races in America. The federal government should be compelled to rectify that imbalance by passing legislation that accomplishes certain stated goals. Then there would have to be a federal court order that required the Congress of the United States to accom- plish these goals within the satisfaction of the Court—pretty much like what the 1964 Civil Rights Act did to southern legislatures. It required the legislatures in those states to appropriate money for programs that helped rectify the imbal- ance. If the legislature didn't rectify problems, if it didn't act in good faith, then the states lost federal funding. I think that kind of a lawsuit has a far greater public appeal, and a greater legal foundation, than does simply suing for money for a generation of black people. Because nobody is going to think that will be effective, other than making a few people rich for a short time—not rich, but getting some money in their pockets for a short time. And then the next generation is going to be in the same spot.

SWEET: You know what's nice about this due-process lawsuit? It does away with a lot of the complaints that "we were also done wrong" from the Irish or other minorities precisely because it recognizes the fundamental difference. African Americans were kept down by the force of law, not custom, and then every effort to lift the burden of the law was met with denial of due process. So under this lawsuit, what you're saying is, We're going to give black folks a fair chance to assimilate, just like we gave that opportunity to assimilate to other groups.

SCRUGGS: That's right, that's right.

HITT: We always come back to the technical hurdles. What's your statute of limitations theory?

SCRUGGS: My statute of limitations theory is: continuing constitutional violation. Happens every day. It's like suing your government the same way you sue your doctor for malpractice for not doing his job. The Constitution tells the three branches of government what they're supposed to be doing, what is supposed to be protected. The case law fills that out, records what is supposed to be done. The government is not doing its duty. So, in essence, it's a malpractice case or a mandamus case.

SWEET: Governmental malpractice. Nice.

HITT: A what case? Mandamus? "We command," right?

SCRUGGS: Right. In other words, we would argue that what they were supposed to do was not a discretionary function of government. You must do it. The Constitution says, "You must." You don't have any discretion, you must do it. That's where I think the remedy lies. Because you force the Congress of the United States to pass laws whether monetary funding for programs or the creation of programs that pass the courts' scrutiny. Just like southern states were forced to do thirty years ago.

HITT: Very interesting rendition. So do to the feds what the feds did to the South.

SCRUGGS: That's right. In that way, you're not couching it as reparations; there's judicial precedent for it: it's been done to all the southern states that were under the Civil Rights Act, okay? I think that's the approach, and we'll have the greatest result in terms of producing, in a few generations, a better society.

HITT: You know, that argument might even have a lot of appeal among southern whites. It kind of sticks it to the federal government, which, after all, won the war only to set 4 million penniless, propertyless, illiterate black men, women, and children adrift in the South. Slavery was evil, but so were the actions of the victors in Washington, D.C., who set in motion the Black Diaspora of 1865 and then walked away from it.

The Meta-Strategy

GARY: You know, all these theories have something to them. But I don't think we can sit down and figure out the way to legally win this case before we file a lawsuit. I think you've got to put together a concept that can get you there, and it's going to be step-by-step.

HITT: We have to file a lawsuit without knowing where we're going?

GARY: We need to get some star power on the legal side, make a strong opening case, and get it going.

SWEET: To Congress.

HITT: Is that where you're ultimately headed? Is the idea to file a case that gathers enough momentum that Congress will step in and settle it?

SCRUGGS: I think so.

GARY: You want to get to a settlement.

SCRUGGS: That's how a lot of these cases go, to the legislature.

PIRES: That's what happened with the Japanese internment case. Congress was so embarrassed by the claims that it passed a reparations-settlement bill. Each aggrieved Japanese American received $20,000.

HITT: But that case was easier, legally, to get started.

PIRES: Actually, harder. There was a Supreme Court decision in 1944 declaring the Japanese internment "constitutional."

HITT: How did they get around that?

PIRES: They got Congress to open an investigation into the facts that the government supplied the Court in order to make that 1944 decision and found that it was full of deception and lies. So the Court decision suddenly was no longer a roadblock to the case.

SWEET: That's what I was saying at the beginning. There's a way in which educating people about history, through this lawsuit, makes it more possible to file and win such a suit.

PIRES: Congress often gets involved in these cases because there are matters of justice that just can't be litigated fairly within the strictures of our common law and our Constitution.

HITT: What I hear you saying is, ultimately, that many class-action suits are just giant goads to get Congress to deal with politics. You are using the elegance of the law to motivate our legislative branch into doing what, arguably, they should be doing anyway.

SCRUGGS: That's right.

PIRES: It's true. We're getting social change from goddamn lawyers. How the hell did that happen?

SCRUGGS: My view of it is that the guys who wrote the Constitution had just thrown off a dictator, a British king who had exploited them as a colony. They had no rights, no democracy to speak of. They were not about to create a system of government that was going to allow for another dictator. So they created a strong separation of powers so that no one person or one group could gang up on another. More freedom, but at the price of governmental inefficiency. This inefficiency has worsened over time to the point that the political branches of government are capable of solving only the most compelling and broad national problems.

PIRES: Like what?

SCRUGGS: War and peace, things like that. And what's happened is that issues like what we're talking about now, big issues that are very important to people, like abortion, like HMOs, you name it, are—

PIRES: Avoided?

SCRUGGS: No, no. They're exploited, by both political parties. So what's happened is that anything that's going to get solved is punted to the court system.

PIRES: I believe that.

SCRUGGS: The courts have become a safety net. Those in charge of the political branches aren't interested in solutions, only in exploiting the issues for fund-raising purposes.

HITT: Perhaps that explains why the makeup of the Supreme Court is, if you think about, the only thing our two presidential candidates deeply differ on.

GARY: Getting this to Congress also solves the statute of limitations problems.

PIRES: And sovereign immunity.

GARY: Congress can do whatever it wants to do in terms of waiving this and that.

PIRES: It can pass any law it wants.

SCRUGGS: Getting a political solution is the cleanest way to get it done. But today's Congress must be forced to act.

PIRES: Congress won't get there until you get there.

HITT: Very Zen.

SWEET: That's why Congress won't pass the Conyers resolution out of committee.

HITT: What's that?

SWEET: Michigan Representative John Conyers Jr. proposed a bill to apologize for slavery. Congress won't even do that.

HITT: Why not?

SWEET: Probably because it also seeks to authorize a congressional study group to look into slavery.

HITT: A study group?

SWEET: You have to remember: The last congressional study group like this was the one looking into the Korematsu decision. It exposed all the injustices underlying the Supreme Court decision permitting the Japanese internment. By the time the study group finished its work, it was clear that a court case was possible. Congress won't apologize or allow the study group, because it's afraid of precisely this lawsuit—that the lawyers in this *Harper's* forum might reconvene, and not just to chat.

PIRES: And maybe file a complaint before a court. You know, it all gets back to the lack of understanding by the people you mentioned at the beginning, Jack. The people who say, "How could you possibly sue for slavery?" True, you've got all these technical legal problems—the statute of limitations, sovereign immunity, class-certification problems, defining the damages, and the rest. But you have to remember that the judiciary is the only branch of our government that has nothing to do. It sits there, waiting. The legislature writes laws, and the executive carries them out. But our judges sit and wait for us to come with a complaint, which is a kind of prayer. It says, "Judge, I have this story to tell. It's a story of an injustice. It's a new story—a new way of understanding an old injustice. And I ask you today to hear this case, to listen to my story." Sometimes they do. Sometimes, if you play it right, they hear your prayer.

The following letter was published in *The Freedmen's Book*, a collection of African-American writings compiled by the abolitionist Lydia Maria Child in 1865. The letter is a response to a slave owner who has written to his former slave at the war's end, asking him to return to work in Tennessee.

To my old Master. Colonel P. H. Anderson, Big Spring, Tennessee.

Sir. I got your letter, and was glad to find that you had not forgotten Jourdon, and that you wanted me to come back and live with you again, promising to do better for me than anybody else can. I have often felt uneasy about you. I thought the Yankees would have hung you long before this, for harboring Rebs they found at your house, I suppose they never heard about your going to Colonel Martin's to kilt the Union soldier that was left by his company in their stable. Although you shot at me twice before I left you, I did not want to hear of your being hurt, and am glad you are still living. It would do me good to go back to the dear old home again, and see Miss Mary and Miss Martha and Allen, Esther, Green. and Lee. Give my love to them all, and tell them I hope we will meet in the better world, if not in this. I would have gone back to see you all when I was working in the Nashville Hospital, but one of the neighbors told me that Henry intended to shoot me if he ever got a chance.

I want to know particularly what the good chance is you propose to give me. I am doing tolerably well here. I get twenty-five dollars a month, with victuals and clothing; have a comfortable home for Mandy,—the folks call her Mrs. Anderson, and the children Milly, Jane, and Grundy—go to school and are learning well. . . . We are kindly treated. Sometimes we overhear others saying, "Them colored people were slaves" down in Tennessee. The children feel hurt when they hear such remarks: but I tell them it was no disgrace in Tennessee to belong to Colonel Anderson. Many darkeys would have been proud, as I used to be, to call you master. Now if you will write and say what wages you will give me, I will be better able to decide whether it would be to my advantage to move back again.

As to my freedom, which you say I can have, there is nothing to be gained on that score, as I got my free papers in 1864 from the Provost-Marshal-General of the Department of Nashville. Mandy says she would be afraid to go back without some proof that you were disposed to treat us justly and kindly; and we have concluded to test your sincerity by asking you to send us our wages for the time we served you. This will make us forget and forgive old scores, and rely on your justice and friendship in the future. I served you faithfully for thirty-two years, and Mandy twenty years. At twenty-five dollars a month for me, and two dollars a week for Mandy, our earnings would amount to eleven thousand six hundred and eighty dollars. Add to this the interest for the time our wages have been kept back, and deduct what you paid for our clothing, and three doctor's visits to me, and pulling a tooth for Mandy, and the balance will show what we are in justice entitled to. Please send the money by Adams's Express, in care of V. Winters, Esq., Dayton. Ohio. If you fail to pay us for faithful labors in the past, we can have little faith in your promises in the future. We trust the good Maker has opened your eyes to the wrongs which you and your fathers have done to me and my fathers, in making us toil for you for generations without recompense. . . . Surely there will be a day of reckoning for those who defraud the laborer of his hire.

In answering this letter, please state if there would be any safety for my Milly and Jane, who are now grown up, and both good-looking girls. You know how it was with poor Matilda and Catherine. I would rather stay here and starve—and die, if it come to that—than have my girls brought to shame by the violence and wickedness of their young masters. You will also please state if there has been any schools opened for the colored children in your neighborhood. The great desire of my life now is to give my children an education, and have them form virtuous habits.

Say howdy to George Carter, and thank him for taking the pistol from you when you were shooting at me.

From your old servant,
Jourdon Anderson

Timeline of Reparations for American Slavery

*1865 General William Tecumseh Sherman issues Special Field Order #15, providing forty-acre tracts of captured land along the Atlantic coast, from South Carolina to Florida, for 40,000 former slaves.
Congress establishes the Freedmen's Bureau in March to oversee the distribution of land.
President Andrew Johnson reverses the "forty acres and a mule" provision, ordering the Freedmen's Bureau to return the land to the pardoned Confederate landholders. Later, the claim of forty acres and a mule is, oddly, dismissed in many mainstream standard history books as myth. For example, the most recently revised edition of *The Civil War Dictionary* begins its entry with this phrase: "Legend that sprang up among the newly-freed slaves. . . ."
*1866 Congress passes the Southern Homestead Act to provide freedmen with land in southern states at a cost of $5 for eighty acres. Act fails dismally; only 1,000 freedmen receive homesteads.
*1867 Republican Representative Thaddeus Stevens proposes H.R. 29, a slave-reparations bill, which promises each freed adult male slave forty acres of land and $100 to build a dwelling. "[The freedmen] must necessarily . . . be the servants and the victims of others unless they are made in some measure independent of their wiser neighbors," Stevens argues.
*1915 Treasury Department is sued for $68 million in remuneration for labor performed under slavery. The government dismisses the case on grounds of sovereign immunity.
*1955 Activist Queen Mother Audley Moore founds the Reparations Committee of Descendants of United States Slaves after reading "in an old Methodist encyclopedia" that "a captive people have one hundred years to state their judicial claims against their captors or international law will consider you satisfied with your condition."
*1962 Queen Mother Moore's reparations committee files a claim in California.
*1969 James Forman, a radical activist and member of SNCC, interrupts Sunday services at Manhattan's Riverside Church and presents his "Black Manifesto" demanding that American churches and synagogues pay $500 million in reparations.

*1987 National Coalition of Blacks for Reparations in America (NCOBRA) established to seek reparations from the federal government in the form or a domestic "Marshall Plan" for black Americans.

*1989 Representative John Conyers proposes H.R. 3745, the first of several unsuccessful proposals for the formation of a commission to study reparations for American slavery.

*1994 Florida agrees to pay $2.1 million in reparations to the survivors of the 1923 Rosewood massacre.

*1995 The Ninth Circuit Court of Appeals rules in *Cato v. United States*, holding that the claim for $100 million in reparations and an apology for slavery lacks a "legally cognizable basis," and concluding that the "legislature, rather than the judiciary, is the appropriate forum" for such claims.

*1999 Representative Conyers proposes H.R. 40, seeking a formal apology for slavery and providing for a commission to study reparations.

*2000 Representative Tony Hall proposes H.R. 356, a formal resolution to acknowledge and apologize for slavery.

A Legislative and Judicial History of American Slavery and Its Aftermath

*1619 Twenty Africans sold as bond servants in Jamestown, Virginia.

*1621 Dutch West India Company given a monopoly of the American slave trade.

*1662 Virginia's general assembly determines that "[c]hildren got by an Englishman upon a Negro woman shall be bond or free according to the condition of the mother," effectively sanctioning the breeding of slaves by slaveholders.

*1663 Maryland provides that African slaves shall serve for the duration of their lives.

*1664 Maryland declares that baptism does not alter slave status.

*1672 King Charles II charters the Royal African Company with exclusive rights to provide the colonies with Africans, putting England at the vanguard of the slave trade by century's end.

*1688 Quakers in Germantown, Pennsylvania, draft an antislavery resolution.

*1705 Virginia confers upon blacks the status of real estate.

*1717 Maryland legislates that if "any free negro or mulatto" marries a white man or woman, he or she becomes a slave along with their children. Whites and mulattoes born of white women who intermarry, however, are consigned to seven years' servitude.

*1724 New Orleans establishes the Black Code, with fifty-five articles designed to regulate the behavior of slaves.

*1777 Vermont becomes the first American territory to declare slavery illegal.

*1778 Virginia outlaws the trafficking of slaves into the commonwealth.

*1779 The Virginia Assembly passes Thomas Jefferson's "A Bill Concerning Slaves," restricting the movements of slaves and requiring white women who bear mulatto children to leave the commonwealth with their children.

*1780 The state constitution of Massachusetts declares colored persons descended of African slaves to be citizens.

*1783 Maryland forbids further importation of slaves.

*1787 The Constitutional Convention determines that for the purposes of representation and taxation slaves will be counted as three fifths of a free man.

*1790 The first census of the United States records 757,000 black Americans, composing 19 percent of the population. More than 697,000 of them are slaves.

*1791 Free Negroes of Charleston, South Carolina, protest severe legal disabilities and request to be treated as citizens.

*1792 Construction begins on the White House in Washington, D.C., requiring an influx of slaves to lay the foundation.

*1793 Congress passes the Fugitive Slave Act, which allows slave owners to seize runaways in any state or territory and sets fines for the harboring of fugitive slaves at $500.

*Three slaves are executed in Albany, New York, for antislavery activities.

*1797 Congress rejects the North Carolina Slave Petition, the first recorded petition for an end to slavery by freed blacks.

*1800 Boston refuses to support black schools.

*1804 Underground Railroad begins when a Revolutionary War officer purchases a slave and takes him to Pennsylvania. The slave's mother later escapes and follows her son north.

*Virginia forbids all evening meetings of slaves.

*1808 Congress prohibits further importation of slaves.

*1810 Maryland denies free blacks the right to vote.

*1817 The American Colonization Society is established to send freed blacks to Africa.

*1820 The Missouri Compromise, admitting Missouri as a slave state and Maine as a free state, prohibits slavery in the rest of the Louisiana Purchase north of the 36th parallel.

*1822 The American Colonization Society establishes the Liberian colony on the west coast of Africa.

*1827 New York enacts gradual emancipation law.

*1831 Nat Turner leads a slave rebellion in Southampton County in Virginia, killing fifty-five whites. One hundred twenty blacks are killed in retaliation in less than two days.

*Mississippi law declares that it is "unlawful for any slave, free Negro, or mulatto to preach the Gospel." Violators receive thirty-nine lashes upon their naked back.

*1832 Alabama law declares that "any person or persons who shall attempt to teach any free person of color or slave to spell, read or write, shall, upon conviction thereof by indictment, be fined in a sum not less than $250, nor more than $500."

*1836 Congress passes a resolution ceding authority over slave laws to the states.

*1847 Liberia declares independence.

*1850 The Compromise of 1850 results in a new Fugitive Slave Act strengthening slaveholders' ability to capture runaways in the northern free states.

*1857 The Supreme Court rules in *Dred Scott v. John F. A. Sanford*, declaring that the Missouri Compromise is unconstitutional, that blacks are not citizens, and that a slave does not become free upon entering a free state.

*1862 Congress abolishes slavery in the District of Columbia and the territories.

*1863 President Abraham Lincoln issues the Emancipation Proclamation, freeing slaves in the Confederate states.

*1865 The Thirteenth Amendment is ratified, abolishing slavery in the United States.

*1866 Congress passes the Civil Rights Act on April 9, granting citizenship and equal rights to black Americans.

*The Fourteenth Amendment is passed, guaranteeing to all U.S. citizens due process and equal protection under the law.

*1867 Congress grants black citizens the right to vote in the District of Columbia and the territories.

*The first of several Reconstruction Acts places Confederate states under federal military rule.

*1869 The Fifteenth Amendment is passed, guaranteeing black Americans the right to vote.

*1875 The Civil Rights Act of 1875 passed, guaranteeing equal rights to black Americans in public accommodations and in service on a jury.

*Mississippi elects the first black, Republican Blanche Kelso Bruce, to the United States Senate for a full six-year term.

*1877 The Compromise of 1877 ends Reconstruction.

*1881 Tennessee segregates railroad cars. Other southern states follow suit.

*1883 The Supreme Court declares the Civil Rights Act of 1875 unconstitutional, holding that the Fourteenth Amendment forbids states, but not citizens, from discriminating against blacks.

*1890 The Mississippi Plan requires black voters to pass literacy and "understanding" tests, leading the effort by southern states to disenfranchise black citizens.

*1896 Supreme Court rules in *Plessy v. Ferguson*, establishing the separate-but-equal doctrine.

*1909 The National Association for the Advancement of Colored People (NAACP) is established to advocate for civil rights for black Americans.

*1910 Baltimore approves the first city ordinance designating the boundaries of black and white neighborhoods.

*1913 President Woodrow Wilson institutes federal segregation of workplaces, restrooms, and lunchrooms.

*1917 Marcus Garvey establishes a Universal Negro Improvement Association branch in the United States and launches the "Back to Africa" movement.

*1934 Costigan–Wagner Antilynching Bill defeated in Congress.

*1948 Supreme Court rules in *Shelley v. Kraemer*, one of several housing-discrimination cases, that enforcement of restrictive covenants by state courts is unconstitutional.

*President Harry S. Truman integrates the armed forces.

*1954 Supreme Court ruling on *Brown v. Board of Education of Topeka, Kansas*, strikes down the separate-but-equal doctrine.

*1957 Congress passes the Civil Rights Act of 1957—the first since Reconstruction—creating a Civil Rights Division in the Justice Department and the Civil Rights Commission to study all aspects of segregation.

*1960 The Civil Rights Act of 1960 outlaws interference with desegregation orders and voter rights. The Supreme Court declares segregation in bus and railway terminals unconstitutional in *Boynton v. Virginia*.

*1964 The Civil Rights Act of 1964 creates the Equal Employment Opportunity Commission and prohibits discrimination by businesses and employers.

*1965 The Voting Rights Act is passed to enforce the Fifteenth Amendment. 250,000 blacks register to vote by the end of the year.

*1968 The Civil Rights Act of 1968 prohibits discrimination in housing.

*1978 Supreme Court ruling in *Regents of the University of California v. Bakke* strikes down quota system in university admissions.

*1995 The Regents of the University of California vote to end affirmative action in university admissions.

*1996 California votes in favor of Proposition 209 to ban affirmative action in government employment and college admissions.

*1998 Washington citizens vote to ban affirmative action in government employment and college admissions. Similar efforts follow in Florida.

*1999 After an investigation reveals that black drivers on the New Jersey Turnpike were five times more likely than white drivers to be stopped by New Jersey State Police, the Justice Department appoints a state monitor.

[Harper's] *Editor's Note*

As this issue was going to press, the four forum participants were contacted by Professor Charles Ogletree of the Harvard Law School and asked to attend a meeting with other lawyers, including attorneys from Johnnie Cochran's law firm, Cochran, Cherry, Givens & Smith, in order to continue this conversation. Although Ogletree declined to discuss the details, he confirmed the existence of a working group and its intention: to file a reparations lawsuit for the injustice of slavery and its aftermath against the government of the United States.

NOTE

1. " 'Making the Case for Racial Reparations: Does America Owe a Debt to the Descendants of Its Slaves?' — A Forum," *Harper's Magazine*, vol. 301, November 2000, 37–41.

12

Economic Calculations

According to Dalton Conley, associate professor of Sociology at New York University and director of NYU's Center for Advanced Social Science Research, Black economic inequality may be understood as the result of differences in the wealth held by African-Americans as compared to white Americans, not in terms of income differences. Moreover, differences in wealth have a largely historical origin. Slavery's effects are felt not just in loss of wages but perhaps more importantly in the diminished wealth of slaves and their descendants. In a short opinion piece in the *New York Times*, Conley writes,

> One way is to recognize slavery as an institution upon which America's wealth was built. If we take this view, it is not important whether a white family arrived in 1700 or in 1965. If you wear cotton blue jeans, if you take out an insurance policy, if you buy from anyone who has a connection to the industries that were built on chattel labor, then you have benefited from slavery. Likewise, if you are black—regardless of when your ancestors arrived—you live with slavery's stigma . . .
>
> The typical white family enjoys a net worth that is more than eight times that of its black counterpart, according to the economist Edward Wolff. Even at equivalent income levels, gaps remain large. Among families earning less than $15,000 a year, the median African-American family has a net worth of zero, while the corresponding white family has $10,000 in equity. The typical white family earning $40,000 annually has a nest egg of around $80,000. Its black counterpart has about half that amount.
>
> This equity inequity is partly the result of the head start whites enjoy in accumulating and passing on assets. Some economists estimate that up to 80 percent of lifetime wealth accumulation results from gifts from earlier generations, ranging from the down payment on a home to a bequest by a parent. *New York Times*, February 15, 2003.

Dalton Conley: "Wealth Matters," from *Being Black, Living in the Red*[1]

If I could cite one statistic that inspired this [study], it would be the following: in 1994, the median white family held assets worth more than seven times those of the median nonwhite family. Even when we compare white and minority families at the same income level, whites enjoy a huge advantage in wealth. For instance, at the lower end of the income spectrum (less than $15,000 per year), the median African American family has no assets, while the equivalent white family holds $10,000 worth of equity. At upper income levels (greater than $75,000 per year), white families have a median net worth of $308,000, almost three times the figure for upper-income African American families ($114,600).[2]

Herein lie the two motivating questions of this [study]. First, why does this wealth gap exist and persist over and above income differences?

Second, does this wealth gap explain racial differences in areas such as education, work, earnings, welfare, and family structure? In short, this study examines where race *per se* really matters in the post–civil rights era and where race simply acts as a stand-in for that dirty word of American society: class. The answers to these questions have important implications for the debate over affirmative action and for social policy in general.

An alternative way to conceptualize what this book is about is to contrast the situations of two hypothetical families. Let's say that both households consist of married parents, in their thirties, with two young children.[3] Both families are low-income—that is, the total household income of each family is approximately the amount that the federal government has "declared" to be the poverty line for a family of four (with two children). In 1996, this figure was $15,911.

Brett and Samantha Jones (family 1) earned about $12,000 that year. Brett earned this income from his job at a local fast-food franchise (approximately two thousand hours at a rate of $6 per hour). He found himself employed at this low-wage job after being laid off from his relatively well-paid position as a sheet metal worker at a local manufacturing plant, which closed because of fierce competition from companies in Asia and Latin America. After six months of unemployment, the only work Brett could find was flipping burgers alongside teenagers from the local high school.

Fortunately for the Jones family, however, they owned their own home. Fifteen years earlier, when Brett graduated from high school, married Samantha, and landed his original job as a sheet metal worker, his parents had lent the newlyweds money out of their retirement nest egg that enabled Brett and Samantha to make a 10 percent down payment on a house. With Samantha's parents cosigning—backed by the value of their own home—the newlyweds took out a fifteen-year mortgage for the balance of the cost of their $30,000 home. Although money was tight in the beginning, they were nonetheless thrilled to have a place of their own. During those initial, difficult years, an average of $209 of their $290.14 monthly mortgage payment was tax deductible as a home mortgage interest deduction. In addition, their annual property taxes of $800 were completely deductible, lowering their taxable income by a total of $3,308 per year. This more than offset the payments they were making to Brett's parents for the $3,000 they had borrowed for the down payment.

After four years, Brett and Samantha had paid back the $3,000 loan from his parents. At that point, the total of their combined mortgage payment ($290.14), monthly insurance premium ($50), and monthly property tax payment ($67), minus the tax savings from the deductions for mortgage interest and local property taxes, was less than the $350 that the Smiths (family 2) were paying to rent a unit the same size as the Joneses' house on the other side of town.

That other neighborhood, on the "bad" side of town, where David and Janet Smith lived, had worse schools and a higher crime rate and had just been chosen as a site for a waste disposal center. Most of the residents rented their housing units from absentee landlords who had no personal stake in the community other than profit. A few blocks from the Smiths' apartment was a row of public housing projects. Although they earned the same salaries and paid more or less the same monthly costs for housing as the Joneses did, the Smiths and their children experienced living conditions that were far inferior on every dimension, ranging from the aesthetic to the functional (buses ran less frequently, large supermarkets were nowhere to be found, and class size at the local school was well over thirty).

Like Brett Jones, David Smith had been employed as a sheet metal worker at the now-closed manufacturing plant. Unfortunately, the Smiths had not been able to buy a home when David was first hired at the plant. With little in the way of a down payment, they had looked for an affordable unit at the time, but the real estate agents they saw routinely claimed that there was just nothing available at the moment, although they promised to "be sure to call as soon as something comes up. . . ." The Smiths never heard back from the agents and eventually settled into a rental apartment.

David spent the first three months after the layoffs searching for work, drawing down the family's savings to supplement unemployment insurance—savings that were not significantly greater than those of the Joneses, since both families had more or less the same monthly expenses. After several months of searching, David managed to land a job. Unfortunately, it was of the same variety as the job Brett Jones found: working as a security guard at the local mall, for about $12,000 a year. Meanwhile, Janet Smith went to work part-time, as a nurse's aide for a home health care agency, grossing about $4,000 annually.

After the layoffs, the Joneses experienced a couple of rough months, when they were forced to dip into their small cash savings. But they were able to pay off the last two installments of their mortgage, thus eliminating their single biggest living expense. So, although they had some trouble adjusting to their lower standard of living, they managed to get by, always hoping that another manufacturing job would become available or that another company would buy out the plant and reopen it. If worst came to worst, they felt that they could always sell their home and relocate in a less expensive locale or an area with a more promising labor market.

The Smiths were a different case entirely. As renters, they had no latitude in reducing their expenses to meet their new economic reality, and they could not afford their rent on David's reduced salary. The financial strain eventually proved too much for the Smiths, who fought over how to structure the family budget. After a particularly bad row when the last of their savings had been spent, they decided to take a break; both thought life would be easier and better for the children if Janet moved back in with her mother for a while, just until things turned around economically that is, until David found a better-paying job. With no house to anchor them, this seemed to be the best course of action.

Several years later, David and Janet Smith divorced, and the children began to see less and less of their father, who stayed with a friend on a "temporary" basis. Even though together they had earned more than the Jones family (with total incomes of $16,000 and $12,000 respectively), the Smiths had a rougher financial, emotional, and family situation, which, we may infer, resulted from a lack of property ownership.

What this comparison of the two families illustrates is the inadequacy of relying on income alone to describe the economic and social circumstances of families at the lower end of the economic scale. With a $16,000 annual income, the Smiths were just above the poverty threshold. In other words, they were not defined as "poor," in contrast to the Joneses, who were.[4] Yet the Smiths were worse off than the Joneses, despite the fact that the U.S. government and most researchers would have classified the Jones family as the one who met the threshold of neediness, based on that family's lower income.

These income-based poverty thresholds differ by family size and are adjusted annually for changes in the average cost of living in the United States. In 1998, more than two dozen government programs—including food stamps, Head Start, and Medicaid—based their eligibility standards on the official poverty threshold. Additionally, more than a dozen states currently link their needs standard in some way to this poverty threshold. The example of the Joneses and the Smiths should tell us that something is gravely wrong with the way we are measuring economic hardship—poverty—in the United States. By ignoring assets, we not only give a distorted picture of life at the bottom of the income distribution but may even create perverse incentives.

Of course, we must be cautious and remember that the Smiths and the Joneses are hypothetically embellished examples that may exaggerate differences. Perhaps the Smiths would have divorced regardless of their economic circumstances. The hard evidence linking modest financial differences to a propensity toward marital dissolution is thin; however, a substantial body of research shows that financial issues are a major source of marital discord and relationship strain.[5] It is also possible that the Smiths, with nothing to lose in the form of assets, might have easily slid into the world of welfare dependency. A wide range of other factors, not included in our examples, affect a family's well-being and its trajectory. For example, the members of one family might have been healthier than those of the other, which would have had important economic consequences and could have affected family stability. Perhaps one family might have been especially savvy about using available resources and would have been able to take in boarders, do under-the-table work, or employ another strategy to better its standard of living. Nor do our examples address educational differences between the two households.

But I have chosen not to address all these confounding factors for the purpose of illustrating the importance of asset ownership *per se.* Of course, homeownership, savings behavior, and employment status all interact with a variety of other measurable and immeasurable factors. This interaction, however, does not take away from the importance of property ownership itself.

My premise is a relatively simple and straightforward one: in order to understand a family's well-being and the life chances of its children—in short, to understand its class position—we not only must consider income, *education, and* occupation but also must take in account accumulated wealth (that is, property, assets, or net worth . . .) While the importance of wealth is the starting point of the study, its end point is the impact of the wealth distribution on racial inequality in America. As you might have guessed, an important detail is missing from the preceding description of the two families: the Smiths are black and have fewer assets than the Joneses, who are white.

At all income, occupational, and education levels, black families on average have drastically lower levels of wealth than similar white families. The situations of the Smiths may help us to understand the reason this disparity of wealth between blacks and whites. For the Smiths, it was not discrimination in hiring or education that led to a family outcome vastly different from that of the Joneses; rather, it was a relative lack of assets from which they could draw. In contemporary America, race and property are intimately linked and form the nexus for the persistence of black–white inequality.

Let us look again at the Smith family, this time through the lens of race. Why did real estate agents tell the Smiths that nothing was available, thereby hindering their chances of finding a home to buy? This well-documented practice is called "steering," in which agents do not disclose properties on the market to qualified African American home seekers, in order to preserve the racial makeup of white communities—with an eye to maintaining the property values of those neighborhoods. Even if the Smiths had managed to locate a home in a predominantly African American neighborhood, they might well have encountered difficulty in obtaining a home mortgage because of "redlining," the procedure by which banks code such neighborhoods "red"—the lowest rating—on their loan evaluations, thereby making it next to impossible to get a mortgage for a home in these districts. Finally, and perhaps most important, the Smiths' parents were more likely to have been poor and without assets themselves (being black and having been born early century), meaning that it would have been harder for them to amass enough money to loan their children a down payment or cosign for them. The result is that while poor whites manage to have, on average, net worths of over $10,000, impoverished blacks have essentially no assets whatsoever.[6]

Since wealth accumulation depends heavily on intergenerational support issues such as gifts, informal loans, and inheritances, net worth has the ability to pick up both the current dynamics of race and the legacy of past inequalities that may be obscured in simple measures of income, occupation, or education. This thesis has been suggested by the work of sociologists Melvin Oliver and Thomas Shapiro in their recent book *Black Wealth/White Wealth*.[7] They claim that wealth is central to the nature of black–white inequality and that wealth—as opposed to income, occupation, or education—represents the "sedimentation" of both a legacy of racial inequality as well as contemporary, continuing inequities. Oliver and Shapiro provide a textured description of the divergence of black–white asset holdings. They touch on some of the causal factors leading to this growing gap, such as differential mortgage interest rates paid by black and white borrowers. . . .

The Race-Class Debate

A brief review of the discourse on racial inequality may help to put the thesis of this book in historical perspective. The concept of equality most often used in public discourse was inherited from the French Revolution: *equality of opportunity*. Under this concept, equality would be achieved if each individual in a society enjoyed the right to compete in a contest unimpaired by discrimination of any kind. This form of equality would clearly be incompatible with an active, "color aware" form of racial oppression such as the refusal to serve someone at a lunch counter or the denial of a job to an individual based on his or her physiognomy. Further, this concept fits very well with the game like image many Americans have of the capitalist system. If the game is fair, our whole society is bettered by it. By contrast if the rules are stacked in favor of one group, society is not making maximal use of its human resources. For example, if African Americans are barred from higher education, society as a whole may be deprived of the skills of a great surgeon or engineer who could not attend a university because of skin color. With this premise, arguments for equality of opportunity can often be made on the basis of efficiency rather than equity.

Because of this ideological safety valve, equality of opportunity is perhaps the least threatening type of equality to many in the white majority who see a place for all at the starting gate as an underlying premise of the capitalist system. Lingering conscious or unconscious ideas of white superiority may have additionally blunted fears. According to this logic, whites would not have much to lose by allowing blacks into the economic game; if whites are inherently superior, why should they fear the entry of blacks into the contest? The belief in white superiority that had formed part of the public discourse since the early days of Western imperialism, we can speculate, may have provided a sense of security to some of the more privileged whites who did not fear for their class position, particularly during the period of rapid economic growth after World War II.

For these reasons, equality of opportunity served as the underlying philosophy and rallying cry that drove the liberal political triumphs of the 1950s and early 1960s, capped by the 1964 Civil Rights Act and the Voting Rights Act of 1965. With such legislation, equality of opportunity—in name at least—had been achieved. In theory, after 1965, discrimination in hiring, housing, and other aspects of life was illegal. It was at this point, according to sociologist William Julius Wilson[8] and others, that an overt phase of racial oppression ended in the United States and was replaced by economic subordination.

While legal equality of opportunity might have been established and some income gains made, institutionalized racism persisted nonetheless, and the scars of centuries of overt repression remained. A second type of equality had yet to be realized: *equality of condition*—more progressive and less ideologically acceptable to the American public than equality of opportunity. According to political scientist Jennifer Hochschild, "Three-fourths or more of both races agree that all people warrant equal respect, that skill rather than need should determine wages, that 'America should promote equal opportunity for all' rather than 'equal outcomes.'" She adds that most Americans think that everyone should attempt to amount to more than their parents and that "trying to get ahead is very important in making someone a true American."[9] Clearly, upward mobility and socioeconomic success are fundamental to at least the rhetoric of what it means to be American. By such a definition, African Americans may, in fact, be the most American of all, for by some socioeconomic indicators, they have made incredible progress since the passage of civil rights legislation. By other measures, however, they are not so "American"—that is, for whatever reason, upward mobility has been more difficult.

Although as a group African Americans have made progress in a number of socioeconomic areas, the base from which they were starting in the 1960s was dismally low. For instance, in 1964, only 9.4 percent of blacks held professional or managerial positions, compared to 24.7 percent of whites.[10] The median family income in the black community was less than half that in the white community. By the end of the decade (1969), 41.2 percent of black children still lived in poverty, compared to only 9.9 percent of white children.[11] Even when we compare blacks and whites with similar educational credentials, African Americans suffered from lower incomes and worked in less prestigious occupations than their white counterparts.[12] Statistics aside, the televised ghetto riots of the late 1960s may have been evidence enough for many American observers that substantial racial inequities remained in the United States.

Overall, conditions were worse for blacks than for whites across America. In addition, the mechanism by which inequality was transferred from generation to generation was different in the African American community. In their classic 1967 study, *The American Occupational Structure,* sociologists Peter Blau and Otis Dudley Duncan observed that the relationship between the occupations of black fathers and the occupations of their sons was weaker than the similar relationship among whites: regardless of class origin, African American individuals seemed destined to end up in the lower, manual sector of the economy. Blau and Duncan called this condition "perverse equality." In the same vein, the higher an African American attempted to rise in the occupational hierarchy, the more discrimination the individual faced. "In short," wrote Blau and Duncan, "better educated Negroes fare even worse relative to whites than uneducated Negroes."[13]

Despite a lack of equality of condition, many sociologists and historians agree that the period of the 1950s and 1960s was a time of important gains for African Americans. For instance, between 1949 and 1969, the median income (adjusted for family size) increased by 173 percent among African Americans, in contrast to a 110 percent increase for whites. (Keep in mind, however, that blacks were starting from a base income that was slightly more than a third that of whites in 1949.)[14] Additionally, between 1940 and the early 1970s, the black middle class grew at a faster rate than the white middle class. Based on a definition of "middle class" as having a family income twice the poverty line (note the income-based conception of class), the percentage of African American households in this group rose from a minuscule 1 percent in 1940 to 39 percent in 1970.

The period since 1970—the era of "economic subordination," according to Wilson—has been difficult to interpret in terms of race. Some of the positive trends continue—for middle-class African Americans; other statistics, however, tell a different tale, a story of poor African Americans getting poorer. In deciphering the current state of race in America, it may help to view racial inequality in the context of the life course, starting with birth. Black infants, for example, are much more likely than white infants to be born with a low (under 2,500 grams) or a very low (under 1,500 grams) birth weight. In 1994, medical complications associated with low birth weight were the primary cause of death among black infants and the third leading cause for white infants. Correspondingly, the mortality rate among black infants that year (15.8 per thousand) was well over twice that among white and Hispanic babies (6.6 and 6.5 per thousand, respectively).[15]

Looking beyond infancy, we find that over half of all African American children under the age of six live in poverty, three times greater than the proportion in the white community.[16] When we move up the age ladder, the news gets better before it gets worse again. In examining educational statistics, we find that the high school completion rates for blacks and whites are essentially the same among younger adults (ages twenty-five to thirty-four, the group for whom civil rights advances should have had an effect), with 85 percent of African Americans attaining at least a high school education, compared to 88 percent of whites. Even more encouraging is that the proportion of adults in this same age group who receive some college education (not necessarily a degree) is higher for blacks than for whites (3.2 and 2.8 percent, respectively). When we examine college completion rates, however, we find that African Americans are only about half as likely as whites to complete a bachelor's degree (14 and 28 percent, respectively). The college attrition rate for black students has become a major problem on American campuses.[17]

When we move out of school and into the labor market, the situation deteriorates. The black–white wage ratio has begun to widen *slightly* for all education levels since the 1980s.[18] Labor force participation and unemployment differentials have also increased.[19] For example, in 1994, the unemployment rate for blacks was 13.9 percent, whereas it was only 6.2 percent for non-Hispanic whites. The black unemployment rate has only rarely dipped below double digits since the dawn of the civil rights era, and it surpassed 20 percent during the 1982–83 recession. Even when African Americans are able to land a job, it is likely to be a less desirable position. In 1997, only 16 percent of employed African Americans held professional or managerial jobs, compared to 31 percent of employed whites. By contrast, black workers were overrepresented in the service sector, with its lower wages: 26 percent of employed African Americans worked in service industries while only 15 percent of their white counterparts held jobs in this sector.[20]

Income trends reflect the occupational position of black workers. In 1997, the median income for black families was 55 percent that of white families ($26,522 compared to $47,023). In this same year, 26 percent of black families lived under the poverty line, whereas only 6 percent of white families did so. Educational differences do not explain these income gaps. For instance, among individuals who are high school graduates (but have not completed additional education), median incomes are $14,881 and $18,446 for blacks and whites, respectively. When we consider only men, the disparity widens. Black male high school graduates earned a median income of $18,898 in 1997 compared to $26,028 for white males. In other words, in 1997, African American male high school graduates earned 73 cents to the dollar earned by white male high school graduates. For more educated groups, wage ratios are not much better.[21]

The labor market difficulties that African American men continue to face have repercussions further up the age ladder. As mentioned earlier, the black–white wealth gap is even wider than the income difference. Other areas of life are affected as well. For instance, in 1997, only 46 percent of black families consisted of a married couple (with or without children). This figure is 56 percent of that for whites (81.1 percent).[22] Some argue that this dearth of marriage in the African American community is partly a result of a shortage of marriageable (read: well-employed) black men.[23] There seems to be a causal loop in the logic of the current discourse on race in the United States: if black families have two full-time workers, they can maintain economic equity with whites, but blacks face economic obstacles in getting and staying married (as chapter five discusses). Race, family, and life chances seem to be inextricably linked in a vicious circle of inequality over the life course.

Given all these trends, it is understandable why liberals and conservatives are constantly at odds on issues such as the impact and continuing value of affirmative action or the reasons for persistent gaps in socioeconomic attainment between blacks and whites. Both sides can point to statistics to support their arguments, and the debate reaches a stalemate.[24]

The most provocative thesis regarding the state of racial equality today remains that issued by William Julius Wilson back in 1978 in his book *The Declining Significance of Race,* which was championed and attacked by a variety of scholars from both sides of the political debate. Wilson argued that the civil rights victories of the 1960s led to a situation in which overt racial oppression is largely a thing of the past (equality of opportunity), but in which the socioeconomic (read: class) differences between blacks and whites disadvantage

African Americans relative to their white counterparts in terms of their chances for success in life. In its most distilled form, his argument is simply that class has eclipsed race as the most important factor determining the life chances of African Americans. As Wilson himself puts it in the first sentence of his classic work: "Race relations in America have undergone fundamental changes in recent years, so much so that now the life chances of individual blacks have more to do with their economic class position than with their day-to-day encounters with whites."[25]

Understandably, Wilson's controversial argument about the declining significance of race has come under careful scrutiny. Many researchers have tested his hypothesis that class is more determinant than race of the life chances of black Americans. Support has been found for his claim in terms of occupational mobility both within and across generations[26] although race still remains salient in predicting earnings for given education levels[27] and net worth.[28] Furthermore, many scholars have documented the continued importance of race in both the economic and the symbolic realms—for many black Americans.[29] There is some disagreement about the exact mechanism by which race affects the life chances of black Americans: some claim that it has a direct impact net of socioeconomic background characteristics; others argue that it does not. Most are in agreement that race influences the way socioeconomic background (class) affects the outcomes of individuals (a sort of compromise of the race–class debate). In other words, a consensus seems to be emerging that blacks who come from middle-class background are doing better than ever before while poor, predominantly inner-city blacks are being left further and further behind. In other words there an "interaction" between *race* and class background.

The race–class debate is far from settled, however. At the time Wilson penned that provocative statement (1978), it had not even been fifteen years since the end of the era of overt, legally tolerated racial oppression. If class has eclipsed race for any group, it would have done so those born since the 1960s. . . .

[In *Being Black, Living in the Red,* I] first . . . present. . . . . . statistical analyses, addressing the question of why blacks own so much less property than whites. Some scholars have argued that whites have merely enjoyed a head start in property accumulation as a result of overt economic and political advantages they have held for centuries. The other side of the debate has claimed that contemporary issues such as residential segregation and differential credit access are the major culprits in accounting for the racial difference in property holdings. *Results from an analysis that links two generations show that among the youngest cohort of blacks and whites, historical (that is, parental) wealth disadvantages are the most salient factors, although contemporary dynamics may become important over the life course.* [Emphasis is the editors'.]

[Later on I] demonstrate how this wealth difference affects the life chances of young blacks and whites. For instance, [I] show that when we compare black and white individuals, while factoring out the effect of blacks' lower average parental incomes and wealth levels, we find that African Americans actually complete higher levels of education than their white counterparts. . . .

NOTES

1. Dalton Conley, "Wealth Matters," *Being Black, Living in the Red* (Berkeley: University of California Press, 1–24 passim [chap.1].

2. Data from the Panel Study of Income Dynamics (PSID), *1994 Wealth Supplement*. The PSID is an ongoing study conducted by the Survey Research Center, Institute for Social Research, at the University of Michigan; see the PSID Web site at www.isr.umich.edu/src/psid. For further statistics on median and mean net worth at various income levels, see Table A2.1 in the Appendix of [Conley's] book.

3. These family descriptions were extrapolated from profiles of specific families who were interviewed for this study. The age, racial, income, family size, wealth, housing tenure, and divorce descriptions of these families come directly from cases *4348* and *1586* of the PSID 1984 wave (inflation-adjusted to 1996 dollars). The names and other details are fictitious but are in line with previous research that would suggest such profiles.

4. Neither family received health insurance from an employer. Since the Smiths' income was under 185 percent of the poverty line, their children were eligible for Medicaid. (In most states, the Joneses' children would also have been eligible for Medicaid since that family's wealth was in the form of a home, which is excluded from the asset limits of many states.)

5. See, e.g., G. Levinger and O. Moles, eds., *Divorce and Separation: Contexts, Causes, and Consequences* (New York: Basic Books, 1979); and R. Conger et al., "Linking Economic Hardship to Marital Quality and Instability," *Journal of Marriage and the Family* 51 (1990): 643–56.

6. Throughout this book, the terms "black" and "African American" are used interchangeably, as are the terms "Hispanic" and "Latino." Black people of Caribbean origin make up a negligible portion of the data sample.

7. M. Oliver and T. Shapiro, *Black Wealth/White Wealth: A New Perspective on Racial Inequality* (New York: Routledge, 1995).

8. W. J. Wilson, *The Declining Significance of Race: Blacks and Changing American Institutions* (Chicago: University of Chicago Press, 1978).

9. J. L. Hochschild, *Facing Up to the American Dream: Race, Class, and the* Soul *of the Nation* (Princeton, N.J.: Princeton University Press, 1995), 55.

10. Hochschild, *Facing Up to the American Dream*, 55.

11. S. Danziger and P. Gottschalk, *America Unequal* (New York and Cambridge: Russell Sage Foundation and Harvard University Press, 1995), 90.

12. P. Blau and O. D. Duncan, *The American Occupational Structure* (New York: Free Press, 1967).

13. Blau and Duncan, *The American Occupational Structure*, 239.

14. Much of this betterment can be traced to geographic mobility. In fact, the major explanation for black socioeconomic advancement during the 1940s and 1950s was the movement of African Americans from the rural South to the industrial North with its higher wages. See, e.g., M. A. Fosset, O. R. Galle, and J. A. Burr, "Racial Occupational Inequality, 1940–1980: A Research Note on the Impact of Changing Regional Distribution of the Black Population," *Social Forces* 68 (1989): 415–27.

15. J. Ventura et al., "Report of Final Natality Statistics, 1996," *Monthly Vital Statistics Report* 46 (suppl. 2., 1997).

16. See National Center for Children in Poverty, *One in Four: America's Youngest Poor* (New York: Columbia University School of Public Health, 1995).

17. Statistics are from K. DeBarros and C. Bennett, "The Black Population in the United States: March 1997 (Update)," *Current Population Reports,* Series P-20, no. 508 (Washington, D.C.: U.S. Government Printing Office, 1998).

18. See, e.g., J. Bound and R. B. Freeman, "What Went Wrong? The Erosion of the Relative Earnings and Employment of Young Black Men in the 1980s," *Quarterly Journal of Economics* 107 (1992): 201–32; P. Moss and C. Tilly, "A Turn for the Worse—Why Black Men's Labour Market Fortunes Have Declined in the United States," *Sage Race Relations Abstracts* 18 (1993): 5–45.

19. C. Jencks, "Is the American Underclass Growing?" in *The Urban Underclass,* eds. C. Jencks and P. Peterson (Washington, D.C.: Brookings Institution, 1991).

20. DeBarros and Bennett, "The Black Population in the United States: March 1997."

21. DeBarros and Bennett, "The Black Population in the United States: March 1997."

22. DeBarros and Bennett, "The Black Population in the United States: March 1997."

23. W. J. Wilson, *The Truly Disadvantaged:. The Inner City, the Underclass, and Public Policy* (Chicago: University of Chicago Press, 1987).

24. See, e.g., S. Thernstrom and A. Thernstrom, *America in Black and White: One Nation, Indivisible* (New York: Simon & Schuster, 1997).

25. Wilson, *Declining Significance of Race,* 1.

26. M. Hout, "Occupational Mobility of Black Men: 1962 to 1973," *American Sociological Review* 49: 308–22; I. S. Son, S. W. Model, and G. A. Fisher, "Polarization and Progress in the Black Community: Earnings and Status Gains for Young Black Mates in the Era of Affirmative Action," *Sociological Forum* 4, no. 3 (1989): 309–27.

27. See two articles by C. Link, E. Ratledge, and K. Lewis: "Black–White Differences in Returns to Schooling: Some New Evidence," *American Economic Review* 66 (1976): 221–23; and "The Quality of Education and Cohort Variation in Black–White Earnings Differentials: Reply," *American Economic Review* 70 (1980): 196–203.

28. J. C. Henretta, "Race Differences in Middle-Class Lifestyle: The Role of Home Ownership," *Social Science Research* 8: 63–78.

29. J. Feagin and H. Vera, *White Racism: The Basics* (New York: Routledge, 1995); C. West, *Race Matters* (New York: Vintage, 1994).

VI

ALTERNATIVES

The final division of this book, part 6, "Alternatives," is composed of excerpts from Martha Minow's book, *Between Vengeance and Forgiveness.*

Martha Minow is William Henry Bloomberg Professor of Law at Harvard University Law School. Representative among her publications are

- *Engaging Cultural Differences: The Multicultural Challenge in Liberal Societies,* with R. Shweder and H. R. Markus (New York: Russell Sage Foundation, 2003)
- *Imagine Co-Existence: Resorting Humanity after Violent Ethnic Conflict,* ed. Antonia Chayes (San Francisco: Jossey-Bass, 2003)
- *Breaking the Cycles of Hatred: Memory, Law and Repair,* ed. Nancy L. Rosenblum (Princeton, N.J.: Princeton University Press, 2002)
- *Between Vengeance and Forgiveness: Facing History after Genocide and Mass Violence* (Boston: Beacon Press, 1998)

In these pages Minow presents us with a penetrating examination of the merits and defects of various strategies of response to catastrophic social injustices including reparations itself, criminal prosecution, removal from office of responsible parties, apologies, public memorializations, etc. Minow observes that whether or not reparations are made, the public process of considering the issues has immense, perhaps indispensable, political, social, and personal importance. Though centered on injustices such as genocidal campaigns, war crimes generally, and apartheid in South Africa, her book remains one of the best overall discussions of the range of response between forgiveness and vengeance written to date.

13

Between Vengeance and Forgiveness[1]

Martha Minow: From *Between Vengeance and Forgiveness*

Reparations

. . . The South African Truth and Reconciliation Commission launches not only an inquiry into what happened, but also a process intended to promote reconciliation. Other truth commissions seek information to support prosecutions. The information unearthed by the TRC may lead to some legal charges and trials, but its central direction, enhanced by its power to grant amnesty to perpetrators on the condition that they cooperate fully, moves away from prosecutions toward an ideal of restorative justice. Unlike punishment, which imposes a penalty or injury for a violation, restorative justice seeks to repair the injustice, to make up for it, and to effect corrective changes in the record, in relationships, and in future behavior. Offenders have responsibility in the resolution. The harmful act, rather than the offender, is to be renounced. Repentance and forgiveness are encouraged.[2]

By design, the TRC includes a committee devoted to proposing economic and symbolic acts of reparation for survivors and for devastated communities. Monetary payments to the victimized, health and social services, memorials and other acts of symbolic commemoration would become governmental policies in an effort to restore victims and social relationships breached by violence and atrocity. The range of money, services, and public art suggests the kinds of steps that can be pursued in the search for restorative justice.

Restorative justice has academic and political advocates in many countries. They draw on diverse religious and philosophical traditions.[3] Christian sources stress the universality of human suffering and the redemptive power of forgiveness. Jewish sources look to Talmudic treatments of restitution and repair.[4] New Zealand and Australia have drawn upon Maori traditions to develop state experiments in restorative justice.[5] Japanese justice includes an informal track of confession, repentance, and absolution in the service of new roles for offenders and victims.[6] Current South African discussions point to traditional African notions of community repair as the goal of justice.[7] Some commentators look to therapeutic methods and ideals.[8]

Leading statements of the restorative justice vision focus on responses to ordinary crime.[9] Restorative justice emphasizes the humanity of both offenders and victims. It seeks repair of social connections and peace rather than retribution against the offenders.[10] Building connections and enhancing communication between perpetrators and those they victimized, and forging ties across the community, takes precedence over punishment or law enforcement.[11]

These aims of restorative justice reflect a practical view about human psychology. Unlike retributive approaches, which may reinforce anger and a sense of victimhood, reparative approaches instead aim to help victims move beyond anger and a sense of powerlessness. They also attempt to reintegrate offenders into the community. South Africa's TRC emphasizes truth-telling, public acknowledgment, and actual reparations as crucial elements for restoration of justice and community. The TRC proceeds on the hope that getting as full an account of what happened as possible, and according it public acknowledgment, will lay the foundations for a new, reconciling nation instead of fomenting waves of renewed revenge and divisiveness. Archbishop Desmond Tutu explained the TRC's goals in these terms: "Our nation needs healing. Victims and survivors who bore the brunt of the apartheid system need healing. Perpetrators are, in their own way, victims of the apartheid system and they, too, need healing."[12]

The authorizing legislation directed the TRC reparations committee to assemble requests and proposals from individuals and communities. The TRC in turn has recommended legislation to establish monetary payments, medical treatment, counseling, information about murdered relatives, and the naming of parks and schools. The aim of such reparations is "to empower individuals and communities to take control of their own lives."[13] Other reparation efforts after mass atrocities stress restoring particular stolen properties, paying money damages, or securing public apologies from governmental authorities.

One danger with any reparations effort is the suggestion that because some amends have been made, the underlying events need not be discussed again. Equally troubling to many survivors are assertions that monetary reparations can remedy nonmonetary harms, such as the death of a child, the loss of an arm, the agony of remembered torture, or the humiliation and shame of being wrongly detained and interned. The amounts of money likely to emerge from political processes, especially in economically depressed societies such as South Africa, can offer only token gestures whose small size underscores their inadequacy. As statements of actual value, they trivialize the harms. More basically, money can never bring back what was lost. Even the suggestion that it can may seem offensive. Restitution of stolen art, bank accounts, or ancestral bones may return the physical objects but not the world in which they were taken. Apologies may restore some dignity, but not the lives as they existed before the violations.

The process of seeking reparations, and of building communities of support while spreading knowledge of the violations and their meaning in people's lives, may be more valuable, ultimately, than any specific victory or offer of a remedy. Being involved in a struggle for reparations may give survivors a chance to speak and to tell their stories. If heard and acknowledged, they may obtain a renewed sense of dignity. The reparations themselves cannot undo the violence that was done. Yet even inadequate monetary payments or an apology without any reparations can afford more opportunities for a sense of recognition and renewal for survivors, observers, and offenders than would an unsuccessful struggle for an apology, for reparations, or for the restitution of property, or a relative's bones. When the victimized and their supporters push for monetary compensation, for restitution of wrongly appropriated artifacts or property, or for official apologies, they also are engaged in obtaining acknowledgement of the violations and acceptance of responsibility for wrongdoing as much as they press for a specific remedy.

Repair for the Irreparable

Monetary payments of the sort offered by Congress to survivors of the Japanese-American internment symbolically substitute for the loss of time, freedom, dignity, privacy, and equality. The offer of money or some other goods at best ends the inaction and silence after the violation. And yet money remains incommensurable with what was lost. Even as an ideal, and certainly in practice, reparations fall short of repairing victims or social relationships after violence.

This inevitable shortfall makes me wonder about the assumption that the most obvious need of victims is for compensation. So asserts Howard Zehr, a theorist of restorative justice in the context of domestic criminal violations. "Financial and material losses may present a real financial burden. Moreover, the symbolic value of losses—their meaning often acknowledged by story-telling and public memory—may be as important or more important than the actual material losses. In either case, repayment can assist recovery. "[14] Zehr acknowledges the limitations of restitution; no one can give back an eye destroyed by violence. Yet, he argues, paying for expenses might ease the burdens: "At the same time, it may provide a sense of restoration at a symbolic level."[15]

The return to a symbolic dimension seems crucial because, in fact, most victims of crime rate their needs to know what happened and why more highly than their desires for compensation or restitution.[16] Even those who start with a monetary motivation may find more value in the opportunity to tell their stories and to get help for their trauma. A daughter of a Holocaust survivor explains,

"My father is a survivor of Nazi concentration camps. He has been receiving monetary compensation from the German government for many years. A few years ago he heard about the possibility of getting an increase in reparations if he could demonstrate that his experiences caused significant mental trauma. My father pursued that route—interested in money, not healing—and failed to get an increase in reparations. However, in so doing, he had to seek psychological counseling in order to demonstrate his mental trauma. The indirect effect of that process was that he received some very needed counseling—counseling he would not have otherwise sought. He came to realize, after some 50 years, that he has some serious psychological problems that he needed to confront rather than repress. The process was also significantly important to my mother who had to deal with her husband's trauma and who, herself, was a refugee of the War."[17]

Practical, therapeutic benefits from telling their stories and acknowledgment may accrue even for those who seek reparations without consulting a therapist.

The core idea behind reparations stems from the compensatory theory of justice. Injuries can and must be compensated. Wrongdoers should pay victims for losses. Afterward, the slate can be wiped clean. Or at least a kind of justice has been done. This is a commonplace notion of justice in the context of bankruptcy, contracts, and even personal injury law. Extending this idea to victims of mass violence substitutes money or other material benefits—such as insurance, or scholarships—for the devastation inflicted by wrongful incarcerations, or tortures, or murders. This means crossing over differing lexicons of value. Domestic civil justice systems deal with this problem with crude measures of lost earning capacities due to injuries, or random figures to represent the loss of daily contact with a child, a spouse. Some people try to bring rigor to the project of estimating the present value of unjust enrichment from slavery, or from expropriated lands.[18]

Yet no market measures exist for the value of living an ordinary life, without nightmares or survivor guilt. Valuing the losses from torture and murder strains the moral imagination. If a genocide destroys an entire people, the more basic difficulty is knowing whom to compensate. Even if small numbers of a nation survive, compensating them for the loss of their entire world defies computation and comprehension. Symbolic expressions become the only possibilities. German reparations could be directed to the fledgling state of Israel more easily than to disparate fragments of Jewish refugee communities around the globe.[19]

A sense of inappropriateness of putting a value on losses from mass atrocity may lead some to resist the exercise. Consider what happened when Prime Minister Ryutara Hashimoto of Japan offered a letter of apology and monetary reparations to some 500 survivors of the 200,000 "comfort women,"[20] the euphemism for sexual slaves imprisoned and exploited by the Imperial Army during World War II.[21] Only six of the women accepted the offer.[22] Most others rejected it largely because the fund came from private sources rather than from the government itself.[23] Even those who accepted the money, however, emphasized that no monetary payment could remedy the horrors and humiliations they experienced from the rapes, violence, and destruction of their dignity.[24] Some of the women—from Korea, Taiwan, China, the Philippines, and Indonesia—found more gratification when the U.S. Justice Department placed the names of sixteen Japanese individuals involved in enslaving the women for sex on a "watch list" of suspected war criminals barred from entering the United States.[25] Some argued that only prosecutions by the Japanese government would adequately express governmental contrition and redress the abuse.[26] Others supported treatment of the "comfort women" in school textbooks as a kind of reparation through memory.[27]

Some individuals treat an offer of monetary reparations as affording them the chance to make statements of personal strength and dignity. But sometimes the harms extend even into people's abilities to express claims and needs. In South Africa, observers of the Truth and Reconciliation Commission have been struck by how most of the victimized who testify express exceedingly modest requests for reparations. A death certificate for a relative whose death was denied by the apartheid regime; a tombstone: these are common requests gathered by the committee on reparations. One woman who was shot repeatedly while hanging wash on a line asked for removal of the bullets that remained in her vagina.[28] No less, and no more. Some who testify ask for subsidies for their children's education, or to have a park or a school named after victims of torture and murder.

When are small, modest requests a reflection of the lowered expectations of the persistently oppressed? When are they, instead, dignified assertions made by individuals who have no illusions about the possibility of external repair for their losses? When are small requests scrupulous attempts to avoid the implication that torturers can ever remedy the harms that they inflicted? And when are meager requests instead the general expressions of people more committed to building a new collective future—out of what everyone knows to be limited resources—rather than dwelling on an aching past?[29]

These questions recapitulate a debate among feminists over whether an ethic of care reveals women's subordination or instead a vibrant alternative moral perspective. One version of this debate pitted psychologist Carol Gilligan against lawyer Catharine MacKinnon. Gilligan defended an ethic of mutual care and reciprocity over one of individual rights, while MacKinnon argued that an ethic of care emerges when someone has a foot on your neck.[30] I suspect that no abstract resolution of this kind of debate could ever be trustworthy. Only careful judgments embedded in particular historical and personal contexts can illuminate the relationship between moral views and power relationships.

Even so, distinguishing the self-abnegating act from the large-souled gesture may be impossible for an outside observer. This problem highlights the special difficulties in relying on reparations where psychological and political realities push in the direction of modest if not trivial gestures. Yet I do not want to underestimate the power of humble acts of reparations. They can meet burning needs for acknowledgment, closure, vindication, and connection. Reparations provide a specific, narrow invitation for victims and survivors to walk between vengeance and forgiveness. The ultimate quality of that invitation depends on its ability to transform the relationships among victims, bystanders, and perpetrators.

In South Africa, the specific details of reparations for individuals and for the entire society will be decided by the newly constituted government, whose leaders are in so many cases themselves survivors of policy brutality and torture. Archbishop Desmond Tutu recently announced a proposal for a one-time grant

of money to victims designed to assist access to services such as medical services as one of a five-point proposal for reparations.[31] If voted by the legislature,
such payments will not in any immediate or full sense be an instance of perpetrators making reparations, as is the case where an individual criminal offender
offers time or money to the victim or victim's family. Indeed, any collective
forms of reparations dilute the direct connection an individual offender could
make with victims. When Germany made financial contributions to the developing state of Israel after World War II, it provided symbolic expression of national guilt.[32] South Africa's situation makes the process more one of mutual aid
than of making amends, although using the instruments of government to respond to the victimized palpably could demonstrate a dramatic shift in the
meaning and aims of governmental power in that country.

Two other forms of reparations bypass valuation problems. Restitution, the return of the specific, misappropriated object, and apology, the verbal acknowledgment of responsibility for wrongdoing, deserve attention for this reason, and
for their growing use in the contexts of mass atrocities. But restitution and apology raise their own difficulties.

Restitution

In some respects, the demand for returning the actual thing that belonged to the
victim would seem the easiest case for reparations. Valuation problems are absent. Restitution returns the very property, bank account, artifact, or work of art
wrongly taken from the owner. But securing the return especially after many intervening years can be extremely difficult. Restitution can involve harms to and
objections by intervening owners who claim innocence about the underlying
harms. Jeremy Waldron builds a powerful argument against demands for reparation that call for substantial transfers of land, wealth, and resources to rectify
past wrongs. His examples include claims by members of the Taranaki Maori
tribes to the west coast of New Zealand, and similar claims by native peoples to
lands appropriated by colonizing groups.[33] Waldron argues that regardless of
the merits of such claims in terms of historical entitlement, two kinds of intervening events make restitution of the property unwise solutions. The first—
which I find less than compelling—requires an excursion into counterfactual hy-
potheticals. What if tribal owners of land that was wrongly appropriated in 1865
had actually retained the land? Waldron speculates that if those owners had free
choice, they might have sold it, or passed it on to children, or lost it in a poker
game in the intervening years.[34] Although this line of inquiry has a quality of abstract fair-mindedness, it neglects the basic point of wrongdoing: that one group
was unjustly enriched by its injury to the original residents of the land. Waldron
himself acknowledges that if the original owners had not lost their lands, and
subsequently made rational choices about it, then their descendants would have
been better off without the colonization than they actually have been.[35]

Then the second kind of intervening events take center stage. Some innocent
individuals obtain and build their lives around lands that were wrongly stolen

from the original inhabitants. Waldron objects that restoring the actual property after it has passed through a chain of ownership, including whole lines of innocent owners, means committing a current injustice to rectify a past one. Yet I believe this problem is both overstated and amenable to practical remedy. After the expropriation of native peoples, none of the subsequent settlers should be described as wholly innocent. All of them benefited from the expropriation. Yet it would seem unduly burdensome and accidental to mandate the particular dwellers of plots of land in 1998 return them to descendants of original owners while leaving intervening owners and sellers untaxed. Taxing a larger group, even the entire society, to pay monetary compensation to the original owners— or to help buy out the current owners—would spread the burden more fairly.

Perhaps imagining just such a social tax, Waldron suggests that any "[r]eparation of historic injustice really is redistributive: it moves resources from one person to another." He treats this as objectionable because it neglects the innocence of intervening parties.[36] If present-day redistribution is the practical face of restitution for long-ago misappropriations, Waldron argues for a full-blown estimate of all redistributions needed in light of the present-day needs of everyone. The narrower redistributions based solely on claims traced to historic injustice would both neglect some people with pronounced needs and afford new resources to some people who currently do not need them.[37] This argument understates the sheer importance for the victimized and for onlookers of rectifying past wrongs, independent of people's current needs.

Present-day redistributions, even if they work to redress long ago misappropriations, and even if they can be designed to spread the burden among all intervening owners, still carry a dilemma. This is a dilemma seen especially clearly in contemporary South Africa and Eastern Europe, where massive patterns of poverty and inequality present immediate and urgent issues of injustice. In these contexts, historically oriented restitution efforts are both too partial and too inadequate to the survival tasks of rebuilding national economies and civil societies. Yet even this articulation understates the dilemma. These nations have embraced protections for individual liberty and property as well as commitments to address the human rights violations of the past. For them, restitution presents a potentially impossible choice. And newly created private markets in Eastern Europe produce fresh patterns of extreme inequality even before rectifying prior wrongful appropriations of property-lands and goods held by Jews, dissidents, or out-of-favor politicians.

As Joseph Singer explains, "The new South African Constitution protects the property rights of the white minority while allowing for, and in some cases, requiring, restitution or reparations for lost property and past violations of human rights. . . . How can South Africa both move ahead, and at the same time, compensate the victims of *apartheid,* while respecting the property rights of the white minority—a minority whose rights are founded on an almost unbelievable injustice?"[38] Given the history of white appropriation of native African lands, as recently as the 1960s the constitutional project of protecting property rights risks shielding wrongful appropriation of lands in the past.

Once again, it is crucial to return to symbolic dimensions of reparations. Let us bracket the genuinely difficult tensions between compensating past victims without creating new ones and protecting new regimes of private property without simply entrenching the most recently dealt hand in a crooked game. Instead, restitution can be rooted in perceptions of symbolic meaning. As Waldron notes, a different set of concerns accompany claims by dispossessed groups for the return of burial grounds or lands with religious or symbolic significance.[39] When the realm of meaning takes center stage, the economic calculus and confusions fade in importance. This same recognition of the realm of meaning could accompany property that has no asserted religious significance, but instead marks either the identity of the wronged group or the unrepented advantages of the rest of the society. Restoring such property, or making symbolic gestures in this direction, could revive the dignity of the wronged group, and could express the commitment of the others to acknowledge the violations, to make amends, and to break with the atrocity and its legacy. If the disputed property itself is not returned, some material exchange would lend more meaning to acknowledgments of violations.

Social and religious meanings rather than economic values lie at the heart of reparations. Lands that include burial grounds or religious sites especially become worthy candidates for restitution because of their distinctness. They are unique and non-fungible. Similarly, there are no substitutes for plundered artwork, seized artifacts, and the bones of ancestors. Restitution becomes the proper remedy where there is no other remedy for a distinct and worthy claim. Even when contrasted with arguments made by museums about their comparative advantages in preservation and sharing with a broad public, the claim by an original owner for the return of a painting—and the claim by descendants for the remains of their ancestor—call for restitution as a moral, if not legal, matter.[40] If some of these rightful claimants then make arrangements to lend the objects back to museums, the symbolic dimension of the return will become all the more transparent.[41]

Failures to return the symbols of family and community identities and continuity may inspire revenge. In his novel *Talking God,* Tony Hillerman explores a museum's refusal to return human remains to Native American tribes because of the museum's devotion to research and public display.[42] The museum attorney receives a large bulky box, with a letter describing its contents as "a couple of authentic skeletons of ancestors" from the cemetery behind the Episcopal Church of Saint Luke. Enclosed are the disinterred remains of the lawyer's own grandparents. This fictional account captures both the rage and the tit-for-tat exchanges that atrocities can inspire. . . .

Apology

The symbolic dimensions of reparations express implicitly or explicitly an apology for wrongdoing or for failing to do more to resist atrocities. Apologies implicit in acts of reparation acknowledge the fact of harm, accept some degree of responsibility, avow sincere regret, and promise not to repeat the offense. As any parent who has tried to teach a child to apologize knows, however, the problems with apology include insincerity, an absence of clear commitment to change, and incomplete acknowledgment of wrongdoing. A distinct problem in the context of genocide and mass violence arises when an offer of apology comes from persons who have no ability actually to accept or assume responsibility, or who have only remote connections with either the wrongdoers or the victims. Who is in a position to apologize, and apologize to whom? Perhaps most troubling are apologies that are purely symbolic, and carry no concrete shifts in resources or practices to alter the current and future lives of survivors of atrocities.

The U.S. reparations for Japanese-American survivors of the evacuation and internment included a statement of apology. President Ronald Reagan signed into law the bill that expressed the nation's apology as well as authorized financial compensation. Reagan said, "No payment can make up for those lost years. What is most important in this bill has less to do with property than with honor. For here we admit wrong."[43] Two years later President Bush signed letters of apology and checks to individual survivors.[44]

In May 1997, President Clinton offered an apology to survivors of the forty-year study by the U.S. Public Health Service that withheld proven medical treatment from a group of African-American men with syphilis.[45] The study had sought to document the course of the untreated disease. President Clinton acknowledged that the government's behavior was "clearly racist."[46] In that act of public contrition, the president spoke for the government in an effort to restore the faith of the survivors and other witnesses in both government and the medical establishment. Some have called for a similar governmental apology for slavery, while others maintain that an apology for that multicentury, multistate practice would be too trivial or too late.[47] Who is in the proper position to call for, to offer, and to accept such apologies? These questions become especially pronounced in the case of slavery, given its massive evil and the remoteness of current government officials to the events, and the continuing contests over slavery's legacy in America.

Other recent public apologies include Prime Minister Tony Blair's apology for his country's role in the Irish Potato Famine from 1845 to 1851. Although Australian Prime Minister John Howard failed to apologize for his government's long-standing policy of stealing some 100,000 Aboriginal children from their parents to be raised by white families and in orphanages, Australia has now instituted an annual Sorry Day, held on May 26, the anniversary of the release of the best-selling human rights report, *Bring Them Home*.[48] Japanese Prime Minister Tomiichi Murayama apologized for suffering inflicted in World War II; East German lawmakers apologized for the Holocaust after their government had denied responsibility for decades; and Pope John Paul I I apologized for violence during the Counter Reformation[49] and gave a partial apology for the church's role during World War II.[50] The Canadian government apologized to its native Aboriginal population for past governmental actions that suppressed their languages, cultures, and spiritual practice.[51] President Chirac of France apologized to the descendants of Alfred Dreyfus, the Jewish army captain who was falsely arrested, convicted, and degraded for spying in the 1890s.[52] These public acknowledgments of wrongdoing and statements of contrition reflect a growing international interest in restorative steps toward justice, and perhaps the mounting influences of television talk shows on a public culture of private feelings. Apologies are actual actions officials can take to promote reconciliation and healing in the contexts of political and interpersonal violence. They may also be the most inexpensive and least difficult actions available to them.

At heart, the apology depends upon a paradox. No matter how sincere, an apology cannot undo what was done, and yet "in a mysterious way and according to its own logic, this is precisely what it manages to do."[53] An apology is inevitably inadequate.[54] Nevertheless, forgiveness, while not compelled by apology, may depend upon it. The mystery of apology depends upon the social relationships it summons and strengthens; the apology is not merely words.[55]

Crucial here is the communal nature of the process of apologizing. An apology is not a soliloquy.[56] Instead, an apology requires communication between a wrongdoer and a victim; no apology occurs without the involvement of each party. Moreover, the methods for offering and accepting an apology both reflect and help to constitute a moral community. The apology reminds the wrongdoer of community norms because the apology admits to violating them.[57] By retelling the wrong and seeking acceptance, the apologizer assumes a position of vulnerability before not only the victims but also the larger community of literal or figurative witnesses.

Expressions of regret and remorse usually are vital to an apology offered by one individual to another. Distinguishing the superficial from the heartfelt is important to sorting the apology from the dodge. Nicholas Tavuchis, who has developed a sustained sociology of apology, argues that "[t]o apologize is to declare voluntarily that one has no excuse, defense, justification, or explanation for an action (or inaction)."[58] He offers in detail the example of Richard Nixon's resignation speech to illustrate how a statement of regret can fall short of an apology. Nixon never mentioned much less acknowledged specific charges. Instead he tried to explain his decisions in light of lost congressional support for his policies, poor judgment, and errors committed in pursuit of higher national interests.[59] Any diversion from accepting responsibility is not an apology. Because of this stringent requirement, an apology may indeed afford victims and bystanders something that trials, truth-telling, and monetary reparations or property restitutions cannot. Full acceptance of responsibility by the wrongdoer is the hallmark of an apology.

Equally important is the adoption of a stance that grants power to the victims, power to accept, refuse, or ignore the apology. The victims may in addition seek punishment, offer forgiveness, or conclude that the act falls outside domains eligible for forgiveness.[60] In any of these instances, the survivors secure a position of strength, respect, and specialness. Although some current Jewish leaders welcomed the Vatican's recent statement on the Church's responsibilities during

World War II, others used the occasion specifically to reject the statement as insufficient. Survivors and their families do and should occupy a position of personal power and social power to articulate the lived meanings of the values at stake in the acknowledged violation.

All of this renders problematic a statement described as an apology but neither offered by the wrongdoers nor presented directly to victims. Again Tavuchis is eloquent: "[A]n authentic apology cannot be delegated, consigned, exacted, or assumed by the principals, no less outsiders, without totally altering its meaning and vitiating its moral force."[61] No one can apologize or forgive by proxy. This is what makes the representative apology offered by an elected official so tricky. If the official was not in power at the time of the atrocity, the apology is at best offered from the office, not the person. Sorrow is at best offered then in a formal, official sense.[62] The apology similarly operates in an official sphere, fixing the record to include acknowledged transgression. An apology by a government actor to a group within the nation—or by one government to another—necessarily involves different social relationships than an apology offered by one individual to another or even to a group.

Official apologies can correct a public record, afford public acknowledgment of a violation, assign responsibility, and reassert the moral baseline to define violations of basic norms. They are less good at warranting any promise about the future, given the shifts in officeholders. Unless accompanied by direct and immediate actions (such as payments of compensation) that manifest responsibility for the violation, the official apology may seem superficial, insincere, or meaningless. Indeed, in the current moment, "[apologising] is now the rage the world over, especially in the US, where it has long been a standard means of winning favour without paying any real price for one's mistakes."[63] Moreover, individuals who are otherwise insecure may apologize profusely and excessively.[64]

Whether offered by an individual or a public official, an apology does not compel forgiveness. Forgiveness itself is and must remain unpredictable.[65] Survivors acquire and retain the power to grant or withhold forgiveness. They, and others, know that some acts are unforgivable. Albert Speer, the only Nazi leader at the Nuremberg war crime trials who admitted his guilt, also wrote, "No apologies are possible."[66] Usually, though, it is survivors who remind the community about what can, and cannot, be forgiven. The authority to view a violation as beyond forgiveness marks one of the survivors' contributions to the community's moral sense.

Reparations offer money or resources in symbolic redress for violations. Restitution returns wrongly appropriated property, artifacts, and human remains. Restitution may be most warranted when the stolen objects themselves carry unique, significant meanings to the victimized. Apologies explicitly acknowledge wrongdoing and afford victims the chance both to forgive or to refuse to forgive. Official apologies following mass atrocities lack the direct connection between perpetrators and victims that help enact the social dimensions of repair. If unaccompanied by direct and immediate action, such as monetary reparations, official apologies risk seeming meaningless.

Reparations, restitution, and apologies present distinct promises and problems as responses to mass atrocity. Each deserves consideration; each belongs in the lexicon of potential responses to collective violence. Yet nothing in this discussion should imply that money payments, returned property, restored religious sites, or apologies seal the wounds, make victims whole, or clean the slate. The aspiration of repair, in each instance, will be defeated by any hint or hope that then it will be as if the violations never occurred. For that very suggestion defeats the required acknowledgment of the enormity of what was done . . .

Other Possibilities

Where a government countenanced or committed atrocities, one alternative remedy is to remove from government offices and pensions those individuals who were directly involved in the offenses. The continued presence and exercise of power by people who participated in the regime of atrocity ironically provides both constant reminders and routinized forgetting of what happened. Sometimes called a purge, and sometimes "lustration," the removal of categories of people from public office or benefits can have a purification effect, but can also sweep in too many people, unfairly.[67]

The case of Jeffrey Benzien, the security police officer in South Africa who invented a particularly cruel and painful technique of torture, seems especially troubling because he still works as a police officer, and will retain that post if he secures amnesty. Some process of removing from power and privilege the very perpetrators who wielded it to torture others would permit a new beginning for the government and the citizenry.

Eastern European countries that have turned to this kind of response encounter the difficulty of identifying accurately who should be removed or barred from government posts, and what should count as unacceptable levels of commission, omission, or complicity. Tina Rosenberg recounts the painful story of Rudolf Zukal, a noted dissenter under the Czechoslovak Socialist Republic, who was fired from his academic post and forced to work as a bulldozer driver cleaning mud from lakes for twenty years, after he refused to sign a statement endorsing the 1968 Soviet invasion of Prague.[68] One triumph of the "Velvet Revolution" was Zukal's resurrection as a national hero and parliamentary leader—under the application of the resolution to screen out of public office all collaborators with the old regime. Zukal had voted for that resolution. Yet his own name then surfaced on the unacceptable list. His name, and the assertion that he was an informer, appeared in secret police files because of conversations he had had, while on a nine-month fellowship during his academic years, with a Czech undercover security agent who posed as his friend while they both participated in the international community in Vienna.[69] Forced to step down from Parliament, Zukal's case illustrates difficulties with a purge practice in a regime of secret spies and subtle collaborators.

Amnesty across the board for government actors, insurgents, and dissidents is another potential response to mass violence. Sometimes justified in the name of getting on with the future, amnesties can be constructive acknowledgments of the past. Yet amnesty is cowardice if it grows out of fear of the continuing power of the wrongdoers, or even fear of the costs of naming the wrongs. As one observer puts it, "[a]n amnesty is credible only as a humane means to remember, not as legislation of forgetfulness."[70]

For those societies recovering from governmentally sponsored totalitarianism, granting each citizen a right to inspect his or her own state espionage file can restore a sense of control, or at least help the individual understand the scope of invasion under the regime.[71] As painful as it may be to discover that a friend or family member was an informant, such knowledge enables victims to shatter the patterns of power enabled by secrecy. Opening secret internal security records for use in public criminal and civil investigations and the work of private historians affords a more general public exposure to particular hidden information, as well as to the scale and methods of secrecy and threat. The decision to open the Stasi (secret police) files in East Germany is a contribution to victims and to the possibility of reckoning with the past. Yet nothing in this process invites or requires informers to come forward to confess or repent. Initial signs indicate that "[t]he line of demarcation between perpetrators and victims seems to be stronger now than shortly after the fall of the Wall."[72]

A very different sort of response, but one that still looks to the future, is to build new institutions. Domestically, building democratic institutions and a culture of human rights may be the crucial task. The adoption of the Fourteenth and Fifteenth Amendments to the United States Constitution after the Civil War, for example, marked a project of commemoration, "an effort to fix the meaning and purpose of the war in an enduring form. The conquering nation sought through the means of law to construct some tangible proofs that the war had achieved a moral reformation justifying its cataclysmic violence."[73] Beyond individual nations, however, individuals, nongovernmental organizations, and collections of nations try to create international institutions—from the United Nations to the permanent international criminal court—as living memorials to atrocities and vital vows for change.[74]

More literal and concrete forms of commemoration and monuments use sculptures and paintings, museums, plays, and poems. Shared spaces and experiences enabled by public art do not produce singular or coherent memories, but they can enable ways to hold and reveal, in common, competing memories.[75] Memorials can name those who were killed; they can depict those who resisted and those who rescued. They can accord honor and confer heroic status; they can express shame, remorse, warning, shock. Devoting public spaces to memories of atrocities means devoting time and energy to decisions about what kinds of memories, images, and messages to embrace, critique, and resist.

Again, the period after the United States Civil War offers examples. Hundreds of towns and cities in both the North and the South engaged in vigorous debates and then plans for soldier monuments.[76] Some advocates of such public art argued "that people are forgetful and need their social memory bolstered by powerful mnemonic aids," while others instead maintained "that memory is safe in the present but monuments are needed to transmit it across generations," and still others advanced "a startling counterargument—that the memory of heroism is undying and will outlast the monuments, which are therefore built simply as proof of memory's reality and strength."[77] Whether anxious or celebratory, people arguing over those and similar monuments tend to assume that a common memory, secured by tangible presences in public spaces, is vital to people's strength and independence. Indeed, more dangerous than disputes over memory would be complacent divestment of the obligation of memory once memorials are mounted.[78]

Whose story and whose interests are served by the design of particular monuments? Historian Kirk Savage argues that the post–Civil War monuments afforded whites a chance to reconcile after the war while excluding or subordinating the freed slaves. Yet once proposed, and even once constructed, public art permits debates over memory, and potentially conflicting and multiple meanings and perspectives on the underlying events. The memorial erected in Boston to Robert Gould Shaw, for example, depicts the white leader of black soldiers as a hero, although he was one of hundreds of men killed in a hopelessly outmatched battle at Fort Wagner, South Carolina, in 1863. In recent years, African-American activists have protested the lack of individuality in the faces of the black soldiers and the elevation of Gould as hero in the war over slavery without even naming the members of the 54th Regiment, the Union army's first African-American regiment.[79] Yet competing claims about what to memorialize—and what the war meant for race relations—started with the initial discussions concerning the 54th Regiment memorial after the war.

Shaw's own family vetoed the proposal for a sculpture of Shaw alone on a horse set on a pedestal of soldiers.[80] The resulting design places Shaw at the center of a relief but not as a leader of the troops, who themselves can be seen by viewers as either brave or confused, in solidarity or subordinated.[81] Racial power relations persisted; only the words of whites who spoke at the dedication ceremony were carved in the memorial, even though several African-Americans also spoke there.[82] The names of the African-American soldiers killed in the 1863 battle were not added to the memorial until sufficient protests mounted in 1982. Yet, precisely at that time, the monument itself helped to unite members of the Boston community after bitter conflicts over school desegregation.[83] On the hundredth anniversary of the monument, the city held a public symposium and series of events to revisit the history and meanings it commemorates. The entire cover of the current informational brochure about the memorial is a closely cropped photograph of the face of one of the African-American soldiers, inset with a small photo depicting Shaw.

Public disputes over proposed and existing memorials may occasion the productive if painful kind of struggle for memory as do fights over reparations. Again, the U.S. Civil War provides examples. Some 120 years after Southern communities mounted tributes to Confederate leaders, African-Americans and some white critics called for tearing them down, much as French and Russian Revolutionaries dismantled royal monuments—and the post–Soviet Russians toppled massive sculptures of communism's demigods. Vividly capturing and recasting memory, fights over monuments in the streets and in debates usefully disturb congealed memories and mark important junctions between the past and a newly invented present. Historian Eric Foner has urged such struggles to make room for new, or countermemorials, rather than destruction of the old; and the juxtaposition of old and new would itself render new meanings to memories. Thus, he argues, "[r]ather than tear down the statues of Confederate generals or Monument Avenue in Richmond, Va., why not add a marble likeness of Gabriel, who in 1800 plotted to liberate Virginia's slaves" or one of African-Americans who fought in the Union army, or the seventeen African-Americans elected to Congress during Reconstruction?[84]

Maya Lin's Vietnam Memorial also evoked vigorous and even angry debate, while inspiring the addition of more memorials and art responding to the U.S. involvement in Vietnam. Designed initially in response to a class project, Lin's plan called for a simple, polished wall engraved with the names of the 58,196 Americans who died in the Vietnam War. Lin also intended the memorial to work with the land, and to be placed in a space that would draw visitors down a sloping path alongside the wall that itself gradually rises in height. The experience of walking alongside the wall, then, would catch visitors by surprise as they noticed how the gradual descent leads downward to an encounter with mounting lists of names, rising in the air.

The image of a gash in the land offended many who sought a more heroic and conventional tribute to those who served in that socially divisive war. Veterans groups organized to finance a representational sculpture of men in combat. Then a group of women veterans organized to fund a similarly realistic sculpture. Now the three sit in close proximity on the Mall in Washington, D.C., and provide the most frequently visited site in that city of frequently visited sites. The wall has become a familiar image in film, television shows, and popular culture. Perhaps to the surprise of some, the literal and figurative reflections offered by its gleaming wall of names afford a dignified and moving tribute to those who died and to the nation that struggled over its involvement in the war. The competing memorials include not only the additional sculptures but also offerings of distinctive personal objects, at times gathered in their own exhibitions as further art commemorating the war and the war dead.[85] The failure to acknowledge the Vietnamese citizens who died occasions further debates over the memorials, and calls for additions or alternative commemorations.[86]

Pained and extended discussions have transpired in Europe, in Japan, and in the United States over potential and actual memorials and monuments commemorating World War II, the Holocaust, and the atomic bomb.[87] Should such memorials be literal or abstract? Should they honor the dead or disturb the very possibility of honor in atrocity? Should they be monumental, or instead disavow the monumental image, itself so associated with Nazism? Preserve memories or challenge as pretense the notion that memories ever exist outside the process of constructing them? James Young, historian and critic of Holocaust memorials, writes of a large cube of black stones placed "like a black coffin" in Münster,

Germany, and dedicated to "the missing Jews of Münster."[88] Some opposed it on aesthetic grounds, others because it hampered limousine drop-offs. It was demolished in March, 1988. Young comments: "An absent people would not be commemorated by an absent monument." More debate and dissent followed. The artist built a new version of the monument for a new home in another German city.[89]

Although that example did not involve preplanned elimination of the monument, other recent tributes do, as artists and communities struggle for forms of commemoration that in and of themselves shock complacency and settled categories for remembering. Can the art itself express inexpressibility, and disrupt the consignment of memory to a settled physical space, outside the responsibility of those currently alive to struggle for memory? Jochen and Esther Gerz designed what they designated as a countermonument in response to an invitation by the city of Harburg, Germany, to create a "Monument Against Fascism, War, and Violence—and for Peace and Human Rights." A twelve-meter-high pillar positioned in a pedestrian shopping mall, the Harburg Monument Against Fascism, called for citizens and visitors to add their names on the monument and thereby "commit ourselves to remain vigilant.[90] The monument was designed then to descend gradually into the ground, and eventually completely disappear. Its inscription offered this prediction of the monument's future: "One day it will have disappeared completely, and the site of the Harburg monument against fascism will be empty. In the end, it is only we ourselves who can rise up against injustice."[91] Indeed, after a series of lowerings over five years, this never beautiful or restful monument entirely disappeared, returning the burden of memory to tourists. Provocation, not consolation, is the goal of such countermonuments.[92]

In addition to monuments, other artistic responses to mass atrocity explore the possibilities of provocation and disturbance. Historian Lawrence Langer emphasizes that art by survivors themselves can afflict "our desire to redesign hope from the shards of despair with the vision of an anguish that is recordable but not redeemable."[93] Art of the unthinkable should disturb as well as commemorate.[94] Similarly, critic David Roskies explains how art of the Holocaust makes readers "partners in poetic resurrection with specific names"[95] and yet other works recall ancient archetypes, remote from specific events and persons.[96] Holocaust art so often avoids human figures and shocks with disharmony and disorientation. "Though in the past, enormous evil could be dealt with figuratively, these artists seem to be arguing that the new order of atrocity—the transformation of humans into things, the utter anonymity of their death, the total denial of choice—precludes a recognizable human landscape."[97]

Commemoration could work with time rather than space. Thus, some seek to build new rituals, such as days of remembrance. Copying the techniques of established religions, states and private groups create liturgies of remembrance, mourning, and collective reconstruction.[98] Australia created Sorry Day as a national day of apology for the misappropriation of native children.[99] Yom Hashoah has become a day of remembrance for the Holocaust, with public events held globally each year for a day in April.

The production of new historical narratives and accounts that build bridges between past and present and resist the temptations of victors' justice while maintaining a moral stance is one more response to genocide and collective violence. "Catastrophe, in fact, has always been a part of the process of rethinking the past."[100] History is never one story, and the telling of history involves a certain settling of accounts.[101] No telling can fully escape the preoccupations of the moment or the political concerns of the authors. For generations after an atrocity, the historical project poses the difficulty of wresting the past from fictions and legends.[102] Moreover, narratives that imply closure and mastery almost certainly distort genocide and torture.[103] Yet work by journalists and historians, rather than political figures and government officials, can collect and connect seemingly disparate accounts of the violence, its causes, and its consequences. Historians can, and should, combine distance and empathy with all involved, even the perpetrators, in order to pursue the aspiration of truthfulness.[104]

In addition, specific historical work addressing shifting responses to atrocity can help set in relief the choices made in different settings at different times. International law scholar Theodor Meron has worked to recover responses to atrocity long predating the contemporary scene by a fresh consideration of the military law of Europe in the Middle Ages and then in the nineteenth-century law of war.[105] Meron suggests that contemporary international human rights law, such as recognition of the crime against humanity, should be understood as an expansion of the parameters of chivalric rules, to apply not just within but between tribes, religions, and ethnicities.[106] By focusing on the history of responses to atrocity rather than atrocity alone, scholars can underscore the continuing human project of dealing with—and preventing—mass inhumanity.

Deliberate programs of education, teaching materials, books, exhibits, and events, for adults and for children—all of these are vital responses to mass violence. Margot Strom founded the educational group, Facing History and Ourselves, to develop curricular materials and to build teachers' capacities to teach about the conditions that led to the Holocaust and about the human potential for responding to early signs of intergroup violence and abuse. Demonstrating the crucial role of dehumanization of particular groups of people before genocide or mass violence occurs can alert young people to the dangers of group exclusions and degradations in their own worlds.[107] Strom emphasizes that such educational efforts should avoid freezing the events in a museum of the past and also resist preoccupation with perpetrators. Instead, the education efforts should teach "that history is largely the result of human decisions, that prevention is possible, and that education must have a moral component if it is to make a difference."[108] Rather than substituting one propaganda for another, education about genocide and mass violence should help young people think critically and independently, or, as one school administrator puts it, "to know the past as fact and to confront its implications in ways that make us all seek to change the future for better. If there are no simple answers to the hatred and violence from the past or in the present, there are the countering forces of intellectual honesty, integrity, justice, and empathy."[109]

Carol Gilligan, who is herself involved with Facing History and Ourselves, warns that "education is too often teaching, not knowing; teaching cannot be just about facts, but must be about empathy, participation, finding common humanity, asking kids where does the hate come from, relevance."[110] Effective education must connect the histories of mass atrocities with students' own lives and personal experiences. Such education programs are likely to clash at times with other messages the school, parents, and the community give about particular histories, the significance of remembering, and duties to respond to violence. Here Margot Stern Strom responds: "by denying our students access to this history, we fail to honor their potential to confront, to cope, and to make a difference today and in their futures."[111]

One intriguing response to the Holocaust was the Thanks to Scandinavia scholarship fund, founded "in gratitude for the humanity and bravery of people throughout Scandinavia who protected persons of the Jewish faith during and after the Second World War."[112] The fund combines this tribute to rescuers with education by financing fellowships for American and Scandinavian students to join together to explore Scandinavian democracy, culture, resistance to Nazism, and contemporary human rights issues.

NOTES

1. Martha Minow, *Between Vengeance and Forgiveness* (East Sussex: Beacon Press, 1999).

2. Howard Zehr, *Changing Lenses: A New Focus for Crime and Justice* (Scottsdale, Pa.: Herald Press, 1990), 211–14.

3. Many advocates of mediation emphasize dimensions of restorative justice; critics suggest that mediation assumes the presence of a community of interest that may not exist. See, for example, John Paul Lederach and Ron Kraybill, "The Paradox of Popular Justice: A Practitioner's View," in *The Possibilities of Popular Justice: A Case Study of Community Mediation in the United States*, eds. Sally Engle Merry and Neal Milner (Ann Arbor: University of Michigan, 1993), 357, 376.

4. See, for example, Baba Kamma 94b. For an English translation, see E. W. Kirzner, trans., Baba Kamma 94b, 547–50, in the series *The Babylonian Talmud: Seder Nezikin*, trans. Rabbi Dr. I. Epstein (London: Soncino Press, 1935).

5. See Jim Consedine, *Restorative Justice: Healing the Effects of Crime* (Lyttelton, New Zealand: Ploughshares Publications, 1993).

6. John O. Haley, "Confession, Repentance and Absolution," in *Mediation and Criminal Justice*, eds. Martin Wright and Burt Galaway (London: Sage Publications, 1989).

7. See [Minow's] chapter 4, n. 136, for a discussion of *ubuntu*.

8. See generally David B. Wexler and Bruce J. Winick, *Law in a Therapeutic Key: Developments in TherapeuticJurisprudence* (Durham, N.C.: Carolina Academic Press, 1996).

Vengeance and Forgiveness

9. See, for example, Consedine, *Restorative Justice;* Burt Galaway and Joe Hudson, eds., *Criminal Justice, Restitution, and Reconciliation* (Monsey, N.Y.: Criminal Justice Press, 1990); Zehr, *Changing Lenses.*

10. See Consedine, *Restorative Justice,* 157–58. See also Albert English, "Beyond Restitution," in *Restitution in Criminal Justice,* eds. Joe Hudson and Burt Galaway (Lexington, Mass.: Lexington Books, 1977), 91; Daniel W. Van Ness, "New Wine in Old Wineskins: Four Challenges to Restorative Justice," *Criminal Law Forum* 4 (1993): 151.

11. See Mark S. Umbreit, "Holding Juvenile Offenders Accountable: A Restorative Justice Perspective," *Family Court Journal* 46 (1995): 331.

12. Archbishop Desmond Mpilo Tutu, Foreword in *To Remember and To Heal: Theological and Psychological Reflections on Truth and Reconciliation,* eds. H. Russell Borman and Robin M. Petersen (Cape Town: Human & Rousseau, 1996).

13. "Truth Commission Announces Reparation Plan," *African News,* 24 October 1997.

14. Zehr, *Changing Lenses,* 26.

15. Zehr, *Changing Lenses,* 26.

16. Zehr, *Changing Lenses,* 26.

17. Helena Silverstein, e-mail to author, 6 June 1997.

18. See, for example, Richard F. America, ed. *African Development and Reparations: Redistributive Justice and the Restitution Principle* (forthcoming).

19. West Germany's initial offer of reparations to Israel triggered domestic opposition, but did establish a framework for acknowledging crimes of racial, religious, and political persecution committed in the name of the German people. See Robert G. Moeller, "War Stories: The Search for a Usable Past in the Federal Republic of Germany," *American Historical Review* (October 1996): 1009, 1016–18.

20. An important and difficult legal and moral issue arises when a government claims that individual claims for reparation can be disposed by treaties or accords between nations. Japan so claimed, pointing to its postwar accords with the home countries of "comfort women." In the absence of a fair process representing such claimants, this kind of nation-to-nation resolution seems painfully inadequate.

21. Seth Mydans, "WWII Victim Accepts Japanese Reparation," *Dallas Morning News,* 13 December 1996, A 61.

22. Mydans, "WWII Victim Accepts Japanese Reparation," A61.

23. Mydans, "WWII Victim Accepts Japanese Reparation," A61.

24. Mydans, "WWII Victim Accepts Japanese Reparation," A61. In contrast, one letter writer argued that reparations would be more important than apologies. C. Suzkuki, "Concentrate on Reparations," *South Morning Post,* 13 September 1995.

25. Sonni Efron, "Justice Delayed 50 Years," *Los Angeles Times,* 13 December 1996, A1.

26. Sonni Efron, "Justice Delayed 50 Years" (quoting Kim Yoon Sim).

27. Sonni Efron, "Justice Delayed 50 Years."

28. Remarks of Dr. Pumla Gobodo-Madikizela, Human Rights Violation Committee member, at the 112th Annual Human Rights and Justice Conference, sponsored by Facing History and Ourselves and the Harvard Law School Graduate Program, 10 April 1997.

29. See text at note 13 (noting the TRC chief reparations principle to promote the abilities of individuals and communities to take control of their own lives). Finding a way to rebuild a society deformed by apartheid seems to defy simple notions of compensation. A lawyer for the Mfengu clan, who were forcibly removed by the regime from their land in 1977 and sent to untillable homelands, recently asked: "How do you compensate for some 18 million honest people who went to town to search for work in attempts to escape poverty and destitution in the homelands, and were imprisoned because of pass law offenses . . . How do you compensate for the results of Bantu education, a system designed to make African children inferior so that they are only trained to minister to the needs of the white man? How do you compensate for the regional destabilization war, the land mines? How do you compensate for 3.5 million people who were forcibly removed and had their lives destroyed?" Quoted in Dele Olojede, "Building a Better South Africa: Far to Go on Its Long Road," *Newsday*, 1 June 1997, A4.

30. See, for example, Ellen C. Dubois, Mary C. Dunlap, Carol J. Gilligan, Catharine A. MacKinnon, and Carrie J. Menkel-Meadow, "Feminist Discourse, Moral Values, and Law—A Conversation," *Buffalo Law Review* 34 (1985): 11, 74–75. Catharine MacKinnon called for a change in the power structure that would allow a woman to define power in ways that she cannot currently articulate, "because his foot is on her throat." Carol Gilligan argued that women articulate values of care and connection that have value independent of women's social and political status. MacKinnon responded that it is "infuriating" to call those values women's "because we have never had the power to develop what ours really would be."

31. Message from Archbishop Desmond Tutu, 31 March 1998, TRC Web site, www.truth.org.za.

32. See Nicholas Balabkins, *West German Reparations to Israel* (New Brunswick, N.J.: Rutgers University Press, 1971).

33. See also Paul Brodeur, *Restitution: The Land Claims of the Mashpee, Passamaquoddy, and Penobscot Indians of New England* (Boston: Northeastern University Press, 1985); Anthony DePalma, "Canadian Court Ruling Broadens Indian Land Claims," *New York Times*, 12 December 1997, A3 (based on oral evidence of traditional ceremonies and oral histories, Canadian Supreme Court rules that native peoples have broad claims to land they once occupied and natural resources and therefore deserve compensation or rights to resources).

34. Waldron, "Superseding Historic Injustice," 9.
35. Waldron, "Superseding Historic Injustice," 11.
36. Waldron, "Superseding Historic Injustice," 13.
37. Ironically, some of the very claimants for restitution have thrived and no longer place the use of the lost property at the center of their lives. Waldron, "Superseding Historic Injustice," 18–19. "I may of course yearn for the lost resource and spend a lot of time wishing that I had it back. I may even organize my life around the campaign for its restoration. But that is not the same thing as the basis for the original claim. The original entitlement is based on the idea that I have organized my life around the use of this object" (p. 19). Here Waldron is directly addressing theories of property entitlement based on autonomy and showing their insufficiency in establish-

ing violable rights. A separate line of critique of Waldron's own approach would question any link between entitlement claims and failures of resilience. In his analysis, those who had failed to move onto new ways of life arguably would have more viable claims to the misappropriated resource. Those who are more adaptable would have lesser claims. This seems to create perverse incentives as well as relying on a needs-based rather than a fairness-based view of Justice, contrary to Waldron's general approach.

38. Singer, "Reparations," 248.

39. Waldron, "Superseding Historic Injustice," 19.

40. See The Native American Graves Protection and Repatriation Act, 25 U.S.C.A. sections 3001–3013, 18 U.S.C.A. section 1170 (1990) (American Indian and Native Hawaiian human remains and burial objects found on tribal or federal lands belong to the legal descendants or else to the relevant tribe); and Jane Perlez, "Austria Is Set to Return Artworks That Nazis Plundered from Jews," *New York Times,* 7 March 1998, A1. Perlez quotes the director of an Austrian museum on the promised return of artworks to the Rothschild family: "We are open to the restitution of everything given to the museum in an immoral trade. This should have been done 30 or 40 years ago. We have to fulfill a specific moral debt" (A27).

41. See Perlez, "Austria Is Set to Return Artworks," A27 (reporting that Baroness Bettina der Rothschild reports bitter feelings but also a sense of noblesse oblige that may prompt the family to agree to some loans).

42. Tony Hillerman, *Talking God* (New York: Harper & Row, 1989), 1–6.

43. Nicholas Tavuchis, *Mea Culpa: A Sociology of Apology and Reconciliation* (Stanford, Calif.: Stanford University Press, 1991 [citing Reagan]).

44. Tavuchis, *Mea Culpa,* 108.

45. See Editorial, "Apology Now; Vigilance, Too," *Cleveland Plain Dealer,* 26 May 1997, B8.

46. Editorial, "The Tuskegee Apology," *St. Louis Post-Dispatch,* 21 May 1997, C6; Joan Beck, "Apology Can't Erase Tuskegee Horror," *St. Louis Post-Dispatch,* 30 May 1997, B7. The president's apology occurred after a widely acclaimed television documentary on the subject entitled *Miss Evers' Boys.* See John Carman, "The Emmy Nominees Are—What, You Again?" *San Francisco Chronicle,* 12 September 1997, C1.

47. Compare DeWayne Wickham, "Why Clinton Must Stop Dodging Slavery Apology," *USA Today,* 16 December 1997, A15, with Bill Nichols, "Should the Nation Apologize? Critics Argue Substance Is Need, Not Symbolism," *USA Today,* 18 June 1997, A1.

48. "A World Apart," *Sydney Morning Herald,* 10 March 1998, p. 13.

49. See Nichols, "Should the Nation Apologize?" A1.

50. Vatican's Statement on Holocaust 1998, reported in "New Catholic Line on the Holocaust," *Jerusalem Post,* 17 March 1998, 3; "The Vatican and the Holocaust: The Overview; Vatican Repents Failure to Save Jews from Nazis," *New York Times,* 17 March 1998, A1; "Act of Repentance: Vatican Issues Statement on the Holocaust," *Newsday,* 17 March 1998, A7.

51. Alexander Chancellor, Foreword to "Pride and Prejudice: Easier Said Than Done," *The Guardian,* London, 17 January 1998, 8.

52. Chancellor, Foreword to "Pride and Prejudice."

53. Tavuchis, *Mea Culpa,* 5.

54. Some harms, though, can only be repaired by an apology, such as "defamation, insult, degradation, loss of status, and the emotional distress and dislocation that accompany conflict." Hiroshi Wagatsuma and Arthur Rosett, "The Implication of Apology: Law and Culture in Japan and the United States," *Law and Society Review* 20 (1986): 461, 487–88.

55. Tavuchis, *Mea Culpa,* 115.

56. Tavuchis, *Mea Culpa,* 121.

57. Tavuchis, *Mea Culpa,* 8.

58. Tavuchis, *Mea Culpa,* 17.

59. Tavuchis, *Mea Culpa,* 55

60. Tavuchis, *Mea Culpa,* 20.

61. Tavuchis, *Mea Culpa,* 49.

62. Tavuchis, *Mea Culpa,* 104.

63. Chancellor, Foreword, "Pride and Prejudice," 8.

64. Tavuchis, *Mea Culpa,* 40.

65. See Hannah Arendt, *The Human Condition* (Chicago: University of Chicago Press, 1958), 241: "In contrast to revenge, which is the natural, automatic reaction to transgression and which because of the irreversibility of the action process can be expected and even calculated, the act of forgiving can never be predicted; it is the only reaction that acts in an unexpected way and thus retains, though being a reaction, something of the original character of action. Forgiving, in other words, is the only reaction which does not merely re-act but acts anew and unexpectedly, unconditioned by the act which provoked it and therefore freeing from its consequences both the one who forgives and the one who is forgiven."

66. Paul L. Montgomery, "Albert Speer, 76, Architect of Hitler's Nazism Is Dead," *International Herald Tribune,* 13 September 1981, 13.

67. See Rosenberg, *Haunted Land,* 67–111.

68. Rosenberg, *Haunted Land,* 3.

69. Rosenberg, *Haunted Land,* 35–39.

70. Smith, "Work on Forgetting," 10.

71. See Geiger, "Consequences of Past Human Rights Violations," 46 (describing The Stasi Record Act and its purposes).

72. Geiger, "Consequences of Past Human Rights Violations," 51.

73. Kirk Savage, "The Politics of Memory: Black Emancipation and the Civil War Monument," in *Commemorations: The Politics of National Identity,* ed. John R. Gillis (Princeton, N.J.: Princeton University Press, 1994), 127.

74. The complex positioning of domestic politicians and global leaders in the international arena is well illustrated in the debate over the international criminal court. See John R. Bolton, "Why an International Criminal Court Won't Work," *Wall Street Journal,* 30 March 1998, A19 (describing support from Clinton administration and objections raised by others within and beyond the United States); Barbara Crossette, "Helms Vows to Make War on U.N. Court," *New York Times,* 27 March 1998, A9; Farhan Haq, "Rights: Progress Slow on Formation of Intl. Criminal Court," *Inter-*

Press Service, 2 April 1998 (some in United States will resist international criminal court on grounds it would erode U.S. sovereignty).

75. See James E. Young, *Texture of Memory,* 6. Public art can "create shared spaces that lend a common spatial frame to otherwise disparate experiences and understanding . . . the public monument attempts to create an architectonic ideal by which even competing memories may be figured." For a thoughtful inquiry into the nature of public monuments and the political debates they can trigger, see Sanford Levinson, *Written in Stone: Public Monuments in Changing Societies* (Durham, N.C.: Duke University Press, 1998).

76. Savage, "Politics of Memory," 129.

77. Savage, "Politics of Memory," 130.

78. "Once we assign monumental form to memory, we have to some degree divested ourselves of the obligation to remember." Introduction, "Darkness Visible," in *Holocaust Remembrance: The Shapes of Memory*, ed. Geoffrey H. Hartman (Oxford: Blackwell, 1994), quoting James Young.

79. Michael Kenney, "Historic Mistakes Carved in Stone," review of *Standing Soldiers, Kneeling Slaves: Race, War, and Monument in Nineteenth-Century America,* by Kirk Savage, *Boston Globe,* 5 December 1997, E12; Christine Temin, "Boston's Conscience Turns 100," *Boston Globe,* 25 May 1997, N1.

80. Savage, "Politics of Memory," 136; "Facing History and Ourselves, "*The New England Holocaust Memorial Study Guide* (Brookline, Mass.: Facing History and Ourselves, 1996), 10–13.

81. Savage, "Politics of Memory," 136–39.

82. "New England Holocaust Memorial Study Guide," 11. Booker T. Washington was among the speakers at the dedication ceremony.

83. "New England Holocaust Memorial Study Guide," 112.

84. Eric Foner, "The South's Hidden Heritage," *New York Times,* 22 February 1997, I21.

85. See Freida Lee Mock, *Maya Lin: Strong Clear Vision* (1995 Oscar-winning documentary film about Maya Lin); Robert Atkins, "When the Art Is Public, the Making Is, Too," *New York Times,* 23 July 1995, p. I; Edward Guthman, "Freida Lee Mock's *Strong Clear Vision* Director Says Lin Stands on Its Own," *San Francisco Chronicle,* 8 November 1995, D1; Jay Pridmore, "Revealing Displays Make Vietnam Museum Noteworthy," *Chicago Tribune,* 9 September 1994, p. 14.

86. See Todd Gitlin, "The Fabric of Memory," review of *Tangled Memories: The Vietnam War, the AIDS Epidemic, and the Politics of Remembering,* by Marita Sturken, *New York Times,* 1 March 1997, sec. 7, p. 16. "National myth-making is full of selective memory, and memory can be a way of forgetting. Thus, as Ms. Sturken points out, Maya Lin's brilliant Vietnam Memorial in Washington, recording the names of 58,196 dead Americans, writes off at least two million Vietnamese dead and converts the war into solely an American tragedy."

87. See Young, *Texture of Memory,* 8–15, 17–25 (documenting disputes over Holocaust memorials); Alan Cowell, "A Memorial to Gay Pain of Nazi Era Stirs Debate," *New York Times,* 29 December 1996, p. 11; Alan Cowell, "In Berlin, Wartime Ghosts Hinder Projects Memorializing Past," *New York Times,* 15 January 1997, p.11.

88. Young, *Texture of Memory*, 17.

89. Young, *Texture of Memory*, 18–19.

90. Young, *Texture of Memory*, 30 (quoting Harburg monument).

91. Young, *Texture of Memory*.

92. Young, *Texture of Memory*, 30–31. See also Sara R. Horowitz, *Voicing the Void: Muteness and Memory in Holocaust Fiction* (Albany, N.Y.: SUNY Press, 1997). She explores narratives and fictions that depict or express "enforced muteness" as both the source of atrocity and its effects.

93. Lawrence L. Langer, *Admitting the Holocaust* (New York: Oxford University Press, 1995), 52.

94. Langer, *Admitting the Holocaust*, 107. See also Hartman, *Holocaust Remembrance*, 17–19.

95. David Roskies, *Against the Apocalypse* (Syracuse, N.Y.: Syracuse University Press, 1999), 257.

96. Roskies, *Against the Apocalypse,* 289.

97. Roskies, *Against the Apocalypse*, 303.

98. Rabbi J. B. Soloveichich argued that the traditional mourning period in Judaism, between the seventeenth day of the Hebrew month of Tammuz to the ninth of Av, include the chanting of Lamentations, an extremely bleak text. The process of mourning was designed to bring individuals into the collective memory of historical destructions of the two sacred temples and to ease people back into everyday routine. Roskies, *Against the Apocalypse,* 36–39.

99. "A Day to Honour the Stolen Generations," *Canberra Times,* 7 April 1998, A12.

100. Roskies, *Against the Apocalypse*, 310.

101. Alex Boraine, Janet Levy, and Ronel Scheffer, *Dealing with the Past* (Capetown: Institute for Democracy in South Africa, 1994).

102. Hartman, *Holocaust Remembrance*, 10.

103. Hartman, *Holocaust Remembrance*, 5.

104. Ash, "Truth about Dictatorship," 40. See also Hannah Arendt, *The Human Condition* (Chicago: University of Chicago Press, 1958), 279: "[E]ven if there is no truth, man can be truthful, and even if there is no reliable certainty, man can be reliable."

105. See Theodor Meron, *Henry's Wars and Shakespeare's Laws: Perspectives on the Law of War in the Later Middle Ages* (Oxford: Clarendon Press, 1993). Meron turns to Shakespeare's histories, notably *Henry V,* to illustrate the chivalric rules governing medieval armed conflicts. See also Lawrence Weschler, "Take No Prisoners," *New Yorker,* 17 June 1996, 50, 55 (reporting Meron's work).

106. Meron, *Henry's Wars and Shakespeare's Laws.* See also Allan A. Ryan Jr., "Battle Cries: Why War Trials Matter," *Boston College Magazine,* summer 1996, 46, 47, for a discussion of medieval chivalry in contrast with contemporary human rights law that gives greater emphasis to the protection of noncombatants and civilians.

107. African scholar Ali A. Mazrui argues that "violations of human rights are preceded by the process of psychic subhumanization." Ali A. Mazrui, "Human Rights and the Moving Frontier of World Culture," in Alwin Diemer et al., *Philosophical*

Foundations of Human Rights (Paris: UNESCO, 1986), 243 . *See* also chapter 2, "Holocaust and Human Behavior (We and They)," in *Facing History and Ourselves Resource Book* (Brookline, Mass.: Facing History and Ourselves National Foundation, Inc., 1994), 58–109, hereinafter cited as *Facing History and Ourselves*.

108. Margot Stern Strom, preface to *Facing History and Ourselves*, xvi.

109. Ron Gwiazda, assistant to the headmaster of the Boston Latin School, quoted in *Facing History and Ourselves*, xxv.

110. Planning meeting, Harvard Facing History Conference, January 1997.

111. Strom in *Facing History and Ourselves*, xix.

112. See Thanks to Scandinavia, Inc., "Human Rights Study in Denmark," June 1997.

Bibliography

Aaron, Henry J. "Symposium on the Economic Status of African-Americans." *The Journal of Economic Perspectives* 4, no. 4 (1990): 3–7.

Allen, Ernest, Jr., and Robert Chrisman. "Ten Reasons: A Response to David Horowitz." *The Black Scholar* 31, no. 2 (2001).

Allen, Robert L. "Past Due: The African American Quest for Reparations." *The Black Scholar* 28, no. 2 (1998): 2–17.

Alter, Torin. "Review of George Schedler's *Racist Symbols and Reparations: Philosophical Reflections on Vestiges of the American Civil War.*" *Social Theory and Practice* 26, no. 1 (2000): 153–71.

America, Richard F., ed. *The Wealth of Races: The Present Value of Benefits from Past Injustices.* Vol. 132, *Contributions in Afro-American and African Studies.* Westport, Conn.: Greenwood Press, 1990.

Andelson, Robert. "Black Reparations: A Study in Gray." *Personalist* 59 (April 1978): 173–83.

Askelan, Andrew. "A Justification of Compensation to the Descendants of Wronged Parties; an Intended Analogy." *Public Affairs Quarterly* 12 (1998): 363–68.

Atfield, Robin. "Unto the Third and Fourth Generation." *Second Order: An African Journal of Philosophy* 8 (January–July 1979): 55–70.

Baier, Annette. "The Rights of Past and Future Generations." In *Responsibilities to Future Generations,* ed. Ernest Partridge, 171–86. Buffalo: Prometheus Books, 1980.

Baraka, Amiri. "The Case for Reparations." *Black Collegian* 29, no. 1 (1998): 26–27.

Barkan, Elazar. *The Guilt of Nations: Restitution and Negotiating Historical Injustices.* New York: W.W. Norton & Company, 2000.

Bayles, Michael D. "Reparations to Wronged Groups." *Analysis* 33 (June 1973): 182–84.

Becker, Lawrence C. "Future Generations." In *Reciprocity.* London: Routledge, 1986.

Bedau, Hugo. "Compensatory Justice and the Black Manifesto." *Monist* 56 (1972): 20–42.

Berlin, Ira. *Many Thousands Gone: The First Two Centuries of Slavery in North America.* Cambridge, Mass.: Harvard University Press, 1998.

Berry, Mary F. "Reparations for Freedmen:, 1890–1016: Fraudulent Practices or Justice Deferred?" *The Journal of Negro History* 57, no. 3 (1972): 219–30.

Bigelow, John, Robert Pargetter, and Robert Young. "Land, Well-being and Compensation." *Australasian Journal of Philosophy* 88 (1990): 330–46.

Bittker, Boris. *The Case for Black Reparations.* New York: Random House, 1972.

Bolner, James. "Toward a Theory of Racial Reparation." *Phylon* 29, no. 1 (1968): 41–47.

Boxill, Bernard. "The Morality of Reparation." *Social Theory and Practice* 2 (Spring 1972): 113–23.

Boxill, Bernard R. *Blacks and Social Justice.* Lanham, Md.: Rowman & Littlefield, 1992.

———. "The Morality of Reparations II." In *A Companion to African American Philosophy,* ed. Tommy Lott, 134–47. Malden, Mass.: Blackwell Publishing, 2003.

Branch, Watson. "Reparations for Slavery: A Dream Deferred." *San Diego International Law Journal* 3 (2002): 177–206.

"Bridging the Color Line: The Power of African-American Reparations to Redirect America's Future." *Harvard Law Review* 115, no. 6 (2002): 1689–712.

Brooks, Roy L., ed. *When Sorry Isn't Enough: The Controversy over Apologies and Reparations for Human Injustice.* New York: New York University Press, 1999.

Brophy, Alfred L. "Comment: The World of Reparations." *Journal of Law in Society* 3, no. 3 (2002): 105–15.

Browne, Robert S. "The Economic Basis for Reparations to Black America." *Review of Black Political Economy* 21 (1993): 99–110.

Bull, Malcolm. "Slavery and the Multiple Self." *New Left Review*, no. 231 (September 1998): 94–138.

Chafve, William H., Raymond Gavins, and Robert Korsad, eds. *Remembering Jim Crow: African Americans Tell About Life in the Segregated South.* New York: The New Press, 2001.

Chicago, City Council of. "Chicago City Council Reparations Resolution 2000" [cited 9/9 2003]. Online at http://h-net.msu.edu/cgi-bin/logbrowse.pl?trx=vx&list=h-afro-am&month=0005&week=c&msg=p704BA6SN4WbmamD3I/HSQ&user=&pw= (accessed September 9, 2003).

Chisholm, Tuneen E. "Sweep around Your Own Front Door: Examining the Argument for Legislative African-American Reparations." *University of Pennsylvania Law Review* 147, no. 3 (1999): 677–727.

Clarke, Stephen R. L. "Slaves and Citizens." *Philosophy* 60 (January 1985): 27–46.

Cohen, Joshua. "The Arc of the Moral Universe." *Philosophy and Public Affairs* 26, no. 2 (1997): 91–134.

Cole, Eve Browning. "'Women, Slaves, and Love of Toil' in Aristotle's Moral Philosophy." In *Engendering Origins*, ed. Bat-Ami Bar On. Albany, N.Y.: SUNY Press, 1994.

Conley, Dalton. *Being Black, Living in the Red: Race, Wealth, and Social Policy in America.* Berkeley: University of California Press, 1999.

———. "The Cost of Slavery." *New York Times*, February 15, 2003, 25.

Cooper, D. E. "Collective Responsibility—Reply to Downie." *Philosophy* 43 (1968): 258–68.

Corlett, J. Angela. "Reparations to Native Americans?" In *War Crimes and Collective Wrongdoing,* ed. Aleksandar Jokic. Madden, Mass.: Blackwell, 2001.

Cose, Ellis. *The Rage of a Privileged Class: Why Are Middle-Class Blacks Angry?* New York: HarperCollins Publishers, 1993.

Crocker, David. "Retribution and Reconciliation." Institute for Philosophy & Public Policy, 2003. Online at www.puaf.umd.edu/IPPP/Winter-Spring00/retribution_and_reconciliation.htm (accessed September 9, 2003).

Cuffel, Victoria. "The Classical Greek Concept of Slavery." *Journal of the History of Ideas* 27 (1966): 323–42.

Davis, Adrienne. "The Case for United States Reparationss to African Americans." *Transforming Anthropology* 10, no. 1 (2001): 39–43.

Davis, David Brion. *In the Image of God: Religion, Moral Values, and Our Heritage of Slavery.* New Haven, Conn.: Yale University Press, 2001.

Dershowitz, Alan M. "Review of David Horowitz: Uncivil Wars: The Controversy over Reparations for Slavery." *Los Angeles Times* 2002, 13.

Downie, R. S. "Collective Responsibility." *Philosophy* 44 (1969): 44–50.

Dray, Philip. *At the Hands of Persons Unknown: The Lynching of Black America.* New York: Random House, 2002.

Dwyer, Susan. "Reconciliation for Realists." *Ethics and International Affairs*, vol. 13 (1999).

Ellinikos, Maria. "American MNCs Continue to Profit from the Use of Forced and Slave Labor—Begging the Question: Should America Take a Cue from Germany?" *Columbia Journal of Law and Social Problems* 35, no. 1 (2001).

Epstein, Richard A. "Against Redress." *Daedalus* (2002): 39–48.

Etzioni, Amatai, ed. *Civic Repentance.* Lanham, Md.: Rowman & Littlefield, 1999.

Farr, James. "'So Vile and Miserable an Estate': The Problem of Slavery in Locke's Political Thought." *Political Theory* 14 (May 1986): 263–89.

Feinberg, Joel. "Collective Responsibility." *Journal of Philosophy* 65 (1968): 674–88.

Fletcher, George P. "The Storrs Lectures: Liberals and Romantics at War: The Problem of Collective Guilt." *Yale Law Journal* 111 (2002): 1499.

Forman, James. "Black Manifesto: To the White Christian Churches and the Jewish Synagogues in the United States of America and All Other Racist Institutions." In *The Black Manifesto and the Challenge To White America,* ed. Arnold Schuchter. Philadelphia: J. B. Lippincott Co., 1970.

Forrest, Peter. "Collective Responsibility and Restitution." *Philosophical Papers* 27, no. 2 (1998): 79–91.

Freeman, Gerene L. "What About My 40 Acres & a Mule?" Online at www.yale.edu/ynhti/curriculum (accessed September 9, 2003).

Frye, Jerry K. "The 'Black Manifesto' and the Tactic of Objectification." *Journal of Black Studies* 5, no. 1 (1974): 65–76.

Fullinwider, Robert. "The Case for Reparations." Report of the Institute for Philosophy and Public Policy (2000). Online at www.puaf.umd.edu/IPPP/Summer00/case_for_reparations.htm (accessed September 9 2003).

———. "Slavery, Reparations and Moral Clarity." Paper presented at the conference, The Moral Legacy of Slavery, at Bowling Green State University, Bowling Green, Ohio, October 18 and 19, 2002.

Garver, Newton. "Aristotle's Natural Slaves: Incomplete 'Praxis' and Incomplete Human Beings." *Journal of the History of Philosophy* 32, no. 2 (1994): 173–95.

Gilbert, Margaret. "On Feeling Guilty for What One's Group Has Done." In *Living Together: Rationality, Sociality, and Obligation.* Lanham, Md.: Rowman & Littlefield, 1996.

Glausser, Wayne. "Three Approaches to Locke and the Slave Trade." *Journal of the History of Ideas* 51, no. 2 (1990): 199–216.

Glover, Trudy. *Forgiveness and Revenge.* New York: Routledge, 2003.

Goldman, Alan H. "Reparations to Individuals or Groups?" *Analysis* 35 (April 1975): 168–79.

Goodey, C-F. "Politics, Nature, and Necessity: Were Aristotle's Slaves Feeble Minded?" *Political Theory* 27, no. 2 (April 1999): 203–24.

Gross, Barry R. "Is Turn About Fair Play?" *Journal of Critical Analysis* 5 (January–April 1975): 126–35.

Hall, Art Alcausin. "There Is a Lot to Be Repaired before We Get to Reparations: A Critique of the Underlying Issues of Race That Impact the Fate of African-American Reparations." *St. Mary's Law Review on Minority Issues* 1 (1999): 1–47.

Hanke, Lewis. *Aristotle and the American Indians: A Study in Race Prejudice in the Modern World.* Chicago: Regnery, 1959.

Hansard. Slavery: Legacy the Official Record from Hansard of the Debate Initiated by Lord Gifford QC in the House of Lords of the British Parliament on 14th March 1996 Concerning the African Reparations. *Official Hansard,* Africa Reparations Movement, 1996. Online at www.arm.arc.co.uk/LordsHansard.html (accessed 9 September 2003).

Hare, R. M. "What's Wrong with Slavery?" *Philosophy and Public Affairs* 8 (Winter 1979): 103–21.

Harriott, Howard H. "The Evils of Chattel Slavery and the Holocaust: An Examination of Laurence Thomas's 'Vessels of Evil.'" *International Philosophical Quarterly* 37, no. 3 (1997): 329–47.

Harris, Lee A. "Political Autonomy as a Form of Reparations to African-Americans." *Southern University Law Review* 29 (2001): 25.

Hayner, Patricia. *Unspeakable Truths: Confronting State Terror and Atrocity.* New York: Routledge, 2001.

Hill, Walter B., Jr. "The Ex-Slave Pension Movement:: Some Historical and Genealogical Notes." *Negro History Bulletin* 59, no. 4 (1996): 7–11.

Hirsch, James S. *Riot and Remembrance: The Tulsa Race War and Its Legacy.* Boston: Houghton Mifflin, 2002.

Hopkins, Kevin. "Forgive U.S. Our Debts? Righting the Wrongs of Slavery." *The Georgetown Law Review* 89 (2001): 2531–56.

Horowitz, David. "Ten Reasons Why Reparations for Blacks Is a Bad Idea for Blacks—and Racist Too" (2001). Online at www.frontpagemag.com (accessed January 6, 2003. [Use "search."—eds.]

Hunting, Claudine. "The Philosophes and the Question of Black Slavery: 1748–1765." *Journal of the History of Ideas* 39 (July 1978): 405–18.

Hutchinson, Earl Ofari. "Debt Wrong: David Horowitz Is Incorrect. It's Time for the U.S. To Pay Up for Slavery." *FrontPageMagazine*, June 5, 2000. Online at www.frontpagemag.com/Articles/ReadArticle.asp?ID=3108 (accessed September 10, 2003).

Islam, Lost Found Nation of. *Reparations Petition for United Nations Assistance under Resolution 1503 (XLVIII) on Behalf of African Americans of the United States of America.* Hampton, Va.: United Brothers and Sisters Communications System, 1994.

Kershnar, Stephen. "The Case against Reparations." *Philosophy in the Contemporary World* 8, no. 1 (2001): 41–46.

———. "Are the Descendants of Slaves Owed Compensation for Slavery?" *Journal of Applied Philosophy* 16, no. 1 (1999): 95–101.

———."The Inheritance Based Claim to Reparations." *Legal Theory* 8 (2002): 243–67.

Lawson, Bill. "Nobody Knows Our Plight: Moral Discourse, Slavery, and Social Progress." *Social Theory and Practice* 18, no. 1 (1992): 1–20.

Levin, Michael. "Aristotle on Natural Subordination." *Philosophy* 72, no. 280 (1997): 241–56.

Lewan, Todd, and Dolores Barclay. "'When They Steal Your Land, They Steal Your Future'; History: Study Details Black Landowners' Losses, Now Worth Millions." *Los Angeles Times,* December 2, 2001, 1.

Lewis, David Levering. "An American Pastime." Review of Philip Dray, *At the Hands of Persons Unknown: The Lynching of Black America*, and James H. Madison, *A Lynching in the Heartland: Race and Memory in America. New York Review of Books*, November 21, 2002.

Lloyd, Genevieve. "Individuals, Responsibility, and the Philosophical Imagination." In *Relational Autonomy, Agency, and the Social Self*, eds. Natalie Stoljar and Catriona Mackenzie. New York: Oxford University Press, 2000.

Loewenberg, Robert J. "John Locke and the Antebellum Defense of Slavery." *Political Theory* 13 (May 1985): 266–91.

Lott, Tommy, ed. *Subjugation and Bondage: Critical Essays on Slavery and Social Philosophy*. Lanham, Md.: Rowman & Littlefield, 1998.

Loury, Glen. "Why Should We Care About Group Inequality." *Social Philosophy and Policy* 5 (Autumn 1987): 249–71.

Loury, Glenn C. "It's Futile to Put a Price on Slavery." *New York Times*, May 29, 2000.

———. *The Anatomy of Racial Inequality*. Cambridge, Mass.: Harvard University Press, 2002.

Lyons, David. "Unfinished Business: Racial Junctures in U.S. History and Their Legacy." Paper presented at conference, The Moral Legacy of Slavery, Bowling Green State University, Bowling Green, Ohio, October 18 and 19, 2002.

"Making the Case for Racial Reparations: Does America Owe a Debt to the Descendants of Its Slaves? A Forum." *Harper's Magazine* 2000, 37–41.

Madigan, Tim. *The Burning: Massacre, Destruction, and the Tulsa Race Riot of 1921*.
New York: St. Martin's Press (Thomas Dunne Books), 2001.

Manne, Robert. "The Stolen Generations." In *Australian Essays 1998,* ed. Peter
Craven. Melbourne: Bookman, 1998. Online at www.tim-richardson.net/misc/
stolen_generation.html (accessed September 9, 2003).

McGary, Howard, and Bill E. Lawson. *Between Slavery and Freedom: Philosophy
and American Slavery*. Bloomington: Indiana University Press, 1992.

McGary, Howard, Jr. "'Reparations' and 'Inverse Discrimination.'" *Dialogue* 17
(October 1974): 8–10.

———. "Justice and Reparations." *Philosophical Forum* (Boston) 9 (Winter–Spring
1977–78): 256–63.

McWhorter, John. "Against Reparations: Review of Robinson, *The Debt.*" *New
Republic*, July 23, 2001.

Minow, Martha. *Between Vengeance and Forgiveness: Facing History after Genocide
and Mass Violence*. Boston: Beacon Press, 1998.

Mulgan, Richard. "Citizenship and Legitimacy in Post-Colonial Australia." In *Citizenship and Indigenous Australia: Changing Conceptions and Possibilities,* eds.
Nicholas Peterson and Will Sanders. Cambridge: Cambridge University Press, 1998.

Nicholas, Mary Pollingue. "The Good Life, Slavery, and Acquisition: Aristotle's
Introduction to Politics." *Interpretation* 11 (1983): 171–84.

Nickel, James W. "Should Reparations Be to Individuals or to Groups?" *Analysis* 34
(April 1974): 154–60.

O'Neil, Charles J. "Aristotle's Natural Slaves Re-Examined." *New Scholasticism* 27
(July 1953): 247–79.

O'Neill, Onora. "Rights to Compensation." *Social Philosophy and Policy* 5 (1987):
72–87.

Page, Clarence. "African-Americans Still Haven't Escaped Shackles of Slavery." *St.
Paul Pioneer Press,* July 5, 2000.

Painter, Nell Irwin. "Soul Murder and Slavery: Toward a Fully Loaded Cost
Accounting." In *U.S. History as Women's History,* eds. Alice Kessler-Harris, Linda
K. Kerber, and Kathryn Kish Sklar, 125–46. Chapel Hill: University of North
Carolina Press, 1995.

Park, Ernie. "Reparations and Inverse Discrimination." *Dialogue* (Journal of Phi
Sigma Tau) 17 (April 1975): 75–76.

Patterson, Orlando. *Slavery and Social Death: A Comparative Study*. Cambridge,
Mass.: Harvard University Press, 1982.

———. *Rituals of Blood: Consequences of Slavery in Two American Centuries*. New
York: Basic Books, 1998.

Paul, Ellen Frankel. "Set-Asides, Reparations, and Compensatory Justice." *Nomos* 33
(1991): 97–139.

Poole, Ross. "National Identity, Multiculturalism and Aboriginal Rights: An Australian
Perspective." In *Canadian Journal of Philosophy Supplemental Volume 22* (1996),
eds. K. Nielsen, J. Couture, and M. Seymour, 407–40.

Preus, Anthony. "Aristotle on Slavery: Recent Reactions." *Philosophical Inquiry* 5,
nos. 3–4 (1993): 33–47.

"A Price for Pain?: Economic *Analysis* of Proposed Reparations for Descendants of Slaves." *The Economist*, April 13, 2002.

Rao, Pappu SS Rama. "The Theory of Compensatory Justice: A Case for the Third World." *Philosophy and Social Action* 7 (April–June1981): 5–18.

Reed, Adolph L., Jr. "The Case against Reparations." *The Progressive,* December 2000, 15–17.

"Reparations Movement." *Congressional Quarterly Researcher* 11, no. 24 (2001): 529–52.

Rescher, Nicholas. "Collective Responsibility." *Journal of Social Philosophy* 29 (1998): 46–58.

Robinson, Randall. *The Debt: What America Owes to Blacks.* New York: Penguin Group (Dutton), 2000.

Rodney, Walter. *How Europe Underdeveloped Africa.* Washington, D.C.: Howard University Press, 1982.

Rohatyn, Dennis A. "Black Reparations: A Black and White Issue?" *Personalist* 60 (1979): 433–37.

Rotberg, Robert I., and Dennis Thompson, eds. *Truth v. Justice.* The University Center for Human Values Series (ed. Amy Gutman). Princeton, N.J.: Princeton University Press, 2000.

Schedler, George. "Minorities and Racist Symbols: A Response to Torin Alter." *Philosophy in the Contemporary World* 7, nos. 2–3 (2000): 5–10.

——. "Principles for Measuring the Damages of American Slavery." *Public Affairs Quarterly* 16, no. 4 (2002): 377–404.

Scheffler, Samuel. "Relationships and Responsibilities." *Philosophy and Public Affairs* 26, no. 3 (1998): 189–209.

Scheiber, Harry N. "Taking Responsibility: Moral and Historical Perspectives on the Japanese War-Reparations Issue." *Berkeley Journal of International Law* 20 (2002): 233–49.

Schuchter, Arnold, ed. *Reparations: The Black Manifesto and Its Challenge to White America.* Philadelphia: Lippincott, 1970.

Schutrumpf, Eckart. "Aristotle's Theory of Slavery — A Platonic Dilemma." *Ancient Philosophy* 13, no. 1 (1993): 111–23.

Sedler, Robert A. "Comment: Claims for Reparations for Racism Undermine the Struggle for Equality." *Journal of Law and Society* 3, no. 1 (2002): 119–59.

Sher, George. "Ancient Wrongs and Modern Rights." *Philosophy and Public Affairs* 10 (1980): 3–17.

Simmons, A. John. "Historical Rights and Fair Shares." *Law and Philosophy* 14 (1995): 149–84.

Smith, John David. "The Enduring Myth of 'Forty Acres and a Mule.'" *The Chronicle of Higher Education,* February 21, 2003.

Smith, Morton. "On Slavery: Biblical Teachings Versus Modern Morality." In *Biblical Versus Secular Ethics,* ed. R. Joseph Hoffman. Buffalo, N.Y.: Prometheus Press, 1988.

Smith, Nicholas. "Aristotle's Theory of Natural Slavery." *Phoenix—The Journal of the Classical Association of Canada* 37 (1993): 109–32.

Smith, Nicholas D. "Aristotle's Theory of Natural Slavery." *Phoenix* 37 (June 1983): 109–22.

Smith, Wilson. *Professors and Public Ethics: Studies of Northern Moral Philosophers before the Civil War*. Ithaca, N.Y.: Cornell University Press, 1956.

Sparrow, Robert. "History and Collective Responsibility." *Australasian Journal of Philosophy* 78, no. 3 (2000): 346–59.

Sterba, James. "Understanding Evil: American Slavery, the Holocaust, and the Conquest of the American Indians." *Ethics* 106, no. 2 (1996): 424–48.

Taylor, C. C. W. "Aristotle's Theory of Natural Slavery." *Analysis* (1983): 40.

Thomas, Laurence. "American Slavery and the Holocaust: Their Ideologies Compared." *Public Affairs Quarterly* (1991): 191–210.

Thompson, Janna. "Land Rights and Aboriginal Sovereignty." *Australasian Journal of Philosophy* (September 1990): 313–29.

——. "Inherited Obligation and Generational Continuity." *Canadian Journal of Philosophy* 29, no. 4 (1999): 493–515.

——. "Historical Obligations." *Australasian Journal of Philosophy* 78, no. 3 (2000): 334–45.

——. "Injustice and the Removal of Aboriginal Children." *Australian Journal of Professional and Applied Ethics* 2, no. 1 (2000): 2–13.

——. "Historical Injustice and Reparations: Justifying Claims of Descendents." *Ethics* 112, no. 1 (2001): 114–35.

——. *Taking Responsibility for the Past: Reparation and Historical Justice*. Cambridge, UK: Polity, 2002.

——. "The Apology Paradox." *Philosophical Quarterly* 50, no. 201 (2000): 470–75.

Tichy, Jindra, and Graham Oddie. "Is the Treaty of Waitangi a Social Contract?" In *Justice, Ethics and New Zealand Society*, eds. Graham Oddie and Roy Perrett. Melbourne: Oxford University Press, 1992.

Topey, John. "Making Whole What Has Been Smashed: Reflections on Reparations." *The Journal of Modern History* (University of Chicago) 73 (June 2001): 333–59.

Tracinski, Robert W. "America's 'Field of Blackbirds'": How the Campaign for Reparations for Slavery Perpetuates Racism." *Journal of Law in Society* 3, no. 1 (2002): 145–59.

Tully, James. "Rediscovering America: The Two Treatises and Aboriginal Rights." In *An Approach to Political Philosophy: Locke in Context*. Cambridge: Cambridge University Press, 1993.

Turner, Jeffrey S. "The Images of Enslavement and Incommensurability in Plato's 'Meno.'" *Interpretation* 20, no. 2 (1993): 117–34.

Vander-Zanden, James W. "The Ideology of White Supremacy." *Journal of the History of Ideas* 20 (June 1959): 385–402.

Vlastos, Gregory. "Slavery in Plato's Thought." *Philosophical Review* 50 (May 1941): 289–304.

Waldron, Jeremy. "Superseding Historical Injustice." *Ethics* 103 (1992): 4–28.

Welchman, Jennifer. "Locke on Slavery and Inalienable Rights." *Canadian Journal of Philosophy* 25, no. 1 (1995): 67–82.

Westley, Robert. "Many Billions Gone: Is It Time to Reconsider the Case for Black Reparations?" *Boston College Law Review* 40 (1998): 429–78.

Wheeler II, Samuel C. "Reparations Reconstructed." *American Philosophical Quarterly* 34, no. 3 (1997): 301–18.

Williams, Bernard. *Shame and Necessity*. Berkeley: University of California Press, 1993.

Williams, Juan. "Slavery Isn't the Issue." *Wall Street Journal*, April 9, 2002, p. 26.

Wilson, Catherine. "Natural Domination: A Reply to Michael Levin." *Philosophy* 74 (1998): 573–93.

Winbush, Raymond A., ed. *Should America Pay? Slavery and the Raging Debate over Reparations*. New York: HarperCollins (Amistad), 2003.

Index

About the Editors

Ronald Salzberger is Professor of Philosophy at Metropolitan State University, Saint Paul, Minnesota, where he has taught moral, social, and political philosophy since 1980. He received his Ph.D. in philosophy from Harvard University.

Mary C. Turck is Director of Publications for the Resource Center of the Americas in Minneapolis, Minnesota. She has written a number of children's nonfiction books, including *The Civil Rights Movement for Kids*. She earned a J.D. from Loyola University of Chicago.

Mary Turck and Ron Salzberger are wife and husband and live in Saint Paul with their daughters, Molly and Macy, and their cats and dogs.